23,00

D0811724

Personality Description
in
Ordinary Language

Personality Description
in
Ordinary Language

D. B. Bromley

Department of Psychology
The University, Liverpool

JOHN WILEY & SONS

London · New York · Sydney · Toronto

Library of Congress Cataloging in Publication Data:

Bromley, Dennis Basil, 1924–
  Personality description in ordinary language.

  Bibliography: p.
  Includes index.
  1. Personality.   2. Personality—Case studies.
I. Title.
BF698.B697   155.2   76-40293

ISBN 0 471 99443 X

Printed in Great Britain by William Clowes & Sons Limited, London, Beccles and Colchester

Acknowledgements

In rough chronological order, many thanks are due to the following persons and institutions: to the University of Liverpool, especially the library staff; to Dr. W. J. Livesley for getting the developmental research under way many years ago, for reading and commenting on the final draft, and for his continued interest; to the Medical Research Council for a grant in aid of research between 1970 and 1974; to the Medical Research Council volunteers on Merseyside for their work as research subjects; to Miss Pamela Yeomans, Mrs. B. June Fazakerley and Mrs. Jean Taylor for their patient work in data collection and content analysis; to Mrs. Dorothy Southern, Miss Elspeth McTear and Miss Maureen A. Thomas for endless typing and retyping; to Mr. C. Bilsbury, Dr. G. F. Wagstaff and Dr. K. Stenning for reading and commenting on an early draft of the whole manuscript; to Dr. J. Russell for commenting on a draft of Chapter 1; to Professor Miriam Allott for commenting on a draft of Chapter 10. Naturally, any errors of observation and understanding are entirely my own and I should be grateful for having my attention drawn to them.

My wife as usual has been more than reasonable and helpful during my prolonged preoccupation with research and writing.

The book contains quotations from the following sources:

Toulmin, S. E., *The Uses of Argument*, by kind permission of Cambridge University Press, London.

Klages, L., *The Science of Character*, by kind permission of George Allen and Unwin (Publishers), London.

Peters, R. S., *The Concept of Motivation*, by kind permission of Routledge and Kegan Paul Ltd., London, and the Humanities Press Inc., New York.

Tolstoy, L., *War and Peace*, Everyman's Library Edition, by kind permission of J. M. Dent & Sons Ltd., London, and E. P. Dutton & Co. Inc., New York.

Watt, I., *The Rise of the Novel*, by kind permission of Chatto and Windus Ltd., London.

Forster, E. M., *Aspects of the Novel*, by kind permission of Estate of E. M. Forster, Edward Arnold (Publishers) Ltd., London.

Contents

Preface

This book describes an approach to the study of personality and adjustment which is radically different from the traditional psychometric and laboratory approaches. It demonstrates that the study of individual cases in psychology and social work is grounded in commonsense and ordinary language. It shows what sorts of methods and standards are appropriate in the study of individual cases at professional and semi-professional levels of inquiry; it also suggests how the findings might be applied in practice and incorporated into a systematic body of knowledge about personal adjustment.

The phrase 'common sense' is used to refer to general understanding which is intelligent and informed, but not necessarily technical, professional or scientific. Similarly, the phrase 'ordinary language' is used to refer to natural ways of speaking and writing in everyday life, as contrasted with specially contrived notations, displays and terminologies.

The emphasis throughout is on the psychological aspects of personality description. The level of linguistic analysis is fairly simple, and readers who are acquainted with, say, Ryle (1949), Waldron (1967), Austin (1970), Palmer (1971), Black (1972), Minnis (1973) and Leech (1974), or with comparable sources, may see further psycholinguistic implications.

The first chapter gives a summary of the developmental psychology of understanding oneself and others, derived in the main from Livesley and Bromley (1973); the sections dealing with self/other comparisons and with the developmental transition to adult and professional descriptions of personality provide convenient connecting links with that book.

Chapter 2 describes the syntax of simple and complex sentences, and examines some of the lexical and semantic aspects of personality descriptions.

The third chapter makes a critical reappraisal of the classical study of trait names by Allport and Odbert (1936), and argues against the undue emphasis on traits in the psychometric approach to personality.

The fourth chapter examines the concept of 'trait' and the concept of 'motive', and attempts to show the connections between conceptual analysis and the main empirical method—content analysis. The psychometric and statistical aspects of content analysis, however, are not considered; the emphasis throughout is on semantic distinctions.

The next three chapters give a systematic, detailed, empirically based, lexical and semantic analysis of personality descriptions. They confirm the restrictive nature of 'trait psychology' and offer a wider and more promising set of concepts for analysing personality and adjustment. This is achieved by a close examination and discussion of the lexical and semantic properties of words and phrases in thirty categories of information commonly found in the ordinary language of personality descriptions. These categories cover the 'internal', 'external', 'social' and other aspects of personality, and are richly illustrated by reference to representative examples of words and phrases. Taken in conjunction with an appropriate method and theory for studying individual cases (described in later chapters), these content categories offer a comprehensive conceptual framework for the description and analysis of personality. This close examination of lexical and semantic issues in the ordinary language of personality descriptions illustrates some of the advantages and disadvantages of content analysis as a method of investigation, but clearly confirms the importance of linguistics in the study of personality and adjustment.

In Chapter 8, the ordinary language of personality description is shown to be related to the logic and language of professional case-studies in social work and clinical psychology. Examination of this relationship brings out some issues in the philosophy of behavioural science, with particular reference to the nature of explanation. A 'quasi-judicial' method of investigation is shown to be an appropriate *scientific* procedure for the study of individual cases—the method is described in detail.

Chapter 9 sets out a 'general theory' of personality and adjustment based on the concepts, methods and findings described in the preceding chapters and takes into account the meta-theoretical issues raised by Maddi (1972).

In the last chapter, the case-study method in psychology and social work is compared and contrasted with characterization in fiction.

The chapters are carefully cross-linked and the overall aim of the book is to provide a general conceptual and methodological framework for the scientific study of personality and adjustment, based on an analysis of the ordinary language of personality descriptions and on a procedure capable of dealing with the professional study of individual cases in clinical psychology and social work.

The book should appeal to students and professional workers in the social, medical and behavioural sciences who are interested in personality and adjustment, especially the theory and/or practice of individual case-work; it should also be of some interest to people concerned with the philosophy of psychology and with psycholinguistics. The book is not as technical as it may appear to be at first glance, and should be comprehensible and useful to non-psychologists who work professionally with people, for example lawyers, criminologists, counsellors, social workers, journalists, writers and teachers generally.

CHAPTER 1

The Development of Self-understanding and Understanding Others

I. Introduction

The term 'person perception' refers to the perceptual and cognitive processes that occur when our interest is directed towards a person and the circumstances he is in. We select and organize information about him, interpret it, and attribute characteristics to him and to his situation. These characteristics may be seen as constant or as variable features of the person and his environment. The reciprocal cognitive processes of accommodation and assimilation—associated with the work of Piaget—usually make it possible for us to achieve a stable and flexible framework of ideas about a person in the context of his surrounding circumstances.

The term 'personality description' refers to any set of statements which purports to offer a sensible answer to questions like, 'What sort of person is he (she)?', 'What do you think of him (her)?', 'What information can be given in the way of a personality appraisal?'. A personality description, therefore, is simply a verbal account of the impression formed of a person. The terms 'self-perception' and 'self-description' are used when the person has formed an impression of himself and his circumstances, and describes that impression in words.

The language of adult and professional personality descriptions is not as technical or as complicated as one might suppose, but there have been remarkably few attempts to elucidate its lexical, syntactical, semantic and other linguistic features, or to clarify the theory and practice of personality appraisal (excluding personality measurement). Hence there are no familiar points of departure for a study of the 'natural' language of personality description. The most convenient way to begin, however, is to review briefly some aspects of the developmental psychology of personality description as described in Livesley and Bromley (1973).

It will become clear that the language of personality appraisal in adult and professional life has its origins in the language and social learning of childhood and adolescence, and remains closely tied to 'commonsense' and the ordinary language of everyday life. Describing the psychology of person perception, i.e. impression formation and understanding others, in childhood and adolescence is a convenient way to begin because it leads quickly to an understanding of the normal adult framework for the social construction of *human* reality. The intention in the rest of the book is to show how commonsense and ordinary language relate to the concepts, methods and findings in the professional and scientific study of personality and adjustment.

The foundations of person perception are laid in infancy and early childhood. The infant's early experiences with people condition his perception of the outside world, so that he grows up naturally inclined to assign human tendencies and characteristics to people; he has to learn *not* to assign them to the non-human aspects of his environment. These early foundations of person perception are still not well understood, in spite of some early pioneering work: see Piaget (1926, 1929). The young child quickly acquires a facility for understanding, and a language for describing, actions and mental states. That is to say, he acquires words and sentences like 'John kicked the ball', 'John won't eat his dinner', 'John wants to go out to play'. By the age of about five or six years, the average child has a good command of the language required for a behaviour narrative, including the associated mental states. This facility with the language of overt behaviour and on-going mental states, however, is not adequate to deal with more complex and extended forms of behaviour, or with the associated dispositional character- istics and tendencies (motives, traits, abilities and beliefs). In other words, a young child below the age of about seven years has little if any facility with the language of *personality* description. The developmental psychology of person perception is the process which takes the child from this concrete level of understanding ordinary actions to the abstract and general level of understand- ing personality and adjustment found in adults.

In spite of the lack of *formal* instruction in self-understanding and understanding others, the average child gradually acquires the experience, the language and the social skills necessary for him to cope with the ordinary aspects of human nature in everyday life. It is not difficult to demonstrate, however, that there is frequently no great depth or breadth in his understanding, which is in any event culturally biased and full of fallacies, superstitions and misconceptions. He is frequently unable to cope effectively with simple problems regarding his own behaviour or the behaviour of other people. His ignorance and incompetence are often sustained by the prevailing culture which fails to recognize that human nature can be approached rationally and empirically, i.e. scientifically.

Naturally, a great deal of learning goes on outside the classroom. The child interacts with other people, routinely with many, intensively with a few, and is thereby obliged to form impressions of them (and of himself). These self-impressions and impressions of others—and the 'self-other comparisons' associated with them—are to a large extent latent or implicit in behaviour, but may become more or less explicit as the individual reflects upon his experience and tries to put it into words. Social interaction brings about a considerable amount of shared experience, a common language and a common frame of reference for the description and analysis of human behaviour and personality. This provides what we might call the 'commonsense' and 'ordinary language' of personality description.

The frequency and diversity of personality descriptions is easily illustrated by listening to serious conversations about people, by reading human interest stories and 'personality profiles' in newspapers and magazines, by reading case-studies prepared for professional purposes, and by reading history, biography and fiction. There are, of course, other ways of portraying personality: in simple terms through mimicry and caricature; in complex terms by dramatic enactment in films or on the stage. But we are concerned almost entirely with the representation of personality by means of ordinary (written) language. There are standardized psychometric methods of representation, such as adjective check-lists, Q-sorts, trait rating scales and questionnaires. The information conveyed through such standardized notational systems can be translated into ordinary language without much difficulty; indeed, they depend absolutely on the infrastructure of ordinary language.

As we shall show, personality descriptions can be analysed in terms of their *contents* and *organization*. The contents consist of words and phrases—the lexicon—classifiable into a larger or smaller number of categories of information (depending upon the level of analysis required), each of which can be regarded as a distinguishable aspect or 'facet' of the person being described. They refer not only to more obvious facets, such as appearance, traits, abilities and motives, but also to less obvious ones, such as the person's material circumstances and possessions, comparisons with other people, and actual incidents in his life. The organization of a personality description can be described partly in terms of the literary structure and 'informal logic' of the description as a whole, partly in terms of the syntax and semantics of its component sentences, and partly in terms of the words and phrases that comprise its 'content'. All these aspects of the language will be dealt with in detail in later chapters.

Personality descriptions are not conjured out of thin air, even in fiction; they have a social context, and claim some sort of rational or empirical validity however indirect. But we must not make the mistake of supposing that a personality appraisal necessarily gives rise to an explicit personality description. The impression we form of another person is expressed basically in the way we *behave* in relation to that person, i.e. our personal reactions. But we may not reflect on our reactions or make them explicit in words: and so, although we have formed a 'latent', 'implicit' or 'tacit' impression of the other person that guides our behaviour in relation to him, we do not 'realize' it until we achieve some sort of explicit (verbal or symbolic) representation of the thoughts, feelings and motives that constitute our latent, implicit appraisal; this explicit verbal representation is a personality description.

It does not necessarily follow, of course, that the explicit personality description fully and accurately represents the implicit appraisal, or that either of these corresponds well with the facts of the other person's existence. Nevertheless, whether we 'realize' it or not, our reactions to another person are initiated and guided by an implicit personality appraisal or 'schema'; although, naturally, our specific reactions are influenced by the actual stimulus situation. For example, a vague distrust may lead us to suspect another person's motives, although the demand characteristics of the social situation may prevent us from questioning his behaviour. In passing, we should note that it does not follow that a person who is shrewd and effective in the social encounters of everyday life is necessarily good at formulating valid explicit personality descriptions.

Our main interest is in the cognitive and psycholinguistic processes that produce our impressions and descriptions of ourselves and other people. The sociology of language and cognition, and the social psychology of interpersonal perception, are of secondary importance to us.

Person perception and the ordinary language of personality description are part of a shared social construction of reality. It follows, therefore, that there must be some connection between the perception of self and the perception of others, and between the language of self-description and the language we use to describe others. These related issues are dealt with in detail in a later section.

As far as interpersonal perception is concerned, we can attribute impressions of others to others, i.e. P_1 can appreciate that P_2 may have an impression of P_3, P_4 and so on. P_1 can also appreciate that P_2 may attribute an impression of himself or another to P_3 (the third party). Such recursive impressions are called meta-perspectives: see Laing, Phillipson and Lee (1966) and Flapan (1968). They are interesting in their own right, and appear to have some practical application in social and clinical psychology; but they do not, in our estimation, constitute the basic problem in person perception. The basic problem is the perception and description of oneself and others; meta-impressions (second-order impressions) are a subsidiary issue, mainly because they cannot be adequately described and analysed until the basic problem has been solved, partly because they are a relatively small (although sometimes important) part of a first-order impression. Second-order impressions are derived from first-order impressions, i.e. the meaning of P_1's impression of P_2's impression of P_3 depends upon P_1's impression of P_2.

There are several closely related areas of personality study which are important but only indirectly and partially relevant to our concern with personality description in ordinary language. They include: person perception, e.g. Heider (1958), Tagiuri and Petrullo (1958), Cline (1964), Warr and Knapper (1968), Hastorf et al. (1970); attribution theory, e.g. Jones et al. (1972), Newtson (1973, 1974); and personal construct theory, e.g. Kelly (1955), Mischel (1964), Bannister and Mair (1968), Bannister (1970), Crockett and Meisel (1974). They are referred to only in passing.

II. The Process of Impression Formation

The process at work in forming an impression of another person is as follows: our personal interest directs our attention towards a person; we perceive his behaviour and circumstances—and their consequences—selectively (and perhaps indirectly), and organize our experience in such a way as to give it a meaningful interpretation; not only do we associate facts with and attribute characteristics to the person, on the basis of direct and indirect evidence, but we also suppose that further facts and characteristics are implied. This 'implicit' impression constitutes a sort of attitude towards the stimulus person, and may become 'explicit' to the extent that we can make assertions about him. It may be possible to infer one person's impression of another from the way he behaves towards him; but it does not follow that he is 'aware' of the impression he has formed of that person, and it does not follow that what he thinks and says and does with regard to that person are consistent one with another. We note that research into attitudes has demonstrated that beliefs, opinions and actions are not always congruent with one another.

The term 'interpretative inference' refers to the way an observer makes sense of his initial observation. The term 'extended inference' refers to the implications derived from a network of ideas bound together by varying degrees of association and referred to as a 'lay', 'naive' or 'implicit' theory of personality: see Wishner (1960), Vernon (1964) and Rosenberg and Sedlak (1972). For example, the initial impression 'warm' is likely to give rise to the extended inferences 'generous', 'happy', 'humorous', and not to 'frivolous' or 'dishonest'.

The impression we have of a particular person at a particular time is not exactly the same as the impression we have of that person at another time. Indeed, our impressions of a person can change quickly and drastically. Although social and psychological factors provoke changes in person perception, our impressions of other people, nevertheless, tend to become reasonably stable and consistent; otherwise it would be difficult to identify people and to interact effectively with them. A personality impression depends upon a number of factors including: the objective characteristics of the stimulus person and his environment, the selection and order of appearance of information about him, the observer's personal characteristics and state of mind, and the social context in which the impression occurs.

The contents of a personality description can be quite diverse, as we shall see. They express fairly simple ideas about a person's name, appearance and employment, as well as more complex ideas about his personal conflicts, social relationships, and so on. These ideas tend to be organized into a consistent and meaningful system, even at the cost of eliminating or distorting discordant elements. If we are unable to 'rationalize' our impression of a person, we tend to regard *him* as inconsistent, peculiar or strange. If we are required to make our impression explicit by writing a personality description, the tendency towards consistency and meaningfulness is greatly increased by the lexical, syntactical and semantic constraints of ordinary written language. Thus, we feel obliged to describe the person in words and phrases that go together, to construct sentences that conform to English grammar, to make statements that make 'psychological sense', and to express what we mean clearly. The reader has almost certainly observed the profound influence that language exerts on behaviour in general and on personality appraisal in particular, e.g. reliance on familiar phraseology, clichés, and conformity to prevailing opinions.

One important but troublesome feature of the language of personality and adjustment is the distinction between terms which refer to *covert psychological processes* and terms which refer to *overt behavioural processes*—see Hampshire (1960) for a philosophical discussion of this issue. Each of these broad conceptual categories appears to be essential and to be closely related to the other, and yet it has proved remarkably difficult to co-ordinate them within one overall framework (but see Chapter 9). The consequence has been that personality theories have developed along two rather distinct lines, descriptive and dynamic, corresponding to a concern with overt and covert characteristics respectively; consider in this connection the distinction between 'peripheral' and 'core' characteristics discussed by Maddi (1972).

Our developmental studies show that children develop a language for the description of actions and states of mind long before they develop a language for the description of psychological dispositions and behavioural 'characteristics': see Livesley and Bromley (1973, pp. 228–86). Moreover, one of the important developments in the transition from juvenile to adult levels of personality description is an increase in the use of dispositional terms and an increase in the scale, precision and complexity of descriptions of behaviour and psychological processes.

It is possible that we have here a clue to the relationship between behaviour and psychological processes, in that some behavioural terms refer to relatively short-term responses or actions, whereas a great deal of our behaviour is organized into complex patterns of considerable duration, and exhibits consistencies and regularities. Mentalistic terms, like 'pleased', 'angry', 'uncertain', are adjectives referring to temporary states of mind associated with the organization of relatively simple on-going patterns of behaviour. Dispositional terms like 'intelligent', 'ambitious', 'artistic', 'hard-working', 'independent', are adjectives referring to motives, traits, abilities and attitudes; these are relatively stable, latent dispositions associated with the organization of complex and recurrent forms of conduct. Crockett (1965) seems to suggest that abstract psychological constructs—such as dispositions—are superordinate concepts that 'generalize' the particular facts of observed behaviour (and presumably enable us to infer further facts about behaviour).

Without pretending that this sort of analysis solves the so-called body–mind problem, we can at least see that in ordinary language and commonsense the so-called 'logical gulf' between mentalistic or dispositional terms on the one hand and behavioural terms on the other normally presents no problem—or rather the problem is solved by means of definitions and common usage. The problem does arise, however, and sometimes acutely, when doubts or disputes arise as to the meaning of a person's behaviour. Even if the observational evidence is not in dispute, it is still possible to interpret the 'same' behaviour in different ways, e.g. as love or duplicity, autonomous or directed, courageous or stupid, intended or accidental, moralistic or power-seeking, neurotic or malingering.

Some mentalistic functions are associated with what might be called second-order or reflexive behaviour, i.e. with behaviour towards one's own behaviour. Thus, hesitations, second-thoughts, plans, reflections, pretences, resolves, and so on, are responses to self-directed actions (or at least responses to representations of such actions). Even this much discussion shows that the problem of reconciling the language of behaviour with the language of psychological processes is a technical problem in philosophy and psycholinguistics as well as a practical problem in personality description.

Contextual factors play an important part in our attribution of characteristics (and causal relationships) to the person and his circumstances. For example, we tend to judge a person in comparison with certain other people, and our judgments are affected by the sorts of information available to us, by the credibility of our informants, by the order of presentation of the information, and so on. Experiments show that even the order of presentation of a small set of trait words may affect the choice of traits thought to be implied by that set. In ordinary language, however, it is unusual for a personality description to be constructed as a short list of unqualified trait adjectives; so, from our point of view, it is doubtful whether such experiments contribute much to the advancement of knowledge about person perception and the language of personality description. At best they provide simple demonstrations of associative networks and of the effects of combining two or more terms. Studies using trait- or mood-adjective rating-scales show that people differ in respect of the central tendency and dispersion of their ratings: see Cronbach (1955), Gage and Cronbach (1955) and Smith (1966). The use of adjective check-lists shows that people differ in the frequency with which they use the various items.

It seems reasonable to suppose that human beings employ all kinds of schemata to organize their behaviour and experience in relation to other people; some of these schemata are simple social stereotypes, others are complex individualized impressions. Ideally, a schema is stable enough to allow the subject to react consistently, but flexible enough to allow him to learn from experience. In practice, our impressions of others are often either too unstable or too inflexible, and so lead us to behave inconsistently or obstinately.

III. The Developmental Psychology of Personality Description

A. Background Literature

Since Piaget's pioneering work there have been relatively few investigations into the child's understanding of human nature (compared with numerous investigations into the child's understanding of the physical world, and of logic and other normative areas), but see Jersild (1951), Estvan and Estvan (1959),

Yarrow and Campbell (1963), Lewis and Brooks (in press). Shantz (in press) reports that although the developmental psychology of social cognition (the way we understand ourselves and other people) was relatively little studied prior to 1963, there has since been considerable interest in this topic. She summarizes and integrates a great deal of the literature up to 1974, dealing with various aspects of the perception of others in juvenile development: see also Peevers and Secord (1973).

Watts (1944) has described the results of some non-systematic investigations into the developmental psychology of personality description. He reported that, below the age of about seven years, children's descriptions of other people are usually confined to statements about appearance, unusual characteristics, and whether they are liked or disliked. From about the age of seven, children's vocabulary for describing behaviour and psychological processes increases in size and differentiation. The word 'nice', for example, differentiates into 'well-mannered', 'polite', 'courteous' and 'agreeable'; 'good' differentiates into 'honest', 'truthful', 'unselfish' and 'steadfast'; and 'kind' differentiates into 'generous', 'sympathetic', 'helpful' and 'good-natured'. One would expect other primitive terms, like 'naughty', 'clever', 'temper', 'funny', 'bossy' and 'silly', to show a similar sort of differentiation.

Watts found that between the ages of seven and eleven years, children's descriptions of other people are usually simple and disjunctive, i.e. they reveal either approval and liking or disapproval and disliking. At first, they usually deal with only one salient characteristic and its immediate effects, but later they may deal with a small number of similarly evaluated characteristics. Between the ages of about eleven and thirteen years children develop the ability to write rather more complex *conjunctive* descriptions, i.e. descriptions which include terms for different sorts of characteristics some of which are liked and some disliked. Few children below the age of eleven seem to realize that a person may exhibit *both* good and bad characteristics, e.g. faithfulness and stupidity, grumpiness and generosity, affection and dishonesty. Even at the age of thirteen and fourteen years, about half the children in Watts's study could not accept that differently valued characteristics could co-exist in the same person. Thus, we reach a relatively late stage in juvenile development before we realize that other people can exhibit both desirable and undesirable characteristics; and it is usually after the age of about thirteen years that we are able to co-ordinate or reconcile these contrasting characteristics in a personality description.

Livesley and Bromley (1973, pp. 209–11) found that personality descriptions focusing mainly on external qualities occurred predominantly in the youngest age group (eight years) and relatively infrequently at later ages. On the other hand, contrary to Watts's findings, descriptions in terms of single traits and univalent trait clusters were fairly common in eight-year-olds; even divalent trait clusters were fairly common from age nine onwards. The most obvious developmental trend was the increasing ability to describe people in terms of clusters of similarly evaluated traits.

Gollin (1958) used a film to portray a character behaving in contrasting ways (friendly and hostile). The ability to make an inference, i.e. go beyond the information given, and to form a concept, i.e. relate and integrate contrasting information, increased with age. In general, girls were better than boys, and higher social class children better than lower social class children.

Richardson, Dornbusch and Hastorf (1961) showed that descriptions of personality in ordinary language could be analysed, by means of content analysis, to demonstrate the conceptual categories used by children in understanding themselves and other people. The great advantage of ordinary language over contrived or artificial language (as in check-lists, rating scales and questionnaires) is that its descriptions can draw upon a very wide range of lexical units and syntactical structures, and can be constructed to fit the stimulus person closely, taking circumstances into account. In addition, ordinary language can provide an overall structure of meaning, and a variety of qualifying words and phrases to indicate, for example, the frequency or intensity of personal characteristics, and the way these characteristics vary with circumstances—see Chapter 2. Richardson, Dornbusch and Hastorf distinguished 69 first-order categories of information, e.g. age, religion, humour, mental abilities; considerably more than the thirteen categories identified by Beach and Wertheimer (1961) referred to below, and more than twice the number that we find it convenient to distinguish: see Chapters 5, 6 and 7.

Beach and Wertheimer (1961) collected twelve personality descriptions of designated stimulus persons from 36 male and 30 female student subjects. Thirteen content categories were identified and grouped into four classes:

Objective Information: appearance, background, general information (job, income, etc.).

Social Interaction: behaviour towards the subject, behaviour towards other people, other people's reactions to (and acceptance of) him, subject's reactions to (and acceptance of) him.

Behavioural Characteristics: temperament, self-concept and emotional adjustment, morals and values.

Performance and Activities: abilities, motivation, activities and interests.

The content categories listed above overlap considerably with those obtained by other investigators, and particularly with those that we have used with both children and adults. Although in theory people can select from a wide range of lexical terms and syntactic structures when formulating their personality descriptions, in practice they tend to rely on a much narrower range.

It is clear that the analysis of the contents of personality descriptions can be carried out in different ways, *there is no one definitive system of analysis*. At best, one might devise a general purpose hierarchical system in which smaller, lower level, units of analysis are grouped into larger, higher level, units. An added complication is that one might wish to cross-classify items; for example, a statement like, 'Drives his wife to work each day' says something about the stimulus person's activities of daily living, his relationship with his wife, and his abilities. Personality can be described in an infinite variety of ways; there is no ultimate 'objectivity'—except as a sort of ideal 'truth' to which actual descriptions are an approximation.

The development of an adequate, i.e. reliable, valid and useful, taxonomy is important scientific work, as the history of chemistry and zoology show. We cannot pretend that the relatively simple system that we have devised for classifying statements in personality descriptions, see later chapters, provides a perfect taxonomy of personality characteristics; but at least it is a step in the right direction, and discussion of its merits and defects should lead to advances in the conceptual analysis of personality and adjustment. Improvements in and standardization of the terms used to describe and analyse personality and adjustment are bound to help in practical work with people in clinical psychology and social case-work provided such terms do not become detached from ordinary language or from the social context to which they belong.

The results of Richardson, Dornbusch and Hastorf (1961) seemed to demonstrate that when two subjects described two different children there was a 38 per cent overlap in the categories used; when two subjects described the same child there was a 45 per cent overlap; and when one subject described two children there was a 57 per cent overlap. These results confirm the expectation that the contents of personality descriptions are influenced by cultural factors, stimulus person factors and personality (subjective) factors.

Yarrow and Campbell (1963) studied children aged eight to thirteen years at a summer camp. They obtained several personality descriptions through interviews, and distinguished seventeen content categories. On average, the children used eleven units (discrete actions, single characteristics, or evaluations) in each description, with a range from 1 to 27. Eighty-five per cent of the descriptions contained evaluations, with details of the other child's social behaviour, e.g. 'shares things', 'friendly', 'bossy'. Statements about abilities, physique, identity and physical appearance occurred in about half the descriptions. Statements about social interactions included those referring to sociability, conformity, social talk, physical play and affiliation. When the social interaction categories were grouped into four types—aggression, affiliation, assertion, submission—nearly half the children referred to one of these types and hardly any used all four. Nearly one-third of the children could describe contrasting tendencies in a stimulus person.

There were some slight changes in frequency of mention of some categories of information from the first interview at the beginning of the camp to the second interview at the end. There have been few investigations into serial changes in the contents and organization of personality descriptions, but see Bromley (1966), and Worrall and Worrall (1974). Some of the simpler serial changes are similar to those found in memory studies using serial recall; but obviously one would expect serial changes to be correlated with changes in the determining factors, i.e. those relating to the stimulus person, the subject, and the environment.

Yarrow and Campbell (1963) found little evidence of age differences (ages eight to thirteen), except that older children mentioned characteristics relating to aggression and domination, and, more important, older children gave more complex and better organized descriptions. There were no sex differences in the complexity of the descriptions but the girls more often mentioned nurturant characteristics like 'shares things' and 'comforts me', whereas the boys were more likely to mention deviant characteristics like 'stubborn'. Active and friendly children gave more complex descriptions and made more inferences.

Scarlett, Press and Crockett (1971) observed, for boys, a shift between the ages of six and eleven years from relatively concrete and egocentric constructs, e.g. 'We play together', 'He hits me', to relatively abstract and objective constructs, e.g. 'He hits people all the time', 'He is kind'. The relative abstractness and generality of such statements cannot be ascertained by inspection, however; some sort of empirical analysis is called for: see Bilsbury (in preparation). Boys were described at greater length than girls; liked children were described at greater length than disliked children by the older boys.

It is apparent from several of the above studies that the length of the personality description must affect any measures of content and organization, so fluency is an important variable in the statistical analysis of personality descriptions.

Studies in the developmental psychology of personality descriptions thus indicate that the ability to understand and describe other people increases with age, in that descriptions by older children are more extensive, contain a greater variety of information, and are better organized, i.e. more complex and comprehensive. There is little evidence that children below the age of seven years can conceptualize psychological dispositions; although by that age the average child has a good vocabulary for describing on-going behaviour, including both overt action and covert mental processes. His lack of psychological conceptualization means that he cannot describe or understand covert *dispositional* characteristics like motives, traits, abilities and attitudes; so that he cannot deal with complex behaviour patterns which extend over any considerable time or across many situations. For example, he finds it difficult to *summarize* a behaviour narrative. Similarly, although the younger child can refer to the particular objects, persons and events in a situation, he cannot conceptualize them as abstract environmental conditions characteristic of a *general class* of situation.

The structure of human behaviour—its organization and episodic nature—is not 'given' in perception, but is learned through experience of actual behaviour *in the context of an accompanying language*, i.e. a descriptive and explanatory commentary. So the way we perceive behaviour is partly a function of the terms and concepts we have acquired through social learning and language learning. Human nature as we know it is a *social construction*, and its susceptibility to error can be illustrated by reference to the errors, confusions and superstitions with which our various accounts of human behaviour are riddled.

The young child's egocentrism restricts his account of the other person, as does his tendency to evaluate the person either positively or negatively. As the child grows older, and more mature biologically and socially, his understanding of other people's psychological characteristics, and their complex behaviour patterns, improves; he tends to accommodate his thinking to the beliefs, attitudes, values and language that form part of the social construction of human reality in his culture.

By the age of about six years, a child becomes aware that another child may think differently from the way he himself thinks; by the age of about nine he realizes that other children can think about his thoughts; a little later he can speculate about another child's thoughts and at the same time compare them with his own. Meta-perspective (recursive) thinking is difficult to carry to three or more steps; the major achievement is the reciprocal (one or two step) meta-perspective: see Feffer (1970), Flavell (1968) and Selman (1971).

The pattern of development during childhood and adolescence is naturally affected by a variety of considerations: sex differences, social-class differences, differences in intelligence, cultural differences, differences in personality and experience. In this respect the development of self-understanding and understanding others is similar to other aspects of child development; there is an underlying competence or capacity for development, but its realization and expression (performance) depends on a whole variety of environmental considerations.

Age differences in personality descriptions are particularly noticeable during the juvenile period (but not in adult life); sex differences seem to be related to values and interests; social-class differences are associated with values and facility with words. Personality characteristics, e.g. neuroticism, prejudice, introversion, sociability, probably exert selective effects on the attention we pay to a person and on the way we interpret the stimulus person's behaviour; differences in intelligence are associated with vocabulary size and syntactical complexity.

Ordinary language provides us with the means of formulating descriptions for *any* person about whom we have information; children's personality descriptions tend to vary somewhat with the kinds of stimulus person they are describing, e.g. they tend to write more about males than females, and more about persons they like than persons they dislike; descriptions of disliked persons tend to contain more justificatory statements.

The language of self-description is similar to that of descriptions of others, except for the greater emphasis on covert psychological factors in self-description: see Livesley and Bromley (1973, pp. 228–41).

B. *Methodological Issues in the Content Analysis of Written Descriptions*
Psychological development can be understood more clearly when one knows something of the adult state towards which juvenile development moves. Similarly, fully developed, i.e. adult, psychological functions can be more clearly understood when one knows something of the juvenile developmental processes that led up to them.

In our main study of person perception in childhood and adolescence, we obtained written personality descriptions (one self-description and eight descriptions of other stimulus persons) from each of 320 children subdivided into eight age groups from seven to fifteen years. The sample was further subdivided into boys and girls, and into higher and lower levels of intelligence.

We analysed the *contents* of these personality descriptions in considerable detail, and noted some aspects of the way the descriptions were *organized*. We examined the main effects of age, sex and intelligence (and their interactions), on the *contents* and *organization* of these personality descriptions. We compared self-descriptions with descriptions of others, and compared descriptions of different sorts of stimulus persons, e.g. males vs. females, adult vs. children, liked vs. disliked.

The children were asked to avoid describing physical appearance, as it was already known that this kind of information is commonly mentioned in children's descriptions of others, and the investigators wished to explore the limits of the children's perception and understanding.

The spoken language of personality description is difficult to study because of the obvious problems associated with recording, transcribing and analysing the spoken word. But, in addition, there are the less obvious problems of recording and interpreting the paralinguistic aspects of speech, and of identifying and explaining the influence of the social context in which spoken language occurs. Some of these problems are mentioned briefly in Livesley and Bromley (1973, pp. 241–65), and have been encountered directly in an intensive study of the language of personality description as spoken by educationally subnormal children: see Bilsbury (in preparation).

Written personality descriptions have a number of advantages from a research point of view. They can be obtained under relatively standard conditions and provide a permanent record. They can, if desired, be transferred word for word to a computer store as empirical data for whatever statistical treatments, e.g. word counts and contingency analyses, are needed to test the validity of the investigator's theories. Written descriptions leave the individual subject free to select and organize the information he thinks is relevant to describing the stimulus person; his responses are not unduly influenced by methodological artefacts, and the analysis of his responses is not restricted by the conceptual framework of any particular theory, e.g. personal construct theory: see Bannister (1970). A written description makes great demands on the cognitive and linguistic abilities of a subject and tends to produce a wide range and a high level of response; a written description is also a fairly formal, considered, individualized performance, relatively free from the effects of momentary social circumstances, e.g. suggestion, duplicity, embarrassment.

In comparison with these major advantages, the disadvantages of using written descriptions to study the language of personality and adjustment are of minor importance. However, one must recognize that some subjects are more fluent with the spoken than with the written word. Written descriptions, like spoken descriptions, can never reveal all that the subject knows or thinks about a stimulus person; not only because the descriptions are not expected to be exhaustive, but also because the subject 'knows more than he can say', i.e. much of his impression is latent or implicit and cannot be expressed in words (even with close and helpful interrogation, see Bilsbury, in preparation). Actions sometimes speak louder than words, and we have said elsewhere that a personality impression is basically an *implicit* schema for the organization of behaviour related to the stimulus person.

By far the most difficult problem in the use of free descriptions, whether spoken or written, is that of conducting a reliable, valid and useful analysis of their contents. It is not necessary to justify the method of content analysis as a general procedure; there is sufficient evidence of its merits: see Holsti (1969), Gottschalk and Gleser (1969), Stone *et al.* (1966). But it is necessary to justify the particular procedures used in the content analysis of personality descriptions. Unfortunately, there is no short answer to the question of to what extent the method we have used in the study of juvenile and adult descriptions is reliable, valid and useful. In fact, the origins of this book lie in the attempt to develop a rational and objective method for the analysis of complex adult personality descriptions.

There is enough evidence from previous studies to demonstrate that the types of content we have identified are very similar to those identified by other investigators, and that any catalogue of contents must be to some extent a matter of convenience. At present, the development of a definitive and comprehensive system of descriptive categories remains a remote possibility. The system we shall propose has proved successful in carrying out case-studies: see Chapter 8. There is also enough evidence to show that reliable methods of content analysis can be developed. The basic problem is that of defining reliable and objective criteria for including a word or phrase in a particular content category, so that independent observers can classify the material in the same way. This may require setting up content dictionaries, and training observers, but it is obvious that reliability is a technical problem of tactics and research resources, not a problem of theory or principle.

The problem of objectively classifying the words and phrases that form the contents of personality descriptions is more apparent than real. In the first place, written descriptions are limited in length and the writer may not have disclosed his meanings fully or precisely. Further interrogation would almost certainly provide enough contextual and associated information to clarify the meaning of most words and phrases, and therefore the content category to which each belongs. In the second place, the personality description as a whole provides a context which narrows the range of meanings that any one word or phrase might have.

The most useful unit of analysis is the word or phrase which states a single fact or idea. Analysis in terms of single words has its uses, e.g. in studies of sentence length, vocabulary, concordance, and so on, but these applications will be dealt with in a separate publication. Similarly, analysis in terms of themes has its uses, e.g. in studies of social attitudes and values, but these applications have not so far been of concern to us.

The research literature on person perception has been surprisingly silent on the practical applications of the findings that have been reported. By contrast, we hope to show that there are many useful applications for a language of personality description that combines scientific rigour with commonsense familiarity. We think this kind of utility can be achieved by combining a critical analysis and reappraisal of the ordinary language of personality description with a critical analysis and reappraisal of professional and scientific methods of personality assessment, e.g. in clinical psychology, social case-work, and elsewhere: see Chapters 8 and 9.

C. Results of the Main Study in Juvenile Development

The contents of the children's written descriptions were analysed into 'statements', first of all by identifying small semantic units; these consisted of a word or a phrase conveying an idea or a single item of information, e.g. 'She is pretty', 'He has a new rabbit', 'polite', 'I like him': see Livesley and Bromley (1973, pp. 122–31). Such statements can be identified with reasonable reliability; although, as we have said, the content analysis of complex adult descriptions demands the compilation of a classified catalogue of words and phrases, if the analysis is to be objective and reliable (see later chapters).

The number of words per description varied not only from child to child, but also from one stimulus person to another for the same child. Consequently, some parts of the analysis had to control for fluency by measuring the relative proportion (rather than the absolute number) of statements in each content category.

An important aspect of the juvenile development of understanding human behaviour is the ability to distinguish, and see the connections between, 'dispositional' and 'behavioural' terms. This is an issue to which we have already referred, and is sometimes discussed in terms of the distinction between psychological (central) statements and non-psychological (peripheral and behavioural) statements. As regards cognitive level, it is also discussed in terms of the distinction between abstract and concrete thinking—hence the relatively late age at which children become able to understand psychological (as opposed to behavioural or external) characteristics. Among the psychological (central) categories of statement are those referring to personality traits, habits, motives, values, abilities, beliefs and attitudes; among the non-psychological (peripheral or behavioural) categories of statement are those referring to appearance, identity, routine actions, actual incidents or life events, and possessions. Whereas the latter set depend upon particular empirical facts (which can be observed), the former set depend upon general theoretical rules or regularities (which have to be inferred). Looked at in this way, the importance of dispositional terms for understanding and describing personality is obvious; they constitute inference rules which enable us to make claims that go beyond, or ahead of, the observational evidence: e.g. 'She will probably accept an invitation to go shopping, *since she enjoys looking at the shops.*

In younger children, the simple present tense is often used to refer to behavioural regularities, e.g. 'He steals' or 'He lies'. These are probably the simplest behavioural invariances, and are not very different from younger children's use of terms like 'kind', 'bad tempered', 'clever', by means of which an impression is stabilized and 'conserved'. The regular and reliable attributes that describe 'personality' are relatively general and abstract in comparison with the overt peripheral and behavioural characteristics to which they refer. It is through the use of dispositional terms that our concept of the other person is simplified and stabilized; they provide a frame of reference in terms of which the person's actual behaviour and manifest characteristics can be understood and reacted to; they also make it possible to incorporate contextual (situational) factors relevant to understanding the person's behaviour and characteristics.

Analysis of the personality descriptions written by children of different ages in the main investigation revealed that on average they wrote nine 'statements' (words or phrases—units of analysis) per description. There was a fairly rapid increase in the length of the descriptions between the ages of seven and eight— probably associated with the acquisition of elementary literacy; this was followed by a more gradual increase up to the age of fifteen years (partly associated with restrictions on the length of descriptions imposed by the test instructions and format). Girls tended to write more than boys, and more was written about male, as compared with female, stimulus persons; there seemed to be surprisingly little difference, however, in the lengths of the descriptions written by children of higher, as compared with children of lower, intelligence. Various small interaction effects proved to be statistically significant but of little theoretical or practical importance.

If we now consider only those statements that refer to covert (central, psychological) characteristics, we find that children of higher, as compared with children of lower, intelligence use more central statements; and that more central statements are used to describe children than to describe adults. It is interesting to observe that younger children use more central statements to describe females whereas older children use more to describe males; this perhaps reflects developmental differences in social attitudes and values. If we consider the *proportion*, rather than the *number*, of central statements per description we find similar developmental effects. There were, therefore, several main effects for the three 'between-subject' variables (age, sex and intelligence), and for the three 'within-subject' variables (adult/child, male/female and liked/disliked stimulus person). In addition, several interaction effects were observed, for example, the tendency for children to make more central statements about opposite sex stimulus persons, and the relative lack of central statements describing adult females. In general, however, interaction effects were small and apparently of no great psychological significance.

An examination of age differences in the children's use of 33 different categories of information, see Livesley and Bromley (1973, pp. 123–26), showed that eleven of them increased with age: general personality attributes; specific behavioural consistencies; beliefs, attitudes and values; stimulus person's attitude towards himself; reputation; effects upon, and relations with, others; other people's behaviour towards the stimulus person; relations with opposite sex; subject's behaviour towards the stimulus person; comparison (of stimulus person) with others; collateral facts and ideas. These categories are mainly concerned with covert (central, psychological) characteristics and social relationships, and one would expect that increased age during the juvenile period would be associated with the greater intelligence and experience needed to comprehend ideas of these kinds.

Some categories of information that one might have expected also to increase with age did not do so, perhaps because their frequency of occurrence was low, e.g. life-history, motivation and arousal, orientation. The increase with age in collateral facts and ideas, especially when associated with a *decrease* with age in irrelevant and unclassifiable facts and ideas, shows that children become increasingly aware of the total situation within which a stimulus person exists, and become increasingly concerned to illustrate, to explain, and to find corroboration for, their appraisal of the stimulus person. Even among adults, one commonly finds a tendency to include in a personality description some information which is merely collateral, i.e. aside from the main issue; it requires not a little concentration to exclude associated information that is not *directly* relevant to a personality description. In fact, in our subsequent study of adult personality descriptions, we have attempted to minimize the number of statements classified as 'collateral' on the grounds that the subjects are showing the investigators what sorts of information are relevant in a personality description, not vice versa.

The developmental trend in personality descriptions during the juvenile period is from (i) relatively brief, simple, unorganized, unreflective, concrete, egocentric, evaluatively disjunctive, descriptions of others, based on overt characteristics and incidentally associated facts, to (ii) relatively longer, complex, organized, reflective, abstract, objective (socially shared), evaluatively conjunctive, impressions of others, based on covert characteristics and relevant associated facts.

Older children become more aware of the external, contextual (situational) influences on behaviour, as well as more able to attribute stable (dispositional) characteristics to people. Similarly, whereas younger children are more 'impressed' by a few superficial and unusual aspects of behaviour and appearance, older children learn to observe regularities and relationships in the person's behaviour as a whole.

Analysis of the contents of the children's descriptions into 33 categories made it possible to study systematically types of statement which occurred rather infrequently, i.e. with a likelihood of occurrence less than one in 100, since there were over 23,000 statements altogether from 320 children, and nearly 3000 for each age group except the youngest. Had the children not been instructed to omit statements about physical appearance, which a number of them were unable to do, many interesting aspects of children's descriptions of others would have remained unobserved, e.g. motivation and orientation, beliefs, attitudes and values, and self-image.

By contrast, some types of statement occurred, on average, relatively frequently, namely, specific behavioural consistencies (15 per cent), and general personality attributes (13 per cent). Others occurred with somewhat lower frequencies: identity (9 per cent), evaluations (8 per cent), mutual interactions (7 per cent) and appearance (7 per cent).

The differences between boys and girls in the use of the various content categories (types of statement) appeared to be of little psychological importance. The more intelligent children made greater use of general personality attributes, whereas the less intelligent children more often referred to family and appearance. The use made of the various types of statement to describe different sorts of stimulus person, e.g. 'liked' or 'disliked', was more or less what one would have expected on commonsense grounds.

We have seen that in the early stages of development children use concrete terms to refer to particular overt actions and appearances. In time, however, they learn to use more abstract terms to refer to covert characteristics and social relationships of a general sort. Eventually, these come to be regarded as internal dispositions, abilities and principles, with causal and organizational effects on behaviour. Motivational terms are rarely found in young children's personality descriptions, which is not surprising considering that human motivation continues to pose problems even for scientific description and philosophical analysis, and considering that there is no sharp dividing line between motivational and non-motivational terms in personality description: see Chapter 4.

The children's use of trait names was examined in some detail. This is of particular interest because of its relevance to our review of the Allport and Odbert monograph: see Chapter 3. Traits form part of the class of covert (central, psychological) dispositions, but also cut across several other content categories, e.g. motives, abilities and attainments, and evaluations. The use of trait names increased with age, and girls used them more than boys. Surprisingly, the use of trait names appeared not to be associated with differences in intelligence at each age level. Traits were more prominent in descriptions of males and children than of females and adults, especially in the older age groups.

On average, the 320 children in the Livesley and Bromley study used nearly two trait names per description (rising from nearly one in the eight-year-olds to nearly two in the nine- and ten-year-olds and then to over two in the older children). The number of *different* trait names used in each set of eight personality descriptions was 5·2 for the eight-year-olds, rising to a maximum of 15·4 for the fourteen-year-olds. Girls used 12·7 as against 10·0 for boys; this observed sex difference is interesting because the two groups had been equated for verbal ability. Children of higher intelligence used 12·1 as against 10·6 for children of lower intelligence; the highest individual score was 35. An increase in the *size* of the vocabulary of trait names is associated with an increase in the average frequency of *use* of traits in personality descriptions. Superficially, this makes it appear that those subjects who have larger trait vocabularies are using them in a less discriminating way, i.e. attributing the *same* trait to *different* people. However, this is unlikely and there may be another explanation for this effect.

A greater ability to attribute a trait need not be associated with a very much larger trait vocabulary, since a child can use different combinations of trait names and different syntactic structures to modify the meaning of a trait name. The less commonly used trait names are acquired relatively late in development and by more intelligent and better educated children.

Livesley and Bromley (1973, pp. 172–79) show that the numbers of traits used by different numbers of children are distributed according to Zipf's law—briefly, many children use a few of the traits, but many of the traits are used by only a few children. Also some trait names, e.g. nice, kind, naughty, are acquired early in development, whereas others are acquired late, e.g. modest, loyal, sly, dirty-minded.

We shall see that the attempt to accord trait names a special status in the language of personality descriptions is probably unwise. In any event trait names comprise only about 20 per cent of the total contents of a personality description written by an older child, and it is obvious that there is much more to describing a person than listing his traits.

Although trait implications have been studied in some detail in the literature of person perception, and although the contents of written descriptions have been the subject of investigation at least since Watts's exploratory studies, yet the *organization* of personality descriptions appears to have been ignored. The term *organization*, used in connection with written descriptions, refers to the way in which words and phrases, the contents, are arranged in syntactical structures so as to represent, as nearly as possible, the meaning intended. As we shall see, this is a large and rather complicated topic, so we shall reserve detailed examination of it until Chapter 2. Livesley and Bromley (1973, pp. 195–208), however, studied some aspects of juvenile development in relation to the organization of personality descriptions, and carried out a content analysis of the terms which modify the meaning of the words and phrases in the content categories already referred to. A complete content analysis should, by definition, account for every word or phrase in the description.

Eight kinds of qualifying or organizing terms were identified: (a) those referring to the frequency, intensity, duration, or likelihood of occurrence, of a personality characteristic, e.g. '*very* understanding', '*always* kind', '*easily* gets nervous'; (b) those indicating some uncertainty about an attribute, e.g. '*never seems* to laugh', 'a *sort of* cousin of mine', 'nervous I *suppose*'; (c) those using the word 'because' explicitly to explain something about the stimulus person, e.g. 'I dislike her *because* she talks about things which are none of her business'; (d) those implying a causal or explanatory relationship but not using the word 'because', e.g. 'He is kind *only if* he is in a good temper', 'He is quiet *when* in company'; (e) those which limit the implications normally associated with a personal characteristic or circumstance, e.g. 'good at work *but* slow', 'degrades other people's achievements *yet* never praises his own'; (f) those which define or illustrate the meaning of a term as it applies to a particular person, e.g. 'If she does argue, *she does not get aggressive*', 'She is greedy *in that* she never shares things'; (g) those which distinguish real from apparent characteristics, actual from possible characteristics, and present from past characteristics, e.g. 'He *pretends* he knows', 'He is *not really* stupid', 'She is *not* as nice *as I thought she was*'; (h) those which make use of figures of speech, e.g. 'He *flares up* easily'.

The amount of qualifying and organizing material associated with covert (central, psychological) characteristics was, of course, relatively small. Nevertheless, it was possible to demonstrate significant differences associated with age and intelligence, but not with sex differences. As children become adolescent, it appears that their vocabulary of covert (central, psychological) terms increases slowly (unless they are in the kind of learning environment that encourages the acquisition of such vocabulary), whereas their ability to combine, qualify and organize these words and phrases increases rapidly. It is this stage of psychological development in person perception that reveals to us the connections between juvenile and adult levels of personality description. When the transition to an adult level of performance has taken place, there are still wide differences of ability between individuals—arising from variations in intelligence, education, experience, interest, and so on—which help to reveal to us the connections between commonsense levels and professional levels of personality description.

IV. The Transition to Adult and Professional Descriptions

The transition to a normal adult level of personality description can be summarized briefly as follows. There is an increase in the variety of words and phrases available for describing human behaviour and psychological processes; these words and phrases are used in a more discriminating and flexible way by being qualified and organized within a number of relatively simple syntactical structures. In addition to the general age trends already mentioned, there is an increased awareness of the complexities of covert psychological processes and of the effects of situational factors, and a greater ability to *explain* human behaviour. Juvenile egocentricity does not disappear altogether, but is overlaid by a recognition of the need for objectivity (social consensus or empirical validation) in personality appraisal; the personality impression is no longer simply an implicit or subjective experience but an explicit and social communication.

By adolescence the average person is able to appreciate that someone is the 'same person' in spite of substantial changes in behaviour, appearance and circumstances; he is also able to see the constancies, relationships and regularities running through variations in a person's behaviour; and he is less inclined to make absolute, i.e. unqualified, assertions. The process of personality appraisal is no longer so 'natural', i.e. based on relatively unlearned affective reactions and on psychological mechanisms like mimicry and identification. Instead, there is a greater reliance on observation and reasoning and a greater preference for formal explicit procedures (although these are often unsatisfactory, e.g. reliance on physiognomic typologies or social stereotypes).

The transition to a normal adult level of understanding others paves the way for professional and scientific methods of personality appraisal. The study of person perception and personality description has a special relevance for clinical psychology and social case-work: see Adinolfi (1971). Our immediate concern, however, is not with the practical problems of personality assessment but with the basic *academic* aspects of personality study, i.e. with conceptual and methodological issues, which it seems to us have been neglected in comparison with the practical aspects of personality measurement and personality management.

A professional and scientific level of understanding requires the ability to carry out formal or quasi-formal operations with systems of psychological concepts, i.e. it requires an understanding of the 'grammar' of human behaviour; it also requires the ability to co-ordinate reason with observation (conjecture and refutation), so as to minimize errors in understanding others: see Chapter 8.

V. A Theory of Self/Other Comparisons

A theory is needed to describe and account for the developmental process whereby the child co-ordinates his understanding of overt behaviour with his understanding of covert psychological processes, i.e. mental states and dispositions. This co-ordination is achieved through the mastery of the ordinary language of personality and behaviour. The child learns the language of personality description in much the same way as he learns the language of other subject matters. We can assume that in the early stages of development the child is not capable of reflexive thought and is aware only of those aspects of the other person's existence or behaviour that directly affect his well-being. But at an early age he begins to learn that certain kinds of behaviour, both his own and those of others, are referred to by means of certain words and phrases. These verbal 'accounts' include behaviour narratives, personality descriptions, psychological analyses, and so on, which the young child associates with certain kinds of conduct in certain kinds of situation. The accounts may be given directly by the person whose behaviour is observed, e.g. an older child, or they may be given by an informant, e.g. an adult, who is in a position to describe and/or comment on that behaviour. At this stage, therefore, the young child is learning the names of certain kinds of behaviour, e.g. 'closing the door', 'crying', and learning about the social and linguistic contexts within which such phrases occur, e.g. the rules of social conduct and the rules of English grammar. Thus, the words and phrases just mentioned might occur in a domestic or school setting in association with sentences like: 'Closing the door is naughty', 'John is crying because he doesn't want to go to school'. Thus, simple behaviour phrases become embedded in the context of an assertion, question or command, and associated with terms related to other aspects of human behaviour, e.g. ethical evaluations (good, bad, naughty), causal connections (if—then, because, when), social comparisons (better, worse, different, same), and so on.

The child is exposed to the language of human behaviour and psychological processes from an early age and probably encounters little difficulty in comprehending and mastering its lexicon, syntax and semantics. The child is, in a sense, conditioned to think and talk in *psychological* terms, which means that he should have less difficulty in understanding *human* nature than in understanding other aspects of nature and logic.

The close connection, in ordinary language, between behavioural terms, e.g. 'crying', 'won't give', 'telling people what to do', and mentalistic terms, e.g. 'afraid', 'wants', 'thinks', and dispositional terms, e.g. 'cowardice', 'stubborn', 'bossy', enables the child to appreciate the relationship between overt behaviour and covert psychological processes. In a similar way he comes to appreciate that behaviour (and the covert processes which underlie and organize it) can be directed towards (or away from) objects, events, persons and circumstances in the real world; and that behaviour can be positively or negatively evaluated, and lead to beneficial or detrimental consequences. Our theory assumes that a normal child develops two co-existing cognitive/linguistic systems (schemata): one represents and refers to the tangible world of behaviour (his own and that of other people); the other represents and refers to the intangible world of thoughts, feelings, desires and sensations, and of traits, abilities and beliefs. The two systems become co-ordinated.

When a child observes the behaviour of other people, a commentary on that behaviour is often provided—either by the people actually observed, e.g. other children, or by a third party, e.g. a parent or teacher. The commentary which accompanies the child's observation of the behaviour in question may consist of statements which describe it, or statements which interpret it, e.g. by reference to mental states such as thoughts, feelings and desires, or by reference to dispositions such as traits, habits, attitudes, beliefs and abilities. The commentary may also provide a causal analysis, in terms of situational or psychological factors, or give an ethical evaluation or personal reaction. In this way, the young child learns to map his first-hand experience of the behaviour of other people on to the forms of language provided for him by other people (or vice versa). He may receive information from various sources, and may encounter problems in reconciling conflicting accounts (or equivalent accounts in different phraseology).

The child begins to make the connections between the behaviour of others that he can observe for himself and the language he is being provided with to describe and make sense of that behaviour. At this stage of development, however, the psychological terms, mentalistic and dispositional, are not properly understood; at best they are regarded by the child as in some important way connected with the behaviour he observes or with what he is 'experiencing', i.e. usage precedes understanding.

When the child is capable of observing his own behaviour, a commentary on that behaviour is also often provided, either by a parent or teacher or by another child. Again, the commentary may consist of statements which describe his behaviour, or statements which interpret it, or statements which express ethical evaluations or personal reactions. Typically too, the commentary includes references to the child's environment—to the objects, persons, conditions and events of which it is comprised—towards which (or away from which) the child's behaviour is directed.

At some stage the child begins to make comparisons between his own overt behaviour and the overt behaviour of other people. He becomes aware, in a primitive way, of the similarities and differences between these two sorts of behaviour; and his attention may be drawn to them by the intervention of adults and other children (who make statements about similarities and differences between the child and others, or who express themselves in non-verbal ways). Again, the language in which such comparisons and contrasts are made includes terms referring not only to overt behaviour and manifest characteristics like size and cleanliness, but also to covert characteristics and processes: thoughts and feelings, traits and abilities, and so on.

The child has already experienced 'the naming of parts', i.e. he has learned to label particular sorts of behaviour like 'closing the door', 'feeding the cat', 'putting on coat', 'being greedy', and 'saying goodbye'. He sees that his own behaviour can be labelled in this way, and that the language he has been using to refer to the behaviour of other children can be used to refer to his own behaviour (and vice versa). Naturally, he may also 'sense' attitudes and relationships which are not made verbally explicit. Without being able to reflect clearly on the process, he accepts that the terms of reference in the commentaries about the behaviour of others also apply to his own behaviour.

Some forms of behaviour are seen by the child as desirable, others as undesirable; he is therefore led, for example by imitation and modelling, to increase and diversify his repertoire of responses. At the same time, because of the commentaries that accompany his own behaviour, and that of other people, he increases and diversifies the language he uses to refer to and make sense of his own behaviour and that of others.

A further aspect of this stage of development is that the acquisition of a language for the description of overt behaviour and covert psychological processes is accompanied by an increase in the verbal control of behaviour, experience and personality. As we have seen, the development of the child's behaviour and language is not left to nature and chance, but is subject to close and detailed control through formal education, family upbringing, and the informal but pervasive influences of other people in daily life.

As the child becomes aware of similarities between his own behaviour and that of others, and learns to attach the same labels to both, he also comes to see that the same interpretative commentary may be applied to both. In this way, he comes to associate *psychological* terms like 'angry', 'pleased', 'wants', 'frightened', 'clever', 'clumsy', with his own *behaviour* and *experience*.

It is difficult to know whether the child goes through a stage of development in which he can apply the psychological terms correctly to his own *overt behaviour* without also, at the same time, being aware of and labelling his own *internal psychological* states appropriately. Whatever the mechanism, the developing child becomes increasingly aware of the relationships between covert psychological processes (both mentalistic and dispositional), overt behaviour and situational factors. This awareness is forced upon him by his tacit acceptance of ordinary language for the description and analysis of his own behaviour and the behaviour of others.

At some stage, the child must make self/self comparisons, i.e. try to align and integrate the two sorts of schemata (behavioural and psychological). It is perhaps not unreasonable to describe this alignment and integration as 'equilibration': a process in which the child's schema for the comprehension of overt behaviour is co-ordinated with his schema for the comprehension of covert psychological states and dispositions. More simply, the child learns the connections between experience and action: between thoughts, feelings and desires on the one hand, and behaviour and its outcomes on the other.

If all goes well, and the child is not unduly stressed or misled, a normal kind of equilibration is eventually achieved characterized by insight and adequate adjustment. In other circumstances, however, an abnormal or precarious kind of equilibration is achieved, characterized by neurotic defensiveness and inadequacy. In normal people, the psychological characteristics and states of mind that a person attributes to himself will, by objective standards of appraisal, be valid, i.e. he will have insight into his own nature, he will 'know himself'. In maladjusted people, by contrast, self-attributions will be invalid to a greater or lesser degree, i.e. there will be a lack of insight—a mismatch between the person's behaviour and the interpretation or explanation that the person has for his own behaviour. Similarly, maladjusted people will tend to misunderstand others.

The development of social cognition eventually reaches the stage at which—in virtue of our accumulated experience, technical knowledge and command of ordinary language—we are able to make routine self/self comparisons, self/other comparisons, and other/other comparisons without difficulty for both sorts of schema. We must not lose sight of the psychological benefits we derive from these comparisons. Our awareness of the behaviour of other people sensitizes us to similar sorts of behaviour in ourselves, and vice versa. When we have learned to label our own states of mind correctly, to relate them to our behaviour and to comment on them, we are in a better position to attribute similar states of mind to others whose behaviour is similar to our own. Disclosures by others of their own psychological processes enable us to identify similar states of mind in ourselves. Explanations by therapists or confidants help us to see relationships in our own behaviour and psychological states to which we have been blind.

The various sorts of self/other relationships described above are shown diagramatically in Figure 1. It is obvious that understanding oneself and understanding others are interdependent processes.

Figure 1 suggests a sort of longitudinal displacement in the development of social cognition, in that overt (behavioural) comparisons between self and others *precede* covert (psychological) comparisons. Since ordinary language incorporates both behavioural and psychological terms (as well as environmental and moral terms), various sorts of within-self, or within-other comparisons can be made; that is to say, we can compare the behavioural, psychological, environmental and ethical characteristics of one and the same

25

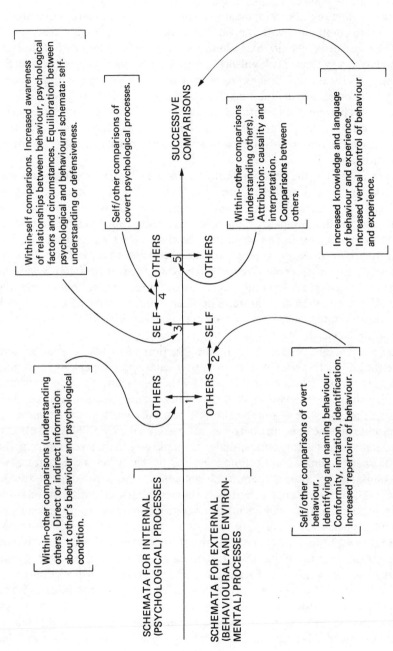

Figure 1. Successive psychobehavioural comparisons within and between self and others (in a social and linguistic context) as the basis for the growth of self-understanding and understanding others

person. This is what is meant by the equilibration of the schemata for understanding behaviour and psychological characteristics; but the actual developmental sequence depends largely on social and language learning.

Our description of the development of intra- and interpersonal comparisons is perhaps more compatible with the views of Vygotsky (1962) and Mead (1934) than with those of Piaget (1926). In his account of the development of thought and language, Vygotsky distinguishes the inner and outer aspects of speech: inner speech is for oneself, outer speech is for others. Vocalization and thought are regarded as separate functions: through social interaction, vocalization becomes speech (but words without thoughts fulfil only an affective, social signalling role); through social interaction, personal experience becomes communal (but thoughts without words, or other means of representation, remain autistic).

Egocentric speech, the child's talking out loud to himself, evolves into two rather distinct forms of speech: 'inner' and 'outer'. The development of 'inner speech' enables the child to think with socially derived word meanings and concepts, and the development of 'outer speech' enables him to communicate his thoughts to others. It is in this sense that the child's *thinking* is socialized. The gradual internalization of speech enables the child to articulate (become increasingly aware of and able to reflect on) his own mental states; it provides the link between his overt actions and covert states of mind. It therefore enables the child to infer comparable mental states in others—not so much by analogy with his own mental states, but rather *by tacit acceptance of the ordinary language of behaviour and personality*.

In the early stages of development the function of words is to direct and regulate the child's thinking in relation to particular objects, persons (including himself), events and relationships. Gradually the child learns to understand and to use the words properly—he comes to understand their syntax and their meanings. The words are acquired before the concepts which give them meaning are acquired; but the concepts become anchored, as it were, by the words and their referents. Some words correspond in a simple way to their referent, e.g. the names of objects, persons and actions; and this probably helps to structure the child's thinking—making it literal and concrete in the early stages—and to regulate his actions. Words referring to mental states and dispositions, for example, can be referred to and defined concretely in terms of overt actions, e.g. '*Clever* means when you get all your sums right', 'You mustn't go with a strange man—that's *rude*' (*sic.*, one four-year-old girl to another!). Words and phrases (meanings) provide the child with the guidance he needs in analysing and regulating his own actions and states of mind, and those of other people.

The early stage of development is characterized by syncretic thinking. The young child can form strings or loose aggregates of words and phrases and even refer to causal sequences, but he cannot organize these ideas into a coherent rational framework. He can impose order and system onto his ideas and his verbal descriptions only to the extent that he has mastered the abstract and general concepts of behaviour and personality. As the child develops he acquires more words and phrases and *integrates* them into more complex descriptions; at the same time, he acquires more higher level concepts and *differentiates* them into their component meanings. The child's own actions and experiences are an integral part of this development, which takes place, as we have indicated, in a sociolinguistic context.

Eventually, by adolescence, the average child has acquired the concepts and terms he needs to understand and influence his own behaviour and that of others. His understanding, however, is relatively informal and spontaneous, i.e. not based on systematic knowledge and formal instruction. It is sufficient to deal with the routine activities of daily living but not with the unfamiliar or abnormal aspects of human nature (including his own).

The child has to learn abstract and general concepts about *human nature* just as he has to learn them about other aspects of nature. For example, he must learn quite abstract concepts like: 'action', 'habit', 'motive', 'attitude', and 'ability', as well as less abstract ones like: 'running', 'being clean', 'trying', 'liking', and 'mending a fuse'. We must remember that although abstract concepts and the words that go with them can be formally taught, their meaning has to be supplied from the child's practical experience in using them.

According to Vygotsky, written language is radically different from spoken language (whether internal or external) in the extent to which it articulates rational thought; this assertion supports our argument that children's *written* descriptions of personality reveal the extent of their understanding of human nature better than do their *spoken* accounts.

CHAPTER 2

Ordinary Language and Personality Descriptions

I. Content, Organization and Meaning

A personality description can be analysed into its constituent words and phrases; these are its *contents*. These contents, however, are not usually presented as a simple list except in certain kinds of laboratory experiments in person perception: see, for example, Warr and Knapper (1968), Anderson and Lopes (1974). Instead, they are presented as 'systems'—often quite simple, but sometimes very complex. These systems are a function of the grammar, style and idiom of the language in which the personality description is expressed. Thus, the constituent words and phrases express an interrelated pattern of ideas in which the 'meaning' of the constituent parts depends upon their relationships with each other. This is referred to as the *organization* of the personality description.

The foregoing account does no more than draw our attention to the fact that personality descriptions—as they are formulated in ordinary language at least (as opposed to technical, artificial, special-purpose descriptions, like rating scales, Q-sorts or check-lists)—have a 'grammar' and the properties of a 'gestalt'. Gestalt properties are well-known in psychology and are recognized by linguists to be important in most aspects of language. We are concerned with the particular ways in which the form or organization of words and phrases in statements and complete descriptions can express ideas or meanings about personality.

The content of a personality description can be studied by means of lexical analysis. Such analysis, however, has rarely been used in the psychological study of personality. The classical example is the monograph published by Allport and Odbert in 1936 entitled 'Trait Names: A Psycholexical Study', which is critically reviewed in Chapter 3. This document was one of the sources which contributed to the trait approach to personality adopted, for example, by Cattell and Guilford and directed towards the identification of a limited number of relatively independent 'factors' or 'dimensions' of personality. After pruning and simplifying the Allport and Odbert list of 'traits', and grouping together words with closely related meanings, Cattell (1943, 1946, 1947) investigated the extent to which these 'psychological attributes' were associated.

Traits were regarded as stable dispositions within a person leading him to behave in characteristic ways; there would be some consensus among a person's acquaintances regarding his psychological attributes as shown, for example, by their agreement in response to check-lists and rating scales. The intercorrelations between scores derived from such methods of assessment were then used in factor-analysis or cluster-analysis to identify the main underlying dimensions of personality. Subsequently, more objective methods—personality tests, behaviour samples, situation tests, life-histories, for example—were developed to measure the so-called dimensions of personality more effectively, i.e. with greater reliability, validity and utility. Investigators studying 'person perception' also demonstrated intercorrelations between similar sorts of psychological attributes; but they regarded the associations between traits as evidence of 'implicit theories of personality', in that the associations were seen as lying more in the mind of the observers than in the persons observed: see Mischel (1968).

We said that the *contents* of personality descriptions are revealed by lexical analysis, i.e. by consideration of their constituent words and phrases. By means of content analysis, it is possible to identify, classify, count, find concordances between, and otherwise examine the constituent parts of personality descriptions. Taken in isolation, words and phrases have a range of meanings and uses of the sort that can be discovered by consulting a dictionary, a thesaurus or a book on word usage. But their 'meaning in use' when they are embedded in the context of a personality description is conditioned (or shaped) by the complex pattern of meaning attributable to the description as a whole. The meaning of many, perhaps most, words and phrases can be grossly or subtly modified by their semantic field or context of meaning, as in the following examples: 'Jones is an *intelligent* man and he has an *intelligent* dog'; 'Are you *anxious* about your prospects in the immediate future or are you normally an *anxious* sort of person?'.

It might seem reasonable to deal with the problem of lexical analysis, i.e. *content analysis*, before considering questions of syntax and semantics, i.e. *organization*. Unfortunately, English grammar is not simple or straightforward and we shall be obliged to operate at all three levels: lexical, syntactical and semantic, moving from one to another as the situation demands. We find ourselves in the paradoxical situation of sometimes having to know what the sentence means before we know what the individual words and phrases mean and sometimes having to know what the individual words and phrases mean before we can work out the meaning of the sentence. Consider for example, the following four uses of the phrase 'feelings of inferiority':

'She experiences feelings of inferiority occasionally as a consequence of the discrepancy she senses between how she might ideally have responded to a demanding situation and how she did in fact respond to it; moreover, her feelings of inferiority are self-reinforcing in the sense that she reacts badly to adverse self/other comparisons but fails to react well to favourable self/other comparisons. These are not feelings of inferiority in a psychoanalytic or psychometric sense, nevertheless they are a distinguishable feature of her personality.'

It is clear from this example that statements containing the same word or phrase can vary in meaning, and that these variations in meaning are not just inconvenient peculiarities of ordinary language, but a powerful means whereby fuller and richer patterns of meaning can be formulated and communicated.

In this connection, we should mention that words can be used to formulate ideas or meanings, to communicate them, and to understand them; although the form of words may vary for each of these functions. Different word patterns can carry the same meaning, and the same word pattern can carry different meanings (depending upon context). Different people may mean the same thing or different things when they use a form of words; and on different occasions the same person may mean the same thing or different things when he uses a form of words.

Even after this brief discussion it should be abundantly clear that ordinary language is exceedingly complicated and that it would be absurd to continue to neglect the power it gives us to express our ideas about persons. We shall find, in this and subsequent chapters, that many of the complexities of ordinary language, as they affect personality study, can be understood after careful examination of the three aspects of language mentioned above: lexical, syntactical and semantic.

The procedures for analysing the contents, organization and meaning of personality descriptions written by normal *adults* are somewhat different from those developed by Livesley and Bromley (1973): see Chapter 1. In that book, we were concerned mainly with the contents of *children's* descriptions of persons. Syntax as such was not dealt with, although some aspects of the organization of the children's descriptions were briefly described. The book also dealt briefly with the developmental transition to an adult level of understanding others. We propose to describe the contents and organization of complex adult personality descriptions in greater detail than we examined the simpler juvenile descriptions. This naturally entails some revision of the content categories, categories of organization, and other aspects of the procedures described in Livesley and Bromley (1973).

II. Syntax

A. Introduction
Although content, organization and meaning are all interrelated in a personality description, it is convenient to look first at the problem of organization, i.e. grammatical structure or syntax. Most of the examples we shall use have simple and familiar contents, the meaning of which is fairly clear; thus, in the early

stages of the analysis of organization, we shall not be unduly distracted or confused by problems associated with content and meaning.

The actual words, the manifest content, in an utterance or written phrase sometime fail to meet normal standards for well-formed syntactical structures, in which case there is usually a basic, implicit, underlying structure, the latent form of the 'sentence', which can be referred to when the meaning of the actual words is in question. For example, the exclamation 'An idiot', when used in the context of a conversation about a person P_i, might be construed as 'P_i is an idiot' or 'I think P_i is an idiot' or 'P_i acts like an idiot', or in some other way, depending upon the particular conversational context.

Syntactical analysis identifies a subject and a predicate in each well-formed sentence. The subject is a noun, noun-phrase or pronoun, sometimes qualified by an adjective or an adjectival phrase. Thus: 'he', 'she', 'the man next door', 'Tom', 'my wife' are examples of persons being the subject of a sentence in a personality description. But many other sorts of grammatical subject are possible, for example: 'His most outstanding characteristic'; 'Her appearance'; 'The thing I like least about her'. The predicate may consist of an intransitive verb which completes the sentence, or an intransitive verb with its complement, or a transitive verb with its object. For example: 'He teaches'; 'He teaches well'; 'He likes teaching'. The complement or object of the predicate may itself be a noun, a noun phrase qualified by an adjective, or an adjectival phrase. For example: 'He likes teaching maths to older children'; 'She takes care of her aged father'. The verb may be qualified by an adverb or adverbial phrase. For example: 'He soon became dissatisfied with his job'; 'She tried with all her heart to keep the marriage going'.

The complexity of the sentences can be increased by the use of clauses or phrases, which can be thought of as being analysable in much the same way as a simple subject-predicate sentence. For example: 'His friends tell me that, on some occasions, through no fault of his own, he has been involved in accidents, and this has made him reluctant to work with people he doesn't know well'. In this way, the various words and phrases in a personality description can be put together, interconnected and embedded in the overall structure of a sentence, and the sentences too can be put together, interconnected and embedded in the overall structure of the description.

For the purposes of syntactical analysis, it is sometimes necessary to redraft actual (real-life) 'sentences' because they are only approximations to grammatical sentences. So, in order to carry out an analysis of the *organization* of written descriptions, it is necessary to transform them into well-formed syntactic structures.

The formulation of complex ideas usually requires complex sentences. If a person's language facility is poor—because of low intelligence or lack of education or both—then he will find it difficult to express complex ideas about other people. He will not have the words or phrases, or the knowledge, or the grammatical skill to formulate sentences expressing the complex facts, relationships and conditions pertaining to human behaviour and psychological processes. This is not to say that such a person may not have a kind of native shrewdness in his dealings with other people; he may very well have acquired certain skills and sensitivities in his social relationships. Nevertheless, if his general linguistic facility is poor, it follows that he will find it difficult or impossible to articulate subtle or complicated thoughts, feelings or wishes about himself or other people. This issue, of course, is closely related to the sociology of language; in particular to the notion that there are social class differences in language, such that some individuals are capable of using only a restricted linguistic code whereas others are capable of using an elaborated code: see Lawton (1968), Bernstein (1972), and Bilsbury (in preparation).

The distinction drawn between the latent and manifest forms of a sentence obviously has a bearing on the issue of linguistic facility, regardless of whether we have in mind the broad sociological differences between elaborated and restricted codes, or the normal range of psychological differences between individual people in their ability, inclination or habit when speaking or writing. Even intelligent and well-educated people sometimes write and often speak in ungrammatical ways (because of error, abbreviation, and so on); the actual or 'manifest' expression may not be sufficient *in itself* to make its meaning clear. That a poorly-formed manifest sentence is usually understood without much difficulty derives from the fact that its latent content and its context are understood and taken for granted by people sharing the same sociolinguistic frame of reference.

Another important matter which has a bearing on interpersonal communication and perception is the use of idiom and metaphor. Thus, for example, if I say, 'She ties people in knots', I do not expect to be taken literally, but rather, metaphorically, since what I am trying to say is, 'She says and does things which lead other people to behave in confused or contradictory ways'. Of course, my colloquial expression may not convey this latent sentence; indeed, I may not be able to say exactly what I mean when I express myself metaphorically.

As regards punctuation, this is often so erratic in personality descriptions written by adults that one cannot use it with much confidence when interpreting the meaning of a sentence. Fortunately, the full-stop is used by most adults to mark the end of a sentence.

B. Syntax in Simple Sentences

The following examples, drawn from the author's research data, illustrate relatively simple sorts of sentence found in personality descriptions written by adults. For the moment, we are concerned mainly with the syntactical structure of these sentences rather than with other aspects of grammar.

    Example 1

                'This woman is a teacher.'
                The sentence can be analysed into:
                    Subject: This woman,
                    Predicate: is a teacher.

The subject can be analysed into:

    Noun: woman,

    Determiner: This.

The predicate can be analysed into:

    Verb: is,

Complement $\begin{cases} \text{Article:} & \text{a,} \\ \text{Noun:} & \text{teacher.} \end{cases}$

Example 2

'She is a persistent complainer.'

The sentence can be analysed into:

    Subject: She,

    Predicate: is ... complainer.

The predicate can be analysed into:

    Verb: is,

Complement $\begin{cases} \text{Article:} & \text{a,} \\ \text{Adjective:} & \text{persistent,} \\ \text{Noun:} & \text{complainer.} \end{cases}$

Example 3

'A very pleasing person to know'. As explained in an earlier section, sentences are sometimes ill-formed. In this instance, the subject and verb have been taken for granted, i.e. the subject of the sentence is the person referred to earlier in the personality description, and the verb 'to be' is assumed to take the present tense. Thus:

(She is) 'A very pleasing person to know.'

The predicate can be analysed into:

    Verb: is,

Complement $\begin{cases} \text{Article:} & \text{A,} \\ \text{Noun Phrase:} & \text{pleasing ... to know,} \\ \text{Adjective:} & \text{very,} \\ \text{Noun:} & \text{person.} \end{cases}$

This example is slightly less simple because there is some doubt about its meaning, i.e. it is not clear whether the 'pleasing' refers to a characteristic of the stimulus person or to the observer's state of mind, or to both. One could argue that the relationship is a reciprocal one, i.e. the two sorts of 'pleasing' usually go together, otherwise a qualifying clause would be needed in order to express the meaning of the sentence more clearly.

Example 4

'She is rude to staff and public.'

The predicate can be analysed into:

    Verb: is,

Complement $\begin{cases} \text{Noun Phrase:} & \text{rude to staff,} \\ \text{,,\quad\quad,,} & \text{(rude to the) public,} \\ \text{Conjunction:} & \text{and.} \end{cases}$

Note that the conjunction 'and' does not have merely an additive function, but also enables the meanings of the words so linked to interact and be modified by that conjunction, in this instance by amplifying the intensity of the meaning common to both terms.

Example 5

'He has a forward but pleasant manner.'
The predicate can be analysed into:

	Verb:	has,
Complement	Article:	a,
	Noun:	manner,
	Adjectival Phrase:	forward . . . pleasant,
	Conjunction:	but.

Note that the conjunction 'but', like the word 'and' in Example 4, has the important function of qualifying the meaning of the word 'forward', in the sense that it inhibits the further psychological characteristics that would be attributed to the stimulus person if the word 'forward' were not so qualified, as in 'He has a forward manner'. The associative networks linking various psychological attributes have been the object of investigation in studies of implicit personality theory, see Bruner, Shapiro and Tagiuri (1958), Wishner (1960), as well as in studies of objective personality assessment: those of Cattell (1943, 1946, 1947) are among the earliest.

The foregoing examples show that some of the syntactical structures in written personality descriptions are quite simple and can be expressed by means of a general formula. The following arbitrary notation will be adopted: S = subject (a noun or noun phrase, usually the stimulus person or some aspect of the stimulus person); V = verb (a verb or verb phrase, usually 'to be' or 'to have', with its auxiliary); A, B, C, etc. = attributes or objects of various sorts (a noun or noun phrase); Q = qualifying words or phrases (adjectival or adverbial); J = qualifying words or phrases (conjunctival). The examples of sentences given above can then be expressed as follows:

Examples	Structure
1, 2, 3	$S + V + A$
4, 5	$S + V + AJB$

Naturally, the subject (S) and the verb (V), can also be qualified (Q), e.g. 'Her best feature (SQ) seems to be (VQ) . . .'; 'His first job (SQ) never provided (VQ) any incentive . . .'. The verb can be negated ($\bar{V}$), e.g. '. . . is not . . .'; '. . . has not . . .'; '. . . does not . . .'; and the attributes or objects can be qualified, e.g. '. . . an interesting personality . . .' (AQ), '. . . somewhat secretive . . .' (BQ).

From these preliminary ideas and typical examples, we can see that a wide variety of assertions about people, as expressed in personality descriptions, have similar and familiar syntactical structures, as the following, additional, real-life examples illustrate:

'She is very affectionate and fond of people and not afraid to show this.'
Structure: $S + V + AQ + J + B + J + \bar{V} + C(C = AQ + B)$.
(She is) 'Not interested in public affairs, (or) other countries or abstract discussions.'
Structure: $S + \bar{V} + AQ + J + BQ + J + CQ$.
'She is a persistent complainer.'
Structure: $S + V + AQ$.
'She lives alone and is contented with her lot.'
Structure: $S + V + A + J + V + BQ$.
'He finds his work fascinating.'
Structure: $S + VQ + AQ$.
'He loves (being with?) people and talking and is open to accept new ideas.'
Structure: $S + VQ + A + J + V + BQ + VC$.

Even longer sentences frequently have a relatively simple syntactical structure. For example:

'He is very much at ease with adults and is ready to fall in with group ideas and games.'
Structure: $S + V + AQ + J + VQ + C + J + VQ + DQ + J + E$.
'She is very self-sufficient, lives alone, has enough money to cope but is very pleased with all she has done—a nice house etc.'
Structure: $S + V + AQ + V + B + J + VQ + J + D + J + EQ$.

The notation merely illustrates the psychological similarity of certain elements in syntactic structures and we shall not refer to it again. Phraseology of a more complex and varied kind is presented in Chapters 5, 6 and 7 which analyse the contents of personality descriptions and attempt to define classes of similar elements.

C. Syntax in Complex Sentences

We gave some thought to the question of how to present our analysis of sentence structure. If we had discovered that sentences in personality descriptions in ordinary English had unusual syntactical structures we would have used bracketing or tree-diagrams—in line with current linguistic practice—so as to demonstrate their special, formal features. In fact, the sentence structures were in no way unusual, except that they were often grammatically 'ill-formed', and analysis by the traditional method of parsing seemed to be at least as adequate and in some respects better-suited to our main aim, namely, analysis of the lexical and semantic aspects of personality descriptions.

The following examples illustrate the more complex sorts of real-life 'sentence' found in personality descriptions written by adults. They are also drawn from the author's research data. Again, we are concerned only with their syntactical features.

Example 1

'This boy although of tender years is a "typical boy" who although one of five children of similar age is always up to mischief and is constantly being shouted at by his mother.'

The 'sentence' (or group of sentences) can be analysed into:

Subject: This boy, although of tender years,
Predicate: is ... mother.

The subject can be analysed into:

Noun phrase: This boy,
Adjectival phrase: although of tender years,

The predicate can be analysed into:

		Verb:	is,
	Noun phrase	Article:	a,
		Noun (complement):	... boy,
		Adjective:	'typical',
Conjunction of relative clauses	Relative clause	Relative pronoun:	who,
		Verb phrase:	is ... up to,
		Adverb:	always,
		Noun:	mischief,
		Conjunction:	and,
	Relative clause	Verb phrase:	is ... shouted at,
		Adverbial phrase:	constantly being,
		Preposition:	by,
		Noun:	mother,
		Pronoun:	his.

Example 2

'She had her faults, she was somewhat difficult to "get to know" initially, and tended to remain rather aloof, and could be rather selfish on the rare occasion.'

The 'sentence' (or group of sentences, some with the word 'she' deleted) can be analysed into:

Subject: She,
Predicate: had her ... occasion.

The 'predicate' can be analysed into:

Co-ordinate clauses

	Verb:	had,
	Pronoun:	her,
	Noun:	faults,
	Pronoun:	she,
	Verb:	was,
	Noun phrase:	difficult to 'get to know',
	Adjective:	somewhat,
	Adverb:	initially,
	Conjunction:	and,
	Verb:	tended,
	Noun phrase:	to remain ... aloof,
	Adjective:	rather,
	Conjunction:	and,
	Verb:	could be,
	Noun:	selfish,
	Adjective:	rather,
	Adverb:	on ... occasion,
	Adjective:	rare,
	Article:	the.

These examples of more complex sentences provide further illustrations of the syntactical issues already raised. We are now in a better position to examine some of the lexical and semantic issues in personality description. We must bear in mind that a comprehensive account of the language of personality description should explain how 'logical' relationships are established between lexical elements by syntactic structures. A personality description is not merely a list of statements.

III. Lexicon: Introduction to the Content Analysis of Words and Phrases

For our purpose the term 'content analysis' refers to a method for identifying and classifying the words and phrases used in ordinary written language to describe and analyse personality. The discussion which follows will be illustrative rather than systematic and comprehensive, since the main issues are dealt with in detail in Chapters 5, 6 and 7.

In Example 1, above, the term 'teacher' indicates a social role, and roles (coded ROLE) are commonly specified in personality descriptions. Similarly, in Example 2, 'persistent complainer' indicates a relatively enduring behavioural disposition or trait, and such general traits (coded GENT) are also very common in personality descriptions. In Example 3, 'pleasing to know' seems to refer to the effect that the stimulus person has on the writer or on people in general, and so might be either coded O–SP, signifying the way other people respond to the stimulus person, i.e. as in statements about his reputation, or coded S–SP, signifying the way the writer (observer) reacts to the stimulus person, i.e. by feeling pleased at knowing him. In Example 4, 'rude to staff and public' is coded EVAL, which signifies an overall positive or negative evaluation of the person, i.e. it is not the behaviour as such that is mentioned, but rather its negative value 'rude'. In Example 5, 'forward but pleasant manner' contains two elements—'forward' and 'pleasant'; the former is classified as SP–O, because it refers to the stimulus person's behaviour towards others, the latter is classified as EVAL because it refers to an overall positive evaluation of the stimulus person's behaviour.

The sentences above, illustrating syntactical structures, contain the following sorts of lexical items (contents).

Content word or phrase	*Code: content category*
... affectionate ...	GENT: general personality trait
... fond of people ...	MOTA + OBJE: goal-directed motivation
... not afraid to show this ...	ORFE + OBJE: orientation and feeling toward something
... not interested in public affairs ...	MOTA + OBJE: as above (negative)
... persistent complainer ...	GENT: as above
... lives alone ...	SITU: current situation or circumstances
... contented with her lot ...	ORFE + OBJE: as above
... at ease with adults ...	SP–O: stimulus person's response to others
... self sufficient ...	GENT: as above
... all she has—a nice house ...	MATP: material possessions.

It is possible to distinguish thirty different sorts of content category in personality descriptions written by adults. These range from simple statements about the stimulus person's identity and physical appearance through statements about his life history and present circumstances, his personal qualities and states of mind, his social relationships, his relationships with the writer of the description, and comparisons between the stimulus person and other people, to statements expressing some sort of evaluation of the stimulus person. A residual category can be used to catalogue any elements (words or phrases) which cannot be classified by reference to the main set of content categories. In theory, the elements should be classified exhaustively and exclusively, but in practice most words and phrases can take on a range of possible meanings, which can be systematically reduced by embedding the word or phrase in a context of other words and phrases. In artificial or specially adapted languages it may be possible to completely 'disambiguate' a word or phrase, but in loose, free-flowing, ordinary discourse, its exact meaning may be indeterminate, although an approximate meaning may be assigned with reasonable reliability and validity.

The inter-observer reliability of content analysis, of the sort under consideration, can be measured by finding the percentage agreement between two or more trained coders analysing the same personality descriptions with reference to an agreed list of categories, and with reference to a lexicon containing all the more frequently occurring terms and representative samples of terms occurring less frequently. Unfortunately, it is not usual for these conditions to be met in studies using content analysis; so that it is difficult to say what levels of reliability could be reached.

The validity of content analysis can be measured in much the same way as in other kinds of psychometric research, i.e. by reference to face validity, construct validity, criterion validity, and so on. Another way of improving reliability and validity would be to refer to the meaning of the sentence containing a lexical element: if the content category to which it was assigned remained constant in spite of variations in wording this would indicate that the meaning of this particular element had been correctly (validly) interpreted. For example 'She is rude to staff and public' might be reworded as 'Staff and public find her rude'. The question now is (a) whether both statements are coded EVAL or (b) whether the former is coded EVAL and the latter O–SP. If it is agreed that the two statements mean the same thing, then any failure to assign the same coding to both would reduce the validity of the coding method. Similarly, the sentence 'She is a very pleasing person to know' might be reworded as 'It is very pleasing to know her'. The question now is (a) whether both predicates are classified O–SP (or S–SP), or (b) whether the former is classified EVAL and the latter O–SP (or S–SP). Again, any failure to assign the same coding to the same meaning when the sentences have different wordings would reduce the validity of the coding method.

Even these brief remarks about the 'meaning' and 'wording' of sentences confirm that lexical (content analysis) issues in the ordinary language of personality description cannot be completely separated from syntactical or semantic issues. We have just seen that it may be necessary to examine several variations in wording for sentences with the same meaning in order to verify that a given lexical element has been correctly classified. We have also seen that the meaning of a given word or phrase is shaped by its grammatical context—as the meaning of the word 'forward' is shaped by the phrase 'but pleasant manner' immediately following it. Similarly the collocation of 'very affectionate', 'fond of people' and 'not afraid to show this' is an example of how we give emphasis and shape to the patterns of meaning we are trying to formulate and communicate.

In conclusion, then, we can say that in our attempts to express our ideas about other people in written English, we contrive to impose an appropriate syntactical structure on certain lexical terms. We find such terms useful in co-ordinating our experience with (a) events in the real world and with (b) the experience of other people. In trying to formulate a sentence, various possibilities and shades of meaning are possible—depending upon the situation, the language ability of the writer, time constraints, and so on—and when a sentence is produced, it may not express the writer's underlying thoughts, feelings and intentions exactly.

In spite of the existence of one-word 'sentences', clipped English, restricted language codes, and so on, our experience is structured. If our experience needs to be more finely articulated, then more complex syntactical structures are called for, which in turn demand, and help to generate, additions to the lexicon.

The concept of 'structure' can be co-ordinated with that of 'level'; structure is found at levels above and below those that we have so far considered. At lower levels, structural considerations govern the order and choice of words and phrases, as well as punctuation and spelling. At higher levels, structural considerations govern the selection and emphasis of available material, the order and manner of presentation of the material as a whole, the organization of paragraphs, style and so on. These higher levels of organization are important in long descriptions in case-studies, in biographies, and in fiction: see Chapters 8 and 10.

IV. Language and the 'Logic' of Personality Descriptions

The *organization* of a personality description (including a case-study, or life-history) can be regarded as a structure which determines the relationships between the words and phrases of which it is composed, and therefore influences their meaning.

A lengthy personality description might have distinguishable substructures within an overall structure; these would appear as separate issues or topics (sections, paragraphs or headings), such as: academic record, leisure activities, job aspirations, marital relationships. Thus, a common feature of personality descriptions is that the information is organized around one or more issues or topics. The relevance and significance of that information, of course, depends upon the skill of the investigator.

One way of discerning (or demonstrating) such overall structural properties in a personality description is to summarize it as an 'informal argument', by means of the method described below: see also Toulmin (1958). Unfortunately, in practice, the informal logical structure is often incomplete and inadequate so that the 'argument' is obscure, and tedious to work out.

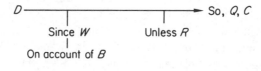

Figure 2

An argument can be thought of as a set of interlocking ideas—analogous to a jig-saw puzzle or meccano set—organized in such a way as to express a meaning or demonstrate a theory. It is possible to distinguish six sorts of components which fit together as shown in Figure 2. Or, in 'standard form', as follows: D, so Q, C, since W, on account of B, unless R.

Type of Statement	Logical Functions
C	States a claim or conclusion.
D	Offers data or foundations, i.e. relevant evidence, for the claim.
W	Refers to a warrant which justifies the step from D to C by appealing to practical standards, canons of argument, or other rules of inference, including analogies and definitions.
Q	Qualifies a claim or conclusion by the use of terms expressing probability or confidence.
R	Rebuts a claim or conclusion by stating the conditions under which it does not hold.
B	Backs an inference warrant or appeals to facts of one sort or another to justify a warrant.

Colloquially

C answers the question 'What are you saying?'
D   ,,   ,,   ,,   'What have you to go on?'
W   ,,   ,,   ,,   'How do you make that out?'
Q   ,,   ,,   ,,   'How sure are you?'
R   ,,   ,,   ,,   'What are you assuming?'
B   ,,   ,,   ,,   'What proof have you?'

Consider the following very simple example:

D: John has a tested mental-age of eight and is about eight-years-old.
C: So, John's intelligence is about average.
Q: Presumably.
W: Since young persons whose MA and CA are equal or nearly equal have average intelligence.
R: Unless the test was wrongly administered or wrongly scored; unless a mistake has been made about John's age; unless John was not feeling well or co-operative, and so on.
B: On account of the accepted theory and practice of intelligence testing which defines intelligence in terms of I.Q.

In a long complex argument, however, such as one finds in a case-study in clinical psychology or social work, there may be many subsidiary arguments which interlock by means of a simple linking device whereby a statement fulfills one function in one argument and another function in another argument. For example, the C of one may become the D of another.

In practice, it is difficult to work out the informal logical structure of a complex argument. As a result, many arguments which appear to be satisfactory do not stand up to close examination. The brief notes, above, can be used to formulate sound arguments and to expose the deficiencies of unsound arguments. Note that a psychological case-study is basically an argument in which a pattern of meaning (construction) is imposed on empirical data (evidence); although it is sometimes presented as if the inferences were *drawn from* the facts of observation. The former is the proper conjectural or 'deductive' mode, the latter is misleadingly called the 'inductive' mode, of argument. Further discussion of this kind of 'informal logic' as it applies to quasi-judicial case-studies can be found in Chapter 8: see also Toulmin (1958) and Bromley (1968, 1970).

Within the overall structural or logical framework described above, several other organizational features are commonly found in personality descriptions, as follows.

Causal or Rational Relationships. Some statements offer reasons or causes for a person's behaviour (see Chapters 4 and 9). The actual psychological mechanisms may not be conceptualized very adequately, although the number of ordinary commonsense explanatory concepts is quite small, e.g. habit, motive, role, circumstance, orientation, (dis)ability. The existence of reasons or causes may be signalled by terms like 'because', 'since', 'so', 'when', 'if', and other more complex conjunctions. Note the following implicit explanations of a person's behaviour: showing an interdependence between psychological processes and qualities, e.g. 'He is nervous and this makes him shy at times', 'He is only kind if he is in a good temper'; or showing an interdependence of psychological processes and circumstances, e.g. 'He has to get cross sometimes', 'He is cheerful considering . . .', 'He is quiet when in company'.

Implications and Reservations. Some statements elicit psychological implications because the ordinary language of personality description is characterized by semantic linkages, e.g. the warm/cold variable in personality ratings. Other statements, however, in effect instruct us *not* to make the usual inferences from a particular quality the person is said to possess, e.g. 'She is always being kind *but* she is nosey', 'She is quite modern *although* sensible', 'He is very good at work *but* very slow'. Structural relationships also govern the way a particular trait is specified. Trait names are highly generalized terms for describing behavioural tendencies. But when they are applied to a particular individual, additional information has to be provided which specifies in greater detail how the trait is expressed in that person's behaviour, e.g. 'She does not always argue, if she does, she does not get aggressive', 'She is greedy because she never shares things although others offer her things'. (Note, in this example, 'because' is used in an evidential rather than a causal sense.)

Perspective and Confidence. Some statements indicate that the writer (speaker) is not too sure of the impression he has formed and that it is difficult to decide whether or not a person possesses a given quality, e.g. 'seems to be', 'sort of', 'I suppose', 'I am told that', 'people say'. Also, a distinction may be made between real and apparent qualities and between past and present dispositions, e.g. 'Although she professes to be your friend, when you are ill she doesn't visit you', 'He is not really . . .', 'She used to be . . . now she is . . .'.

Salience. Some statements say something about the likelihood of occurrence, frequency, intensity and duration of personal characteristics, e.g. terms like 'very', 'mostly', 'sometimes', 'usually', 'always', 'can be', 'scarcely ever', 'quite', 'often'. They make adjustments, as it were, to the structure of meaning.

Figures of speech. Some statements are metaphors (warm, cold, hard, soft, straight), similarities or analogies ('He is like his father', 'Her outlook is the same as his'). We have already referred to these kinds of 'ready-made' phrases; clichés provide an abundant source of simple and practical ways of imposing a 'pattern of meaning' on a person's behaviour.

V. Semantics

A. Definitions, Meanings and Uses
A dictionary contains a definition, and examples of the meanings of, a word, together with other information. It shows how to connect up a given word with other, more basic, familiar words. Understanding a word or phrase, however, depends upon prior experience of the personal characteristics or behaviour to which the word refers, and the circumstances in which it can be used, e.g. the words 'married', 'father', 'jealous', 'shy', 'sulking', 'pretending'.

The problem of defining 'meaning' raises the question of the 'meaning' of operationally defined terms in the study of personality. A term is said to be 'operationally defined' when an explicit measurement can be made upon which all competent observers can agree. For example, introversion, neurosis, creativity and other characteristics, can be defined in terms of performance on standard tests. However, the meaning of such terms is not exhausted by their operational definition; the operational definition is simply a way of *adding* to their meaning a feature which enables such terms to be anchored to empirical observation. The meaning of the operational definition comprises what is known about the reliability, validity and utility of the measurement operation, e.g. the psychological test. Thus, the meaning of the operational definition of a personality characteristic is fairly technical, i.e. not a normal part of the ordinary meaning of the term. Nevertheless, ordinary language is necessary in order to explicate the meaning of an operational definition as well as the wider meaning of the term it defines.

In ordinary language, there are several methods of defining the meaning of words, some of which are familiar to us from traditional work in the study of personality. A word can be defined in terms of a synonymous word or phrase, or by contrast with antonyms. For example, 'jealous' means 'envious', or 'fearful that a rival may take one's place'. A word can be defined analytically, that is, by showing the class to which it belongs and its distinguishing characteristics. For example, 'anxiety' means 'a sort of fear that something unpleasant may happen'. A synthetic definition is one which explains the contextual or functional relationships of the word (as in operational definition). For example 'disobedience' could be defined as 'frequent contravention of parental commands or school rules' or as 'the deliberate refusal to carry out an instruction', or, negatively as 'the score on an obedience test'. The meaning of a word can also be conveyed by citing examples of its use, and by showing what its use implies. For example, in the statement 'She is jealous of her step-daughter', 'jealous' implies 'sensitive to signs of favour'. Such implicative definitions are obviously important in helping to link relatively abstract and general terms (referring to relatively invariant aspects of a person), such as traits or motives, with other terms in the wider conceptual framework. A denotative definition is one which points to examples of the word to which it refers. For example, 'motivation' refers to hunger, thirst and sex. An ostensive definition is one which points to examples of the actual objects, events, relationships, etc., to which the word refers. For example, I might say, 'That's what I mean by aggression' (pointing to a real-life example of it). Finally, words can be defined in terms of the grammatical or logical rules required for using them—e.g., terms like 'very', 'sometimes', 'but', that help to organize and qualify other words in a statement.

In learning how to use language, including learning how to use the language of personality descriptions, the meanings of words are presented to us in all these different ways. Notice that these different ways of learning the meanings of words could be used systematically in educating children in understanding others, by enabling them to represent and communicate their growing experience of the behaviour of other people in more adequate phraseology.

Some words and phrases are vague: e.g. 'butterfly mind', 'odd', 'sort of depressed'. Vagueness, of course, can be useful in the ordinary language of social exchange, but it is an embarrassment in scientific discourse. Wherever possible, therefore, vagueness should be removed—by substituting a well-defined term, as indicated above.

A word or phrase in ordinary language does not have one exactly defined meaning; it may convey different meanings in different contexts. The context, moreover, comprises not just the sentence or passage in which the word or phrase occurs, but rather the overall situation, including the psychological characteristics of the person or persons involved, the constraints and opportunities for action provided by the surrounding circumstances, and sequential and historical factors. For example, the meaning conveyed by the structure and content of a personality description depends upon who provides it, how it is provided, who it is provided for, the reasons for its being provided, as well as upon whether it is early or late in a series or one on its own.

As far as the immediate verbal context is concerned, the psychological significance of a trait name, for example, can be modified by adjacent words and phrases, as the word 'gentle' is modified in phrases like 'gentle but firm', 'gentle and kind', 'gentle with children', 'gentle manner'. In addition, quite elaborate and subtle expressions of meaning are achieved through the use of qualifying and organizing phraseology, such as 'not as gentle as he could be', 'quite gentle when you get to know him', 'surprisingly gentle with pupils considering his apparent bitterness and hostility towards the teaching profession'. Thus, although a word may remain the same linguistic entity in different contexts (and to that extent is not ambiguous), it may be vague unless its context makes it clear. Ordinary language enables us to narrow down the range of reference of a word or phrase.

It could be argued that the use of trait names in traditional methods of studying personality, e.g. by means of adjective check-lists, Q-sorts and rating-scales, has been based on a misunderstanding of the nature of language. Even when trait names are given what appears to be an adequate definition, or even anchored to behavioural criteria, one cannot be sure that one has succeeded in delimiting and fixing the range of reference or 'meaning' of these terms. And even if one were moderately successful in achieving this sort of 'operational definition', it is not clear that the resulting description would correspond well with any real-life characteristic of a stimulus person. Moreover, it is clear that traits, as commonly understood, are not independent of one another; they interact in various ways, perhaps differently in different circumstances. Flexibility and accuracy in the specification of meaning in the description and analysis of psychological and behavioural processes can be achieved through the careful use of ordinary language, although this approach has been neglected in favour of artificial and oversimplified terminologies.

The traditional approach adopted a strategy which was perhaps fully justified in the early history of personality study—a strategy modelled on scientific positivism, relying on standardized methods of observation and measurement, and using technical terms for the description and analysis of personality (with particular reference to understanding abnormal behaviour). This strategy gave rise to the construction of a wide variety of personality tests: questionnaires, inventories, projective tests, and so on. It gave rise to assessments based on specially contrived languages, e.g. those devised by Freud, Murray, Cattell and other theorists in personality research. It is perhaps ironic that Allport, who preached a sort of 'naturalistic' approach to the study of the individual person, should have provided one of the main platforms for later work in the positivist tradition: see Chapter 3. The apparent failure of the positivist approach to give an adequate description and explanation of human personality—see Mischel (1968)—is a major reason for embarking on this difficult and uncertain enterprise of investigating personality descriptions in ordinary language.

Statements about a person may fulfil various functions, depending upon circumstances. For example, statements may (a) assert an observation or a conjecture, an event or a relationship, (b) assert a possibility, (c) express a wish or a value judgment, (d) assert a past, present or future state of affairs, (e) make a joke, (f) express a social relationship, e.g. in taking sides or adopting a role, (g) express a command, warning, doubt, feeling or intention. Consider the following respective examples: (a) 'John hits his wife'; 'John is not usually aggressive'; 'I expect John will feel remorseful'; 'John is like his brother'; (b) 'John seems to have lots of friends'; 'John may be in debt'; (c) 'I wish John would listen to reason'; 'John's manners are awful'; (d) 'John was an only child'; 'John is good at his job'; 'John will be looking for help'; (e) 'With friends like John's who needs enemies?' (f) 'Jill objects to John's attitude'; 'John's behaviour is no business of mine'; (g) 'Tell John that he is wrong'; 'If John isn't more careful, there will be trouble'; 'I doubt whether John is responsible for his actions'; 'I feel that John is deliberately making trouble'; 'John cannot rely on Jill's help from now on'.

Thus the language of personality description and analysis is part of the everyday language of social exchange. It can express the writer's (speaker's) actual assessment and considered beliefs; but it can also reflect the writer's (speaker's) less rational feelings, wishes and expectations in relation to the stimulus person. It can be adapted to his audience—their age, sex, ability, and so on. Statements about persons often function as 'opinions' (rather than as scientific observations, generalizations or hypotheses) in that they fulfil a personal (subjective) function in the social exchange of everyday life—consider the similar function of political opinions described in Smith, Bruner and White (1956).

A personality description can be said to 'represent' the person as the map represents the territory, or as the formula represents a chemical reaction. Or, to use the analogy of the jig-saw, words and phrases are fitted into various combinations of other words and phrases, so as to construct a meaningful description of him; although the meaning one expresses may be incomplete, ambiguous and otherwise imperfect. Perhaps a better analogy would be that of the molecule, where words and phrases are regarded as arranged in a mainly linear but partly branching fashion in a variety of different structures (sentences). The molecules (sentences) in turn form a richly interconnected 'tissue' or 'pattern' of meaning.

One aspect of natural language that we shall largely ignore is etymology. Etymology is a specialized and technical subject outside the range of our immediate concern. It deals with the causes and historical sequences of changes in the meaning of words. Of course, the etymology of certain words in the description and analysis of personality could have implications for the sort of linguistic analysis we are engaged in. The word 'personality' itself, for example, has an interesting origin dating back to the use of a mask (persona) by actors in Greek and Roman times. However, when we discover that the word 'behaviour' is derived from the Old English *behabban*, to detain, restrain, that the word 'kind' is derived from the Old English (*ge*)*cynde*—*cynn*, kin, and that the word 'ambition' is derived from the Latin '*ambitionis*', to go about canvassing, it becomes obvious that the etymology of personality terms requires a book all to itself.

We cannot exclude etymological issues altogether, if only because we have to make comparisons between the literal and figurative (metaphorical) meanings of the same word or phrase. John Locke was the first to point out that some psychological terms seem to be derived metaphorically from the physical world. How is it, for example, that we can use terms like 'cold', 'tough', 'bright' and 'stiff' to refer to psychological characteristics? Can etymology discover whether we derive psychological meanings from physical meanings, or vice versa? Locke's view has been argued against indirectly in Chapter 1, where it was said that our perception and understanding of the physical world might be conditioned by our early infantile experiences in the behavioural world of persons. However, all we can do at this stage is to point out that words and language have an 'ontogeny' as well as a 'phylogeny'.

Few, if any, personality terms are 'iconic', i.e. imitative or representational. Some, however, are created in the image of their human or behavioural counterparts, e.g. 'quisling', 'statesmanlike', 'queenly', 'slavish', 'motherly'. But such terms are metaphorical, rather like the physical terms referred to in the previous paragraph.

Written language appears to be derived from spoken language; written language is much more effective in formulating the abstract and complicated systems of ideas that we are interested in. That they can exert a controlling influence on perception and action suggests that it is perhaps more important to study these cognitive functions (via written descriptions) than to study on-going interpersonal encounters (via the spoken word).

The range of meanings that can be taken on by a word in isolation from other words can be broadly stated and illustrated by means of a dictionary and a thesaurus; but a dictionary definition does not *fix* a word's meaning. The actual meaning of a word or phrase, when it is used in a statement, is shaped by its grammatical context and by the wider situational context. This point has already been made, but deserves emphasis; it raises the further point that the writer (speaker) may fail to say exactly what he means and the reader (listener) may fail to understand, or misconstrue, what is written (said). The wider issues concerning the situational and psychological factors in communication have been dealt with to some extent in social and clinical psychology and we do not intend to expand on these issues.

Ordinary language is 'holophrastic', in that a word or phrase may form a complete unit of meaning, e.g. one word 'sentences' and stereotyped phrases. Words occur in familiar patterns, for example 'not very happy', 'fun to be with', 'a well-paid job', 'outwardly calm'. Metaphors function as complete phrases, for example: 'She ties people in knots'; 'He's a wily old bird'; 'She's living on a knife-edge'. In many instances, such stereotyped phrases become so familiar in common usage that their status as metaphors is not intrusive and their meaning is quite clear.

The rule that words occur in structured sets applies to language in general, and the language of personality description is no exception. It has been clearly established that trait names can be grouped into clusters or factors, and overlap in meaning, or form part of a strong associative network. Mischel (1968) argues that the clusters and factors thus established reflect not so much the actual existence of personality dispositions in people, but rather the cognitive structures we use to make sense of the behaviour of people. This is an interesting distinction, and one is tempted to suppose that the two are isomorphic. However, we must not confuse our representation of the world with the world itself; we must not confuse personality descriptions with personalities.

The way words fit into associative networks and into frequently occurring grammatical patterns is referred to as 'collocation'. The extent to which a word can fit into such collocations is referred to as its 'collocability'; thus it has been said that you shall know (the meaning of) a word by the company it keeps: Waldron (1967). As we have seen, lexical items, capable of taking on a range of meanings, can be fitted into a particular syntactical structure, so that a definite meaning is generated.

Grammatical patterns have semantic significance. It would make sense, for example, to say 'He is normally quiet and shy, but when he is with friends, and especially after a few drinks, he can be boisterous and talkative'. But it would not make sense to say, 'Although he is feeling guilty and anxious about his behaviour he is not sorry or disturbed by what he did'. The 'grammar' of personality descriptions consists of the rules that enable us to explain why some sentences about people make sense, whereas others do not—this is what the psychology of personality and adjustment is about.

As we can see from the above examples, in the context of personality description, certain familiar phrases occur: 'quiet and shy', 'when he is with friends', 'guilty and anxious', and so on. Such familiar and easy usage is associated with the existence of high transitional probabilities in the English language, and with a moderate degree of 'redundancy'. Redundancy, in this sense, means that certain words and phrases could be omitted from a sentence without serious loss of meaning. Language may be looked at in terms of information transmission, channel capacity, redundancy and noise. Such concepts apply to the language of personality descriptions too, see Bieri *et al.* (1966). Redundancy in personality descriptions occurs when words, phrases or statements overlap in meaning, and when there are high transitional probabilities between words in a sentence. It might be possible to account for 'implicit theories of personality' in terms of redundancy in the English language, in the sense that, for example, 'ambitious' implies 'hard-working' because 'hard-working' is part of the accepted meaning of 'ambitious'. Thus a person's 'implicit theory of personality' may be simply a reflection of his way of using the language of personality description. Associative networks (semantic fields) for trait names can be expected to have both a personal (idiosyncratic) and a social (common) aspect.

Although sentences in English are partly redundant, this does not mean that the underlying meaning is fully expressed. A personality description is only the manifest content of a much wider latent content of ideas. Normally, we are neither willing nor able to explicate the whole system of ideas, feelings and intentions that centre upon the stimulus person. Moreover, this system of experience is not static, but lives and changes in response to the stimulus person and in response to our self-examination of the thoughts and feelings we have about the stimulus person. The fact that we give relatively brief and sometimes strongly selective and evaluative descriptions of a stimulus person should come as no surprise. We respond in exactly the same way in other circumstances, for example, if we are asked to say what we think of a book or a film. Not only do we know more than we say, we also want and feel more than we can say.

In order to move towards a more scientific language of personality, we must first understand the practical uses to which personality descriptions can be put. We have already remarked on the obvious fact that personality descriptions can fulfil an adaptive function in social interaction in everyday life; this happens when we make statements about persons which are not intended as contributions to an objective exchange of scientific ideas but as moves in an interpersonal encounter; such statements are made in the interests of conformity, disparagement, dominance, tension release, information seeking, and so on. For example, the remark, 'He seems to spend a lot of time away from home' may be intended not as a factual assertion, but as an attempt to modify another person's impression of a stimulus person by fostering doubt about the way the stimulus person spends his time. Alternatively, it may be a way in which the speaker can reveal that he, at least, questions the accepted view about, i.e. the reputation of, the stimulus person.

There are other occasions, however, when we are genuinely trying to arrive at an objective and valid assessment (impression) of the stimulus person, and where there is at least an approximation to a scientific exchange of ideas. These include case-conferences for the assessment of people with psychological disturbances or social problems, committee meetings to assess the progress of students or of people in their careers, the preparation of case-material for judicial purposes or for a piece of serious biography or journalism. On occasions such as these, the situation demands a clear statement of the issues, the best evidence, sound argument, well-supported findings, and so on. In other words, the situation calls for a 'quasi-judicial procedure', i.e. a rational and empirical method for studying individual cases: see Chapter 8.

B. Denotation, Representation and Structure
Human language has a denotative function in that it can refer to, symbolize or stand for, a wide range of objects, events, processes and relationships. This is not to say that language is fully adequate to denote all that we have experience of; moreover, language is not always firmly locked into the world of facts—it is not only easy but also important for language to express phantasy and supposition. Words can become so remote from tangible facts, however, that they take on a life of their own, as it were, independent of the real world. In such circumstances, the words shape experience and action without the benefit (or hindrance) of reciprocal effects. Misunderstandings about people are traceable in part to the failure of words, ideas, facts and actions to form a coherent system.

What is denoted by a word or phrase is often some constant feature of a person's existence. For example 'John is timid, he is reluctant to take physical risks', 'John prefers red wine'. These two examples illustrate how particular words can be fitted into a general syntactical framework to express relatively invariant psychological characteristics like traits and preferences. 'John wishes he had not come', 'Tom wishes to be excused', 'Mary wishes things would liven up', and so on, are examples of statements with 'desire' as a constant theme. Other examples could be found to show how words are used to refer to other constancies in personality, i.e. to dispositions, capacities, roles, attitudes, and so on. The ability to structure experience in terms of recognizable or relatively invariant (stable) features is a major achievement in the child's cognitive development, and not least in his understanding of the behaviour of people: see Chapter 1.

The dangers of reification are well-known; we sometimes unwittingly assume that 'something' must correspond to the words we use. Such reification has been regarded as a peculiar flaw in the language of personality description. For example, actions can be classified as 'hostile'; the regular occurrence of such actions results in the person's behaviour or attitude being described as 'hostile', and finally 'hostility' or a hostile disposition comes to be thought of as an attribute of or agency within the person. The development of a scientific language for the description and analysis of personality clearly requires rules to prevent unwarranted shifts of meaning, and ways of eliminating vagueness; but it also requires rules which permit shifts of meaning and even vagueness where necessary.

Linguists such as Whorf (1956) argue that the language we use constrains and delimits our experience and understanding of the world. Language, experience and action, however, interact with each other, and there is no reason why we should regard language as the limiting factor. Nevertheless, the words we use can shape our experience and actions, as is easily seen for example by the extent to which Freudian and other psychological terms have entered into common usage and changed our perceptions of and responses to people.

It seems likely that cross-cultural comparisons in the language of personality description, especially comparisons between industrial, scientific societies and pre-industrial, animistic societies, could reveal interesting differences in the way human nature is conceptualized. For example, some societies have extended vocabularies for referring to important aspects of nature, e.g. sand, snow, whereas other societies have relatively small vocabularies. In some languages, it might be difficult or impossible—because of lexical, syntactical or semantic limitations—to represent some states of affairs; consider, for example, notions such as 'unconscious mind', 'not being oneself', 'in two minds'. Unfortunately, the anthropological literature is too extensive for us to consider at this stage of our inquiries.

Words represent experience in different ways. For example, words can describe the formal structure of knowledge, as when we describe the attributes of an object or an event in terms of its class membership; thus, we have words which will list the attributes of 'marital discord' or 'policemen'. Words can describe functional relationships between behaviour and experience, as when we describe a person's subjective attitude or intention; thus we have words like 'waiting', 'anxious' and 'trying'. Words can also express evaluation, i.e. degree of approval or disapproval; thus we have words like 'dreary', 'pleasant', 'unpleasant', 'like' and 'dislike'. These different aspects of representation are not mutually exclusive. A word like 'aggressive', for example, can represent certain formal attributes, a way of behaving, and a moral judgment.

By the careful choice and juxtaposition of words, different shades of meaning can be expressed, e.g. the use of 'murderous' or 'tough' instead of 'aggressive', or the use of 'fairly aggressive' or 'justifiably aggressive'. In the context of everyday social exchange, techniques like irony, sarcasm, exaggeration and euphemism have a recognized place, and the spoken word can sometimes express evaluation and affect more effectively than the written word. We assume, however, that a scientific language of personality descriptions must be a written language from which affect and evaluation have been excluded or at least discounted, except in the ways described in Chapter 8.

Some words can be arranged into an ordered series, as for example, cowardly, timid, brave, rash. A rating scale with explicit descriptive terms at each point constitutes one such scale. Such ordered sets may be used for making comparisons between people or for describing changes within the same person. However, as will be seen from the above example, such linear scales may be difficult to explain in grammatical terms; and, in any event, relationships between such ordered series in ordinary language are likely to be multidimensional—hence the attempt to devise Guttman scales in personality measurement. The example shows that the order of words in a series depends upon the criteria used to define their meaning, that is, upon whether one is considering psychological disposition or social desirability.

Another kind of relationship can be seen in negation, e.g. 'shy' versus 'not shy'. Such forced-choice or two-valued judgments have been used extensively in personality measurement. But a negation does not necessarily mean the same as a recognized antonym, e.g. 'shy' versus 'sociable'. The insertion of intermediate categories between the two contrasting terms results in what are, basically, ordered multiple-choice scales similar to rating scales.

Hierarchical relationships also occur among personality words. Eysenck's description of neuroticism or introversion, for example, as 'types' of behaviour subsuming certain 'traits', which in turn subsume certain 'habits' and 'actions', is one example of such a hierarchy: see Eysenck (1970). The notion of a 'ladder of abstraction' in the use of ordinary language is familiar and applied to personality descriptions quite naturally, for example, in citing examples of actions which illustrate a trait, or in grouping a series of life-history events into an overall educational or occupational status.

We shall not attempt to give a full account of the semantics of personality description. Readers who are particularly interested in this aspect of language, however, may detect the outline of a more comprehensive semantic analysis throughout the text. The work of transforming this into a firm and detailed framework lies in the future.

CHAPTER 3

A Lexical Analysis of Trait Names

I. Introduction

The concept of 'traits' has dominated the study of personality from the beginning. Traits have been thought of as psychological dispositions within a person which lead him to behave in characteristic ways. Allport (1937, 1961), Cattell (1965) and Guilford (1959) have built their approach to personality on this concept. More recently, however, Mischel (1968) has questioned not only the validity of personality measurement but also the assumptions upon which the notion of traits is based.

The theory of traits might be regarded as the natural heir to the 'hormic' theory: both deal with the problem of finding order and meaning in ordinary behaviour. One advantage of traits over instincts as hypothetical behavioural dispositions is that they do not imply relatively fixed action patterns and universality of expression. Instead, they are compatible with the belief that people have individualized ways of behaving and of expressing their personal qualities and states of mind, and that there are differences between individuals with regard to characteristics like agressiveness and sociability.

By the time McDougall's hormic theory had been discarded, the mental testing movement had been successful in devising objective, reasonably valid and reliable measures of intellectual abilities, and in using these measures with demonstrable success in education, industry and the Armed Forces. This success appears to have fostered the belief that analogous concepts, methods, findings and applications were possible in the study of personality and adjustment. Hence it was natural that investigators should try to devise objective methods for the measurement of personal qualities.

Among the personal characteristics which early investigators attempted to measure were: social intelligence, values, humour, dominance/submission, neuroticism, masculinity/femininity and anxiety. The study of personality and adjustment, however, soon found itself in the difficult position of trying to develop objective, quantitative and experimental methods for studying traits (and states) conceptualized in a psychodynamic, clinical framework; one outcome of this was the projective test movement.

In the meantime, Allport and Odbert (1936) had carried out their psycholexical analysis of trait names. The apparent lack of follow-up to this work, apart from that of Cattell (1943 *et sequentia*), is difficult to understand. Allport and Odbert seem not to have fully appreciated the richness and adequacy of ordinary language in personality descriptions. However, their findings were used by Cattell and others for the construction of rating scales and adjective check lists. The problem of personality description seems to have been conceived simply as an exercise in listing and sorting traits. The surprise which greeted the discovery of the size and diversity of the lexicon of 'traits' indicates that there had been no expectation that this would be the case. Presumably, it had been hoped that the list would be at least manageable if not short, and that some obvious taxonomy would be discovered. For a more recent and different sort of psycholexical study, see Glueck *et al.* (1964).

II. A Critical Review of the Allport and Odbert (1936) Monograph

A. Introduction

Our approach to the study of lexical issues in personality will be developed in subsequent chapters. Although it has little in common with previous approaches, it can be usefully contrasted with one classical study entitled *Trait Names. A Psycholexical Study* by Allport and Odbert (1936). Their opening remarks in that monograph state the problem as that of separating out terms which actually denote psychophysical dispositions or traits from terms which are 'mischievous verbal snares'. Mathematical terms are rejected as 'utterly foreign'; but it is argued that neutral, objective terms, suitable for scientific descriptions, can be identified. It is further argued that trait names can be used without circularity (tautology) and without vacuity, i.e. can be used to state substantive inferences.

Apparently, Allport and Odbert were not the first to start on the construction of a lexicon of trait names, but they seem to have been the first to succeed. The lexicon comprises 17,953 terms extracted from Webster's unabridged *New International Dictionary* (1925) and listed alphabetically in four main categories. The authors say that it is a 'thesaurus', but this is not strictly true. It is not a storehouse of knowledge about personality characteristics, and it lacks the special features of a thesaurus proper; it does not provide a detailed classification or arrangement in terms of antonyms, synonyms, frequency or associated meaning, and so on; it does not reveal an underlying conceptual structure or facilitate the organization and expression of ideas about people. It is not even a dictionary, since it does not give the meanings of the trait names, their etymology or their grammatical class. It is simply an alphabetical list of words classified under four headings: (i) neutral terms which might possibly be used to refer to personal traits, e.g. 'bitter', 'excitable'; (ii) terms which might possibly be used to refer to moods or emotional reactions or other temporary states or activities, e.g. 'mocking', 'pining'; (iii) terms expressing social judgments, judgments about personal character, or terms referring to the effect that a person has on others, e.g. 'stupid', 'hated'; (iv) miscellaneous terms referring to physique, capacities or developmental condition, together with metaphorical and doubtful terms, e.g. 'elastic', 'oblique'. We shall discuss the validity and usefulness of this classification in due course.

The theory on which the selection of items was based is somewhat obscure and does not seem to have been adhered to in practice. For example, it is asserted that, '. . . Each single term specifies in some way a form of human behaviour . . .' (p. vi). But it is difficult to reconcile this principle with the inclusion in the list of words such as 'dumpy', 'jemmy', 'non-absorbent', 'statistical', 'ajar', 'outlying', 'seismic', 'apocryphal', 'bedlam', 'bevel', 'bifocal' or 'caloric'. Even a casual glance at the list reveals that the words have a wide range of usage; their common factor being that most of them *might*, either directly or indirectly, refer to some aspect of human nature: persons, their behaviour or psychological processes, social evaluations, ethical and legal judgments, situations, causes and effects, abilities, achievements, social relationships, and so on.

One cannot but admire the diligence that went into the compilation of such a comprehensive listing of terms. However, many of them are so obscure and rare or inappropriate for normal usage—e.g. 'hereticating', 'muticous', 'tenebrific', that little is gained by including them—in fact, they detract from the usefulness of the list by making it unwieldy and by obscuring conceptual boundaries between groups of words. Whatever else the list as a whole might be called, it ought not to be called a list of 'trait names'.

Another stated principle is that, '. . . each term is a record of commonsense observation, inexact perhaps, but nevertheless constituting an authentic problem for the science that has taken as its task the purification and codification of commonsense views of human nature . . .' (p. vi). It is difficult to see what is meant by this assertion. We do not know whether or not the sort of behaviour referred to by some of the terms has ever occurred, or whether each term has ever, in fact, been used to refer to an actual occurrence of behaviour. The words were selected from a dictionary on the grounds that they *could be* so used, not that they *had in fact been used*. Hence, although it is beyond doubt that commonsense observation of the behaviour referred to by some of the words has occurred—otherwise we should not find it possible to communicate effectively—it seems likely that other words have little or no utility as semantic tokens in the context of communication about human behaviour. The above principle completely misrepresents the function of a word list, and even misrepresents the function of the dictionary from which it is derived, because dictionary meanings describe how a word is to be used in relation to other words; a dictionary does not provide an exhaustive account of the verbal meaning of a word, i.e. its connotation.

One use to which Allport and Odbert thought their word list might be put was for the construction of '. . . schedules of one sort or another for the systematic investigation of personality . . .' (p. vi). They had in mind, no doubt, check lists, rating scales, personality profiles, interview schedules and questionnaires; and they supposed that their list provided the lexical universe from which subsets of terms could be selected.

Allport and Odbert believed that they had been largely successful in separating '. . . neutral words . . . from . . . censorial and evaluative terms' (p. vii). The latter terms were concerned with character and social desirability, i.e. with ethics (morality) and normative social behaviour, though the authors imply that they constitute a '. . . vocabulary of terms signifying the subjective impressions which one individual may make upon another' (p. vii). This remark is revealing in two ways. First, it suggests that these terms cannot figure in an objective assessment; but we know that there can be consensus, that objective criteria for assessment can be set up, and that rigorous judicial procedures are available, for making such moral judgments: see Chapter 8. Second, it suggests that 'subjective impressions' are composed entirely of normative judgments that are different from 'objective assessments' composed of judgments of another sort— presumably judgments based on inferences from observed behaviour shorn of any moral implication. The authors seem to have taken the distinction between 'subjective' and 'objective' judgments for granted, since they do not define these terms or discuss them. The term 'subjective' means 'dependent upon one's personal awareness', whereas the term 'objective' means 'independent of one's personal awareness'. The words are used to contrast what is 'in the mind' with what is regarded as being 'in the real world'—and this appears to be the distinction that Allport and Odbert are taking for granted. But there are many aspects of reality which are not directly demonstrable by simple tests and observations; they call for conceptual analysis and theorizing tied to indirect and often elaborate empirical investigation.

As a consequence of the necessary conceptual analyses and theorizing, which are derived from subjective cognitive processes, the distinction between theory and fact has become blurred, so that the distinction between 'subjective' and 'objective' is similarly blurred. The term 'objective', when used in the context of scientific method, now refers to a sort of general agreement, between competent investigators using standard procedures, on the interpretation or construction to be placed on the admissible evidence or data. Objective knowledge then exists independently of any particular person's awareness. Thus Allport and Odbert failed to see, or at least failed to make clear, that their so-called 'neutral words' could not be assigned as descriptive terms by reference to any simple personal observation or demonstration—except perhaps tautologically by means of an operational definition—otherwise they would be subjective. The terms themselves cannot be classified as 'objective' or 'subjective' for the simple reason that the words 'objective' and 'subjective' refer to *procedures* for deciding whether a term is being used subjectively or objectively. Thus, for example, my own experience in relation to a person may lead me to make the judgment that he is kind; this is a subjective judgment (although Allport and Odbert list it as a neutral, objective trait), since I can be proved wrong or perhaps cannot show that the judgment can be made independently of my personal experience. Furthermore, as we shall see in Chapter 8, one can make 'objective' judgments about morality by setting up the appropriate quasi-judicial (scientific) procedures (which is not the same as proving that one moral code is right and another wrong). The question of which terms in personality descriptions can be assigned objectively is a procedural and empirical question, not one to be answered on *a priori* grounds on the supposition that affectively neutral behavioural dispositions really exist.

Allport and Odbert's second subset of words '. . . contains terms designating mood, emotional activity, or casual and temporary forms of conduct, such as are not ordinarily considered permanent or consistent dispositions, and yet at the same time serve to differentiate one man's conduct from another's' (p. vii). It is difficult to see how these words constitute a homogeneous subset, comprising as they do words as diverse as 'blinking', 'bored', 'delivery', 'flagging' and so on. The authors continue, 'In the strict sense of the word, these terms do not symbolize personality at all, for personality always seems to imply some form of *lasting* mental structure. But the line is difficult to draw, and so for the sake of completeness, these words descriptive of present activity or mood are included' (p. vii). The terms were thought to refer to modes of affect, action and will, and to be particularly descriptive of the '. . . forms of specific but variable behaviour resulting from . . . (authentic personal dispositions) . . . as modified by the effective stimulus of the moment . . .' (pp. vii–viii).

Taken literally, the words in the second subset should cover every imaginable sort of human activity, and it does include many such—'approving', 'awakening', 'caressing', 'garnering', 'logrolling', and so on. But one looks in vain for 'reading', 'writing' and 'adding' (the word 'calculating' is listed as a neutral trait). One finds emotional states such as 'fretting', 'horrified', 'relieved' and 'mollified', but looks in vain for 'amused' ('amusing' is listed as a social evaluation), 'guilt' ('guilty' is listed as a social evaluation), and a few others. We notice in passing that 'gloomy' is listed as a personal trait together with 'uncertain', 'confident', 'jealous' and 'cheerful'; and that 'peculiar' is listed as a social evaluation together with 'horrid', 'immature', 'important', and 'purged'. All of these terms occur with reasonable frequency as predicates in statements like, 'I feel . . .' or 'He feels . . .' or comparable grammatical forms, e.g. 'He is . . .'.

The fourth subset in Allport and Odbert's list was intended to contain miscellaneous terms not classifiable under the other three headings. It includes metaphorical and rhetorical terms, terms referring to physique and medical conditions, nationality, social role and status, age, and other less obvious characteristics.

In the final paragraph of their preface, Allport and Odbert say that only the first of their four subsets of words are 'trait names' in the strict sense, but that not all psychologists will want to adhere to this strict sense. Hence, in the title of the monograph, 'trait names' refers to all 17,953 terms. The usefulness of the classification, in their opinion, does not depend on any particular theory about human traits, and the data, as it were, are supposed to speak for themselves.

Unfortunately, things are not so simple. Words, particularly words about human nature, are not like phenomena in the natural world—complete with stable properties independent of human experience. Words, their associated meanings and grammatical functions, are man-made, and are themselves constituent elements in man's conception of man. Allport and Odbert's lexicon is largely derived from that commonsense conceptual framework which enables us to say what we think should be said about ourselves and other people, and provides the epistemological basis for the further evolution of our understanding of human behaviour which emerges as the joint product of conceptual analysis and empirical investigation.

The first part of the main discussion of trait names in Allport and Odbert's monograph opens with a quotation from p. 74 of Klages, *The Science of Character*, Klages (1929, trs 1932), which is well worth repeating in the context of our present approach to the language of personality descriptions, as follows.

> Language excels in unconscious insight the acumen of the most talented thinker, and we contend that whoever, having the right talent, should do nothing but examine the words and phrases which deal with the human soul, would know more about it than all the sages who omitted to do so, and would know perhaps a thousand times more than has ever been discovered by observation, apparatus, and experiment upon man. (Klages, p. 1)

The spirit of this quotation matches our feelings about the language of personality descriptions very well, since we have argued that men's intimate dealings with other men over thousands of years of social evolution must have been associated with a parallel conceptual evolution in men's understanding of human nature, and that this understanding must have found expression in language, literature and commonsense. However, we know that men's understanding of other aspects of nature has often been sadly deficient, distorted and erroneous; and they have often confused phantasy with reality, as in myths, legends and magical thinking. It would not be surprising, therefore, to find that men's understanding of *human* nature has also been inadequate and wrong, and that perhaps only since the Enlightenment has there been any substantial scientific advancement in understanding man as a species and men as individuals.

Allport and Odbert refer to Bentham's theory of fictions, see Ogden (1932), in which Bentham explains how the act of naming confuses real entities with imaginary fictions, especially in relation to the study of human nature, e.g. the confusion of 'neutral' with 'censorial' terms.

Allport and Odbert present the problem of conceptualizing reality as one that permits only two options: one is either working with fictions or with facts. They do not seem to accept the idea that there might be different degrees of approximation to objective knowledge or the idea that what passes for a fact one day might be shown to be a fiction on the next. Furthermore, they appear to take for granted, as axiomatic, that 'such mental processes or dispositions', i.e. traits, exist and 'can be determined by observation or by inference' (p. 1). We note the disjunctive use of the word 'or' in this quotation, as if they were independent routes to knowledge. They argue that with a '... suitable term ...', '... depicting personality as accurately and as faithfully as possible ... corresponding to authentic psychological dispositions ...', '... the ability to understand and to control one's fellows is greatly enhanced'. If we accept that terms are not altogether arbitrary, some being more effective than others as semantic tokens, and if we accept that there are such things as 'authentic psychological dispositions' corresponding to these terms and substantiated by appropriate empirical data, then it seems reasonable to suppose that '... the ability to understand and to control one's fellows ...' would be greatly enhanced (p. 1). This argument is unfortunately a circular one, since understanding and control demonstrate and validate the 'authenticity' of the terms and concepts we use to describe nature. The difficulty is that we often cannot tell the difference between a fact and a fiction without carrying out elaborate conceptual analysis and empirical investigation; but without fictions there would be no way of looking for facts, and without facts there would be no exposure of fictions and no relationship with the real world. As Kant said, 'Theory without experiment is lame; experiment without theory is blind'. Popper's description of the process of conjecture and refutation provides an adequate modern account for the procedural basis of scientific method: see Popper (1972).

The cultural and historical aspects of the language of personality description are touched upon briefly by Allport and Odbert. Working from information on etymology and the history of language, they remind us that words like 'devotion', 'pity' and 'patience' gained their meaning in association with the spread of Christian beliefs. Astrology gave rise to 'lunatic', 'jovial', 'saturnine' and 'mercurial'. The graeco-roman doctrine of the elements and humours gave rise to 'temperament', and to 'sanguine', 'choleric', 'melancholic', 'phlegmatic', 'good-humoured', 'bad-humoured', 'hearty', 'heartless' and 'cordial'. The Reformation of the 16th century and its aftermath gave rise to traits like 'sincere', 'pious', 'bigoted', 'precise' and 'fanatic', and to terms referring to the self, such as 'self-regard', 'self-assurance', 'self-love', 'self-confidence', 'self-esteem' and 'selfish'. The 17th century saw the emergence of 'fatuous', 'callous', 'countrified' and 'disingenuous'. The literature of the 18th century gave rise to 'day-dream', 'depression', 'ennui', 'chagrin', 'apathy' and 'diffidence', and modified the meaning of 'reverie', 'excitement', 'constraint', 'embarrassment' and 'disappointment'; in court circles, the terms 'prim', 'demure', 'gawky', 'enthusiastic', 'interesting' and 'boresome' were used. Political awareness has given us 'liberal', 'democrat', 'radical' and 'tory'. Modern slang has given us 'racketeer', 'yes-man', 'corker', 'wet', 'bum', 'slob', 'screwy' and 'mixed-up'. The social and behavioural sciences have given us 'neurotic', 'psychotic', 'introverted' and 'schizophrenic', and have modified the meaning of 'alienated', 'deprived' and 'intelligent'.

We have no difficulty in agreeing with the view that the language of personality description, like other sorts of language, changes with the times. We would go further, however, and argue like Wittgenstein (1953) that language is a form of life, and as such is constantly evolving selective adaptations in response to the opportunities and constraints imposed on it.

Allport and Odbert (pp. 3–4) complain that it is difficult to identify traits objectively, i.e. with reference to observable data agreed upon and interpreted in the same way by competent investigators working independently of one another. The relationship between the imputed disposition and the overt action is not always simple and direct: a disposition can give rise to many different overt actions, depending upon circumstances; similarly, the same overt action may express different dispositions. Many trait words are closely related in meaning, or related in a grammatical sense, to other trait words—as shown by experiments in rating or in language usage. But empirical studies are needed in order to demonstrate that the *language* of personality description (and explanation) represents the *facts* correctly.

Allport and Odbert (pp. 4–6) stress, as we have been stressing, that the language of commonsense expresses an abundance of common knowledge about human behaviour and must have evolved into a reasonably coherent medium of social exchange adequately representing the reality of human nature, and adequately geared to the practicalities of human relationships and activities. But, however much we are drawn to such a view of the language of personality description, we must remember that it is only partly true. Even a cursory examination of the history of ideas shows that 'commonsense' is regularly contradicted and corrected by 'scientific sense'—the earth is not flat, it is not the centre of the solar system, animal species were not all created at the same time, the faculties of the mind do not correspond to those in phrenology, human beings are not always aware of the motives and reasons for their actions, human behaviour cannot be analysed in terms of instincts, women are not on average inferior to men in intelligence, abnormal behaviour is not caused by witchcraft, character is not determined by the position of the planets at one's time of birth, and so on. The persistence, in 'commonsense', of scientifically outmoded beliefs like these, and of fads, fallacies, superstitions and other epistemic disorders is a sad fact of human existence brought about by inadequacies in people and in their education.

As psychologists, we are not concerned with bringing scientific knowledge into line with commonsense, but with bringing commonsense into line with scientific knowledge. Then why study the ordinary (commonsense) language of personality descriptions? There are several reasons. First, it is only by studying ordinary language that we can discover whether or not it has anything to contribute to scientific psychology. In this connection, we should point out that discoveries in psycholinguistics are contributing to our understanding of cognitive processes. Second, although scientific discoveries in psychopathology have revolutionized our understanding of insanity and showed that commonsense was greatly in error, yet there are some deviant forms of behaviour which resist analysis in terms of the available 'medical models', and might yet yield to more 'commonsense' methods of analysis, e.g. in terms of social learning, emotional functions, or even semantic confusions. Third, some psychologists might say that our understanding of the average person in the ordinary activities of everyday life has not been revolutionized by 20th-century psychology; which implies that all the effort that has been expended on the study of personality and individual differences has contributed little to our understanding and control of human nature in general. This view would, of course, be questioned by other psychologists who would point to the limited but real successes achieved by selection, guidance and training methods in industry, education and the Armed Forces, by counselling methods for a wide range of minor maladjustments, and by survey and organizational methods in social relationships. These and other areas of modern psychology have given rise to concepts, methods and findings which are far more soundly based and effective than commonsense could be shown to be. Nevertheless, with regard to the study of personality and normal adjustment, there is a feeling of dissatisfaction—a suspicion that current approaches are not particularly useful or enlightening. It follows, therefore, that there are sufficient grounds to justify an examination of the ordinary language of personality description. Even if commonsense proves to have little or nothing to offer scientific psychology, we should at least be able to demonstrate the poverty of commonsense in comparison with the psychological study of personality and adjustment, and to suggest ways of remedying this deficiency.

In passing, we should mention that reliance upon commonsense and ordinary language in the practicalities of human relationships in everyday life does not *prove* anything except the need for a common currency for social exchange. The fact that, in everyday life, we talk and behave 'as if' traits (dispositions) really existed does not commit us *scientifically* to that point of view; similarly, we can talk and behave in daily life 'as if' existing family relationships were 'natural' and yet, in our scientific work, we can question this belief.

On p. 5 of their monograph, Allport and Odbert reveal that they see both lexical content and grammatical form as closely related to psychological processes; although the ideas they cite in support of this argument (the relation of grammatical expression to temperament and psychosis) seem not to have been verified.

We need not enter into discussion of the philosophical viewpoints known as Realism, Idealism or Nominalism—since our modern philosophy of science view point has already been stated—except perhaps to note that the *geistewissenschaftliche* approach of Dilthey and Spranger was idealist in the sense that it attempted to identify *ideal* forms of behaviour and personality analogous to the ideal forms of geometry.

The description and analysis of any one person's qualities and adjustment must be in terms that are applicable to people in general, the 'idiographic' and 'nomothetic' approaches to personality (see Allport, 1937, and Jones, 1971) must be compatible with each other. All that this means is that the rules of any procedure for describing and explaining personality should be applicable equally to all the individual cases that fall within their scope, and that there should be some logic in any differential application of the rules in, say, psychometric assessment or psychoanalytic treatment. For example, the diagnosis of 'anxiety state' or the attribution of traits like 'highly intelligent' or 'good tempered' must be phrased in such a way as to be equally applicable to all cases covered by the rules for using such terms, except in so far as further rules may be introduced, as in the judicial process, to delimit the applicability of any procedure. Thus we may need additional rules to exclude young children, females, physically ill people, people from another culture, and so on, from the scope of any particular method of assessment or analysis. In the judicial process, such rules for routine procedure, as well as rules for handling difficult and exceptional cases, have reached a high degree of efficiency. But although the study of individual persons and their adjustment can be described as a 'quasi-judicial' process, see Chapter 8, no equivalent refinement of concepts, procedures and terms has yet been achieved; nor have psychological case-studies yet generated a satisfactory body of 'case-law' based on systematic comparisons and contrasts between representative or model cases.

The failure of personality study to provide a coherent conceptual framework for the description and explanation of the normal person's adjustment to his environment can be accounted for in at least two ways. First, it can be argued that the whole problem has been misunderstood and wrongly formulated, and arises largely because of semantic confusions. Our present deep investigation into the language of personality description is, in part, an attempt to rethink the whole issue of 'personality study'. Second, it can be argued, more simply and straightforwardly, that our individual patterns of personal adjustment have evolved (or been shaped) in response to the particular demands of the situations we have been faced with, so that the major part of the consistency and regularity in our personal behaviour is the product of our genetic constitution and the reinforcement contingencies of our environment. This second view is so well-known as an alternative to personality study in its traditional form that no further discussion is necessary at this point: see Mischel (1968). By 'traditional form', of course, we mean the description and analysis of personality in terms of dispositions or traits—especially those which have been investigated by psychometric methods. It is interesting to note that Allport and Odbert (pp. 11–13, 15–16) reject the psychometric and factor-analytic approaches to personality on the grounds that they result in the identification of population characteristics, not individual characteristics; but they fail to recognize that a 'case-law' approach would avoid this result. The authors assert that 'True traits must be discovered in each individual life separately through the use of more direct clinical and experimental methods' (p. 13). Unfortunately these 'more direct methods' were never satisfactorily developed—partly because the quasi-judicial basis of personality study was not recognized. Once this quasi-judicial, and scientific, basis is recognized, the concepts, methods and findings of a wide range of approaches to personality study can be seen in a much better perspective.

For Allport and Odbert, traits were personal dispositions which underlie or determine a broad but relatively well-defined range of actions. They have an 'individualized' quality which may be absent from simpler, more automatic and habitual responses; and they have 'directive', 'psychological' and 'organizing' qualities which may also be lacking in simpler responses. The defining properties of personal dispositions correspond with a number of other psychological concepts, e.g. attitudes, interests, values and principles—provided they have a general range of application and are peculiar to the individual person.

An important semantic confusion in Allport and Odbert's monograph arises in connection with their contention that '... no two men possess precisely the same trait' (p. 14) and that '... such unique patterns ...' i.e. traits '... do exist ...' (pp. 14–15). The concept of uniqueness has a central place in Allport's approach to personality. Particular things are unique by definition, however, so that nothing is gained by asserting that some particular response, habit, trait or other characteristic is unique: one's nose, fingerprints and income tax return are all unique in that sense. But when we come to describe and analyse these particular phenomena, as opposed to merely contemplating them, we must recognize their abstract and general properties, otherwise we cannot represent them or deal with them. Once we clear up this semantic confusion, the concept of 'uniqueness' as it applies to personality characteristics presents no difficulty. It simply means that particular features of an individual personality are singular or peculiar to that person. Taken to its logically absurd limits, such an interpretation of the uniqueness of personality characteristics would mean that the individual's traits (and even the person himself!) were never 'the same' from one occasion to another. Allport and Odbert, however, recognize the practical necessity of using the same trait name to refer to roughly comparable dispositions in different people.

The detection of similarities and differences between people, and consistencies and inconsistencies in the behaviour of one person, requires some common basis of comparison, which implies abstract and general terms of reference. Language cannot *reproduce* particulars, it can only *represent* them or indicate them. Thus, the 'uniqueness' that Allport regards as the main issue in the study of personality must either be *represented* by means of abstract and general terms or be *indicated* by whatever means are available, such as pointing, giving examples or further descriptive terms, or presenting observational data. Otherwise, uniqueness can only be 'experienced' at first hand. In geography, for example, 'hill' and 'valley' are general terms and can be used to refer to all kinds of hill and valley, no two of which are alike, but there is no difficulty in distinguishing and describing any particular hill or valley.

It is obvious that no trait word can ever represent all the particular features of a personal disposition. However, by a careful choice of trait words, suitably qualified and phrased, one can identify and represent with sufficient accuracy for most everyday or scientific purposes the actual personal disposition referred to. Similarly, by means of language generally and the presentation of evidence directly, one can indicate, i.e. show or denote, the particular personal dispositions referred to (and represented by the trait word or phrase). A 'personal disposition' is simply a readiness to act in a particular sort of way, and is revealed by consistencies and regularities in the behaviour of an individual.

The above interpretation of the uniqueness of personality and personal dispositions makes it easy to understand how trait names are used in the ordinary language of personality descriptions. There is no mystery. Provided we agree on the definition of a trait word and on the sorts of empirical evidence that would justify the use of that trait word—either in isolation or in association with other words and phrases—we can use it either to characterize a particular person or to describe similarities and differences between people, or to draw attention to something in human nature which cannot be adequately represented in words. Given this sort of reasonable usage, moreover, it is possible to represent subtle and complex effects produced by the interaction of several dispositions within one and the same person. For example, one might say, 'The most vulnerable aspect of her affection for him is the jealousy evoked by having to share his affection with others, which tends to revive a latent hostility towards people upon whom she is dependent'. Provided one is able to define and amplify these terms, and draw attention to the available evidence, and expand the theory which enables one to make inferences of this sort, there is no problem. It is not necessary to introduce metaphysical notions such as 'common', 'unique' or 'cardinal' traits.

On p. 16 of their monograph, Allport and Odbert confess to having no list or classification of traits as such; they do not think that traits can be satisfactorily measured; and they see no objection to traits 'overlapping' (presumably in meaning). They regard trait names as '... merely oblique representations of dispositions that are known to exist' (p. 16), and they give the example of a man characterized by different observers as 'cautious', 'timid' and 'cowardly'. The observer's differing views can be resolved, we have argued, by examining the relevant evidence, by adopting a common theoretical framework, and by studying the language they are using to describe the person.

Allport and Odbert (p. 17) attempt to deny the charge that trait psychology is committing the same error, reification, as faculty psychology, i.e. assigning definite powers to the mind to correspond with the terms available in language, such as 'attention', 'memory', 'will'. Their argument is confused, however, by statements like the following: 'But traits are no such powers of the mind, but are merely facts of mental organization peculiar to each individual' (p. 17). Nevertheless, the key question, as to how the existence of traits is to be established, is hardly raised. And the authors seem to argue (p. 20) that the existence of personal dispositions cannot be refuted, which is not philosophically acceptable.

Allport and Odbert suppose that the terms referring to personal dispositions— 'shrewd', 'humorous'—can be clearly distinguished from ethical evaluations— 'honest', 'good'—and argue that the latter '... have absolutely no direct reference to personality' (p. 18). Moral qualities, however, are important aspects of personal adjustment: they help to direct and regulate behaviour, and their 'existence' can be assessed fairly rigorously by the application of quasi-judicial methods of investigation. Moreover, most personal dispositions have a 'social desirability' value, which further obscures the difference between what Allport calls 'personality' and 'character'.

Trait names are diverse and exhibit secular change, through obsolescence and innovation. This could mean that some personality attributes have gone out of existence (because of changes in human nature and its environment), or simply that new and improved ways of conceptualizing human nature have appeared.

The use of compound words, phrases and metaphors shows that single words are not able to depict personal characteristics very accurately, but must be embedded in complex grammatical structures; these in turn must be embedded in a context of real or possible actions giving the language of personality description a 'pragmatic' aspect.

B. Classification of Trait Names

Allport and Odbert remind us that interest in the language of personality description dates back at least to the time of Galton who in 1884 remarked that *Roget's Thesaurus* contained at least 1000 words pertaining to character.[1] In 1910, Partridge listed 750 adjectives describing mental traits.[2] In 1926, Perkins estimated that there were about 3000 names of traits and ideals in *Webster's New International Dictionary*.[3] In 1926, Gesell reported an unfinished attempt to classify adjectives describing six aspects of human behaviour: intellect, energy, social, autonomy, temperament and morality.[4] In 1932, Klages estimated that there were 4000 German words describing inner states.[5] The references cited in Allport and Odbert are as follows:

1. Sir Francis Galton, 'Measurement of Character' in *Fortnightly Review*, **42**, 1884, p. 181.
2. G. E. Partridge, *An Outline of Individual Study*. New York: Sturgis and Walton, 1910.
3. M. L. Perkins, 'The Teaching of Ideals and the Development of the Traits of Character and Personality'. *Proceedings Oklahoma Academy Science*, Univ. Okla. Bull., N.S. No. 348, Vol. VI, 1926, pt. 2.
4. A. Gesell, *Mental Growth of the Pre-School Child*. New York: Macmillan, 1926, p. 419.
5. L. Klages, *The Science of Character*. Tr. 1932, p. 71.

It is interesting to note that, because of their concern with personal dispositions, Allport and Odbert were inclined to play down characteristics of a non-psychological nature—as if they were somehow unimportant determinants of adjustment and mental state. For example, they complain that over half of the 3000 entries in *The Trait Book*, published by the Eugenics Record Office in 1919 as a vocabulary for the analysis of personality, referred to physical peculiarities (acne, ingrowing toe-nails), and many others to racial or occupational characteristics; only a few psychological traits were included.[6] The problem of what information is relevant to the description of personality and adjustment is dealt with in detail in Chapters 5, 6 and 7 and in summary in Chapter 8. We describe and discuss thirty different categories of information, including those just mentioned, and show that trait names have an important but by no means exclusive role in the descriptive language of personality. In 1933, Baumgarten listed 1093 traits in German selected from dictionaries and the writing of characterologists. Allport and Odbert maintain that she failed to separate 'neutral' from 'censorial' terms. She also selected only words in common use, and therefore listed only about one-quarter as many 'traits' as Allport and Odbert.[7] These references are cited as follows:

6. Eugenics Record Office, *The Trait Book*. 2nd Ed. Cold Springs Harbor: Eugenics Record Office, Bulletin No. 6, 1919, pp. 127.
7. F. Baumgarten, *Die Charaktereigenschaften*. Beitr. zur Charakter-und Persönlichkeitsforschung, Vol. 1. Berne: A. Francke A.G. 1933, pp. 81.

Allport and Odbert's list contains 17,953 words describing personality characteristics and individual behaviour. They comprise four and a half per cent of the 400,000 terms in *Webster's New International Dictionary* (1925 edition). Allport and Odbert claimed that they were able to identify trait names and classify them into four categories with a reasonable degree of reliability. The main criterion for including a term was whether it could be used differentially to 'characterize' the behaviour of an individual person. On this criterion, the authors include 'mincing' and 'dyspeptic' but exclude 'walking' and 'digesting'. On examination, however, we find that 'dyspeptic' and 'digesting' are included in the category of metaphorical and doubtful terms. Further examination confirms the authors' confession that '... the application of this criterion involved a considerable degree of arbitrariness' (p. 24), for it is difficult to see the differential character of 'baiting', 'balancing' and 'bartered', or of 'celebrating', 'castaway' and 'charging'.

The differential character of the terms listed would have been more effectively demonstrated had the authors presented them as a thesaurus rather than a dictionary. For example, the word 'deliberate' stands on its own as a personal trait in their first list and there is no immediate indication as to how it might be used to specify a differential characteristic. When the same word is looked up in *Roget's Thesaurus*, however, its relationships with other words in the English language are shown. For example, it can be used as an adjective to describe slowness of movement, or as a verb to describe diligent thinking or attention, or as an adjective to describe leisurely calm action, or as a verb to describe taking council and advice or, in its noun form 'deliberation', it can refer to carefulness, caution and premeditation. A thesaurus is a method for finding words to express ideas; the problem here is to find the form of words which best express the particular differential characteristic, i.e. the feature which is a mark of that person's individuality and makes him recognizably different from other persons with whom he can reasonably be compared.

The 'differential character' of the traits listed by Allport and Odbert seems to consist of nothing more than the ability to find other traits with which they can be compared and contrasted, as 'deliberate' can be compared with 'measured', 'slow', 'thoughtful', 'calm', 'careful', and contrasted with 'fast', 'spontaneous', 'erratic' and 'unthinking'. Which of these words—in isolation or combination, with or without supporting phrases—best expresses the idea in question in an actual situation is a matter for empirical investigation and conceptual analysis.

Wherever possible the authors use adjectives and participles, limiting the nouns and adverbs to those for which no corresponding adjective or participle exists, or where the meaning is different. Various forms of a word are given, but only if they are used in different ways. Rare, archaic and slang terms are included in order to obtain a comprehensive record.

It seems reasonable to suppose that any obvious system of classifying the traits would have occured to the authors. Hence, we can presume either that a list of traits cannot or does not reflect the natural, factual structure of personality and human adjustment, that the natural structure is not obvious, or that there is no natural structure to present (this last possibility would mean that the language of traits refers to fictions rather than facts). Our own position in this matter is clear: we regard the language of traits as a useful and important part of the language of personality descriptions; we do not regard it as being an exclusive or special language; we do not restrict traits to single words. The validity and utility of traits as concepts in the description and explanation of personality are matters for empirical study and conceptual analysis.

The trait names listed by Allport and Odbert were categorized into four subsets. The first subset contained 4504 words (25 per cent of the total) designating traits proper, i.e. consistent and stable sorts of psychological disposition, e.g. 'aggressive', 'introverted', 'sociable'. These are thought of as referring to fairly enduring behavioural characteristics which find recurrent expression in a wide variety of circumstances. They can be used to identify the person, to compare and contrast him with other people, and to predict and influence his behaviour.

The second subset contained 4541 words (25 per cent of the total) designating on-going behaviour and temporary states of thought, feeling and intention, e.g. 'abashed', 'teasing', 'pacifying', 'rejoicing', 'gibbering', 'frantic'. Some words like 'fascinating', 'fraternizing' and 'obstructing' may refer either to intention or effect on others (see below), or both.

The third subset contained 5236 words (29 per cent of the total) mostly designating ethical evaluations, i.e. moral character. The essential feature of these terms is that they should refer to a judgment made about a personal characteristic and not to the characteristic itself. Thus 'good', 'bad', 'nice', 'nasty', 'worthy' and 'worthless' are ethical evaluations about the person, his behaviour or his psychological characteristics. Allport and Odbert argue that such terms do not themselves normally designate dispositions within the person. On the other hand, 'benevolence', 'tolerance' and 'patience' are personal dispositions which are judged to be socially desirable, i.e. good, nice or worthy;

whereas 'greediness', 'selfishness' and 'disloyalty' are also personal dispositions, but judged socially undesirable. The third subset contains terms of another sort, namely, those that refer to the effect that a person has on other people, e.g. 'dazzling', 'irritating', 'hurtful'. In these instances the word refers to a social judgment *about* the person, his behaviour or his psychological processes; again, it is argued that they do not themselves designate personal dispositions and they are not basically moral judgments. There are two reasons for including words of this sort in the list. First, a person's effect on others is an important aspect of his personality—it corresponds to our content category coded O – SP (see Chapter 7)—and is associated with the concept of reputation. Second, the study of personality—it corresponds to our content category coded O–SP (see Chapter and social deviation.

One difficulty with the third subset is that some concepts which acquire meaning as social judgments, e.g. 'honest', 'unselfish', 'law-abiding' (or their opposites), can become incorporated or adopted as guiding principles of character and, in effect, operate as personal dispositions of the sort listed in the first subset.

The fourth subset contained 3682 words (21 per cent of the total) designating a miscellaneous assortment of physical, social and psychological characteristics not clearly assignable to the other three subsets. Hence, it contained words like 'little', 'myopic', 'frail', 'freshman', 'Irish', 'local', 'murky', 'over-trained', 'pampered'. Some terms in this fourth subset referred to capacities or talents such as 'able', 'gifted' and 'prolific'; but whereas 'intelligent' and 'educated' also belong, 'creative' and 'erudite' are assigned to the first subset, 'stupid' and 'learned' to the third subset. Other terms in the fourth subset are allegorical, figurative, metaphorical, and of doubtful applicability to psychological characteristics, e.g. 'adrift', 'amphibious', 'close-grained'.

Physical terms such as 'hard', 'wooden', 'opaque', 'taut', occur in all four subsets. Animal qualities such as 'foxy', 'worm', 'apish', 'sheepish, 'toadying' are similarly distributed. Hyphenated words prefixed by 'self', e.g. 'self-indulgent', 'self-critical' belong in the first subset.

Allport and Odbert mention the existence of phrases and idioms, but, as they say, 'There appears to be no limit to the possible making of phrases' (p. 30). But it is exactly this capacity for making an infinite variety of grammatical phrases that reveals the limitations of a mere 'list' of trait names. Even a dictionary or thesaurus of personality and adjustment does no more than help increase the lexical scope and precision of ordinary language descriptions. One is more likely to discover the facts and relationships one is interested in by examining *language in use* than by examining word lists.

Finally, Allport and Odbert (p. 31) recognize statements of the sort that we have shown to occur in 'free descriptions' of personality. However, they downgrade them to the status of 'circumlocutions' used by novelists and biographers to characterize a trait which cannot be designated by a single word. Thus, the authors never reach the point of discovering that the language of personality descriptions is a working language with lexical, syntactical, semantic and pragmatic aspects. Instead, they think of it as a long list of trait names, with relatively fixed meanings, from which a number can be selected to describe and interpret observations about individual behaviour.

The main attempt to reduce and simplify the vocabulary of trait names has been made through factor-analysis. Thurstone (1934), for example, obtained ratings of persons on 60 common adjectives from 1300 subjects and found that five factors would account for the intercorrelations. The aim is to identify what Cattell and others would call 'factors' or 'dimensions' of personality; these are thought of as the basic or primary factors necessary for any general taxonomy or structural description of personality and individual differences: see Cattell (1943, 1946). Allport and Odbert, however, minimize the value of this kind of enterprise and stress instead the need for exact and particular descriptions of 'personal dispositions'. Our view is that the conceptual boundaries that are drawn around different aspects of personality do not necessarily delineate real entities (natural structures or functions); they show the *semantic distinctions* we find sensible and useful in relation to the experience we have of ourselves and other people (whether at a common sense, professional or scientific level of understanding).

III. An Attempt to Reclassify Trait Names

Having voiced our criticisms of the attempt by Allport and Odbert to represent the language of personality as a universe of trait names, it might seem illogical to attempt a similar exercise. Nevertheless, we must provide some account of the lexicon of the language of personality descriptions. There are several ways of compiling a lexicon. One way is that taken by Allport and Odbert. A second way would be to select and classify words and phrases from a thesaurus rather than a dictionary, or to attempt to compile a thesaurus. A third way would be to sample words and phrases from the texts of suitable novels, biographies, case-histories, newspaper articles, magazine stories and other sources: see, for example, Glueck *et al.* (1964) and Rosenberg and Jones (1972). A fourth way, one that we have used extensively, is to sample words and phrases from written personality descriptions obtained under controlled conditions: see Chapters 5, 6 and 7. We do not know how these various lexicons would compare with one another or to what extent they would overlap.

We derived a word list from that compiled by Allport and Odbert; it consisted of four sublists corresponding to the four categories devised by those authors. The first and second sublists each contained a random five per cent sample of the more useful terms, i.e. words familiar enough to be recognized, defined and used in the context of a personality description by an intelligent educated adult. The third and fourth sublists each contained a random one per cent sample of the more useful words, selected on the same basis. The procedure was to calculate the sizes of the samples, find the interval numbers necessary to count through each of the four subpopulations of trait names in the Allport and Odbert monograph, and find a random position to start each count.

A. First List

Allport and Odbert's first 'minimum' list is supposed to comprise 'real', i.e. neutral and objective, traits of personality or personalized determining tendencies or consistent and stable modes of individual adjustment. Allport and Odbert admit that comparable trait names may be found in their other three categories of terms, but they prescribe '. . . no list or classification of traits' (p. 16).

The problem is how to impose some kind of conceptual structure or taxonomy on this array of trait names, as a framework for the description of individuals. There have been a number of attempts to classify traits since Allport and Odbert published their important monograph in 1936. These attempts have all assumed that the structure or taxonomy is revealed by the semantic similarities and differences between the words, e.g. by the way words with similar meanings can form a 'cluster', whereas words with contrasting meanings form a polar opposite cluster. The idea that traits are 'dimensional' is demonstrated in the construction of rating scales. Cattell's 16 PF test, see Cattell, Eber and Tatsuoka (1970) is probably the best example of a test based on a taxonomy of traits historically related to the Allport and Odbert list. It purports to measure a series of relatively independent personality characteristics, by reference to responses to verbal statements, and defines them in terms of clusters of bipolar words or phrases. A simpler taxonomy is provided by Eysenck (1970), in which the orthogonal dimensions of stability/instability (neuroticism) and introversion/extraversion give rise to four basic types of person: stable introverts, stable extraverts, unstable introverts, and unstable extraverts, each with a characteristic cluster of personality traits.

Mischel (1968) refers to a number of studies in which representative sets of trait words have been used to construct rating scales. With the use of these rating scales it is possible to intercorrelate the traits and to show that they form clusters. That is to say, traits form subgroups such that the correlations are relatively high between traits within a subgroup, and relatively low between traits in the subgroup and traits outside it. It has been found, however, that this 'clustering' is not necessarily an effect produced by any *real* psychological features exhibited by the persons being rated, since ratings made of strangers show similar clustering effects, and ratings made of the trait words themselves (in terms of their similarity in meaning to other trait words) also show similar clustering effects.

Studies of so-called 'implicit theories of personality' have shown that, in the mind of a judge or a rater, the possession by the stimulus person of one trait tends to imply the presence or absence of other traits, with some measurable degree of probability. We have already seen, however, that in natural language certain words tend to go together or to be related, as synonyms or antonyms, for example, or in other collocations and associative networks. Thus, what was supposed to be the discovery of basic personality structures, i.e. systems of traits within persons, may simply illustrate some of the semantic features of the language of personality description.

The question then is whether such semantic relationships mirror the facts of human personality and adjustment, or whether they provide us with no more than a system of convenient fictions—analogous to the elements of the graeco-roman world or the Ptolemaic epicycles.

It is not necessary to examine further the semantic relationships among trait names by means of multivariate statistical analysis. But are there any other ways of arranging trait names so that some kind of conceptual structure or taxonomy is revealed? It is to this question that we now turn. An examination of the sample derived from the first of the four lists of trait words in Allport and Odbert suggested the following possibilities: (i) many words are associated with hostility/submission; (ii) some words are constructed by means of a comparison with some person or type of person, e.g. 'bishoplike', 'brigandish', 'Dantesque', which suggests, as Allport and Odbert noted, that a large number of metaphors and similies can be constructed; (iii) additional words can be constructed from basic forms by the addition of prefixes and suffixes to indicate relative, as opposed to absolute, qualities, e.g. 'overfond', 'non-communistic', 'respectful', 'saintlike', 'superethical', 'unacademic', 'ultramodern'; (iv) a fair number of terms seem to refer to social dispositions, e.g. '(un)grateful', 'outspoken', 'mixer', 'tolerant'; (v) a fair number of terms have to do with fleshly or sexual attributes, e.g. 'erotic', 'nymphomaniac', 'passionate', 'voluptuous'; (vi) some refer to deviant qualities such as 'depersonalized', 'giddy', 'hypokinetic', 'mad-brain'; (vii) some permit the addition of the prefix 'self', as in 'self-centred', 'self-opinionated', whereas others do not (the prefix 'self', however, adds little to the meaning of the word); (viii) trait clusters corresponding to a variety of 'dimensions' of personality can be formed, e.g. stubborn versus compliant, introverted versus extraverted; some of these correspond to accepted, psychometrically defined, factors.

We have demonstrated the possibility, as have others before us, that some personality traits can be collected into bipolar clusters, though whether every single trait could reasonably be accommodated within a comprehensive classification remains to be seen. The indications are that the meaning of trait names is such that it would probably be impossible to form non-overlapping clusters.

B. Second List

Allport and Odbert's second list comprises terms designating temporary states of thinking, feeling, wanting and doing, which help to differentiate one person's conduct from that of another. They refer mainly to emotions, actions, volitions and cognitions as 'states' rather than 'traits'.

At first glance, the sample derived from the second list suggests no obvious conceptual structure or taxonomy. It is difficult to avoid regarding some terms as nonsensical. To begin with, the words seem to be drawn from relatively unrelated semantic categories; and in our earlier discussion of the full Allport and Odbert list we noted some obscurities and inconsistencies. We note in passing that *Roget's Thesaurus* proved to be of no help in the task of finding classes and relationships of psychological interest.

On closer inspection, however, and with reference back to the criteria for selecting words from *Webster* to fit this category, we see that several subgroups might be distinguished, as follows. (i) There are words possibly designating overt forms of behaviour, e.g. 'bowing', 'brushing', 'clattering', which seem to require little or no element of inference or of doubt as to what is going on. (ii) There are words designating forms of behaviour, e.g. 'begging', 'bribing', 'conceding', about which there may be some doubt because there is an element of inference. The point is that the same overt behaviour may be *construed* in different ways, i.e. as begging (rather than receiving payment for services), as bribing (rather than giving a present without obligation), as conceding (rather than freely offering).

It may be that the examples in subgroup (i) are not as simple as they look but also require that the behaviour in question be construed in one way rather than another, as bowing (not just bending forward), as brushing (not rubbing) and clattering (rather than making an unavoidable noise). If so, then they too belong in Subgroup (ii); Subgroup (i) could then be reserved for words which unambiguously and without inference refer to specified patterns of motor activity (movements) of the sort described in time and motion study. Unfortunately, many of the standard terms of reference in time and motion study, 'reaching', 'grasping', 'positioning', are objective and unambiguous only in the context of other terms, procedures and data: namely, those appropriate to the application of time and motion study techniques to a particular sort of task such as sorting mail or machine sewing. In ordinary language in daily life, we might still be required to interpret the behaviour referred to by these terms, i.e. as reaching (not just gesturing), as grasping (not just touching), and as positioning (not just putting down).

We are forced to conclude that it is difficult to find basic or 'primitive' terms to describe a person's movements or actions as such. The problem is to specify them so rigorously and in such fine detail that reasonable observers would agree about what the person actually did or said. Provided behaviour statements can be shown to be objective, i.e. amply corroborated by further testimony or by behaviour records of some kind, they provide the basic observational evidence which may support or refute some inference (conjecture or construction) about the person.

The awkward fact is that we make two rather distinct types of 'behaviour statement'. Let us call them Type A and Type B. A Type A statement refers to a pattern of movements, including a speech pattern, and a Type B statement refers to what the pattern of movements might signify as a psychological act. Thus, 'Holding the index and second fingers of the right hand upright at arm's length to form a V shape' might be regarded as an adequate example of a Type A behaviour statement. What it signifies as a psychological act depends on the construction to be placed on the behaviour to which it refers. The possible Type B statements might be as follows: 'Giving the victory sign', 'Making an obscene gesture signifying contempt', 'Mimicking the older children'. The validity of such statements would depend upon additional evidence.

The next three subgroups in Allport and Odbert's second list of words refer to well-known mental activities: (iii) thinking; (iv) feeling; (v) wanting. Three examples of each will suffice: (iii) 'doubting', 'forejudging', 'misrelating'; (iv) 'alarmed', 'frightened', 'glad'; (v) 'begging', 'detesting', 'avoiding'. Although some basic perceptual and psychological functions are not included in Allport and Odbert's list, i.e. words like 'seeing', 'hearing', 'looking', 'listening', others like 'feeling' and 'touching' are included.

As we have already seen, words do not carry a fixed quantum of meaning, but are capable of a wide range of meanings depending upon their linguistic context and the surrounding circumstances. Hence, it is perhaps impossible to assign words unambiguously to psychologically meaningful lexical categories; lexical categories are simply convenient lists containing words which are often used with the sort of meaning which enables us to classify them as similar in some respect, e.g. as habits, motives or abilities.

Some words seem to refer to achievements, i.e. to what the person is accomplishing or has accomplished: words like 'blossoming', 'duping', 'evicting' and 'guarding'. But closer examination reveals that they are further examples of Type B behaviour statements. There are obviously hundreds of words in existence, and no doubt hundreds more yet to be invented, to refer to the multifarious activities that people engage in, e.g. 'haggling', 'humming', 'idling', 'impugning', 'japing' and 'jogging'. There seems to be no point in attempting to list them exhaustively, and there seems to be no hope of classifying them.

Another subgroup in the second list contains words which refer to what we might call: (vi) states of being, e.g. 'ennui', 'estranged', 'homesick', 'idle', 'indebted', 'intoxicated' (metaphorically), 'maddish', 'mesmerized', and so on. Some of these terms imply a *relationship* between the person and some object, event or person in his environment.

The words in the second sublist contain the usual sorts of prefixes and suffixes, e.g. 'discontented', 'overconcerned', 'misinterpreting', of which the first two, according to our analysis, would be feelings, and the third a sort of thinking. The use of the prefixes 'out', 'over' and 'under' makes comparative judgments possible. The prefixes 'un', 'in', 'mis' and 'dis' usually form a negative, e.g. 'unhopeful', 'indiscreet', 'misusing', 'disbelieving'.

We notice that several classes of word correspond to some of the content categories described in our analysis of adult personality descriptions: see Chapters 5, 6 and 7. These are: (vii) Orientation and Feelings (ORFE), e.g. 'upset', 'unhopeful', 'piqued'; (viii) Expressive behaviour (EXPR), e.g. 'quivering', 'sauntering', 'haw-hawing'; (ix) Motivation and Arousal (MOTA), e.g. 'intent', 'obstructing'.

Our analysis of the lexical items in the first and second lists—based on a five per cent sample of the acceptable words—has led to some clarification of the language of personality descriptions. We now examine the third and fourth lists.

C. Third List

Allport and Odbert's third class of personality terms purports to list character evaluations. The essential feature of these items is supposed to be that they refer to *external judgments about* the person or his characteristics, not to dispositions within the person. But there are, of course, some dispositions which are essentially moral characteristics, e.g. 'honesty', 'truthfulness', in that they have to do with the ethical principles and beliefs (morals) which guide the person's actions. Moreover, character evaluations must refer to a person's intentions, principles and beliefs in order to judge them against the appropriate ethical standards, and we might therefore think of 'character' as having an inside and an outside aspect. The inside aspect comprises the psychological characteristics (beliefs, dispositions) which give rise to the behaviour; the outside aspect is the objective judgment (intersubjective consensus) of them in terms of an external ethical code. The inside aspect can be assessed *objectively* (by the quasi-judicial procedures described in Chapter 8) in relation to recognized moral standards, although such standards change in relation to cultural and historical conditions.

To say that the samples of words derived from this third list designate 'character evaluations' is rather misleading. It is true that they designate a variety of 'social evaluations', i.e. positive or negative estimations, made by one person of another. But they range over terms of affection, hatred, praise, abuse, denigration, esteem, blame and excuse. At least half the terms seem to make an adverse evaluation; so the main function of the words in the third list is to enable one to make adverse (bad) or favourable (good) comments about a person, his behaviour or his characteristics. Generally speaking, such judgments are related to our approval or disapproval of the stimulus person and to the concordance (or lack of it) between his interest and ours, i.e. liking versus disliking.

D. Fourth List

An examination was made of a one per cent sample of the words in Allport and Odbert's fourth category, which they regarded as largely metaphysical and of doubtful value, although they included words designating physical condition, developmental status and capacities of various sorts.

The demonstration that words as diverse as those listed in Allport and Odbert's fourth category can be used to say something about a person testifies to the richness and flexibility of the language of personality description. It seems incredible that any of the psychometric systems of trait clusters so far developed could assimilate more than a fraction of these wide-ranging terms. Some of them, however, could be assimilated to the category of evaluations, e.g. 'cesspool', 'tainted', 'psychopathic', and others to the category of states of being, e.g. 'uncared-for', 'impoverished', 'alive'. Physical characteristics form a fairly clear subset, e.g. 'hollow-eyed', 'slender', 'wizen-faced'. Some terms seem to involve metaphorical comparisons, e.g 'oviform', 'satiny', 'tuneless'; others involve more literal comparisons, e.g 'pilgrim', 'unministerial', 'veteran'.

IV. Conclusion

Our attempt to reclassify the trait names listed by Allport and Odbert can be summarized in tabular form according to the semantic functions they seem to fulfil: see overleaf. It does no more than underline the difficulty, perhaps even the

---

The semantic functions of trait names in the Allport and Odbert list

---

1A. Words used in behaviour statements Type A (see text); these are 'primitive' terms: the irreducible elements of observed behaviour.

1B. Words used in behaviour statements Type B (see text); these are 'inferences' or 'constructs': their meaning depends upon context and relevant evidence.

2A. Words referring to regular, stable and consistent ways of behaving.

2B. Words referring to the psychological dispositions, 'traits', or inclinations, thought to *underlie* the behaviour described in 2A.[a]

3A. Words describing expressive behaviour: primitive and irreducible terms referring to emotional behaviour.

3B. Words referring to temporary on-going 'states' of mind, cognitive, affective, volitional and relational, thought to *underlie* the behaviour described in 3A.

4A. Words used to refer to ethically-related behaviour *and* to the personal values, i.e. character or morals, that underlie it.

4B. Words used to make a value-judgment about a person's character or morals by referring him, his actions, intentions or dispositions, to some *external, independent* scale of values.[b]

---

[a] The words in 2A and 2B are sometimes interchangeable, so their meaning may be unclear.
[b] The words in 4A and 4B are easily confused with those in 2A and 2B.

---

impossibility, of making a definitive list and classification of the words and phrases used in ordinary language to describe and analyse personality.

As an exercise in the language of personality description, Allport and Odbert's investigation was a piece of inspired guesswork; but because it was not conceived within an appropriate conceptual framework (backed up by suitable empirical methods) it failed to solve any basic problems, and did not lead directly to the formulation of new questions, hypotheses and techniques (except those associated with Cattell). The limitations of the exercise are easily seen in retrospect. For example, it assigns to trait names a key, even an exclusive, role in the description of personality; it assumes that individual words can be designated either as trait names or not (without regard to the diversity of their usage in natural language); it assumes that each trait name has a well-defined and static meaning; it assumes that the appropriate unit of analysis is the single word rather than the phrase; it does not deal with the problem of how words are modified—in meaning and effect—by the linguistic and situational context in which they occur; it does not deal with the problems of frequency of occurrence, common usage or the difference between spoken and written vocabularies; it also misconstrues the function of a dictionary, seeing it as a sort of encyclopedia of terms and their empirical reference, instead of a list of words defined approximately in terms of other words.

The above comments are sufficient to show that we do not accept that traits have an exclusive role to play in the description of personality, and we do not accept that the concept of traits has been correctly formulated by Allport and subsequent investigators.

We have demonstrated, in a somewhat negative way, the contribution that trait names make to the language of personality description. The attempt to separate trait names from the context of ordinary language was understandable but ill-founded. Not only has it failed to produce the promised benefits, but it has given rise to serious misconceptions and erroneous methods in personality assessment. This is not to say that trait names have no place in personality descriptions, see Gough (1960, 1965), but rather that they do not deserve the privileged place accorded to them since 1936. There is evidence that some trait names can be classified into relatively independent subsets—on both empirical and rational, i.e. grammatical, grounds—and used in the construction of standardized and useful psychometric tests of personality; but such measures by no means solve the problem of personality description. The scientific description of personality requires all the resources of ordinary language plus whatever additional resources are available from the technical languages of psychology.

CHAPTER 4

Conceptual Analysis and Empirical Method

I. The Concept of 'Trait'

The main consideration in classifying words and phrases as 'traits' is that they should not specify actual behaviour, for the simple reason that traits refer to broad or *general* dispositions within a person which can be inferred from the coherence of his responses in different situations. Responses as different as laughing, refusing a request and swearing might express the same underlying disposition, e.g. aggressiveness. Thus, to use Allport's term, actions may be different but 'functionally equivalent'; conversely, actions may be the same but 'functionally different'; laughter may express sociability, aggressiveness, ambition or other traits, depending upon its context: the problem is to identify the underlying disposition.

The next consideration is that words and phrases identified as traits should not be judgments of the *effect* that the stimulus person has upon other people; they should refer to characteristics or dispositions *within* the person. To define personality in terms of the effect the stimulus person has on others is to confuse cause with effect, and to confuse the term 'personality' with that of 'reputation'.

Finally, if the characteristic is narrowly specified—in such a way as to restrict its scope of application to a particular sort of situation or to an habitual pattern of response—then it cannot, by definition, have the status of a *general* disposition or trait. Thus, for example, 'careless' can be classified as a trait, but 'careless of his appearance' specifies behaviour rather narrowly; for whereas 'careless' implies 'careless in general' (assuming normal and not loose usage), 'careless of his appearance' obviously does not imply 'careless in general', even though it might be one of a number of observations which eventually lead an observer to that inference. Thus, 'careless of his appearance' is almost (not quite) an observational statement; it lacks the abstractness and generality of 'careless' and has a narrower range of application.

If we conceive of dispositional terms as standing on a ladder of abstraction, then those nearer the bottom of the ladder subsume fewer lower dispositional terms and fewer patterns of actual behaviour. For example, the phrase 'careless of his appearance' might reasonably subsume 'doesn't always bother to shave or to comb his hair', 'wears dirty shoes and odd socks', 'wears worn and soiled clothes', and so on; but it could not reasonably subsume 'leaves his tools lying about', 'doesn't bother to make proper arrangements', or 'makes mistakes'. In other words, it makes sense to exemplify or paraphrase in some ways but not in others. The structure of ordinary language enables us to move sensibly up and down the ladder of abstraction, from behavioural terms to dispositional terms and back again, and to distinguish one kind of dispositional term from another.

It might be argued that, by defining traits as abstract and general dispositions, we are 'saving appearances' and accepting the conceptualization formulated by Allport and others. To some extent this is correct, since we regard the concept of 'trait' as a valuable and, as yet, indispensable part of our approach to the study of personality. In our approach, however, the concept of 'trait' does not occupy the privileged and exclusive position that it occupies elsewhere. Moreover, we try to avoid any presuppositions about the existence and nature of traits—the sorts of presupposition which led Allport to concentrate on the real and essential nature of traits to the neglect of most other aspects of the language of personality description. As far as our method of content analysis is concerned, the notion of traits as general dispositions is merely a conceptual convenience with a recognized element of arbitrariness in it; this arbitrariness is partly concerned with the degree of abstractness and generality above which a word or phrase is conceptualized and labelled as a General Trait (GENT) or 'trait', and below which it is conceptualized and labelled as a Specific Trait (SPET) or 'habit': see later sections for the system of content categories and notation. The conceptual boundaries of 'trait' and 'habit' are neither clear nor fixed in ordinary language.

Some important general dispositions have been largely excluded from the province of personality study. One obvious example is that of 'intelligence', presumably because it constituted a major area of investigation which was already well-developed in terms of concepts, methods and findings, by the time trait psychology emerged as a recognizable movement. In addition to mental ability, however, there are other abilities which are referred to by dispositional terms, e.g. artistic, athletic, tactful, dextrous, courageous, though one might just as well say that dispositions such as tact, dexterity and courage are used as terms which refer to abilities: see Wallace (1966).

Thus, when we compare and contrast the notions of 'disposition' and 'ability' we find that they do not refer to distinct entities within persons. To have a 'disposition' implies some ability to behave in an appropriate way and, to a lesser extent, to have an 'ability' implies some inclination to use it in appropriate circumstances. For example, to say, 'He is generous' implies that he has an ability to share his resources; and to say, 'He has an ability to share his resources' implies that he is generous. All that we are doing here is making a tautology explicit; we are not confused by an alternative context for the use of the word 'ability' which refers to the occurrence of an opportunity which permits the expression of an act (or of a constraint which prevents it): thus, for example, 'He is generous, but he is not able to share his resources (there being none to spare at the moment)' and, similarly, 'He is (in the position of being) able to share his resources (so we shall see whether he is generous or not)'.

The word 'disposition' is from the French and Latin *dis-*, apart, *ponere*, *positum*, to place, and is a noun meaning: the arrangement, plan or distribution of things available and under one's control; natural tendency or inclination. In the language of personality and adjustment the term thus refers to the ability and inclination to do what is possible.

The word 'ability' is from the Latin *habilitas*, to have, to hold, and means having enough strength, skill, power or means to do something. The term 'ability' therefore refers mainly to the means or resources available to the person, whereas the term 'disposition' refers to both the means and the inclination to use or deploy them. The term 'inclination', of course, means to turn to or tend to move in a particular direction, and so be disposed to distribute or arrange one's actions according to a plan or objective.

There are concepts in the study of personality and adjustment whose boundaries overlap with one another. This makes it difficult to assign words and phrases to one category exclusively—in a content analysis—like that of General Trait (GENT), for example. The category Motivation and Arousal (MOTA) also expresses a 'dispositional' concept; it refers to motivation and arousal, i.e. to the needs and desires that people have, to their likes and dislikes, their preferences and aversions. One might say that a motive is a psychobiological disposition within a person that instigates, sustains and directs (aims) his behaviour towards an appropriate object or end state. The aim is the fulfilment of the desire, the satisfaction of the need; the object is whatever the consummatory phase of the behaviour is directed towards.

If we assert that 'P_i is aggressive', do we mean that his behaviour is generally aggressive? Or that he needs to be aggressive? Or that he has the ability to be aggressive? In fact, we can mean any one or all of these, depending upon what we do in fact 'mean' by the assertion that 'P_i is aggressive'. This meaning can be elucidated by amplifying the statement, by restating it in other ways, by citing appropriate examples, and so on, in order to eliminate ambiguities.

The concept of 'disposition' is not as simple as we had supposed—it has both a motivational or directive character and an instrumental or operant character (the pattern of actions and outcomes). The former could be referred to as the 'intentional' or inner aspect of the behaviour as planned, the latter as the actual or outer aspect of the behaviour as executed. The concept of 'intention', together with that of 'motive', 'cause' and 'reason', is dealt with later.

We shall see in the chapters dealing in detail with the content analysis of personality descriptions that dispositional, i.e. motivational or intentional, features are found in at least three other 'internal' aspects of personality. One of these is Expressive Behaviour (EXPR), another is Orientation and Feeling (ORFE), and the third is Moral Principles (PRIN). Moreover, it is difficult, if not impossible, to describe many of the 'external' aspects of personality without saying something, directly or indirectly, about the aims and objects of the stimulus person's behaviour.

We thus confirm the commonsense notion that motives and intentions pervade a person's actions, and that the individual organizes his behaviour, using whatever resources are available to him, in certain characteristic (typical and recurrent) patterns so as to attain a variety of aims in relation to a variety of objects and circumstances. As a consequence, his motives are expressed not only in his general behaviour characteristics or 'traits', but also in his habits, his abilities and achievements, his phantasies, his expressive behaviour, his thoughts and feelings, his morals, his social relationships, and so on, over most facets of his personality.

The problem of describing and analysing personality by means of a content analysis of ordinary language, and in terms of a limited number of conceptual categories (traits, abilities, motives, habits, and so on), may now appear to be insoluble. This is partly because we confuse words with things, and partly misunderstand the nature of language. We have assumed that these conceptual categories refer to entities whose existence can be verified by reference to empirical data. But these conceptual categories are better thought of as convenient lines of demarcation in the construction of 'word maps' about people. Personality descriptions are 'representations' of persons and, as such, can take many forms: a biography, a personality rating, an MMPI or 16PF profile, a case-study, or a short free-description of the sort obtained in our empirical investigations. We find it convenient to identify and refer to certain features of human nature as 'traits', 'motives', 'moods', 'abilities', 'attitudes', and so on, rather as geographers find it convenient to refer to certain features of terrain as ridge, valley, pasture, fault, and so on. The geographer is fortunate in being able to represent the physical terrain by means of a system of conventions and notation in maps. The psychologist has no such notational system for representing persons, unless one accepts the dubious analogy with standardized tests, or the even more dubious analogy with Lewinian topological diagrams. The geographer can also more easily secure consensus among competent investigators, since his concepts are tied more closely to observable data.

Thus, when we say that the concepts we use to describe and analyse personality are convenient fictions we are only asserting what is true of all empirical sciences; they are constructs and hypotheses and therefore liable to falsification and revision, i.e. they are not incorrigible.

How can we be sure that the language we use to represent personality corresponds to (or, rather, can be shown to refer to) something real, something that can be observed or validated independently of language? How can we be sure that our description is not largely fiction, like a medieval map or the biblical account of creation? We can never be *absolutely* sure, because it is always possible that some new conceptualization will make existing views obsolete and even ridiculous. All we can do is to engage in a continual process of revision—of conjecture and refutation, to use Popper's terms—in which we try to improve the internal coherence and external validity of our conceptualization in relation to the relevant standards of practical utility and predictive accuracy.

In studying the ordinary language of personality description and analysis, we are deliberately *not* concerning ourselves with the actual persons referred to, i.e. with the validity and accuracy of descriptions. We are assuming that ordinary language provides a common currency for social exchange and for the symbolic representation of experience about persons in general. We are assuming, of course, that we already understand people reasonably well, or at least that we understand relatively normal people in the ordinary affairs of everyday life. If this were not the case, it would be difficult to see how human relationships could achieve the levels of complexity known to us, in fact or in fiction. But we must not exaggerate the level of understanding reached by the average person; it is probably abysmally low in comparison with what is possible even within ordinary language and common sense. Misunderstandings and failures in the normal course of human relationships are abundant, at least testifying to the possibilities for remedial education and training. Failure to understand and manage persons with unusual characteristics or in unusual situations is to be expected—on the grounds of simple ignorance and lack of intelligence. There is no reason why the ordinary language and understanding of everyday life should be adequate to deal with *abnormal* persons. The fact that we sometimes fail to understand other people, fail to predict or to influence their behaviour, and fail to describe and explain them adequately, suggests that failure is the exception rather than the rule. While it is important to discover why we sometimes fail, it is perhaps as important to discover how we usually succeed.

The study of personality descriptions in ordinary language examines our *commonsense* understanding of other people, in the hope of relating it more effectively to *scientific* knowledge and professional practice. It could be protested that this is rather like trying to relate folklore about the weather to meteorology; the analogy is not altogether an apt one, although there are some points of similarity. However, we must not confuse a scientific description and analysis with a survey of popular wisdom; we are not studying beliefs about human nature but rather the structures and processes of language and cognition in relation to self-understanding and understanding others.

II. The Concept of 'Motive'

Concern with human desires, feelings and intentions is such an obvious feature of the language of personality descriptions that one could expect the behavioural sciences to have made considerable progress in describing and explaining human motivation and affect. To some extent this is true; the psychodynamic approaches to personality and psychopathology have made extensive and revolutionary contributions to our understanding of these aspects of human nature; the psychometric approach has been much less successful; the physiological and comparative approaches to behaviour have also made extensive contributions to our understanding of the biological basis of drives and emotions.

Nevertheless, there is still considerable confusion regarding the description, analysis and explanation of human motivation and emotion in relation to personal adjustment. The main reason is that these phenomena are subjective, and can be dealt with objectively only by means of empirical (behavioural) evidence. Some of the confusion arises from methodological difficulties, i.e. from our inability to set up the investigations needed to answer certain empirical questions; other confusions are 'conceptual', i.e. they arise from our inability to clarify our ideas or to formulate coherent theories.

Our present concern is with the sorts of desires, feelings and intentions to be found in everyday life. This does not exclude consideration of some minor psychological deviations, so well-documented in clinical psychology and psychiatry, since many of us encounter them occasionally in daily life, but it does allow us to treat them as a special case, i.e. as the sorts of behaviour not easily described and explained in the ordinary language of personality descriptions. As a consequence, we must be prepared to accept either that ordinary language can, in principle at least, deal adequately with 'extraordinary' sorts of behaviour, or that a special technical language is needed to describe and explain them. Freudian psychology demonstrates that special languages (expressing novel concepts, relationships and observations) are possible. If such novel concepts and terminologies prove useful and popular, they get assimilated, in one form or another, into the ordinary language of everyday life (even though they may be invalid and misleading).

A useful basis for discussion is *The Concept of Motivation* by Peters (1960). The early part of this book deals with answers to apparently simple questions which are—philosophically at least—central to the language of personality and adjustment, e.g. 'Why did Jones cross the road?' The sort of answer or explanation one gets depends upon the sort of question one asks (and, of course, on the situational context within which that question is asked), but an answer in terms of a goal (or its correlated motive) e.g. 'To buy a newspaper (or because he wanted a newspaper)' is not the only way of explaining this normal human action. Our empirical studies indicate that, in ordinary language, there are at least six different sorts of explanation for human actions. Briefly, in addition to the concept of goal (or motive), explanatory concepts in commonsense include the following: trait (or disposition), role (or social expectation), habit (or custom), circumstance (or environmental constraint), and orientation (attitude, belief or expectation). In addition, there are combinations of these, or more thoroughgoing analyses based on psychological theorizing (not necessarily of a scientific sort). These various explanatory concepts are described in more detail in Chapter 9. We mention them at this point only to emphasize that the concept of 'motive', like the concept of 'trait', has no *special* merit in the explanation of human conduct; *any* sort of fact which reduces or eliminates the puzzlement created by 'Jones crossing the road' may be considered explanatory. Thus, having received the answer, 'To buy a newspaper (or because he wanted a newspaper)' we might still be puzzled—for example, if he could have reached the same goal (or satisfied the same desire) without crossing the road (there being a newsagent on each side of the road). In this situation, we are forced to consider other possible motives, or other sorts of psychological factors, such as those just mentioned. We notice, incidentally, that the same goal may satisfy a variety of motives, and the 'intentionality' of the behaviour is only one sort of evidence relevant to questions of the sort, 'Why did he do that?' Jones's 'wanting' and 'intending to buy' might themselves be instrumental to some deeper-lying motive. Peters (1960) touches on this when he distinguishes 'his' (i.e. Jones's) reasons from 'the' reasons for an action. In other words, he (Jones) may have personal, subjective aims (his reasons) which may or may not coincide with his stated reasons or with yet other objective reasons discovered by empirical and rational inquiry into his behaviour. Ordinary language copes easily with these interesting differences in the description and analysis of motivated behaviour.

People are held responsible for the normal and foreseeable consequences of their actions. This common ethical principle is based on the assumption that adults are fairly rational and organize their behaviour according to the way they construe the opportunities for, and constraints on, the satisfaction of their desires. But people sometimes misconstrue their situation or lack the abilities necessary to deal with it optimally. The result is that sometimes their actions, though well-intentioned, are inappropriate or have unexpected consequences, and have to be 'explained' in terms other than motives.

In dealing with the explanatory powers of the concept of 'character traits', Peters argues that terms like 'honesty', 'punctuality', 'considerateness' and 'meanness' do not refer to the sort of goal human beings seek, but to the 'type of regulation' (p. 5) they impose on their behaviour, i.e. to their 'particular sort of ways' of behaving. According to Peters, the fact that our behaviour is regulated by social prescriptions and values means that we behave according to rules and not just according to the biological demands of a situation—otherwise how do we account for sexual conventions or playing games? The rules, moreover, are usually known to and accepted by the person. The fact that some people are better than others at keeping to the rules is an important aspect of personality and social adjustment and enables us to use terms like 'honest', 'punctual', 'considerate' and 'mean', in at least three ways: as behavioural statements of how a person *acts*; as dispositional statements of how he *tends* to behave, i.e. what can be expected of him; and as evaluative statements signifying the social desirability of such actions and dispositions.

Peters (p. 5) contrasts character traits like those just mentioned with goal-directed motives like 'ambition', 'hunger' and 'sexual desire'. Such motives indicate, in a rather general way, that the person's energies and activities are directed towards (aimed at) certain objects or outcomes: although the exact nature of these aims and objects has to be particularized when referring to the motives of individual people. In the same way, the exact nature of character traits, particular ways of pursuing goals, has to be specified when referring to individual people. The meaning of the terms we use to refer to such characteristics is said to be 'field dependent'.

Motivated behaviour has an appetitive (goal-seeking or intentional) phase and a consummatory (goal-finding or fulfilment) phase. This distinction corresponds to what Peters refers to as 'means' and 'ends' (p. 6) respectively. The terms 'seeking' and 'finding' need a few words of explanation: 'seeking' is used in the sense of 'looking for', 'trying to get' and 'wanting' (though not necessarily with any clear idea of what will terminate the search, or with the intention of accepting only one particular end result); 'finding' is used in the sense of 'arriving at', 'experiencing', 'supplying', 'succeeding in getting', 'concluding' and 'becoming able' (though not necessarily with any implication that what one finds, experiences, gets or becomes able to do will fully satisfy, i.e. meet the requirements of, the underlying appetite, or that the end result will be accompanied by a definite experience of 'pleasure').

Social regulations, either implicit or explicit, govern a wide range of human activities from early life until death. Thus, much of a person's behaviour 'makes sense' when seen in the context of his social roles and social circumstances. In the main, he behaves as people 'expect' him to behave. There are, therefore, two problems. First, 'What genetic and environmental factors make the person a social being?' Second, 'Why is the person's behaviour not completely regulated by society?'. The first of these questions is too general for us to consider; it raises fundamental issues in a variety of scientific disciplines, including the study of human evolution, since, for all we know, the forms of human social adjustment with which we are familiar may be transitory and may give way eventually to new forms about which we can only speculate. The second of these questions is much more relevant to the issues we are presently dealing with, because if we observe, as we often do, that a person's behaviour deviates from that which is socially prescribed, then we need to find, either in the ordinary language of common experience or in the technical language of psychopathology, the explanation for such deviation.

In situations where there are no social prescriptions, or only vague ones, we must look elsewhere for the explanation as to why the person behaved as he did. In situations like these, commonsense relies upon concepts like 'temptation', 'greed', 'stupidity', 'forgetfulness', 'panic', 'carelessness', 'laziness', 'immorality', 'incompetence', 'unnatural desire' and a whole catalogue of socially undesirable human feelings. Such failings, lapses and derelictions usually elicit disrespect and blame, whereas strengths (of character) and dutiful behaviour elicit respect and praise—presumably in the expectation that such treatment will discourage offenders and encourage the virtuous. The existence of forgiveness and the acceptance of blame in everyday social transactions demonstrate that people do not always follow rules. Nevertheless, the failure of a person to abide by commonly accepted social regulations calls for an explanation in a way that his obedience to the regulations does not. At a commonsense level, a great deal of normal behaviour is explained by reference to the rules and expectations governing familiar social relationships; deviant behaviour is explained either

84

by reference to 'character failings' as mentioned above, or by reference to psychopathology (neurosis, brain injury) or by reference to supernatural processes (possession, witchcraft). The notion of 'mitigating circumstances' permits some of the blame for a person's actions to be attributed to the environment: because of stress, provocation, temptation, bad example, and so on. The same sort of consideration applies to dutiful behaviour: the more difficult it is in the face of adverse circumstances, the more praiseworthy the act and the person, because his behaviour reveals the strength of his dispositions or convictions.

The person's awareness of his own desires, capacities and circumstances is an awkward fact which must nevertheless be accounted for in the explanation of human behaviour. It is an awkward fact because people differ in the extent to which they understand themselves, appreciate the circumstances they are in, and think about their actions. A person's awareness varies from one moment to the next and from one situation to another. In so far as a person's assessment of himself and his situation corresponds to the best objective assessment that could be made, we might say that *his* (subjective) reasons for, or explanations of, his own actions correspond to *the* (objective) reasons or explanations. However, the person's assessment is sometimes at fault, in which case we are obliged to say that he is mistaken in thinking that he understands why he behaves as he does, and possibly that he behaves as he does *because* of his misunderstanding. If the latter, the objective assessment would have to take account of the person's misunderstanding, i.e. incorporate it as an element in the description and explanation of that person's action. By contrast, an assessment which does not have the benefit of evidence about the person's awareness may be mistaken if the person's awareness is a key factor in determining his behaviour. Thus, if a person thinks that he can discuss confidential matters with a friend without their being passed on, he may do so, contrary to an observer's expectations.

Man's cognitive and linguistic capacities enable him to reflect on himself and the world, to profit from experience and to try out novel sorts of action. As a result, he is capable of setting goals (being 'future-oriented' to use Allport's (1955) term), formulating plans or strategies and making tactical adjustments so that his actions can serve as means to an end. Goal-directedness is thus more than a mere instinctive searching, and although analogous behaviour is observed in other animals, it seems to achieve conscious intentionality only in human beings. Animals have needs, drives and appetites, but not desires, motives and intentions.

Peters (p. 97) says:

> But men differ from the rest of nature in that they understand some of the laws in accordance with which they act and act differently because of this understanding. They also act in accordance with quite a different set of laws—normative laws—which they themselves create.

Thus, at the human level, because of the interposition of psychological processes, actions can often be explained in terms of motives (or some other psychological factor). But then the motives themselves have to be explained—partly in terms of basic and acquired needs and personal qualities, partly in terms of environmental factors. We have already noted, however, that motives may be closely associated with values, and values may contrast sharply with the biology of survival and reproduction, so that it is not immediately obvious how values come to play such an important role in human behaviour; unless perhaps we think in sociobiological terms of 'cultural' evolution, when the selective advantages of altruism and common values become more obvious.

Another conceptual and linguistic problem is that although 'actions' are, in a sense, composed of 'sensations' and 'movements' or physiological processes, they cannot be *reduced* to them for the purpose of description and analysis. This is because an action has an organic quality, e.g. driving to work, preparing a meal, and is not dependent upon any particular pattern of sensations or movements. Also, an action may have experiential components (wanting, thinking, feeling) not directly related to sensory or motor processes. Actions thus become psychological constructions (conceptualizations) for the organization and interpretation of sensations, experiences and movements. An action is something done or achieved; it may be of interest to examine its sensory and motor components for practical purposes, as in time and motion study, or for research purposes, as in the analysis of human performance; but, at a commonsense level in everyday life, such analysis is usually inappropriate and explains nothing. The explanation of an 'action' must be in psychological terms, because 'action' is a psychological concept.

In order for action to occur at all there must be a host of interrelated and sequential conditions, many of which are taken for granted in psychological explanations, e.g. physiological functions, perceptual and memory processes. Normally, however, it is not necessary, or even possible, to tell the whole story; all that is required is a causal analysis which shows how the events one is most interested in came about and shows, in principle at least, how the analysis might be pursued in greater detail.

Ordinary behaviour is 'ordinary' because it is familiar and usual; it does not normally excite curiosity, puzzlement or wonder. Since it provokes no questions, it appears to need no explanation; and since it needs no explanation it must be comprehensible. If it is questioned, however, and explanations are forthcoming, they can be either mundane or illuminating. Consider, for example, a question like, 'Why did she remind him that the ladder she had borrowed was still in the garage?' One answer might be, 'Because she noticed he was painting the house and might have need of it'. Another answer might be in terms of social exchange, reciprocal obligations and basic personality structure, in suburban life. The first answer would be mundane, the second illuminating. The first answer satisfied the curiosity of a neighbour; the second solves the deeper puzzlement of a social scientist. Both are adequate in their own way, although a psychologist might want to introduce an intermediate type of answer in terms of individual motives, attitudes and traits.

Peters (p. 28) argues that the concept of motivation is sometimes used to provide a causal (material) interpretation of what is basically a logical term, i.e. 'motive'. This is because there are different levels of comprehension: a behavioural science level and a commonsense level. The former attempts a *causal* analysis, the latter attempts to identify motives as one sort of *reason* for action.

The routine satisfaction of ordinary needs differs in a variety of ways from the intermittent satisfaction of prolonged and more deeply felt needs. But whereas Peters (p. 25) seems to argue for the separation of motive and habit, Allport's (1937) view is that motives are 'habits-in-the-making'.

Biological and environmental factors exert wide-ranging and persistent influences on individuals—directing and shaping their behaviour (and the underlying psychological characteristics)—hence the distinction between actions which are deliberately and actively organized from within (plans, instructions, rules) and those that are passively shaped by impulse, compulsion or force of circumstance. The former are regarded as being under the control of the person and therefore his responsibility, whereas the latter are regarded as being brought about by environmental or other factors outside the person's control, e.g. fear, provocation, even habit. The distinction, however, is a conceptual convenience and one must not lose sight of the functional relationships between inner states (hopes, fears, desires) and outer conditions (incentives, disincentives, opportunities, constraints).

When we assign 'responsibility' to a person for his actions we do so on the basis of what we know of his abilities, personal qualities, circumstances, and so on. If a person is pursuing socially prescribed activities there is no point in asking what his motives are since these can be taken for granted (unless one wishes to inquire more deeply into the psychological foundations of social conventions or into the personal affairs of a particular individual). But to inquire further into these motives is to imply, Peters suggests (p. 31), that there might be something discreditable in them, and that such inquiries are searching for 'justification not simply explanation'. He says (p. 31) 'Motives are reasons for action ... when there is an issue of justification as well as of explanation'. But, as we have seen, motives are only one sort of reason for actions: the sort of reason which states the goal towards which the person's behaviour is directed. According to Peters (pp. 35–6) the concept of motive in ordinary language is used to account for, and to evaluate, an action which falls outside the normal range of conventional behaviour; it also implies a goal-directed disposition as *the* reason for the action.

Knowledge of a person's motives is sometimes said to be the key to understanding personality. It is particularly useful when it comes to finding ways of influencing the person's behaviour, whether by incentives, counselling or behaviour modification, since it may show how the same motive can be directed towards different goals or along different paths, e.g. the need for approval, or how one motive can be substituted for another, e.g. group achievement for personal achievement.

Although the term 'motivation' is used to refer to the goal-seeking aspect of human behaviour, it is not clear whether it refers only to the on-going processes or to the initial state which instigates the behaviour in the first place. Peters (pp.

37–8) seems to object to the idea that emotional states trigger motivated behaviour; indeed the idea has little to recommend it, since it does not add to our understanding. Feelings and emotions are transitory states signalling how well or badly things are going for the individual and express fairly well-defined psychological states, such as hope, anxiety, satisfaction and disappointment, which presumably have some adaptive significance. It seems reasonable to assume that directedness is *intrinsic* to normal behaviour and that there are endless directions for behaviour to take—depending upon the individual's past history, his present physical and mental state, the opportunities, incentives, constraints and disincentives of his surrounding circumstances, and so on. Disorganized random behaviour or apathy is so rare as to be indicative of serious psychopathology or stress.

We close this section with four quotations from Peters which emphasize the importance of conceptual analysis for personality description in ordinary language:

> The difficulty about developing a science of psychology is that, in a sense, we already know too much about human behaviour, albeit in a rather unco-ordinated manner. Commonsense, which is incorporated in the concepts of ordinary language, has creamed off most of the vital distinctions. Psychology has the task of systematizing what is already known and adding bits of special theory to supplement commonsense .... (p. 155.)

> For ordinary language enshrines all sorts of distinctions, the fine shades of which often elude the clumsiness of a highly general theory. The analysis of a concept like that of 'motive' is never merely an inquiry into terminology. It is an avenue of approach to distinctions which may well be theoretically as well as practically important. (p. 49.)

> The point of looking closely at ordinary usage, if one is a psychologist, is that it often provides a clue to distinctions which it is theoretically important to take account of. We know *so much* about human beings, and our knowledge is incorporated implicitly in our language. Making it explicit could be a more fruitful preliminary to developing a theory than gaping at rats or grey geese. (p. 50.)

> Above all things, a study of the different psychological concepts of ordinary language encourages a sensitivity to the different *sorts* of questions that can be asked about human actions and the different sorts of answers that are appropriate. (p. 50.)

Our main aims are to describe the empirical studies which make explicit, and perhaps refine, the conceptual distinctions found in commonsense and the ordinary language of personality description, and to systematize the findings in a framework of *scientific* knowledge.

III. Research Method: Content Analysis

The subjects in our empirical investigations comprised twenty men and twenty women in each of the six decades of life from the twenties to the seventies, giving 240 subjects altogether. They were drawn from a panel (register) of adult volunteers recruited from the Merseyside region of England under the terms of a grant from the Medical Research Council between 1970 and 1974 to investigate person perception in adult life and old age. They were tested under standard conditions in small groups in a lecture-room setting; they were asked to read the instructions on the front of a booklet, and listened to the investigator reading and explaining these instructions; their questions were answered, and they were told that the purpose of the investigation would be explained to them in a general way after completion of the exercise. Their instructions were to think of a person they knew reasonably well who fitted the title given at the top of each page, e.g. 'A man I like', 'A girl I dislike', and to write an account of that person, i.e. to say what sort of person he (or she) was, but without spending time describing the stimulus person's physical appearance. The first title in each booklet was 'Myself', followed, in random order for each subject, by titles describing eight sorts of stimulus person (SP): man liked, man disliked, woman liked, woman disliked, boy liked, boy disliked, girl liked, girl disliked. This procedure was the same as that in the study of juvenile development: see Chapter 1.

These personality descriptions, together with other data, provide the empirical evidence for the present investigation, and for a number of related studies still in progress. The descriptions are, on average, about 100 words (or five sentences) long. They can usually be understood without difficulty, although close examination often reveals a certain amount of vagueness. There are, of course, the usual differences between subjects in the quantity and literary quality of the descriptions, and there are variations from one description to another even for the same subject (partly because they are writing about different sorts of stimulus person). Some idea of the content and organization of adult personality descriptions can be gained by reading the six examples presented below; they were drawn at random from a total of 1920 descriptions. The self-descriptions will be reported in a separate publication. The following personality descriptions retain features of the originals: spelling, punctuation, and so on. Occasionally, slight alterations have been made in order to safeguard the identities of the people concerned, but these do not materially affect the examples.

A woman describes a man she dislikes:

> He is middle-aged. Scottish. Cheerful in a banal sort of way. Has a reasonably good job. Thinks women are suitable only for bed and carrying in the coal—and certainly not fit to drive the car. Is stodgy, has no imagination whatever, sings sickly sentimental songs at parties, thinks his opinion on any subject whatever is the only one worth considering. Wears fair-isle pullovers. Is interested in boating and golfing and has the most appalling wife.

A man describes a woman he likes:

This woman is a paraplegic and perhaps fortunate in having parents who can support her financially. However she throws herself enthusiastically into all causes for the disabled and maintains a high standard of jolity which is catching. She is the type of person who makes one feel that you have missed something in life.

A man describes a girl he dislikes:

The person I have in mind is an exhibitionist—always seeking to thrust herself into the company with an air of superiority where none exists. Her moral integrity leaves much to be desired in a young woman and she seems to get a kick out of relating experiences most people would want to keep to themselves—particularly a female. She has a brash personality with a voice to match. I could not envisage anything said to her remaining unrepeated with added embellishments designed to denigrate and perhaps worse. I would not want to associate myself with her more than is absolutely necessary in the course of my contact.

A man describes a boy he dislikes:

This young man is a bore. He will corner a conversation and talk away on mainly one single subject, always the same one, even though he knows that there is only one other person in the company that has even the remotest idea what he is talking about. As I happen to be that person it can become very embarrassing. He has a habit of making jokes about other people in the company often not in good taste and usually very embarrassing to the company. When it is pointed out to him he gets very offended and accuses people of having no sense of humour. He seems to want to be a leading light at the expense of anybody or everybody.

A woman describes a woman she dislikes:

She is very popular with a lot of people, but also very unpopular with others. I dislike her because she is so ungrateful and is very miserly. She has an air of efficiency but underneath is quite incompetent. She is quite pleasant, but can be very hurtfull if she is so inclined. She has beautifully manicured hands and is one of those people who speak with their hands. She spends a lot of time dancing and playing tennis but anything which involves spending money is not persued. Her personality is very uninteresting.

A woman describes a boy she likes:

This boy is a very trustworthy boy always ready to help in any way other people. He is a worker very good at football and is very good in every way at home. He has had several accidents but has overcome them, and got quickly back on his feet.

The six examples constitute a very small sample of the total. Nevertheless, they are sufficient, for the time being, to illustrate the ordinary language of personality descriptions. Although they illustrate differences between individual subjects clearly enough, they obviously cannot reveal systematic differences between age groups, between the sexes, or between the different sorts of stimulus person written about. The investigation of these factors will be described in a separate publication.

The illustrative personality descriptions above have a number of features which are characteristic of material of this sort. First, each description is a cognitive product manifested in 'ordinary language' and thus composed of words and phrases structured, i.e. organized, in such a way as to represent the subject's impression of a stimulus person and to make it meaningful to others. Second, it is a selective, focused and coherent account of a real person, but not an exhaustive account. Third, it is a functional response to the demand characteristics imposed by the research setting, and to this extent it might be different from comparable responses (descriptions) in other settings, e.g. in casual conversation with friends or in a police inquiry. These various features call for rather different sorts of linguistic analysis. The first requires a lexical and a syntactical analysis; the second requires a semantic and psychological analysis; the third requires a situational or pragmatic analysis. We shall find, however, that these different sorts of linguistic analysis overlap and interlock one with another.

The design and general arrangements for the investigation into person perception in adult life and old age were deliberately modelled on those used for the investigation into person perception in childhood and adolescence. The volunteer subjects were somewhat above the average for the population at large in vocabulary, intelligence and socioeconomic status. The differences between the various age groups were not so great as to prevent us from talking sensibly about adult personality descriptions in general; but we must remember that, with all their obvious faults and weaknesses, they are the products of a slightly 'above average' sample of the adult population. The original intention was to make comparisons between different age groups—over a large part of the juvenile and adult phases of life—in terms of a standard set of stimulus persons and a standard set of content analysis categories. Although pilot studies had led us to believe that such straightforward comparisons were possible, we came to see that there was much more in the ordinary language of adult personality descriptions than we had supposed, and that our conceptual analysis would have to go much deeper than it had gone in the investigation of children's descriptions.

We became increasingly concerned about the ambiguity of words and phrases taken in isolation for the purpose of content classification—leading inevitably to unreliability in coding. We felt compelled, eventually, to refine the system of content categories developed in connection with the relatively simple juvenile data, to adopt a more searching and explicit method for classifying the contents of adult personality descriptions, and to be more flexible in attaching meanings to the words and phrases thus classified.

Content analysis is a general method of analysis which attempts to define and categorize, exhaustively and exclusively, the elements in an array. The term 'content analysis' is usually thought of in connection with the detailed examination, by social scientists, of the texts of books, political broadcasts and newspaper articles, and of the contents of films and the products of other media. The method is, however, much more general than this. The term 'content analysis' can be used to refer, for example, to the analysis of projective test data, responses to open-ended survey questions, and narrative accounts of human and animal behaviour in natural settings (as in behavioural ecology and animal ethology).

In the chapters that follow, our lexical and semantic analysis of personality descriptions is presented in terms of 30 'content categories', each describing a different 'aspect' or 'facet' of personality, i.e. a feature common to human beings and therefore capable of being used to draw comparisons and contrasts between people. The system is intended to provide an *exhaustive*, but not entirely *exclusive*, classification of the contents of adult personality descriptions. As we have already seen, other taxonomies are possible, and the conceptual boundaries of our categories are by no means firmly fixed.

The smallest convenient unit of analysis is a word or a phrase. The words and phrases in personality descriptions can be conveniently classified into thirty conceptual categories. In order to emphasize the classificatory nature of the conceptual terms used to label our content categories, they are occasionally printed with initial capitals and given their coded abbreviation, in capital letters, in brackets after them. Either the full word or phrase, or its coded capitalized abbreviation, are used—according to the requirements of the text for ease of comprehension and economy.

Some of the issues raised by the use of the method of content analysis are discussed in subsequent chapters in relation to particular sorts of empirical data. We hope to demonstrate that the analysis of personality descriptions is central to the study of personality; it leads naturally to a 'general theory' of personal adjustment and is compatible with a 'quasi-judicial method' of studying individual cases: see Chapter 8.

The fact that the same word or phrase in a personality description can be classified in different ways, depending upon how one interprets it, raises an important problem in the use of content analysis as a method of investigating personality. This problem concerns the 'exclusiveness' of a category in any system of content analysis that we might devise; that is, whether it is possible reliably to allocate a word or statement to one, and only one, category. The issue can be settled in two ways: (a) by defining and illustrating each category so carefully and thoroughly that each item can be assigned unambiguously or (b) by listing all the items assignable to each category and using the lists as definitive registers.

Failure to solve the problem of 'exclusive' categories is bound to lead to ambiguity and unreliability in the coding of items, but it might be possible to deal with the problem in other ways: e.g. by cross-classification or by assigning a proportion of the ambiguous element to two or more content categories. Both of these solutions would create complications in any subsequent statistical analysis, but at least they demonstrate that the rule of 'exclusiveness' in content analysis is not mandatory but rather commendatory.

The conceptual categories in a system of content analysis are confusable to a greater or lesser extent. For example, a particular word or phrase might seem probably to belong to category A, or less probably to category B or C, but clearly not to belong to D, E or F; another might seem equally likely to belong to category D or E, but unlikely to belong to A, B, C or F. For example, as we shall see, without the benefit of a standard reference list of words and phrases it is sometimes possible to confuse the category of Identity (IDEN) statements with that of Life History (LIFE) statements, but one would be unlikely to confuse an identity statement with, say, a statement about the stimulus person's attitudes, referred to and labelled as Orientation and Feelings (ORFE). Similarly, we shall see that some words and phrases categorized as Physical Appearance (PHYS) are difficult to distinguish from other words and phrases categorized as Expressive Behaviour (EXPR) or Physical and Mental Health (HLTH). The problem is that it is not always clear what a particular word or phrase *means*, even with the benefit of some contextual information. Indeed, ordinary language is notoriously rich in meanings and it is quite normal for one meaning to be expressed in several different words or phrases; and for several different words or phrases to be interpreted in the same way. Conversely, several meanings may find expression, through a process akin to Freud's notion of 'condensation', in one phrase; such convergence of meanings can be contrasted with the divergence of interpretations that occurs when one phrase is interpreted in several different ways. A person's 'ambition', for example, can be indicated by statements about his personality traits, his life-history, his attitude to his family, his relationships with other people, his daily routines and his expressive behaviour. Yet all these (and others) are aspects of a person's existence that we have to distinguish if we are to construct an exclusive and exhaustive system of content categories for describing personality.

We shall not be concerned with statistical questions about the 'reliability' and 'confusability' of the content categories; these will be raised in the subsequent investigations to which we have referred. We shall see that there are limits to what can be achieved by the method of content analysis, apart from difficulties associated with measurement and statistics; but we shall also see that in exploring the limits of content analysis, as applied to personality descriptions in ordinary language, we are also exploring the nature and scope of personality study.

In the three chapters that follow, we define, illustrate and discuss thirty distinguishable but interrelated aspects or 'facets' of personality and adjustment familiar to commonsense. These are based on an extensive and detailed content analysis of personality descriptions in ordinary language. The first group of nine categories deals with 'internal' psychological characteristics, i.e. with covert, subjective features, sometimes called 'dispositional' and 'mentalistic' processes. The second group of nine categories deals with 'external' behavioural characteristics, i.e. with overt, physical manifestations. The third group of twelve categories deals with general and specific social relationships and with evaluation and residual information. The intention is to provide a comprehensive and integrated conceptual basis for a scientific description and analysis of personality.

The content analysis of ordinary language, however, does not, and possibly cannot, provide a *definitive* taxonomy of terms. Personality can be conceptualized in a variety of ways; the contents and organization of a description can be adapted to a multiplicity of purposes. Research workers are free to choose whatever sources of data and methods of analysis seem most appropriate: see, for example, Dana (1970) and Jones and Rosenberg (1974).

Before closing this chapter we should mention that, although the empirical foundations of our systematic content analysis consist of personality descriptions written by adults under standard conditions, as previously described, yet we have taken many opportunities to examine the contents of personality descriptions (written and/or spoken) available from many other sources: political profiles, professional and semi-professional case-studies, gossip, fiction, biographies, autobiographies, other research studies, and so on. We are confident that the concepts and methods we have developed apply equally well to these other materials. As we shall see, especially in Chapters 8 and 9, the whole point of our inquiries is to develop *general* concepts and methods for the *scientific* study of individual cases.

CHAPTER 5

Lexical and Semantic Analysis:
'Internal' Aspects of Personality

I. Introduction

This chapter describes the 'internal' facets of personality as revealed by a lexical and semantic analysis of ordinary language.

Using the method of content analysis described briefly in previous Chapters, nine categories of information—referring mainly to internal psychological processes—were defined, as follows:

Content analysis categories	Abbreviations
General trait	GENT
Specific trait or habit	SPET
Ability and attainment	ABAT
Motivation and arousal	MOTA
Orientation and feeling (or attitude)	ORFE
Object of an attitude	OBJE
Expressive behaviour	EXPR
Principles and moral values (or character)	PRIN
Self-concept	SELF

They are defined, illustrated and discussed in the Sections A to I.

II. Content Analysis Categories

A. General Trait (GENT)

The concept of 'trait' was discussed at length in Chapters 3 and 4: testimony, perhaps, to the importance of this concept in the study of personality. We now examine this concept empirically, with reference to the words and phrases of ordinary language, and discuss the findings.

The dictionary meaning of the word trait is a 'stroke, a touch, a characteristic' from the French *trahere* and the Latin *tractum*, to draw. This perhaps supports the idea that physical appearances—the visual impression and the outward signs—make a major contribution to the personality impression. Unfortunately, etymological issues in the language of personality description are too technical for us to deal with.

Allport (1937, p. 295) defined a trait as 'A generalized and focalized neuropsychic system (peculiar to the individual) with the capacity to initiate and guide consistent (equivalent) forms of adaptive and expressive behaviour'. A personality trait is a general and relatively enduring disposition to behave in a characteristic and consistent way in certain sorts of situation. Traits or dispositions include temperamental qualities, prevailing mood and moral qualities. A trait does not specify the behaviour itself, it specifies the *kind* of behaviour to be expected of the stimulus person. It is important to bear this distinction in mind.

In personality descriptions of the sort we are concerned with, and in personality assessments in general, traits constitute a major category of information. Among the more obvious trait words are the following: intelligent, morose, cruel, conceited, tolerant, good-tempered, creative, affectionate, honest, careless, conscientious, selfish, insincere, kind, religious, humorous, contented, self-sufficient, independent, lazy, malicious, shy, happy, enthusiastic. These are the sorts of terms listed in Allport and Odbert's (1936) now classical psycholexical study of trait names: see Chapter 3. So far, we have restricted our examples, as Allport and Odbert did, to single words (including hyphenated words). However, ordinary language is not limited to single words; and single words are not functionally independent of each other. For example, 'neat and tidy', 'calm and collected', 'as straight as a die', are simple phrases which function as lexical units. Moreover, there are transitional probabilities between pairs of terms—'kind' and 'generous' tend to go together, as do 'honest' and 'truthful', whereas 'tolerant' and 'conceited' tend to exclude one another.

Trait words can be modified in a variety of ways, most obviously by a negation like 'not' or 'never', but also by adjectives like 'almost', 'very', 'usually', and so on. In addition, the basic word-form can be modified by prefixes and suffixes of various sorts, such as 'unhappy', 'cruellist', 'affectionless', 'dishonest', 'insincerity', 'kindly', 'ultra-religious', 'superintelligent', and so on.

Trait words and phrases have no special status in the language of personality descriptions, being subject to the same rules as other words and phrases. The following examples of trait statements are taken at random from the main investigation: '... extravert ... good humour ... practical ...', '... selfish ... inclined to show off ... greedy ... bad-tempered ...', '... patient in adversity ...?', '... kind ... of gentle disposition ... sincere ... friendly ...', '... has sympathy ... easy to talk to ... generous ... kind ...', '... cheerful ... sense of humour ... not overbearing ...', '... forceful ... forthright ... considerate ...

humble ... dependable ... honest ... ambitious ...', '... a bit selfish ...', '... quiet ... reserved ... level-headed ...', '... ambitious ...', '... a touch of ruthlessness ...', '... kind ... compassionate ... can't say no ...', '... happy ... full of fun ... kind ... generous ... gay ...', '... stubborn ...', '... not entirely truthful ...', '... equable ...', '... not at all selfish ... not one for picking quarrels ...', '... practical ... sense of humour ... generous ... kindly ... hospitable ...', '... taciturn ...', '... generous ... easy-going ... never known him once show uncharacteristic irritability ... shy ...', '... calm ... unexcitable ... matronly stability ...', '... anti-social ...', '... sly ... underhanded ...', '... lack of interest or enthusiasm ... apathy ...', '... independent ... definite will of her own ... not assuming ... sense of humour ... good-natured ... bears no grudges ...', '... even-tempered ... never ruffled, whatever the stress of the moment ...', '... works hard ... not easily roused ... friendly ... happy disposition ...'.

What trait words and phrases do in personality descriptions is to indicate the *sort* of behaviour to be expected of the stimulus person; but if no particular situation or context is specified, the expected behaviour must be described in general terms. However, if we know the *sorts* of behaviour to which the stimulus person is disposed, and if we know the *sorts* of behaviour typically elicited by a given situation, then we can predict that the actual behaviour of the stimulus person in that situation will fall within a relatively narrow range of possibilities, e.g. a person who is disposed to physical violence is likely to assault or threaten someone who frustrates him.

Personality dispositions, however, do not function in isolation but in what we can call, for want of a better term, 'psychodynamic systems', in that the nature of a trait depends in part on the other traits in the system. This assertion is not as metaphysical as it may seem, for it says no more than can be said for the 'meaning' or 'function' of a word in a sentence. One can rarely predict behaviour accurately simply on the basis that a trait name has been assigned to a person. One needs to know the nature of this individualized trait or 'personal disposition', see Allport (1961), and the system to which it belongs.

Traits are not 'primitive' or 'irreducible' terms for describing actual overt behaviour, although they must be referred to such terms in the last resort in order for their 'meaning in use' to be disambiguated; their meaning is 'field dependent'. Thus, when one of these dispositional words or phrases is used, we should ask, 'What does it mean?', or better still, 'What did the stimulus person actually do and say (or fail to do or say) to warrant the attribution of that trait?' A trait word or phrase does not refer to behaviour itself but to a 'class' of behaviours; but there is no way of exhausting the psychological meaning of, say, 'generous' or 'ruthless' or any other trait by listing all the actual behaviours included in the class—for the simple reason that the class is infinitely large. Whether the terms 'generous' or 'ruthless' can be properly attributed to a person is partly an empirical issue and partly a conceptual issue. It is empirical to the extent that actual instances of the person's behaviour need to be examined to see whether they have the distinguishing characteristics of the class; it is conceptual to the extent that the nature and scope of 'generosity' or 'ruthlessness' may have to be developed as a sort of psychological theory. Thus, one can find whole books devoted to the description and analysis of concepts like 'aggression', 'achievement motivation', 'intelligence', 'ingratiation', 'introversion/extraversion', and so on. In this connection it is important to realize that an operational definition of a trait is no more than a methodological convenience.

Some trait words refer to the person's moral dispositions, or 'character'; these must be distinguished from the same or similar terms when they are used to refer to an *external assessment* of the person's 'character' in relation to a common set of social values. Since moral qualities are so important in personal adjustment and in personality assessment, the distinction between ethical and non-ethical attributes may be difficult or impossible to make: see also Chapters 7 and 8.

B. *Specific Trait or Habit* (*SPET*)

If a psychological characteristic is largely habitual, restricted or automatic, i.e. not a flexible wide-ranging response disposition, then it can scarcely count as a trait. Thus, the habit of driving one's car to and from work each day is not a trait—it is, rather, an adaptive, habitual 'performance'. This regular performance or habit may be one of many determined in part by traits like 'independence', 'ambition' or 'laziness'.

Some characteristics refer to a relatively narrow range of behaviours, as in 'Careless of his appearance'. With characteristics like this, it is sometimes difficult to decide whether the range of behaviours referred to is sufficiently wide and psychologically significant to justify the attribution of a trait (rather than a habit). Consider the following examples: 'Doesn't often wash his car', 'Goes to church regularly', 'Careful with money'. The key features distinguishing the first and second examples from the third is that the first and second are fairly close to the behaviour itself—the behaviour is used as a clue in the assessment of personality—whereas the third is more remote from behaviour, although it severely restricts the range of relevant behaviours, namely, to those involving the use of money. On this interpretation then, 'Careless of his appearance' seems to count as a 'trait', since it does not actually specify the relevant behaviours; on the other hand, the range of possible behaviours is so restricted that it might be counted as a habit without much ambiguity and therefore be regarded as an evidential clue to a more generalized disposition or condition, e.g. 'carelessness' or 'apathy'.

The term 'habit' refers to a tendency to perform a usual or customary action. The word is derived from the Latin *habitus*, state, dress—*habitare*, to dwell. The fact that one can use the term 'habit' quite sensibly to describe the behaviour of animals in their 'natural habitat' is a good lead into the argument that the concepts and methods of behavioural ecology have a great deal to contribute to the study of personality and adjustment and to the language of personality descriptions: see Chapter 9. For the moment, all we need to notice is that human beings in their 'natural habitat', i.e. in the surroundings to which they have become accustomed, have acquired behavioural routines and 'strategies of adjustment' nicely adapted to the particular ecological niche that they occupy. These routines might be said to have 'evolved' as adaptations to local conditions. The local conditions include not only the physical geography, weather and other natural phenomena, but also the human and man-made environment, all the paraphernalia and symbolism of civilized life. If the external circumstances affecting a person's behaviour stay the same, then his behavioural routines will tend to persist (unless there are changes within the person); similarly, if his external circumstances change, then his behavioural routines will tend to change (unless there are strong inertial factors within the person which resist change).

Even the superficial behavioural routines that we shall refer to as Routine Habits and Activities (ROUT), see Chapter 6, may have some psychological significance as indicators of personality (and of circumstances). Such routines often demonstrate what is called 'convergence', i.e. the tendency for different people to respond in much the same way to similar conditions, reinforced by what is called 'social conformity', i.e. the tendency to behave like other people. In so far as such routines are commonly shared and easily modified in response to changes in circumstances, their value as indicators of 'personality' is reduced. Hence our decision to exclude phrases like 'Doesn't often wash his car' and 'Goes to church regularly' from the category of traits or general dispositions. To say that a form of behaviour is not a trait, however, is not to say that it has no psychological significance. It is one of the inadequacies of traditional personality study that it has concentrated on the measurement of individual differences in traits, instead of concentrating on the particular forms of adaptation of the person to his environment—via the case-study. The recognition that personality study is a branch of human behavioural ecology opens up a new way of conceptualizing it, and enables us to see that the language of personality is more than a psycholexical review of trait names. To speak of a person's routine habits is therefore to refer to his stereotyped responses to standard situations, i.e. to established behaviour patterns by means of which he adjusts smoothly, efficiently and repetitively to the familiar, recurrent circumstances of his environment. Such routines include those associated with washing, dressing, household chores, occupational activities, leisure, and so on. Since knowledge of people's routine habits contributes to understanding them as persons, it forms part of the study of personality and adjustment. In fact, such knowledge is useful not only in its own right, but also as evidence of underlying traits and situational factors.

In addition to the ordinary routines of daily life, however, there are what we might call 'specific reaction patterns' which a person exhibits only occasionally but does so reliably. Consider the following illustrative examples: '. . . poor loser . . .', '. . . glib tongue . . .', '. . . domesticated . . .', '. . . home loving . . .', '. . . secretive about her private life . . .', '. . . helpful to friends and family . . .', '. . . finds his work fascinating . . .', '. . . sulks if she doesn't get her own way . . .', '. . . He can't "rescue" anything that goes astray without a fuss . . .'. Some of the specific reaction patterns referred to by these phrases are obviously rather different from the ones we have labelled 'habits' or 'routines'. The fact that some imply evaluations, e.g. 'poor loser', is not important, since many, perhaps most, of the things we say about people carry an implicit value judgment. They indicate, in a rough sort of way, the sort of behaviour to be expected of a person in a given sort of situation: e.g. 'complaining, vengeful, rude if he fails in a competitive situation', 'fluent and plausible in making excuses', and so on. Some of them refer to the person's thoughts, feelings and desires, see Orientation and Feelings (ORFE) and Motivation and Arousal (MOTA), as elements in a specific reaction pattern; and some are confusable with General Personality Traits (GENT). This illustrates, again, the difficulty we experience in drawing hard and fast lines between the various content categories. It would be interesting to make even more detailed comparisons between phrases provisionally assigned to different content categories than we have so far been making; this kind of philosophical linguistic analysis would almost certainly contribute further insights, but we prefer to find an overall approximate taxonomy of words and phrases before considering the advantages of more detailed analyses.

The following additional SPET statements are taken at random from the main investigation: 'If he is crossed in any way he will resort to physical violence . . . he will not work . . . he lounges about studying the racing page . . .', 'His enthusiasm sometimes runs away with him . . .', 'She soon brightens up when she has told someone . . . what has depressed her . . .', '. . . used his authority to bully younger people who were in no position to answer back . . .', '. . . frequents the club I most use . . .', '. . . every time she has a personal problem she contacts me for advice . . .', '. . . overindulges in both food and drink . . .', '. . . tends to discuss matters which she has not fully understood and to misrepresent them . . . does not apply herself to a task unless she is constantly reminded of it . . .', '. . . mean about money . . . helps herself to things which do not belong to her . . .', '. . . habit of interrupting conversations that I or any of my friends may be having . . .', '. . . works only for money . . .', '. . . (fond of animals) but sometimes plays too roughly with them . . .', 'When she visits there is no "Hello—how are you?" introduction—she just breezes in half-way through a sentence ready for the next . . .', '. . . always rushing . . . inclined to sulk when opposed . . .', '. . . if he doesn't agree he will say so . . .', '. . . inclined to get exasperated with his wife at times but does not lose his temper to the same extent with acquaintances . . .', '. . . if he wants advice he will ask for it and give it some thought . . .', '. . . sensible with his money . . .?', '. . . will ignore or break agreements made as little as twenty-four hours previously . . .', '. . . goes out of her way to find out everybody's business . . .', '. . . always has sensible advice to offer . . .?', '. . . throws herself enthusiastically into all causes for the disabled . . .', '. . . will give her unsolicited advice on any subject . . . makes the most outrageous statements . . .', '. . . keeps up with all the latest dress . . .?', '. . . goes out of his way to help people . . .?', '. . . most lavish with invitations to us to "pop over and see them"—never fixes a date . . .', '. . . he will do nothing to help in any team work . . .', '. . . will give away clothes or possessions merely because a friend has admired them . . .', '. . . often makes his wife uncomfortable in other people's company . . .', '. . . will not give much to charity . . .', '. . . not always kind to her mother . . .', '. . . makes foolish and dangerous remarks ...', '... collapses if someone stands up to her ...', '... does not always bother about personal hygiene ...', '... will leave early without telling anyone he is going ...', '... drives his girl-friend around in his father's car ...'.

That we do not normally think of general traits and specific traits as very different is shown by the ease with which we combine them in phrases; though one of the main differences is that specific habits require longer statements. The longer examples show the limited extent to which significant psychological information can be conveyed in a single word. Some examples show that statements in the ordinary language of personality descriptions are not necessarily to be taken literally; they have a meaning which is generally understood, and it is this accepted meaning which may be at issue when questions about the validity or equivalence of personality statements are raised.

Quite a number of SPET statements refer to behaviour in interpersonal relationships and so are confusable with the Stimulus Person's Response to Others (SP–O) statements: see Chapter 7. Other categories of statement also might be construed as SPETS, e.g. Expressive Behaviour (EXPR) and Motivation and Arousal (MOTA): see later. The problem is to discover the primary meaning communicated by the statement. In the present context we are, of course, excluding its emotional meaning.

A common and effective method of presenting information about a person is to give a general attribute, e.g. '... he is awkward ...', followed by an illustration or amplification, e.g. '... if he asks you to do something, he will say it's not right ...'. The second part of the statement is likely to be the evidential basis of the first part, which, in virtue of its abstractness and generality, is an inference or construction.

Perhaps the main conclusion to be drawn from an examination of a large and heterogeneous array of SPET statements is that, apart from describing habitual and specific reactions to circumstances, they illustrate the problem of defining the boundaries of psychological concepts since their contents are similar to those of other content categories. One might therefore argue that SPET and GENT statements, and possibly other sorts of 'trait' and 'state' statements, are not only about the 'content' of a personality description but about the organization and meaning of behaviour. The phrase 'inner structure and dynamics' might be appropriate to refer to the ways in which we conceive a person's behaviour to be organized psychologically, from within. Thus, statements about traits, habits, motives, affective states, attitudes, abilities, values and the self-concept, are central to personality description. These various covert or 'psychological' functions can be separated, conceptually at least, from the correlated overt behaviour by means of which the person relates himself to his environment. However, such separation is not easy to deal with in terms of content analysis, since the 'inner' and 'outer' aspects of the person are necessarily correlated, in spite of some apparent discrepancies. The inner structure and dynamics 'dispose', i.e. incline and enable, the person to act in certain ways. But circumstances and events in his environment set up opportunities (and constraints) which help to elicit (or inhibit) responses and to serialize them. This whole problem is taken up again in Chapter 9 which proposes a 'general theory' of personal adjustment and argues that the proper study of personality and adjustment is the study of 'persons in situations'.

C. *Ability and Attainment (ABAT)*

We have seen that traits and habits have a motivational quality, in that they seem to 'direct' behaviour. By contrast, Abilities and Attainments (ABATs) seem to be relatively passive 'capacities'. For example, phrases like 'well-informed' or 'able to swim' signify in a general way what the person is capable of, but they do not *necessarily* imply an inclination to seek out or use opportunities to exercise his abilities. The possession of abilities, however, makes it more likely that the individual will exercise them in appropriate situations. A person's 'attainments' (as opposed to his 'abilities') are the performances and accomplishments which enable one to infer his underlying abilities. Thus, 'He swam ten lengths' implies that 'He is able to swim quite well'; but his being able to swim does not imply that he likes swimming or wants to swim or swims regularly.

Abilities and attainments are easily thought of in connection with intelligence and various sorts of problem-solving, with technical, domestic and artistic skills, with social and administrative competence, athletic prowess, and so on. Knowledge of what a person 'can' or 'cannot' do is obviously important in predicting what he is *likely* to do or in explaining why he did *not* behave in a particular way.

In addition to these sorts of abilities and attainments, however, it is possible to think of traits and habits as abilities, e.g. 'He can be very aggressive at times' and 'He is capable of vulgarity given the right company'. Consider also 'He can show affection when he wants to'. The terms 'aggressive', 'vulgarity' and 'affection' in the above examples clearly refer to overt behaviours (occasional performances) rather than to covert dispositions (enduring inclinations), and thus demonstrate yet again that the construction we put on the behavioural evidence is revealed in the language we use to describe a person's psychological characteristics.

Human beings have disabilities and faults as well as abilities and attainments; but we can regard them simply as negations of ABATs and include statements about them in this same category. For example: 'Cannot swim well', 'Did not swim ten lengths', 'Failed the entrance exam', 'Is not able to express his anger', 'Cannot keep his anxiety under control', 'No good at figures', are all examples of disabilities or faults, i.e. negative ABATs, but nevertheless contribute to the description of personality and adjustment.

Statements about abilities given by children about children usually refer to the more obvious types of competence mentioned above, especially those relevant to adjustment to school, i.e. athletic and academic abilities. Comparable statements occur in descriptions of adults written by adults, e.g. '... clever ...', '... dull ...', '... poor memory ...', '... slow thinking ...', '... original thinker ...', '... maths graduate ...', '... knowledgeable ...'. We have seen that there are subtle differences in phraseology in ordinary language which enable one to distinguish between the various aspects of a person's psychological make-up. The average person, however, probably sees little difference between traits, habits, abilities, and other personality characteristics; but then the average person uses nouns, verbs, adjectives and other distinctive 'parts of speech' fairly well without being able to give much of an account of the grammar of the language he is speaking.

The following examples of ABAT statements are taken at random from the main investigation: '. . . very clever mind . . .', '. . . intelligent . . . capable of great things . . .', '. . . very able . . . has already been very successful . . .', '. . . good at football . . .', '. . . not able to keep a confidence . . .', '. . . well educated . . . good speaker . . .', '. . . clever liar . . . if necessary capable of the big bold lie . . .', '. . . a gift for friendship . . . not in the top flight academically . . . has produced excellent results . . .', '. . . not able to make any sort of conversation . . . only able to answer direct questions . . .', '. . . has musical talent . . .', '. . . above average intelligence . . . can talk easily with them . . . can take on responsibility . . .', '. . . artistic . . . clear headedness . . .', '. . . fairly rapid weighing up of situations . . .', '. . . good listener . . .', '. . . an expert at several things . . .', '. . . all the social graces . . .', '. . . well acquainted with modern trends . . .', '. . . she can draw out ideas you didn't know you had . . .', '. . . good at telling tales . . .', '. . . has her whole character under tight control . . .', '. . . doing well in training . . .', '. . . no qualifications for it . . .', '. . . speaks well . . .', '. . . perceptive in his judgment of people . . .', '. . . he can play the politician . . .'.

Statements about Abilities and Attainments (ABAT) say something, either relatively or absolutely, about the person's competence (or lack of competence) in a wide range of performances. Evaluative terms, e.g. '. . . good at . . .', '. . . incompetent . . .', enter into some ABAT statements directly, and positive or negative evaluation is implicit in many.

D. Motivation and Arousal (MOTA)

The concept of 'motive' was discussed at length in Chapter 4 from a mainly philosophical point of view. We now examine this concept empirically, with reference to the words and phrases in ordinary language, and discuss the findings. The concept of Motivation and Arousal (MOTA) includes, for our purposes, the associated, subsidiary concept of preferences and aversions, i.e. likes and dislikes. In the ordinary language of personality description, statements about motivation can be indirect and somewhat obscure. Such statements usually refer to subjective states: motives, purposes, needs, drives, intentions, wishes, wants and aims underlying goal-directed activity. Thus, a question like 'Why is he going to the bank?' may be answered in various ways, e.g. 'He is going to the bank to get money', 'He wants some cash', 'He wishes to buy a present for his wife and intends to draw out some money for that purpose', 'He has been trying to get to the bank all week', 'He's desperate for money', 'The reason is he is short of cash'. The subjective states associated with motivation and arousal also include: impulses, inhibitions (motivational controls), aspirations and ambitions, frust-rations and conflicts, hopes and fears, fulfilments and disappointments, cares and concerns. The common features of such psychological processes are: first of all, goal-orientation; second, striving; third, affective states associated with the onset, progress and outcome of the goal-directed behaviour. In some instances, of course, the end-state is far from clear until the person has acquired the experience necessary to identify adequate aims and objects, e.g. food preferences, personal relationships, sexual outlets, status positions. The term 'arousal' is used loosely to refer to the extent to which feelings and desires are salient in awareness and in the organization of behaviour.

Behaviour is normally directed (rather than undirected) because there is usually a limited supply of goods and services, and opportunities for satisfaction, and an almost insatiable demand for them. Motivation, in other words, is *intrinsic* to the behaviour of organisms, and the main problem is not to understand how behaviour is initiated and sustained but rather how it is inhibited and controlled. There are, of course, abnormalities of motivation, as in apathy, compulsiveness and frenzy. Since behaviour is normally directed, there is no particular mental state that corresponds with a motive or aspiration. Clear-cut emotional states are usually associated with definite deprivation, frustration or conflict on the one hand, and with definite relief, achievement or satiation on the other.

The experiential accompaniments of normal goal-directed behaviour are those familiar to us from everyday life: expecting, hoping, wanting, feeling bored, sorrowful, excited, and thinking, remembering or imagining.

Consider the following statements: '... hopes to start her nursing career ...', '... wanted me to do her a favour ...', '... ambition to write ...', '... wants to get married ...', '... willing to help ...', '... tries to please ...'. They indicate a target-state or end-state—a possible future—towards which the persons actions are directed. Although the statements are not explicit, one can assume that the person would act positively, i.e. intend to bring that state nearer to realization, or at least passively accept circumstances and events which made that state more likely. By contrast, one would expect the person to inhibit behaviour likely to delay realization or make it less likely, and to avoid or resist circumstances which threatened to diminish the likelihood of that state.

Thus, given a certain amount of general knowledge about human behaviour, one can assert a number of psychological implications that follow from a statement about a person's motives (aims or desires). The girl who 'wants to get married', for example, is likely to watch her weight, take care of her appearance, protect her reputation, take an interest in houses, furniture, cooking and seek out opportunities for meeting eligible men, and even curtail her educational and occupational activities.

To say explicitly that someone 'intends' something is to assert that there is a behavioural path that the person is willing and able to tread to reach that future state. For example, 'He intends to go to University ...' implies that the person thinks he has a fairly clear idea of the actions and achievements necessary for University admission and sees himself as capable of gaining admission, though he may be mistaken.

There are other sorts of statement which omit reference to a definite goal or aim, but describe the level of arousal experienced by the person, i.e. the intensity of his motivational state (the direction of which is vague or unspecified), e.g. '... tries hard ...', '... is afraid to try ...', '... gets carried away by enthusiasm ...'. Generally speaking, however, such statements occur in a context which provides information about the target-state.

Statements which include words such as 'like', 'dislike', 'prefer', 'interest', may disclose potential motivational states, as in the following: 'He likes bananas', 'He dislikes aggressive people', 'He prefers blondes', 'He is not interested in the theatre'. Statements like this disclose motivational dispositions, i.e. tendencies to move in one direction rather than another, given the opportunity. The last word in each of these statements describes the object, person or activity in relation to which the person's behaviour may be organized. Similarly, words like 'enjoys', 'satisfied', 'happy', 'contented', 'hates', 'loves', occur in statements describing the person's state of mind during the consummatory phase of a motivational cycle. Consider, for example, 'He is happy when he is gardening', 'She enjoys shopping', 'He is satisfied with his work', 'She is contented with her marriage', 'He hates (and therefore avoids where possible) travelling on buses'.

Although motivated behaviour is directed, i.e. future-oriented, there must be changes in direction from time to time, for obvious reasons. Hence, the normal sequence will be: initiation, goal-seeking, goal-finding. These phases correspond to the appetitive, directive and consummatory patterns of behaviour familiar in animal ethology. The nature of the action, of course, depends upon the physiological and psychological state of the organism, its 'plans' and 'resources', and upon the actual environmental circumstances in which the action occurs. The action sequences do not necessarily run off smoothly, the actions do not necessarily emerge in an orderly way; on the contrary, they are sometimes interrupted, frustrated, and in conflict with each other, apart from being sometimes erroneous and unsatisfying.

The following examples of motivational statements (mostly positive) are taken at random from the main investigation: '... in order to gain his own ends ...', '... is rarely prepared to be of any assistance herself ...', '... endeavours to be the life and soul of the party ...', '... she is fond of young children ...', '... she is a keen motorist ...', '... loves ... outdoor life ...', '... she is a keen gardener ...', '... she wants to tell you what to do ...', '... she likes expensive things ...', '... a strong interest in art ...', '... has interested himself in ... education ...', '... fond of animals ...', '... his liking for a drop of the hard stuff ...', '... he loves his children ...', '... will try the same again ...', '... wanting everybody to be happy ...', '... she was not prepared to put herself out for any individual ...', '... she needed her freedom after a few years ...', '... has always got to demonstrate her individuality ...', '... always willing to help if needed ...', '... tries to take a rise out of me in public ...', '... she ... must control everything ...', '... again it must be him in the limelight ...', '... is prepared to make do with ...', '... doesn't seem to try to solve her problems ...', '... he must have his way ...', '... try to wheedle out of it ...', '... eager to please ...', '... hopes to attain a higher position ...', '... makes no effort to find employment ...', '... is determined to prove his point ...', '... won't join in any conversation ...'.

The above examples are fairly straightforward, in the sense that they seem to raise no special problems in relation to our psychological and philosophical analysis of the concept of motivation. Most of the statements, naturally, make a positive assertion about motivation and arousal by using words or phrases like: 'fond of', 'likes', 'wants', 'keen', 'interested in', 'tries', 'prepared to', 'needs', 'hopes'. But negative statements are also possible, and have the effect of ruling out unwarranted inferences. We also note the occasional use of words and phrases like 'must', 'has to', 'got to', which indicate an element of compulsion *within* the person (the context makes it clear that the constraint is not environmental).

One awkward fact is the occurrence of references, not cited above, to generalized or vague states of enthusiasm or indifference, e.g. '... she is most apathetic about it ...', '... she doesn't seem to solve her problems ...', '... zest for living ...', '... enthusiasm about all things modern ...', '... uninterested in other people's views ...'. It is one thing to define motivation as a goal-directed state of mind and action, and to identify the presence or absence of such states; but it is another to identify vague or generalized states of arousal lacking focus or direction. Nevertheless the concept MOTA includes both motivation and arousal, so that generalized states of enthusiasm or indifference (apathy) can be included in this category rather than assimilated to traits (GENT) or attitudes (ORFE).

Another awkward fact is that motives are often *characteristic* of a person; they direct his behaviour in an enduring and consistent way in different situations. The question arises, therefore, as to whether such characteristic motives are better regarded as traits. To make matters worse, some 'traits' have a definite motivational quality: 'very studious', 'strong will ... hard worker'; so it could be argued that they are better regarded as Motivation and Arousal (MOTA) statements.

For the time being, we have to accept such confusions and uncertainties, since their existence points to unresolved conceptual issues and to arbitrary lines of demarcation between psychological categories. All that we have done is to go back to common sense and ordinary language to rediscover and reaffirm the relevance of information described in these and other content categories which has been neglected because of the emphasis, in the last few decades, on the measurement of traits and the analysis of psychodynamic processes. It may be that commonsense and ordinary language seriously misrepresent human nature (just as in earlier days they seriously misrepresented the physical universe and the world of living things). If this is the case, then we can expect to find serious anomalies, contradictions, confusions, falsehoods, and other signs of invalidity and incoherence, when we make a close examination of commonsense understanding and the ordinary language of personality and adjustment. The traffic in ideas and words between commonsense and scientific understanding is two-way, and we must not be too accepting of the argument put forward by a number of eminent people that the study of human psychological and behavioural phenomena cannot lead to essentially new discoveries because human beings have long had a natural acquaintance with and understanding of human nature, whereas new physical and biological phenomena are constantly being discovered through observation, exploration and experiment.

E. Orientation and Feeling (or Attitude) (ORFE)

In a normal cycle of behaviour there are four distinguishable phases: (i) arousal and motivation, (ii) orientation, including affective and cognitive reactions of an anticipatory and appetitive kind (including decision processes), (iii) volition and overt actions of an executive and consummatory sort and (iv) consequential personal experiences, effects and reactions (including modifications to earlier thoughts, feelings, motives and capacities, brought about by reflection and learning), as well as social and environmental consequences. See also Chapter 9.

Our present concern is with the second phase of the so-called 'activity cycle', namely, 'orientation'. Although many human actions are habitual, in that they occur automatically without much conscious control, yet there are many occasions in daily life when our behaviour has to be thought out: planned, monitored, and modified as required. Many habitual reactions, moreover, are acquired through the gradual elimination of these processes as the person's reactions become better adapted, more finely tuned, to the recurrent and familiar situations to which he has to adapt.

The significance of orientation (ORFE) lies in the way the person represents his situation to himself (and, on occasion, represents himself to himself: see Self-concept (SELF) later). It is obvious that people differ in their ability to assess the situation with which they are faced—and this is important when we remember that many of them regularly face the same situations or the same sorts of situation, e.g. at work or in interpersonal relationships. It is also obvious that an individual's assessment of his circumstances varies from one occasion to another, depending upon his abilities, his experience, his familiarity with the situation, the pace of events, and so on. It follows, therefore, that a person's assessment of, and orientation towards, his environment is not always valid and accurate—in the sense of corresponding exactly to the facts of the situation. A person's actions, however, are normally organized in terms of how he sees the situation (not how the situation really is). Hence, in order to understand why a person behaves as he does, we need to know: (a) the actual facts of the situation he is in, and (b) his subjective appraisal of that situation. If we know how he perceives the situation (what he thinks, wants, feels and expects of it, and so on), then we are in a better position to understand why he *reacts* to it in the way he does. Similarly, if we have information about the actual facts of the situation and can see discrepancies between these objective facts and the person's subjective appraisal of them, then we are in a better position to understand and anticipate the actual effects that his reactions produce, including the reactions of that person to the consequences of his own actions and circumstances.

As regards our dealings with other people in the ordinary affairs of everyday life, the importance of knowing how they see their situation is that it helps us to anticipate what action *they* will take and therefore enables us to take whatever action *we* think is appropriate. Thus, our assessment of another person's view of his situation is part of *our* orientation to *our* situation with regard to that person. To take some simple examples: selecting a birthday present for someone, advising someone on their relationship to a third party, advising someone about a job or a place to live—all of these call for some understanding of the other person's point of view, i.e. his Orientation and Feelings (ORFE).

The phenomenon of 'taking the role of the other person' is so well known in sociology and social psychology that we do not need to discuss it in any detail. We are not, in fact, much concerned with the sociological analysis of this phenomenon, which is concerned mainly with the organization of role sets. We are more concerned with the cognitive and linguistic aspects of one individual's assessment of another individual's view of his situation. The sorts of analysis carried out by Goffman (1963), Laing, Phillipson and Lee (1966), and Harré and Secord (1972), provide a bridge between the sociological analysis and our psycholinguistic analysis of personality appraisal in everyday life.

Our assessment of another person's orientation to a situation is based on the answers we can provide to a number of simple questions, such as, 'What does he think (about the situation)?', 'How does he feel about this?', 'What is his point of view?', 'What does he want (with regard to this situation)?', 'What can he do about it?', 'What options does he think are open to him?' and so on. In a sense, these are questions about the person's 'attitude' to a particular situation, and we are using the term 'orientation' with much the same meaning, i.e. as a mental posture indicating a readiness to act in a certain way. We note, however, that the interrelationships of beliefs, attitudes, opinions, intentions and actions are complex, to say the least.

Several books have emphasized the importance of the sort of preparatory assessment implied in 'intentional behaviour': see Anscombe (1963). Perhaps the best known is that of Miller, Galanter and Pribram (1960), which deals with cognitive planning and the subsequent organization of behaviour. Peters (1960) says it is important to understand how behaviour is organized and regulated by means of rules incorporated in the individual's psychological make-up—rules which help him to assign meanings to situations, to consider possible courses of action, and to act accordingly: see Chapter 4. Harré in Mischel (1974) and Harré and Secord (1972) have attempted to work out a theory of behaviour based on the idea of the individual as an actor or agent whose deliberations (and 'accounts') are a key ingredient in the organization of his behaviour and so must be understood if we are to make sense of it.

When we come to deal with the description of fictional persons in novels (see Chapter 10) we shall see that the analysis of ordinary states of mind is one of the most important features of the writer's craft, since it gives the reader a view of the fictional person 'from the inside' as it were, and enables him to understand why the character in the novel should react in the way he does. It has even been suggested that this awareness of the inner workings of the mind of the fictional character sometimes makes readers feel that they 'know' a character in a book better than they 'know' some of their friends and acquaintances in real life, because in real life we are usually denied such open access to another person's thoughts, feelings and wishes.

As far as the ordinary language of personality appraisal is concerned, the description of orientation and feelings (ORFE) is fairly straightforward. For convenience, however, in relation to the method of content analysis, this category (ORFE) does not include the many statements about the stimulus person's attitude towards another stimulus person (SP–O), or towards himself (SELF), or towards the writer of the description (SP–S); these categories of information are dealt with elsewhere.

We should not neglect the point that orientation and feelings can refer to situations which are in the past, the present or the future. Furthermore, they can refer to situations which are merely possible or imaginable, without ever being realized. The ability to consider matters remote in time, space and possibility is an essentially human characteristic compounded of conceptualization (abstraction and generalization) and language. It is not necessary to explore the philosophical and psychological aspects of this ability, since we are concerned only with how it is referred to, as an ability and process, in the ordinary language of everyday life in trying to describe and explain a person's behaviour.

The statements we make about other people's 'states of mind' are usually in the present tense, although, as we have just seen, their 'state of mind' may be either a reaction to past events, an anticipation of possible events or events in the future, or an experience connected with the present circumstances. Consider the following examples of ORFE statements: '. . . he thinks . . .', '. . . he feels that . . .', '. . . finds his work fascinating . . .', '. . . resentful of . . .', '. . . wonders if . . .', '. . . doesn't seem to recognize that . . .', '. . . finds life very full . . .', '. . . knows her mother is worried . . .', '. . . confused about . . .', '. . . she cannot see how . . .', '. . . seems lost . . .?' These examples illustrate some of the words and phrases in ordinary language that refer to a person's state of mind. We notice that ORFE statements generally imply an object, person, idea or event, towards which the person is 'oriented'. Since there are usually many such objects of interest in the person's life, it follows that his 'states of mind' cannot all be active at the same time. They can, however, be 'attributed' to him as latent dispositions which become active as each situation arises and as he makes ready to respond in a particular kind of way. We also infer from the above examples that some states of mind can be specified fairly precisely and are associated with fairly clear-cut responses to a situation. Other states of mind, however, cannot be specified precisely because the person is ignorant, lacking in confidence or uncertain about his situation. Nevertheless, even knowing only that a stimulus person is 'still undecided', 'confused', or has 'mixed feelings', still helps us to make better sense of, and to predict more accurately, his reactions to a situation—not so much by identifying the particular course of action he is likely to take but rather by identifying those courses of action which he is *unlikely* to take. It seems that many of our assessments of other people's states of mind are concerned with reducing the uncertainty associated with their behaviour and this can be done both by guessing what they will do and what they will *not* do.

The following examples of ORFE statements are taken at random from the main investigation: '... life does not make him happy ...', '... does not care at all for his appearance ...', '... she just won't entertain it because I am a married man ...', '... enjoys life fairly well ...', '... would be quite surprised if anyone accused her of stealing ...', '... the attitude that even though she goes to work there is no need to do anything ... as long as she gets paid ... she is quite happy ...', '... her house is untidy but this does not bother her ...', '... a young outlook on life ...', '... worships the trappings of material success ...', '... he will not face up to his responsibilities ...', '... does not realize how foolish he sounds and acts ...', '... seems to enjoy working on an intellectual level ...', '... enjoys spreading gossip ...', '... enjoys wearing his hair long ...', '... he knows what he wants ...', '... he knows his priorities ...', '... arriving half-an-hour late does not bother her ...', '... proud of his strength ...', '... sure of what he wants ...', '... prepared to listen to arguments against his view ...', '... has no plans for the future ...'.

As we have seen, statements about the stimulus person's orientation in relation to himself, to other people, and to the writer (observer), are assigned not to ORFE but to other content categories—SELF, SP–O, SP–S respectively, e.g. '... aware of her own worth ...', '... expects everyone to take notice of her whim ...', '... does not mind taking an old duck like me to dinner occasionally ...'. It is not always easy to decide to which category a particular statement should be assigned. As we have shown with examples from other content categories, meanings do not *reside in* the words and phrases themselves but are *assigned to* those words and phrases according to context and to the point of view of the reader (listener). Some phrases which look as if they referred to states of mind seem, on further examination, to be statements about traits or ethical principles (character or values), e.g. '... thinks much of money ...', '... he thinks that he should have what(ever) he wants ...', '... apathetic to everything ...', '... appears to enjoy all he does ...', '... has a philosophical approach to life ...'. Some of the statements are idiomatic and metaphorical rather than literal, e.g. '... she thinks the world owes her a living ...', '... she is usually so wrapped up in her work ...'.

Two further points are worth mentioning. First, ORFE statements are, by definition, about states of mind, i.e. ways of thinking and feeling about persons, objects, circumstances and events, therefore they refer explicitly to psychological processes; but they also refer implicitly to behavioural processes, e.g. '... undismayed ... by misfortune ...', '... anxious to do well ...', '... enjoys her housework ...', '... adores her father ...'. (SP–O). If we ask what such statements mean—in the context of an ordinary personality description—there is usually no difficulty in translating the psychological statement into its behavioural counterpart (or equivalent). There appears to be no 'logical' gulf between psychological and behavioural terms, merely a convenient shift from 'inner' to 'outer' manifestations of personal adjustment, made possible by the structure and function of ordinary language. The developmental processes in understanding one's own behaviour and psychological processes and understanding the behaviour and psychological processes of other people are dealt with briefly in Chapter 1.

Second, the fact that meanings do not reside in words and phrases but are a function of the reader's (or listener's) interpretation of them—given the context, situation, and so on—seems, at first glance, to create an insurmountable obstacle in the path of any attempt to establish an *objective* method of content analysis for ordinary language. We have seen that words and phrases can often be assigned to more than one content category; not because of any essential ambiguity in their meaning, but because they can signify different things, depending upon the uses to which the reader (or listener) wishes to put them. Hence, although the content analysis of ordinary language, at least as far as personality descriptions are concerned, cannot be 'objective' in the naive empirical sense of corresponding with external facts, it can be 'objective' in the methodological sense of corresponding with agreed procedural rules for handling observational data. We have already given some indication of what these procedural rules amount to in the content analysis of personality descriptions, namely: clear definitions, multiple criteria, numerous examples, split classifications, or definitive lists of words and phrases for each conceptual category: see Chapter 4.

F. Object of an Attitude (OBJE)

In the normal activities of everyday life our behaviour and attention are usually directed towards some object, circumstance, person or event. For example, a housewife's behaviour may be directed towards the preparation of a meal, a child's behaviour may be directed towards the rules of a game, a man's behaviour may be aimed at settling a dispute between his workmates. In all these examples there is an end-result, an aim or objective, the achievement of which is directed by an overall plan or strategy modified as required by tactical adjustments to local conditions. The behaviour which ensues is the 'realization' or implementation of an underlying psychological policy or programme. The nature of this underlying policy or programme is not well-understood; it can range all the way from an explicit, detailed list of self-instructions, e.g. a pilot carrying out a pre-flight check, to a vague, more or less implicit, intention to 'find someone to talk to' or 'do a little reading' or 'find out what's going on'. Whatever its psychological character, its function is to organize and direct behaviour, and to do so, usually, within an overall system of aims and objectives related to a range of environmental opportunities and constraints by means of an adjustable time-table or schedule of activities.

In our brief references to the relationship of behavioural ecology to the study of persons in situations, we emphasize the extent to which the behaviour of an individual is shaped by, and organized in terms of, the surrounding environment. This is not to say that the person is merely a creature of circumstance; on the contrary, people are active agents in relation to their environment. Human action and experience is directed towards *something*, and in order to 'make sense' of the person's conduct we must know the aim and object of his behaviour. Now, in order to specify what it is towards which the person's behaviour is directed, we need to refer to various objects, persons, ideas, events and circumstances in the person's environment: to pots and pans, quarrels and reconciliations, and so on, throughout the vast range of things with which human beings are concerned.

All this is obvious at a commonsense level of understanding other people and describing them as persons. But the scientific study of personality has attempted to abstract the person from his environment (from the circumstances in which, in our point of view, his behaviour is very firmly embedded), and has attempted to devise methods of describing and analysing personality *independently* of the environment in which the person lives his life. We regard this enterprise as largely if not entirely misconceived and believe that the proper focus of personality study is that of 'persons in situations'. The person's circumstances, in other words, require detailed analysis in order for us to see why and how the person's behaviour and experience are organized and directed in the way they are. A case-study, for example, deals with the relationships between a person and his environment. A psychometric assessment, by contrast, provides no more than a rough specification, in relative terms, of a number of operationally defined psychological variables whose reliability, validity and utility are questionable, to say the least. The psychometric approach to the study of personality is, however, a very different kind of scientific enterprise from the one in which we are engaged; but we can defer consideration of this particular issue and deal with it briefly in connection with the study of individual cases: see Chapter 8.

We have excluded from the category of OBJE statements those that refer to other people, to the stimulus person himself, and to the writer of the personality description. These other categories of statement are classified as Stimulus Person's Response to Others (SP–O), Self-concept (SELF), and Stimulus Person's Response to the Subject (SP–S), respectively. The only reason for categorizing statements in this way is that persons constitute an easily identifiable and important class of 'objects' towards which behaviour is frequently directed. Although, as the title of category OBJE indicates, human beings can relate to an infinite variety of objects, events, ideas and circumstances, it is difficult to find any particular classes of 'objects' which are as important to the stimulus person as the 'self' or 'other people'. It would, of course, be perfectly feasible to further subdivide these categories so as to be able to categorize statements referring to the way the stimulus person relates to, say, his work, school, home, God, the neighbourhood, leisure, and so on; these are his 'attitudes'. Attitudes have been studied thoroughly and for many years by social psychologists, but they are of interest to us only in so far as they are 'realized' in the actions and experience of an individual person; we are interested in his attitude to himself, to his wife, to other key people in his environment, and to other key aspects of his circumstances, e.g. his disability, his work, money, or whatever it is towards which his attention and energies are directed. In other words, we are not concerned with 'social' attitudes, i.e. attitudes common to groups of people; we are interested only in 'individual' attitudes towards 'objects' of individual concern. The fact that such attitudes may give rise to 'collective' social phenomena is another matter which is of no immediate interest to us as far as the study of personality description is concerned.

Naturally, OBJE statements cannot function *separately* from motivation and arousal (MOTA) and orientation and feelings (ORFE). Thus statements in personality descriptions are categorized as ORFE + OBJE or MOTA + OBJE, and they are assigned to the appropriate *psychological* function, i.e. to ORFE or MOTA. There is no independent content category for OBJE.

The following MOTA + OBJE statements are taken at random from the main investigation: '... endeavours to be the life and soul of the party ...', '... likes expensive things ...', '... he is fond of animals ...', '... he has interested himself in the modern problem of education ...', '... will try the same again ...', '... has not got the guts to leave home ...', '... very much pro-female ...', '... does not seem to like home-life ...', '... even if he does not want to do it ...', '... interested in people and affairs outside his immediate circle ...', '... he means well ...?', '... avoids all unpleasant tasks ...', '... designed to denigrate and perhaps worse ...?', '... enthusiastic in his approach to life ...', '... has an aversion to dogs ...', '... has a liking for antique furniture ...', '... likes his home ...'.

The following ORFE + OBJE statements are taken at random from the main investigation: '... does not care at all for (about?) his appearance ...', '... enjoys life fairly well ...', '... seems to take a delight in spreading rumours ...', '... is not afraid to hold an unpopular opinion ...', '... always willing to help if needed ...', '... willing to put herself out in a good cause ...', '... always ready for a giggle and a joke ...', '... a philosophical approach to life ...', '... knowing ... that ... home is the best place for him ...', '... his attitude to life is somewhat soured ...', '... accepts the discipline of study ...'.

In some instances it is not clear whether the motivational or experiential aspect of the behaviour is being referred to. For example, does the statement, 'He loves animals' mean 'He directs his behaviour toward the welfare of animals' or 'He is delighted by (has affection for) animals' or both? Similarly, does the statement, 'He enjoys company' mean 'He takes pleasure in (delights in) company' or 'He seeks out company' or both? Generally speaking, although one or the other meaning, motivational or experiential, was in the mind of the person making the statement, he would probably agree that the other could apply too.

Statements about orientation and feelings (ORFE) or motivation and arousal (MOTA) apparently unrelated to any object, event, idea or circumstance (OBJE) are not altogether ambiguous, e.g. 'She feels anxious', 'She is insecure', 'He feels a bit out of place', 'He is apathetic'. Such statements either indicate some sort of general trait (GENT), i.e. a disposition to behave in a way which is relatively independent of the situation, or they depend for their meaning on contextual factors (other statements in the description, or information that is understood and therefore taken for granted, make clear what it is towards which attitudes and desires are directed).

G. Expressive Behaviour (EXPR)

The dictionary definition of the word 'express' is 'to press or to force out', 'to emit', 'to represent or make known'. In psychology, the term 'expressive behaviour' refers to largely involuntary manifestations in conduct of inner psychological processes—thoughts, feelings, desires; it also refers to those behavioural signs which are not actions in themselves but simply surface indications of an inner state. As regards the first of these, a distinction has been drawn between two aspects of one and the same action—a 'coping' aspect (*what* is done) and an 'expressive' aspect (*how* it is done)—see Allport (1937) and Allport and Vernon (1933). How an action is described in ordinary language depends upon which aspect of the action is deemed to be most informative. For example, 'He closed the door' and 'He shut the door firmly' convey very different accounts of the same action; the former presents a simple behaviour episode, the latter amplifies the episode by describing the 'manner' in which the action was carried out, which in turn implies a correlated state of mind, namely, 'decisiveness, finality, conclusiveness' or alternatively 'rejection, denial, avoidance', depending upon context. As regards the second sort of expressive behaviour, surface indications independent of instrumental action, one might distinguish natural expressions, the smile of pleasure, the nose wrinkled in disgust, intention movements, from those which 'betray' the person's inner states and dispositions, a trembling lip, a blush or stammer.

The psychological significance of an action is therefore assessed by reference to these two aspects: *what* is done (or said) and *how* it is done (or said). The essence of the expressive aspect of an action, i.e. the manner in which an act is performed, is that it exhibits (or, better, is modified by) the inner psychological state that underlies the action.

The importance of expressive behaviour in social interaction is obvious; it provides a 'non-verbal' or 'paralinguistic' dimension to interpersonal communication, and signals the underlying affective state of an individual with an immediacy and directness required in many sorts of social encounter: see Argyle (1975). Words, by contrast, fulfil a more reflective function; at least in so far as they are not merely expressive. They enable us to represent and consider objects, events and relationships; but they require time and thought, so that words are more deliberate and more detached from the immediate situation than are expressive signals. There is, of course, some overlap between these two sorts of communication. One can achieve some control over various aspects of expressive (non-verbal) behaviour and use them *deliberately* to convey the sort of information usually reserved for verbal communication: eyes cast heavenwards and rolled, for example, signifying, 'The situation has become absurd'. Similarly, one can, to some extent, use words in a purely expressive way, as in the use of swear-words, terms of endearment, of rage, anger, fear, excitement, and so on. The distinction between expressive behaviour and language proper is further blurred by our ability to amplify and elaborate our feelings by recourse to well-thought-out words and phrases, and to increase the conviction and impact of our words by giving them an affective loading, as in poetry, rhetoric and propaganda.

Our present concern is with statements describing relatively simple forms of expressive behaviour (EXPR): characteristic postures, gestures, facial expressions, speech mannerisms, movements and outward appearance, e.g. style of dress. Like some other sorts of information, descriptions of these expressive characteristics help one to identify the stimulus person, i.e. they constitute 'behavioural marks' which distinguish that stimulus person from another. When used in a personality description, statements about expressive behaviour can be used to 'introduce' the stimulus person by focusing on tangible facts like his physical appearance, outward manner and characteristic movements. Normally, however, statements categorized as Expressive Behaviour (EXPR) are not limited to introducing and identifying the stimulus person as a physical or behavioural entity; they also describe or imply something about his *psychological nature*, since expressive behaviour is assumed to reveal something of the person's underlying temperamental qualities and affective states.

For convenience, then, we can distinguish two functions for statements about expressive behaviour: one is for identification, the other is for inference (or attribution). Statements which seem to have no implications as regards psychological characteristics can be assigned to Physical Appearance (PHYS); those which seem to have implications for Physical (and mental) Health (HLTH) can be assigned to this category.

Consider the following typical examples of EXPR statements: '... acid edge to her voice ...', '... dresses well ...', '... wears clothes more suitable to a teenager ...', '... weighed down with cheap jewelry ...', '... fresh and clean ...', '... neat and tidy ...', '... stylish ...', '... sloppy ...', '... sloppy manner ...', '... clumsy ...'. The first phrase illustrates how feelings of contempt or dislike can affect one's tone of voice. The second phrase carries with it a number of vague implications, e.g. of relative wealth, taste or concern for personal adornment; thus expressive behaviour can 'express' more than temperamental qualities, mood or feelings. The important thing is that the behaviour (its outcome or residue) should be a sign of something other than itself. Thus, the third phrase, above, carries the implication that the stimulus person does not conform to the standards of dress prescribed for a person in her age-grade, which in turn implies perhaps a certain moral laxity, lack of insight or other attribute. The fourth phrase, similarly, implies poor taste combined with ostentatiousness, in the sense that being '... weighed down with cheap jewelry ...' *betrays* the person's character. The fifth and sixth phrases occur frequently, and obviously convey more than a literal interpretation, namely, honesty, innocence, and carefulness, thoughtfulness respectively. The word '... stylish ...' means fashionable or distinctive and carries with it implications of being modern, confident, extraverted. Finally, '... sloppy manner ...' and '... clumsy ...' imply carelessness, unreliability, stupidity, and so on, though neither the behaviour nor the implied psychological characteristics are directly specified. We note, therefore, that some EXPR statements are direct reports of observed behaviour (or its outcome), whereas others refer to behavioural tendencies or dispositions, and to states of mind.

The following examples of EXPR statements are taken at random from the main investigation: '... a loud voice ...', '... in a noisy obtrusive way ...', '... she is very smart ...', '... a compulsive talker ...', '... noisy ...', '... does not bother about his appearance ...', '... never smiles ...', '... always presents a bright aspect to the world ...', '... always whining ...', '... bright smile ...', '... she sparkled ...', '... vivacity ...?', '... alive ...', '... gay ...', '... sarcastic ...', '... an ever present cynical grin ...', '... patronising attitude ...', '... his clothes are clean, tidy and traditionally normal ...', '... pleasant and courteous ...', '... still comes up smiling ...', '... tries to be trendy but generally ends up "short back and sides" ...', '... well groomed ...', '... very affected with people she wants to impress ...', '... keeps up with all the latest dress even though it may not suit her ...', '... smart and clean ...', '... hearty ...', '... bright ...', '... a very broad Scots accent ...', '... untidy in habits ...', '... overdresses ... uses too much make-up ... loud-mouthed ...', '... standing back in a disparaging manner ...'.

Thus, we use expressive behaviour to 'read' the affective states of other people, and as clues to their personality (including beliefs, values and motives), temperamental qualities, and circumstances. But in practice, the psychological significance of expressive behaviour depends upon a variety of factors. Weeping, for example, is more common in women than in men; and more common in children than in adults; so that one cannot give it the same interpretation in all cases. Similarly there are probably social class differences in the expression of emotion, e.g. anger.

We learn to recognize standard patterns of expressive behaviour—smiles, scowls, and so on—and to take contextual factors into account, in much the same way as we learn that words have different meanings in different contexts. Expressive signals and their corresponding interpretations thus constitute a sort of non-verbal semiotics, but by no means a simple stimulus-response system. Expressive behaviour is a 'language' with its own complex system of signs, sequences and significances corresponding to the lexicon, syntax and semantics of ordinary language, and it develops through maturation and learning. This fact becomes of the utmost importance when we consider the *individuality* of expressive behaviour. Thus, we are each capable of smiling (or scowling or other expression) in different ways in different circumstances. The people who know us well are capable of discriminating between these different expressions whereas others are not. In much the same way, people who know us well can attach finer shades of meaning to the words we use because they are more familiar with the way we use words. Close acquaintance also increases the likelihood of shared experiences and common characteristics, forming a sort of expressive 'dialect', as occurs among family members, or other groups on close familiar terms with one another, e.g. in the barrack room, the office or Parliament. Conversely, people unfamiliar with the usage of words and expressive behaviour in circumscribed groups or in individual persons are unable to appreciate its full or true psychological significance. Thus we may misconstrue the 'pleasant smile' as 'an invitation to closer acquaintance' or the 'abrupt manner' as 'personal dislike'. Some misinterpretations are widespread: the wearing of spectacles as a sign of intelligence, a large full mouth as a sign of sensuousness, wide eyes as a sign of honesty, and so on. Just as the language of words contains a variety of misleading clichés, so the non-verbal 'language' of expressive behaviour contains a variety of misleading signs.

Affect and expressive behaviour have proved to be difficult areas to study scientifically, especially in relation to self-understanding and undertanding others: see Wessman and Ricks (1966), Tomkins and Izard (1966), De Charms (1968), Ekman and Friesen (1975).

H. Principles and Moral Values (or Character) (PRIN)

The moral aspects of personality are important and need not be excluded from *scientific* analysis simply because ethical principles themselves cannot be derived from the empirical study of human behaviour. Ethical principles are rather like scientific theories, in that they are not so much *derived from* the data, inductively as it were, but rather *imposed upon* the data in an attempt to make 'moral sense' of them. Thus, morality is an attempt to impose order and meaning on human social behaviour and to regulate it according to standards of right and wrong. There are individuals whose role in society is to formulate or administer ethical codes, or to evaluate them critically. Moral issues are prominent in fictional accounts of character: see Chapter 10.

We are not concerned with ethics in general, only with the description of a person's moral character in relation to the ethical code appropriate to him. The quasi-judicial method of studying personal adjustment (see Chapter 8) shows that it is possible to conduct an empirical investigation into whether a person's behaviour is or is not regulated in accordance with certain ethical rules. This is done every day in courts of law throughout the land.

We have asserted that there is no *logical* gulf between psychological processes on the one hand and behavioural processes on the other; the two are related as internal (subjective) and external (objective) manifestations of personal adjustment. Thus, without contradicting the maxim that 'One cannot *derive* ought from is' (in a general sense), we can obviously *compare* 'ought' with 'is' when it comes to matters of character assessment or the attribution of legal responsibility. In other words, empirical data about a person's behaviour may enable one to infer that he is or is not honest, truthful, reliable, loyal, and so on, and to understand and forecast his behaviour. The fact is that we do this sort of thing naturally in everyday life, although our standards of evidence and inference usually fall far short of the ideals held up in courts of law and in other judicial and quasi-judicial settings.

A person's 'moral character' can be defined fairly broadly as his 'philosophy of life' to encompass his basic assumptions about the nature and purpose of human life and his own personal existence. It includes the fundamental assumptions, tenets and preconceptions on which he appears to base his behaviour, especially his relationships with other people, and regardless of whether the person himself is aware of them or can make them explicit. Also included are the person's basic values: in relation to which he feels good or bad, worthy or worthless, guilty or innocent, shameful or proud. His ethical principles include those beliefs and attitudes associated with religion and ideology. Thus, in addition to terms like honest, truthful, reliable, loyal, and so on, which are commonly used in ordinary language to refer to moral characteristics, there are terms like democratic, materialist, aesthetic, religious and scientific. Naturally, specific traits of character and conscience are included: conscientious, unscrupulous, church-goer, insincere, temperate.

Our most obvious difficulty is the same as that faced by Allport and Odbert (see Chapter 3) in that it is difficult, if not impossible, to separate out moral (evaluative) terms from ethically neutral (non-evaluative) terms, and to distinguish clearly between the dispositions or capacities within the person and the judgments made of him by other people. For example, the term 'good' seems to be a social judgment, but can be used to refer to an attribute of character, e.g. 'She is good to her neighbours' meaning not that her neighbours or others judge her to be 'good' (they may or may not), but that she 'does good' and 'is good', i.e. performs valuable services for and takes an interest in her neighbours. This sort of consistent behaviour is normally attributed to a 'disposition' within the person, i.e. to a tendency to act in a certain way in situations of a certain sort. Thus, even when a term is clearly used as a social judgment, it must make some kind of reference, however indirectly, to dipositions within the person. We carry our goodness, evil, reliability and punctuality around with us, as it were, in the form of dispositions to behave in ways that lead, whether intentionally or not, whether justifiably or not, to the social judgments that are made of us.

Now, if it makes sense to account for our behaviour in terms of dispositions, and if, as it seems, almost any kind of behaviour can be thought of in evaluative terms, i.e. as good or bad in relation to some ethical code, then it follows that almost any kind of disposition also can become the focus of social value judgments, as shown by research work on social desirability: see Edwards (1957) and Block (1965). If this is the case, then we cannot make a sharp distinction between moral character and personality. In Allport's classic maxim: 'Character is personality evaluated; personality is character devaluated', Allport (1937, p. 52). We have seen that meaning *does not reside in* words and phrases, therefore it is impossible to assign them validly and objectively, i.e. unambiguously, to either 'character' or 'personality' as Allport and Odbert attempted to do in their psycholexical analysis of trait names.

The solution to this problem seems to be that ethical codes are selective and give greater emphasis to some forms of behaviour than to others—though they can usually be stretched or shrunk as required to include or exclude certain forms of conduct, e.g. pre-marital sexual relations, homosexuality, the use of alcohol and other drugs, aggression, and so on. Therefore, when we refer to a person's 'moral character' we usually have in mind those forms of conduct selected and emphasized by the ethical code proclaimed in the society to which the person belongs, e.g. honesty in commercial transactions, truthfulness in scientific work, loyalty in personal relationships, fairness in matters of social control, and so on. It follows that observers with different ethical pespectives will select and emphasize different qualities of character in the stimulus person they are describing—clear examples can be seen in the differing assessments made of political figures by their supporters and opponents, because at base, political behaviour is a matter of morality. Thus, for example, one man's 'greed' is another man's 'enterprise' and one man's 'jealousy' is another man's 'sense of fair play'. Therefore problems can arise if we are dealing with people in a society where different ethical codes co-exist.

The following examples of statements about principles, character and moral values (PRIN) are taken at random from the main investigation: '... religious ...', '... trustworthy ...', '... has a code of behaviour to which he adheres ...', '... practices what he preaches ...', '... narrow-minded ...', '... loyal ...', '... does not gamble ...', '... I doubt if he knows any loyalties ...', '... without regard to fairness or ethics ...', '... he thinks that any person who is not of his (political persuasion) is less than dust ...', '... has very strong and narrow religious views ...', '... firm in her views, aims and standards ...', '... does not hold any political views ...', '... not an abstainer ...?', '... has a cruel conception of an avenging God ...', '... hates all forms of war ...', '... has keen pacifist convictions ...', '... not religious ...', '... cherishes the moral values that I cherish ...', '... never bigoted ...', '... rather unscrupulous principles ...?', '... narrow-minded bigot ...', '... Fascist ...', '... her philosophy seems to be to take life as you find it ...', '... he purports to be very religious ...', '... a man of integrity ...', '... church worker ...', '... idealistic ...', '... a strong sense of loyalty ...', '... practising Christian ...', '... has doubts about religion ...', '... her motto is that we are all human beings ...', '... has no idea ... of fair play ...'.

These representative examples suggest three further features of the ordinary language of 'character' assessment. First, they are simple, straightforward and limited in variety. Second, they tend to assert the presence or absence of an ethical code, without much concern as to the nature of that code, e.g. 'very religious', 'narrow-minded', 'integrity'. Third, they indicate an awareness of the difference between ethical principles and ethical practices.

I. Self-concept (SELF)

Under the general heading of Self-concept (SELF), we include any words and phrases which refer to the way the stimulus person regards himself, i.e. to his impression of or attitude towards himself. The empirical basis of SELF statements may consist of things said by the stimulus person about himself, and of things done by him which seem to reveal something of the way he regards himself, though often the evidential basis of the statement is not given. For example: '... thinks of himself as ...', '... is self-deprecatory ...', '... has a high opinion of himself ...', '... he has no confidence in his own abilities ...', '... self-satisfied ...', '... full of his own importance ...'.

Like several other content categories the Self-concept (SELF) category does not have exclusive rights over all the words and statements that may be assigned to it. Some of them might very well be used to make assertions about personality traits (GENT) or moral character (PRIN).

We are concerned now only with the ordinary observer's assessment of the stimulus person's self-concept. Before going any further, however, we should perhaps mention the importance of the 'self' as a concept in the study of personality and adjustment. Although it would be misleading to say that the concept of 'self' is firmly established and well-understood, it nevertheless plays a major role in most psychodynamic approaches to personality: see Maddi (1972) and Gergen (1971). In other words, it is generally accepted that a person's impression of himself is a key factor in his adjustment, since it is associated with important functions like ego-involvement, achievement motivation, self-regard, guilt, and so on.

The self-concept has proved remarkably difficult to investigate empirically. In recent years, there have been attempts to study the psychological development of the self-concept, the most relevant to our present purpose being that of Livesley and Bromley (1973, pp. 229–40; see also Chapter 1). It is our contention that a developmental study of the self-concept, as exhibited in self-descriptions in the ordinary language of everyday life, provides us with the most secure empirical foundation for the analysis of the concept of self in the study of personality and adjustment in children and adults.

The following examples of SELF statements are taken at random from the main investigation (they are from descriptions of others, not self-descriptions): '... in order to gain his own ends ...', '... has the attitude that "only the best will do for me"....', '... he is sure of himself ...', '... is very good-looking and knows it ...', '... without self-pity ...', '... knows all—until he tries it ...', '... imagines himself to be worthy of a much higher station in life ...', '... totally self-centred ...', '... has always got to demonstrate her individuality ...?', '... not self-sacrificing ...', '... sharp self-awareness ...', '... self-appointed goals ...', '... likes to feel that she is important ...', '... is full of self-importance ...', '... no thought at all for anyone but herself ...', '... she thinks she is indispensable ...', '... thinks he knows all the answers ...', '... she is quite ruthless in wanting her own way in everything ...', '... well aware of her own worth ...', '... self-centred ...', '... vain ...', 'thinks she is irresistible to men ...'.

Consideration of these and other representative examples reveals that SELF statements in personality descriptions tend to be presented mainly as value-judgments referring to the person's selfishness, self-preoccupation or inflated opinion of himself. Some, however, identify specific characteristics of the self.

Thus, SELF statements by others contribute surprisingly little to the personality description. This is probably because the self-concept is a particularly private aspect of personality, protected by a variety of social strategies and psychological defences, and not easily penetrated except by close friends, confidants or therapists. By contrast, self-descriptions written by the stimulus persons themselves reveal much more information—classifiable in terms of our standard system of content analysis; they emphasize different aspects of personality than do descriptions of others: for example, there is more emphasis on inner psychological processes—motivation and orientation—and less emphasis on adverse value judgments of self-centredness and so on. It is obvious, therefore, that we shall learn more about self as an aspect of personality and adjustment from the analysis of self-descriptions than from the analysis of descriptions of others. We intend making a separate study of self-descriptions in adult life and old age, to be published separately.

CHAPTER 6

Lexical and Semantic Analysis: 'External' Aspects of Personality

I. Introduction

This chapter describes the 'external' facets of personality as revealed by a lexical and semantic analysis of ordinary language.

Using the method of content analysis described briefly in Chapter 4, nine categories of information, referring mainly to external behavioural processes, were defined, as follows:

Content analysis categories	Abbreviations
Identity	IDEN
Physical Appearance	PHYS
Physical and Mental Health	HLTH
Life-history	LIFE
Contemporary Situation	SITU
Prospects	PROS
Routine Activities	ROUT
Material Circumstances and Possessions	MATP
Actual Incidents	INCS

They are defined, illustrated and discussed in the Sections A to I.

II. Content Analysis Categories

A. Identity (IDEN)

The word 'identity' is a noun meaning 'the state of being the same'. When used to refer to a person's identity it means the 'personality' or the 'individuality' of that person, i.e. who or what a person is. The word 'identity' is derived from the Latin *idem* meaning 'the same'. One is reminded of the metaphysical notion that personality is . . .what a man really is. . . : see Allport (1937, p. 48). The related word 'identify' is a verb referring to the process of ascertaining or proving a person's identity, or of assigning him to a class of persons.

The sorts of words and phrases pertaining to and classifiable as Identity (IDEN) include the stimulus person's name and address, sex, nationality, race and religion, age and marital status. These occur, for example, on identity cards, application forms, and official documents of various sorts. One obvious function of information of this sort is to identify the particular stimulus person and distinguish him from other persons with whom he might be confused, e.g. his brother, or a colleague in the same organization. Another, slightly less obvious, function of IDEN statements is to 'introduce' the person at or near the beginning of the personality description. The description, i.e. the symbolic representation of the stimulus person, can thereby be referred to facts in real life, for example, statements can be checked against observation or against another independent description. With the stimulus person's identity established, personal pronouns can be used in statements about him.

In one sense, it is possible to form an impression of a person without knowing who he is; i.e. without being able to state his formal public identity—e.g. an impression formed of a stranger on a train or a person met casually at a social gathering. In these circumstances, the stimulus person's identity has a personal and subjective basis, e.g. 'That funny chap I met on the train' or 'The woman in the black dress who was talking to Nancy at the dinner we went to last week'. Such subjective personal references to identity can range widely over most of the content categories we shall describe, since all one needs to do in order to form an identity (IDEN) statement is to prefix the information with a phrase like 'He is the person who . . .'—for example, . . . owns the big dog up the street', '. . . has those peculiar facial tics', '. . . teaches at the local school', or '. . . wants to be elected'.

The fact that IDEN statements can be so easily composed from such diverse information shows, perhaps, not only how important Identity is as a concept in personality, but also how difficult it may be to assign one exclusive meaning to a word or phrase in a personality description—one of the accepted, but we believe mistaken, rules of the method of content analysis.

Like the formal, public statements of identity, the subjective personal statements serve to introduce the verbal account of the impression formed and to anchor the description to facts in the real world (or, of course, to fictions in the fictional world, e.g. character, plot and situation in a novel: see Chapter 10). It is difficult to see how we could form an impression of a person without some such reference to identity. Thus, in one sense, identity statements constitute the irreducible minimum of information needed in order to form an impression. We need such information in order to 'refer to' a particular person, and especially in order to enable the reader (or listener) to identify that *same* person. Such identification is not only essential to the effective communication of other information about the stimulus person, but also essential to effective action on the part of the reader (or listener) in relation to that person. The clearest illustrations of the essential nature of identity statements are found in accounts of mistaken identity, e.g. in police inquiries, in impersonation, and in failure to recognize 'who' is being referred to in a verbal or written account.

Illustrative examples of Identity (IDEN) statements taken at random from the written descriptions in the main investigation, and referring to different stimulus persons, are as follows: '... middle-aged ...', '... married ...', '... this girl is a near neighbour ...', '... he is I believe a Jamaican ...', '... born in Prague ...', '... a mother ...', '... J.H. is getting on in years ...', '... the wife of a good friend of mine ...', '... the man I am thinking of is dead ...', '... although coming from Newmarket ...', '... about 30 ...', '... a widow ...', '... an adopted daughter ...', '... this young lady ...', '... this boy is only nine years old ...'.

Names and/or addresses are the most obvious public statements of identity, but they are not essential to identification, except where the social situation prescribes them, e.g. formal introductions, court proceedings, safety regulations. Identification, as we have seen, can be achieved by reference to other sorts of information.

It is worth mentioning that 'identification' is a frequent type of social transaction; it has a variety of routinized or standardized forms, for example: signing a cheque or a document; acknowledging a person's presence at a meeting by appropriate forms of interaction; greetings and conversations in informal encounters (in which implicit mutual identifications take place as precursors to familiar patterns of interaction). Another sort of personal identification occurs in the use of pre-arranged or accepted codes, as in voice recognition on the telephone acknowledged by a characteristic response, in the use of code-names and pass-words, or by the use of signals such as the use of a rendezvous or the wearing of an agreed article of clothing.

Identity and physical appearance are closely linked, in the sense that the stimulus person's external morphological characteristics are usually sufficient for him to be identified by people who know him reasonably well, and even by people who do not know 'who he is' in the formal sense described above. Knowing someone 'by sight only' is a common experience, and it is a common practice to attach photographs, usually full face only, to official documents, e.g. student records, to facilitate identification, to reduce the risks of misidentification, and to stimulate the recall and recognition of relevant information. In fact for most kinds of routine social interaction, physical appearance, behaviour setting and role relationships provide sufficient implicit grounds for identification without resort to explicit 'presentations' of personal identity, e.g. by means of name-labels, registers, fingerprints or identity cards.

B. Physical Appearance (PHYS)

Statements about physical appearance are a prominent feature of personality descriptions in ordinary language. Even when subjects under test conditions are instructed not to spend time on this aspect of personality, a proportion of them nevertheless make statements of this kind. The word 'appearance' is a noun which refers to the outward condition of the person who appears: his or her form or aspect, what that person shows or how he looks. The word is derived from the Latin *apparere*—to come forth. The verb 'to appear' means to become visible. There are, however, three rather distinct aspects of the description of a person's 'appearance'. The first is simply the physical properties referred to, e.g. '. . . dark hair . . .', '. . . tall . . .', '. . . slim build . . .', and it is to this aspect that the content category Physical Appearance (PHYS) refers. The second aspect refers to what the person 'seems' to be (as opposed to what the person 'really is'). Thus one might say: '. . . She looks blonde, but actually her hair is dark . . .' or '. . . He is not as strong as he looks . . .'. Reference to the difference between 'real' and 'apparent' characteristics is a major feature of adult personality descriptions; it is expressed not by the use of particular sorts of lexical items but by the use of certain syntactical constructions: see Chapters 1 and 2. The third aspect of appearance has to do with the person's manner or demeanour, for example, '. . . neat and tidy . . .', '. . . fresh and clean . . .', '. . . wears a frown . . .'. This aspect is dealt with elsewhere under the heading of Expressive Behaviour (EXPR). We must also take into account the fact that a person's physical appearance can be the object of an evaluation, e.g. 'nice looking', 'too big', 'weedy'. It thus becomes a problem to decide whether a particular word or phrase is meant to convey a factual statement or an evaluation or both. Evaluations (EVAL) are another sort of content category described and discussed elsewhere.

Words and phrases in the category Physical Appearance (PHYS) include those referring to external morphological features, i.e. the surface characteristics of the body, and any expressive behaviour which is purely descriptive. Such words and phrases in the main investigation include the following examples: '. . . well-built . . .', '. . . lean and lanky . . .', '. . . tall . . .', '. . . small . . .', '. . . large head . . .', '. . . dark hair . . .', '. . . fair complexion . . .', '. . . fat . . .', '. . . big teeth . . .', '. . . rotund . . .', '. . . slim . . .', '. . . chubby . . .', '. . . well-made . . .', '. . . has recently adopted a beard . . .', '. . . sparkling brown eyes . . .', '. . . large boned type . . .', '. . . short in stature . . .', '. . . an albino . . .', '. . . big and bosomy . . .', '. . . heavily built . . .', '. . . wears his hair long . . .', '. . . appears 10 to 15 years younger than she is . . .', '. . . thick-set . . .', '. . . powerful . . .'. These items directly describe the relatively permanent physical characteristic on the basis of which a stimulus person is recognized, i.e. identified.

We have tried to ensure that the category Physical Appearance (PHYS) is relatively objective and neutral, in that the words and phrases classified under this heading have no particular psychological or behavioural implications and have no particular moral or social value. However, it is not possible to disambiguate words and phrases completely and to assign them with absolute confidence to one category or another (except by means of a definitive list), and it is not easy to discount the overtones of psychological or evaluative meaning associated with these terms. Indeed, one familiar use to which information about physical appearance is put is that of a framework for the expression of non-physical attributes. This is achieved by the metaphorical use of language and the equating of emotionally compatible elements. Such usage is particularly common in literature and journalism. Tolstoy, for example, in *War and Peace* introduces his characters in this way:

> The countess was a woman of about five-and-forty, and of rather an Eastern type, with a thin face, and the weary look of a mother of twelve children. (p. 35.)

It is relevant to our present concern to note that the very next sentence in this passage refers to at least two other sorts of information, namely, those categorized as Expressive Behaviour (EXPR) and Physical and Mental Health (HLTH). Statements in these two categories are frequently in close association with statements about Physical Appearance (PHYS). The passage continues:

> Her deliberate speech and movements, which were the result of weak health, gave her a certain dignity that commanded respect. (p. 35.)

A fine example of the use of Physical Appearance as a framework for the expression of non-physical attributes is found in the way Dologhow is introduced:

> Dologhow, a young man of about five-and-twenty, was of middle height with curly hair and blue eyes. He, like all infantry officers at that time, wore no moustache, and his mouth, which was his most striking feature, was therefore visible. It was singularly well-shaped and fine, with the upper lip something in the shape of a wedge closing energetically on the prim lower lip; the corners were marked by a perpetual smile—by two perpetual smiles, one on each side, as it were, and this, added to his look of intelligence and insolence, commanded attention. (p. 31.)

Although categories of information other than physical appearance are used in such descriptions—for example Identity (IDEN), Comparison with Others (SPvO), Evaluation (EVAL), and Expressive Behaviour (EXPR)—the reader is led to believe that the various psychological characteristics attributed to Dologhow are manifested in his physical appearance. The smile, for example, is 'perpetual' and thus becomes a fixed feature expressing a relatively permanent characteristic rather than a variable feature expressing changing states of thought and feeling. The language of personality descriptions in literature is dealt with in detail in Chapter 10.

Journalism, of course, is full of clichés about physical appearance: 'Tall, blond Miss X', 'Granite-faced Mr. Y', and so on. The characteristics are mentioned mostly because they 'fit' the image or stereotype that the journalist is trying to convey: '... paunchy, jowled, bespectacled, balding ...', for example, or '... wiry, thin-faced, sharp-eyed and lank-haired ...'. Physical characteristics which do not fit the psychological image that the journalist is trying to convey may be explained away by phrases like '. . . in spite of his appearance . . .'. The journalist may find himself trapped by his own implicit use of the language of personality descriptions into shaping his account of the person's psychological characteristics to fit the popular stereotype appropriate to the person's physical appearance.

C. *Physical and Mental Health (HLTH)*

That human behaviour and psychological processes have an organic basis is taken for granted by layman and scientist alike, although within each of these groups there are different views about the nature and scope of the relationship between body and mind (brain and behaviour).

Recognition of the important part played by physical health in the overall adjustment and personal qualities of an individual is revealed in personality descriptions by statements categorized as Physical and Mental Health (HLTH), as follows: '. . . health is bad . . .', '. . . has to take things easy . . .', '. . . disabled . . .', '. . . had a stroke recently . . .', '. . . full of energy . . .', '. . . lacking energy . . .', '. . . strong . . .', '. . . physically active . . .', '. . . weedy . . .', '. . . delicate . . .', '. . . had a serious brain operation . . .', '. . . poor stance . . .', '. . . ungainly . . .', '. . . too fat . . .', '. . . bad skin . . .', '. . . poor eyesight, etc. . . .', '. . . trouble with her feet . . .', '. . . limps . . .', '. . . no stamina . . .', '. . . lithe . . .', '. . . agile . . .'.

Such statements carry a wealth of implications; they raise many expectations about the stimulus person's mobility, capacity for work, reactions to stress, relationships with other people, self-concept, and so on.

A personality description which omitted to mention physical facts having a bearing on the person's adjustment would properly be judged to be deficient in this regard. A personality description is deficient to the extent that it fails to mention *any* known fact relevant to assessing the person's actions and state of mind; these are the sorts of fact we are trying to catalogue. We mention this point now, because it is perhaps easier to see in relation to facts categorized as Physical and Mental Health (HLTH) than in relation to other sorts of fact, e.g. MATP or INCS: see later.

Statements about physical health and disease refer to the person's medical state, his physical fitness, his speed, strength and stamina, his physical abilities and disabilities. In addition, they may refer to the person's physical symptoms, to his expressive behaviour (posture and movement), and to his appearance, in so far as they indicate something about his physical health (as opposed to statements categorized as Physical Appearance (PHYS) which indicate something about his identity).

Statements about mental health and disease are included under HLTH in so far as they refer to conditions which may be recognized as organic or functional ailments of the sort dealt with in psychiatry. However, given the present uncertainty about mental health—its conditions and causes—and the arguments about the validity of the 'medical model' for some psychopathological states, the inclusion of statements about mental health in the general category HLTH must be regarded as tentative and questionable. Furthermore, the manifestations of mental 'abnormality' in daily life are not always obvious or clearly distinguishable from the normal range of variations in behaviour. Thus, for example, statements about shyness, bad temper, depression, anxiety, aggressiveness and sexual inclinations may or may not rank as HLTH statements, depending upon whether or not they are regarded as symptoms of an 'illness'. Hence, a close search for evidence relevant to the question of whether a stimulus person is suffering from a psychiatric illness could range over facts classified under a number of categories other than the one we have labelled Physical and Mental Health (HLTH). For example, facts about the Stimulus Person's Response to Others (SP–O), his Orientation and Feelings (ORFE) and his Life-history (LIFE), to name only a few categories, might be indicative of psychopathology.

The following examples of HLTH statements are taken at random from the main investigation: '... has a great deal of energy ...', '... enjoying good health ...', '... has plenty of vitality ...', '... is a paraplegic ...', '... when her health allows ...', '... has a very minor physical defect ...', '... has had a number of operations and is not in particularly good health ...', '... dwells on her past and present illnesses ...', '... having been crippled since babyhood ...', '... athletic ...', '... despite some physical disability ...', '... rather bad eyesight, at least it is bad enough to prevent him driving a car ...'.

In personality descriptions written by ordinary adults, statements about mental health are relatively rare; one would need to analyse descriptions written by social workers and clinical psychologists to obtain diverse examples.

D. *Life-history (LIFE)*

We have already seen that a person's identity (IDEN) is described partly by statements about his life-history, for example his date and place of birth, and partly by statements about his current existence, his age, address, and so on. One cannot always make a clear distinction between past, present and future behaviour. One's 'present' behaviour, for example, spans not just this moment of time but rather the duration of one's current concerns and on-going activities. To take a simple example: if we are getting married or moving house, we are likely to think of that concern or activity as part of our present life, though it might occupy several weeks and eventually pass through all three phases of our temporal existence: future, present and past.

From a psychological viewpoint, therefore, past, present and future merge into one another, not merely in a temporal sense but also in a causal or deterministic sense. The person we are now depends in part on the person we have been and helps to determine the person we shall become. These temporal relationships are complicated by the fact that we can anticipate and plan our future, and we can reinterpret our personal history. Thus, in a real, though not in any absolute, sense, human beings can make their own history and future. This is because the effects of life experiences not only act on us directly, in virtue of our physical make-up (personality has a biological basis), but they also act indirectly, in virtue of our psychological make-up (personality has motivational, affective and cognitive, as well as sensory and behavioural, aspects). A particular event, e.g. losing a limb, falling in love, or achieving a given level of income, can have different effects on people because the event is construed differently, i.e. it has different *meanings*. The psychological significance of such events and, therefore, the influence they have on behaviour, also varies with time: events look different in prospect from how they look here and now, and they look different again when they have become part of our recent or remote life-history.

A person's behaviour is usually (though not always) more explicable in the context of his life-history and future prospects (or long-range aims) than without this context: see Chapters 8 and 9. Strictly speaking, a scientific explanation calls for an analysis of the proximal causes of an event. We take for granted the following assumptions; that these causes are antecedent to the event in question, that the event would not have occurred but for these antecedent causes, and that antecedent causes of this sort tend to produce this kind of event. Unfortunately, analysis of the causes of a person's behaviour tends to have to move beyond concern with proximal or precipitating factors to concern with causal paths reaching back to relatively remote and early determinants. Psychodynamic analysis is a good example of this tendency, and even a behaviouristic analysis is based on the assumption that a person has a 'reinforcement history' which helps to explain why he behaves in certain ways in the present circumstances.

If we regard the notion of 'causal path' as a reasonable and useful concept in the analysis of the behaviour of individuals, then the separation of the person's life into past, present and future phases can be seen as a matter of linguistic convenience. We think of a person's existence as having duration and we think of his behaviour as consisting of patterns of activity which change over time and in relation to his circumstances (which also change over time). Various sorts of causal path can be traced out, depending upon how far back in time one wishes to go, and how complex or ramified an account one wishes to give. Causal paths can be analysed at various levels of abstraction and can be traced selectively as the situation requires. In this respect, the scientific analysis of the causal pathways of individual behaviour is no different from other kinds of scientific analysis. A causal analysis is, after all, an 'explanation', and explanations are intended to provide information that is felt, by someone, to be lacking. Explanations are not unlike maps, and we use different maps for different purposes. Hence, the sort of explanation which is appropriate for one purpose is not appropriate for another. For example, an explanation in psychodynamic terms may not answer the questions being asked by a teacher or a magistrate even though it satisfies the psychotherapist. Implicit and explicit causal statements are commonly found in personality descriptions in ordinary language: see Chapters 1, 8 and 9.

Statements about life-history (LIFE) attempt to provide a context or past record so that the individual's present behaviour can be explained more effectively, and so that his prospects and future behaviour can be stated with greater accuracy. At least, this is the scientific justification for including LIFE statements in the personality description associated with a professional case-study. The inclusion of LIFE statements in a personality description makes it more coherent, convincing and interesting.

Words and statements classified as Life-history (LIFE) for the purpose of content analysis include all those pertaining to the individual's personal history (including any social history circumstances that are relevant), e.g. his childhood and life so far, and any formative experiences and circumstances.

The following examples were taken at random from the main investigation: '. . . lost his father in an accident when he was six . . .', '. . . went to a public school . . .', '. . . has had a hard life . . .', '. . . went into his father's business . . .', '. . . left school at 14 . . .', '. . . married very young . . .', '. . . retired at 60 . . .'. Such items form part of the narrative history of the stimulus person's life. They are factual statements rather than causal analyses or inferences, except where the inference is a general statement about the stimulus person's history.

Statements categorized as Life-history (LIFE) can be distinguished from those categorized as Contemporary Situation (SITU), or Actual Incidents (INCS) or Future Prospects (PROS), for conceptual convenience as separate 'facets' of personality. But in some instances this is difficult and arbitrary. Evaluative terms can enter into LIFE statements. Another difficulty is that, like Identity (IDEN) statements, statements in many other content categories can be construed as Life-history statements. Indeed, some subjects go so far as to present the whole of their personality description as a narrative-cum-story using the past tense. It follows, therefore, that many LIFE statements can be cross-classified. For example, '. . . lost his father at the age of six . . .' could be regarded as a statement about family and kin (FAMK), and '. . . went into his father's business . . .' as a statement about social position (SOPO). However, there is usually some fact about the phrasing or the context which indicates that the statement in question is intended to fulfil a narrative function. In other words, it is offered as a key element in the sequence of events that makes up the individual's life, as part of the causal path leading to the stimulus person's present behaviour (and the circumstances relevant to that behaviour).

The following examples of Life-history (LIFE) statements are taken at random from the main investigation: '. . . has had several accidents but has overcome them, and got quickly back on his feet . . .', '. . . lost her husband 12 months ago . . .', '. . . used to work at a children's hospital . . .', '. . . has recently been married . . .', '. . . has maintained his youthful idealism throughout the years . . .', '. . . trained as a nurse . . .', '. . . had a very effective influence over the three younger children . . .', '. . . has been brought up with every care and consideration . . .', '. . . his was never a happy home . . .', '. . . although quite well known years ago she never made close friends because of her disagreeable character . . .', '. . . represented his school on the running track . . .', '. . . has suffered greatly . . .', '. . . had a quarrel with his brother over some property and lost the case which did not improve his temper . . .'.

Reflection reveals that we often do not know a great deal about the past life even of people we know reasonably well; so that life-history information may not be particularly important at the level of everyday social exchange. Nevertheless, even at this level, we do feel more confident if our personality description is anchored to key events in the stimulus person's life-history. His present behaviour seems to be more comprehensible and we feel better able to forecast his future actions. At a professional or scientific level however, life-history data are usually necessary in any serious attempt to explain, predict or influence the person's behaviour.

E. Contemporary Situation (SITU)

The distinction between past and present becomes somewhat blurred when we consider the extent to which human beings can integrate their thoughts, feelings and desires over time. As we have seen, in situations like getting married or moving house, we are likely to think of ourselves as being in circumstances which persist over a period of time that is short relative to the life-history although long in absolute terms, i.e. when measured in hours or days. These sorts of temporary circumstances set up local conditions which profoundly affect a person's behaviour—they provide the actual situational context in terms of which his present behaviour is organized and directed. Long-range plans and *strategies* of adjustment can sometimes be inferred from recurrent patterns of life-history events; by contrast, local circumstances—the contemporary situation—may elicit *tactical* adjustments at variance with the person's preferred or characteristic reactions: see Chapter 9. Strategies of adjustment are not necessarily rational and deliberate but may be shaped by the individual's reinforcement history and influenced by psychodynamic processes of which he is not aware.

Thus, consideration of the contemporary situation (SITU) helps to show that part of the explanation of why a person behaves as he does must deal with the *present circumstances* which surround him. But we are doing no more than echoing modern behaviourism here, in arguing that actions are shaped by reinforcement contingencies (though, naturally, this is not the whole story) and that a knowledge of the stimulus situation is needed to understand on-going behaviour.

Statements classified as Contemporary Situation (SITU) can be thought of in terms of the constraints and opportunities in the stimulus person's present circumstances; they encompass any physical, social or psychological aspect of his surroundings in so far as it endures long enough and is relevant to understanding his behaviour. Consider the following examples: '... his parents are in business and work long hours ...', '... he works with people younger than himself ...', '... he is constantly being shouted at by his mother ..'. These phrases describe the circumstances affecting the stimulus person's actions. It so happens that these examples describe constraints (or limitations) on behaviour rather than opportunities, and in this respect they are akin to the so-called EFUs or 'environmental force units' conceptualized by Schoggen in Barker (1963).

We usually think of ourselves as active agents, i.e. as having to some extent at least the attributes of autonomy, self-control and intentionality. In a trivial sense, we are active agents in so far as we 'behave' at all, i.e. 'act' as opposed to being 'acted upon' or physically moved. In virtue of a range of inborn and acquired characteristics, human beings are predisposed to act in similar ways in certain situations. Some of these behavioural predispositions are strong and universal, so that the circumstances which elicit the reactions then seem to be 'compelling'.

The notion of universal 'core characteristics' in personality is discussed by Maddi (1972): see also Chapter 9. Consider, for example, common reactions to conflict, frustration, novelty and social norms. In explaining such reactions, we take the internal predisposing factor for granted—as a feature common to all or most people (or to the 'sorts' of people we are talking about)—and search for a relevant external circumstance as the factor which 'precipitates' or triggers the reactions.

One reason for employing statements about the contemporary situation in a personality description is to show that certain environmental conditions elicit (or inhibit) responses which the person is predisposed to make, i.e. they provide the opportunity (or constraint) for the exercise (or inhibition) of such responses. But SITU statements may also be introduced in order to show that the person was, as it were, *compelled by circumstances* to act against his natural inclination, e.g. giving information in response to threat, bribery or torture, being seduced by a more experienced person, or failing in an enterprise through physical exhaustion.

Another reason for employing SITU statements is to explain a change in the organization or direction of a person's behaviour. Human beings are partly the creators of, and partly subject to, their circumstances. Thus, statements about dispositions and abilities and other qualities 'within the person' supply only part of the information needed to understand why a person behaves as he does; hence the limited success of psychometric assessment in predicting actual behaviour. Attitudes, abilities and personal dispositions are normally thought of as relatively enduring psychological characteristics, giving a constant direction and a consistent pattern to the person's actions. But our behaviour may have to be accommodated to local conditions (SITU), and such accommodations call for tactical adjustment. The mnemonic expression: $P_i \times S_j \rightarrow B_{ij}$ states the argument concisely: a particular pattern of behaviour B_{ij} is produced by a particular person P_i in a particular situation S_j.

A situation has a subjective and an objective aspect. The subjective aspect is the construction placed upon it by the stimulus person; the objective aspect is the construction placed upon it by competent, disinterested investigators (which aims to be an account of what the situation really is compared with what the stimulus person thinks it is). Statements about the contemporary situation (SITU) in personality descriptions are intended to provide an objective account, although naturally they suffer from a variety of defects associated with the inability or unwillingness of informants to provide a truly objective and comprehensive statement of the relevant facts (The stimulus person is sometimes the observer's only informant on this matter). When the stimulus person understands his situation correctly and acts accordingly there is no particular problem. However, when the stimulus person misconstrues the circumstances he is in, his actions will be misdirected and inappropriate. This sort of mismatch—between what the person thinks is the case and what it really is—often leads to failures and inadequacies in adjustment and to consequent feelings of anger, anxiety, self-reproach or, more rarely, to relief or amusement. In personality descriptions, we often find statements, classified as Orientation and Feelings

(ORFE), which can be used to describe and explain the stimulus person's subjective views, especially when there is a serious mismatch between the stimulus person's objective Contemporary Situation (SITU) and his subjective Orientation and Feelings (ORFE).

The following examples of statements classified as SITU are taken at random from the main investigation: '... has recently become redundant ...', '... now that her family are grown ...', '... does not have time off very often ...', '... remains in a humdrum situation, the salary for which is quickly being overtaken ...', '... is fortunate in having parents who can support her financially ...'. Notice that in this last example the explicit evaluative term 'fortunate' and the implicit 'do' underlying the explicit 'can'. Further examples are: '... works in ... a glamour job ... although ... very hard and dangerous work ...', '... despite her own trouble ...', '... even when going through a period of stress in his personal life ...', '... his opportunities to be of service to others ...', '... he has returned home ...', '... has now had to retire from this dedicated work ...', '... often under pressure ...', '... despite this very tiresome and troublesome job ...', '... her husband does not earn much so has taken in two lodgers ...', '... this has meant a lot of study in his own time ...', '... has a happy family life ...', '... even a doctor's pay is stretched to keep six children, a wife and an elderly mother-in-law under the same roof ...', '... she had to come by bus six miles and so missed some evening entertainment ...', '... has left school but not working ...', '... with a wife out at work full-time ...', '... now expecting her first baby ...'.

Statements describing the situation a person is in (SITU) are a large and important feature of personality descriptions, and reinforce the belief that the study of 'persons in situations' is a proper focus for the psychology of personal adjustment.

F. Prospects (PROS)

Some actions and psychological processes are characterized by direction and intentionality. To use Allport's phraseology, they are 'future-oriented'. Normal people have plans for and expectations about the future, and their present actions are governed to some extent by the outcome these actions are designed to bring about; they are not only 'being' but also 'becoming': see Allport (1955). There are, no doubt, some instances in which direction and intentionality are lacking, for example in states of confusion or absent-mindedness, and other normal instances in which actions are geared to the immediate situation rather than to a more distant one. There are also various sorts of psychopathology and juvenilism which seem adversely to affect a person's capacity to deal with possible or future states of affairs and restrict him to actual here-and-now-situations, as with certain sorts of brain injury, psychopathy, and as with very young children. Finally, there are ultrastable or rigid patterns of personal adjustment which prevent or hinder the evolution of new forms of being: see Chapter 9. These issues, however, go beyond our immediate concern.

Statements categorized as Prospects (PROS) are infrequent in comparison with statements in other content categories. They usually refer to the stimulus person's future behaviour and its consequences or to his likely achievements or failures; but they may, of course, refer to any aspect of the person's future existence, e.g. his appearance, health, family, social relationships, abilities, including the environmental circumstances (situations) that he may have to deal with. They may also be stated conditionally, i.e. as possibilities or hypotheses.

The following examples of PROS statements are taken at random from the main investigation: '. . . most likely to be a national figure in the years ahead . . .', '. . . will make her mark in this new sphere of activity . . .', '. . . is expected to do well in his final exams . . .', '. . . should do well in the world . . .', '. . . as an adult will become a much nicer person . . .', '. . . if she has the backing of her parents, academically she should succeed . . .', '. . . a phase that will pass as she gets older . . .', '. . . in the hope of more reward later in life . . .', '. . . he is a very unhappy type and will always be so . . .', '. . . would be . . . different . . . if they had a family . . .', '. . . he will work hard . . .', '. . . if we were to ever meet we would get on very well indeed . . .', '. . . his health may not hold out at the pace he sets himself . . .', '. . . unless there is a very considerable change in outlook she will make a very poor wife and mother . . .', '. . . she will . . . enjoy life to the end . . .'.

Statements about prospects (PROS) therefore deal with possibilities and probabilities for the person's future, and with hypothetical or conditional states of affairs. Their relative infrequency suggests a general reluctance or inability on our part, as observers in daily life, to make predictions in the face of uncertain and complex conditions. Nevertheless, this 'facet' of personality is of the utmost importance in clinical psychology and social case-work.

G. Routine Activities (ROUT)

Systematic observation of a person in his normal surroundings, his 'habitat', shows that much of his behaviour can be described in terms of a relatively small number of recurring patterns, including his normal routines and his daily or other periodical activities. The most obvious of these is the sleeping–waking cycle. Associated with the typical sleep patterns are the routines of retiring to bed at night and getting up in the morning. During the day, the individual engages in a variety of routine activities, such as grooming, eating, working and moving from one place to another. Typical examples are: '. . . works from 9 to 5 . . .', '. . . walks to work each day . . .', '. . . plays golf at the weekend . . .', '. . . goes to town on Saturdays . . .', '. . . works most evenings . . .', '. . . has regular club activities . . .', '. . . works full-time . . .'; and in the passive sense: '. . . is visited weekly by her children . . .'.

Little or no consideration is given to such routine patterns of behaviour in traditional approaches to personality study, although there are strong grounds for supposing that they vary widely between individuals and that these differences are relevant to understanding personality. This problem—of conceptualizing the individual's 'ecological niche'—is not one that can be dealt with briefly, and we shall consider it in more detail in Chapter 9. Let us accept that human beings engage in a variety of routine activities, many of which are fairly universal, and so not relevant to describing the *individual* person. The individual person, however, may engage in routine activities or have habits which are either peculiar to him or characteristic of a relatively small number of people. In order to be informative, statements categorized as Routine Habits and Activities (ROUT) should refer to patterns of behaviour which are salient for the stimulus person, and/or useful in understanding him, or useful in distinguishing him from other people.

In personality descriptions written by children, hobbies and interests are frequently mentioned, and activities of this sort are included in the general category of Routine Habits and Activities (ROUT) in the content analysis of personality descriptions written by adults. Statements about routines seem to provide two sorts of information: first, direct information about behaviour itself—what the person actually does with his time; second, indirect, i.e. circumstantial, evidence about the person's dispositions, abilities, circumstances, and so on.

The following examples of ROUT statements are taken at random from the main investigation: '. . . motorist . . .', '. . . gardener . . .', '. . . strong interest in art, literature, and architecture . . .', '. . . goes to bed late . . .', '. . . probably drinks a little . . .', '. . . plays tennis . . .', '. . . takes a keen interest in Scouting . . .', '. . . he is interested in a variety of sports . . .', '. . . supports his Church . . .', '. . . drives a car . . .', '. . . she is engaged in uniformed voluntary Red Cross work . . .', '. . . thinks nothing of spending a Saturday morning on a cold winter's day standing on the side-lines of a football pitch as a linesman . . .', '. . . finds time to read . . .', '. . . has never smoked . . .', '. . . only within the last ten years has he started to drink . . .', '. . . nothing prevents his nights out or his golf . . .', '. . . has no particular interests . . .', '. . . goes nowhere and does nothing in her spare time . . .', '. . . does a lot of gardening . . .', '. . . reads detective stories . . .', '. . . does not drink or smoke . . .'.

It is obvious from these and other examples that statements about Routine Habits and Activities (ROUT) can vary a great deal in their psychological significance. Some do no more than fill out the personality description with a little more superficial detail, whereas others raise deeper issues about the person.

Statements about routines are closely associated with statements categorized as Motivation and Arousal (MOTA), which includes statements about likes and dislikes, preferences and aversions. One naturally assumes that a person's Routine Habits and Activities (ROUT) are motivated positively (or negatively), i.e., that he does them (or not) because he likes (or dislikes) doing them. Hence, we frequently find a ROUT statement co-ordinated with a MOTA statement, e.g. '. . . she loves driving . . .', '. . . likes his pint . . .', '. . . likes to be out of doors . . .', '. . . fond of music . . .', '. . . has an aversion to dogs . . .', '. . . likes to travel on buses . . .', '. . . always wanting to talk . . .'. Such statements presuppose, unless otherwise stated, that the stimulus person acts accordingly. Statements about routines are also associated with statements categorized as Abilities and Attainments (ABAT); obviously one cannot engage in habits and activities without the *ability* to do so, as in '. . . enjoys driving . . .', '. . . keen golfer . . .'.

Consideration of the way a person regularly relates the recurrent impulses and inhibitions arising in his motivational state to the recurrent constraints and opportunities presented by his environment constitutes an important aspect of the sort of personality study we are advocating, i.e. *the study of persons in situations.* However, not all behaviour is regular or recurrent in the sense of 'Routine'. Some actions are irregular and occasional, some are isolated events. It requires a major effort of abstraction and generalization to perceive the consistencies and regularities in a person's behaviour; and we must not confuse crude generalizations based on single instances with well-phrased and carefully qualified generalizations based on good empirical evidence. Irregular and isolated actions are not devoid of psychological significance; they can be studied as empirical phenomena for the light they throw on the characteristics and circumstances of the stimulus person. Naturally, investigators seek to place such apparently isolated actions in some kind of context by showing their similarity to or connection with other sorts of actions and circumstances, e.g. as in a driving accident, a quarrel or a suicide: consider the notion of 'similar facts' dealt with in Chapter 8.

A great deal of our behaviour is standardized, shaped by social prescriptions, so that some aspects of the person's regular and recurrent patterns of behaviour are not indicative of anything other than his social position and his general disposition to social compliance: he behaves as he is expected to behave. Thus, if we are interested in personal qualities which are masked by the social role, it may be necessary to pay closer attention to isolated or irregular and occasional events in the hope that we can catch the person unawares or 'off-guard', as it were, without the mask. It is a mistake, however, to suppose that insight into underlying characteristics will necessarily help us to predict the person's behaviour more effectively—this depends on the sorts of prediction we want to make. People generally do what is expected of them, so that knowledge of a person's social role (see the category SOPO) is an important aid in predicting his behaviour. It is also a mistake to suppose that the occasional or irregular action is somehow more revealing, in the psychological sense, than the regular or routine form of behaviour exhibited by the person. The occasional examples of selfishness, cowardice, stupidity, laziness, and so on, may be less impressive, on account of their infrequency, than the regular manifestations of co-operation, courage, intelligence and effort, even though these regular forms of behaviour are prescribed and sanctioned by the surrounding social arrangements.

Interests and hobbies form a sort of subdivision of ROUT; they are non-vocational pursuits: persistent forms of behaviour centred upon the exercise of a skill, as in gardening or playing bridge. They are more active and systematic than mere preferences, but range widely from embroidery to politics, for example. Statements about interests and hobbies stress the topic, activity or skill itself rather than the underlying motivation or ability. Among the more obvious examples are: '... home decorating ...', '... needlework ...', '... model making ...', '... sport ...', '... prison visiting ...'.

Statements about interests and hobbies figure prominently in children's self-descriptions—presumably because they are closely tied to intrinsic motivation and are highly valued. It is likely that interests and hobbies continue to reflect intrinsic motivation and personal values in adults (and so would be more frequently mentioned in self-descriptions), although the amount of time and effort that they can devote to them is usually much less than in childhood. Adult interests are possibly less personal and more social, i.e. less expressive and more conforming, and to this extent less revealing of inner personal qualities. The leisure-time activities of adults are normally studied in terms of social psychology, although they have a contribution to make to the study of personality.

H. Material Circumstances and Possessions (MATP)

Simple statements about possessions—toys, pets, and so on—are fairly prominent in children's descriptions of personality. Surprisingly, however, statements categorized as Material Circumstances and Possessions (MATP) are relatively infrequent in adults' descriptions: statements referring to property, tools and materials, and other personal effects are classified in this way. Thus, for example, '... pet dog, rabbit, etc. ...', '... an old sports car ...', '... house, garden, allotment ...', '... tools ...', '... wealthy ...', '... not very well off financially ...', '... has everything he needs ...', '... plenty of money ...'.

This category excludes statements about personal relationships, natural talents, qualifications and social responsibilities. The following examples of MATP statements are taken at random from the main investigation: '... her own house ...', '... spends a lot on improving his home and up-dating his car ...', '... the rather sporty car he drives ...', '... fantastic collection of jelly moulds ...', '... seems very well off, extremely comfortable home, runs a car ...', '... wealthy ...', '... well to do ...', '... not poor ...'.

The relevance of statements about Material Circumstances and Possessions (MATP) is that they constitute another aspect of the environmental circumstances within which the person lives his life and in relationship to which his behaviour must be understood. We might suppose that in a society like ours, with relatively wide differences in wealth and income, such statements would be fairly prevalent, and so they are when we are describing people whose economic status is different from that with which we are familiar; they are also fairly common in fictional studies of character. Normally, however, the people who are reasonably well-known to us, and about whom we have well-formed personality impressions, have a similar sort of socioeconomic status, and information about their wealth and income tends to fall into the background and get taken for granted. In the main investigation, therefore, the subjects were writing mainly about people like themselves—adults of slightly above average socioeconomic status—so the few statements about material circumstances and possessions (MATP) that occurred revealed little other than an occasional idiosyncrasy or materialistic outlook on the part of the stimulus person.

I. Actual Incidents (INCS)

An important feature of personality descriptions in daily life is that they are summaries. Not only are they very selective in their treatment of the topic (the stimulus person and his environment), but they are formulated as conclusions without being much concerned with the presentation of evidence or with the formulation of argument. Rather like a news report, a typical personality description presents a summary account of the facts as they are understood, with little reference to the sources (witnesses), evidence or inferential reasoning that provide the 'grounds' for the belief. In this respect, they differ from a scientific case-study: see Chapter 8.

Nevertheless, statements giving a direct report of things said or done by the stimulus person (or things not said or done) are occasionally found in ordinary, brief personality descriptions, for example: '... she asked where I lived ...', '... I once heard her defending an acquaintance ...', '... she came in late that night ...'. These sorts of statement rarely give details or the source and credibility of the informant, but they do provide empirical data or, more correctly, illustrative instances of events; they do not describe general facts, episodes or circumstances, but rather isolated items of information usually intended to illustrate a point in the personality description.

The following examples of statements categorized as Actual Incidents (INCS) are taken at random from the main investigation: '... on a walk we had to make our way through thick undergrowth and brambles which must have been painful on his bare legs, but he only once whimpered and then only briefly; soon he was sunny again ...', '... he was really looking forward to attending a cricket match ... just before he was due to leave home a phone call requested his attendance as a blood donor ... he immediately went to give his blood and missed the cricket match ...', '... she turned up at a (formal) wedding in "hot pants" ...', '... I once caught him with a wild water hen tied up with a bit of rope ...', '... she hardly smiled when I expressed my opinion about it ...'.

Our lives, as represented by statements categorized as Life-history (LIFE) and Routine Habits and Activities (ROUT), are composed of behavioural episodes, Actual Incidents (INCS), arising out of the interplay of our personal characteristics and the circumstances that surround us. Barker (1963) has developed an 'ecological' approach to the study of naturally occurring behaviour which attempts to catalogue episodes in the 'stream of behaviour'. Livesley and Bromley (1973, p. 243–53), however, have shown that the notion of 'units' of behaviour is problematical. The study of 'person' perception depends upon assumptions and findings in the study of 'behaviour' perception: see also Chapter 1.

In an ideal case-study, we would have access to all the incidents or episodes that make up the life of a stimulus person, or have access to a large and representative sample of them. In practice, we have no such access. At best, we have a very small set of observations of key incidents provided by credible and competent observers (perhaps corroborated by the stimulus person himself or by circumstantial evidence). The nearest we come to these conditions is in dealing with biographical and autobiographical materials, and in a very detailed case-study. Characterization in novels shows what can be done with imaginary materials: see Chapter 10.

Representing the stimulus person literally as a catalogue or string of episodes is a cumbersome and unnecessary procedure. Raw data in any science have to be selected and interpreted. Even an historical narrative is selective, in that the events it reports are organized around some theme or interpretation favoured by the historian; and a map in geography does not set out every detail of the territory it represents. Similarly, in the study of personality, behavioural episodes are cited mainly as evidence relevant to some theory about or assessment of the stimulus person, and even a detailed biography or case-study actually cites rather few Actual Incidents (INCS). It is not surprising, therefore, that personality descriptions in ordinary life mention few or no actual incidents.

If we are looking for 'evidence' to illustrate our summary personality descriptions, we must refer to the incidents themselves: to the actual behaviour, circumstances and events making up the person's life. If we want to go beyond a 'mere description' of the person's behaviour to an 'explanation' or 'interpretation' of it, we must introduce inferential or theoretical principles into our account.

Thus the function of statements about Actual Incidents (INCS) in a personality description is usually to demonstrate or illustrate an assertion, and occasionally to present evidence (data) for analysis and interpretation. Often, such statements merely imply the assertion they illustrate (the assertion itself is taken for granted); they can refer to various facets of personality, Expressive Behaviour (EXPR), General Personality Traits (GENT), Life-history (LIFE), SP's Response to the Subject (SP–S), and so on, illustrating again that conceptual boundaries in the ordinary language of personality descriptions are very fluid— or 'fuzzy'.

CHAPTER 7

Lexical and Semantic Analysis: 'Social' and Other Aspects of Personality

I. Introduction

This chapter describes the 'social' facets of personality as revealed by a lexical and semantic analysis of ordinary language.

Using the method of content analysis described briefly in Chapter 4, twelve categories of information, referring mainly to social processes and relationships, were defined and grouped as follows:

Content Analysis Categories	Abbreviations
Social Relationships:	
Social position	SOPO
Family and Kin	FAMK
Friendships and Loyalties	FRIL
Stimulus Person's Response to Others	SP–O
Others' Response to the Stimulus Person	O–SP
Comparison with Others	SPvO
Relationships with the Subject:	
Stimulus Person's Response to the Subject	SP–S
Subject's Response to the Stimulus Person	S–SP
Joint Action with the Subject	SP+S
Comparison with the Subject	SPvS
Evaluation and Residue:	
Evaluation	EVAL
Collateral or Irrelevant Information	COLL

They are defined, illustrated and discussed in Sections II, III and IV, subsections A to L.

II. Content Analysis Categories: Social Relationships

A. Social Position (SOPO)

Each person occupies a position in society. This position is defined by the set of roles that he occupies and the statuses that he has at a particular time. These roles and statuses are associated with his membership in a variety of social groups ranging from the small informal primary groups, family, friends, and so on, to the large formal secondary groups such as profession, political party, church. These social organizations give rise collectively to norms and prescriptions for behaviour which have the general effect of standardizing people's actions and co-ordinating them one with another, e.g. shopkeepers and customers, teachers and pupils and parents. There is no need to go into the social psychology of roles and statuses, since these are reasonably well understood and documented in the plentiful literature of social psychology.

In order for a statement in a personality description to reveal something about a person's Social Position (SOPO), it must mention fairly specific words or phrases like: 'teacher', 'housewife', 'secretary', 'shopkeeper', 'organist', 'TV organizer', 'gardener', 'member of the WVS', 'headmaster of the local primary school', 'friend of Mrs. Murphy', 'member of the most exclusive club', 'captain of the firm's football club'. Such items refer to social, occupational and domestic roles, voluntary and leisure-time roles, family and neighbourhood roles; they refer to one or more of the sets of social activities carried out by the stimulus person in relation to other people in the context of fairly well-established social expectations and prescriptions. These expectations and prescriptions are supported by a variety of incentives and sanctions, and by socialization processes stretching back to infancy which result in the internalization of rules and values governing social conduct, as experienced, for example, in feelings of obligation.

Knowledge of a person's social roles enables us to make inferences and predictions about him without knowing much or anything of his 'personality' (in the sense of his personal dispositions), since his roles direct and constrain his behaviour.

The status accorded to any particular role is a dual function of the importance assigned by people to that role and the esteem in which the person occupying it is held (in virtue of the effectiveness with which he appears to fulfil the obligations associated with the role). Status is therefore a measure of social evaluation—it is not something that can be assigned by an *individual* but is rather a product of the consensus between *people* as to how a person's social performance shall be regarded. Statements about status, therefore, are usually categorized as Other People's Response to the Stimulus Person (O–SP) and include statements about reputation. The concept of reputation is a surprisingly neglected one both in the study of personality and the study of social psychology; this important topic bridges these two areas and will be the subject of a separate publication.

Evaluative judgments of a general sort, not particularly associated with the performance of a social role, are classified as Evaluations (EVAL). For example, a phrase like 'conscientious worker', taken in its general sense, refers to the way the stimulus person goes about his business: fulfilling requirements and attending to detail. Phrases like 'highly respected worker' or 'not well thought of as a businessman' on the other hand, imply a kind of 'court of judgment' or 'reputation', in the sense that there is some consensus among a group of people regarding the esteem in which the stimulus person is held.

The following examples of SOPO statements are taken at random from the main investigation: '... a former sergeant-major ...', '... used to work at a children's hospital ...', '... headmaster ...', '... teacher ...', '... high up in the scientific world ... was the superior of a friend of mine ...', '... an assistant in a shop ...', '... a journalist ...', '... he is now senior tutor at a college ...', '... now works for a leading public service department in what might be termed a glamour job ...', '... an active union member ...', '... secretary of the works football team ...', '... a member of a prominent, politically known family ...', '... no gainful employment ...', '... was in a supervising capacity ...'.

Naturally, SOPO statements can refer to the past and may therefore have to be considered as possible life-history (LIFE) statements. Social position can also be the 'object' of ORFE and MOTA statements, as in 'keen to improve her position at work'. This further confirms the 'confusability' or 'unreliability' of content categories that are not well-defined and extensively (or even exhaustively) itemized.

A difficulty arises when the 'role activity' rather than the 'role title' is used in a statement, e.g. 'He teaches' rather than 'He is a teacher' or 'She runs the house and looks after her husband and children' rather than 'She is a housewife'. We have already seen that ordinary language is sometimes ambiguous and capable of expressing the same idea in different words, and that it has a number of characteristics such as ellipsis and metaphor which complicate the task of content analysis. As a general rule, one should assume that the particular word or phrase used in a personality description is designed to convey a particular meaning, and that different words and phrases have different meanings, e.g. that 'He teaches' does not mean exactly the same as 'He is a teacher'. However, if, on examination, one cannot usefully distinguish between two such items, and assign one to ROUT and the other to SOPO, then there is no alternative but to classify them under the same heading. Whether two such items are or are not regarded as equivalent, i.e. interchangeable, depends in part on associated contextual material. We have already dealt in Chapters 1 and 2 with the ways in which words and phrases in ordinary language are 'organized' by means of syntax and expressive or stylistic features.

B. Family and Kin (FAMK)
Statements about Family and Kin (FAMK) refer fairly straightforwardly to facts, and are not greatly informative unless they indicate that the stimulus person's family situation is unusual. Typical examples of FAMK statements

would be as follows: 'close to his family', 'has few relatives', 'has a sister', 'does not get on with his mother'. Statements like these refer to the specific ties that the stimulus person has, or had, with family and kin, and to his role within the immediate kinship network.

It is not unusual to find that a great many statements in a personality description make some kind of reference to the stimulus person's family and relatives, so it is sometimes difficult to distinguish between FAMK statements and statements in other categories, such as Life-history (LIFE) and Contemporary Situation (SITU): e.g. '... was brought up later by a favourite aunt ...', '... still lives with his mother ...'.

Statements about FAMK seem to fulfil two rather contrasting functions in ordinary descriptions of personality. One is similar to that of Identity and General Information (IDEN), in that it provides some sort of foundation or anchorage point for other sorts of information, e.g. 'has two children'. The other function is to draw attention to, or to explain special effects attributable to, an unusual family situation, e.g. 'her family seem to keep her in the background'. Although the implications of mundane FAMK statements may not be worked out explicitly in the personality description—or even by the recipient of the information—implications of one sort or another are conveyed, as shown, for example, by the raising of questions or the detecting of contradictions or omissions in the personality description.

The following examples of FAMK statements are taken at random from the main investigation: '... has two daughters ...', '... is the eldest of four children ...', '... has two very good parents ...', '... she has married sons and daughters ...', '... has three adopted children ...', '... young family of three children aged 2 to 8 years ...', '... her sister ...', '... having had two children of her own ...', '... had a very patient father ...', '... with no family ...', '... one of a large family ...', '... she is the youngest child in her family ...', '... her husband is a busy doctor ...', '... of a poor family herself ...', '... he has a good wife and a large family ...', '... his children are quite clever ...', '... his wife is still alive ...', '... her mother has had a lot of illnesses ...', '... has fathered ten children ...', '... he has no family—that is no children of his own ...'.

As in the lists of examples illustrating other content categories, there is sometimes doubt as to whether a statement belongs to a category or not. It should be pointed out that FAMK statements are essentially *factual* descriptions of kinship networks and family circumstances. Statements describing psychological relationships and interpersonal behaviour within the family are assigned to other categories, e.g. SP–O, O–SP, or illustrated in later subsections.

C. Friendships and Loyalties (FRIL)

The notion of friendship is basically that of a love relationship or attachment between persons: a relationship characterized by intimacy and favoured treatment. The notion of loyalty is similar in that it describes an essential feature of love and friendship, namely that of being true and faithful to, or firm in one's allegiance to, another person. Loyalty is regarded as a kind of quasi-legal bond which ties one person to another, presumably because of some reciprocal relationship of mutual advantage and obligation. The notion of friendship is not far removed from that of family and kin—not only may the former become the latter, but also the nature of the relationship is often similar in both. Friendships may substitute for family and kin in situations where family and kin are remote in a geographical or other sense; they also provide a mechanism for outbreeding and social mobility.

Although there are several important psychological and behavioural similarities between Family and Kin (FAMK) on the one hand and Friendships and Loyalties (FRIL) on the other, it is convenient, for the purposes of content analysis, to distinguish between them. Thus, FRIL statements refer to stable, close, personal relationships, to trust, support and mutuality, but in respect of non-family ties only. Such statements refer to the stimulus person's affection for and loyalty to individuals outside the family, e.g. 'He is friendly with . . .', '. . . no friends . . .', '. . . few friends . . .', '. . . looks after his colleagues . . .', '. . . enjoys the company (protection, support) of . . .'. We need to distinguish statements like these from statements which simply describe the Stimulus Person's Response to Others (SP–O) or Others' Response to the Stimulus Person (O–SP), including the person (writer) whose personality description is being analysed, i.e. SP–S and S–SP: see later. We also need to distinguish FRIL statements from statements like 'friendly' and 'makes friends easily' which are dispositional statements falling into the category GENT or SPET.

The following examples of FRIL statements are taken at random from the main investigation: '. . . her boy-friend . . .', '. . . hardly ever entertains friends . . .', '. . . he has very few close friends . . .', '. . . generous (to his family) and friends . . .', '. . . she is a friend of my younger daughter . . .', '. . . as far as I know she has no enemies . . .', '. . . now she is no longer friends with the . . . host . . .?', '. . . (able to discuss) . . . world problems with his friends . . .', '. . . she had made no close friends at school, or in her job . . .', '. . . a friend of my own son . . .', '. . . he has only one friend . . .'.

Friendships and loyalties naturally vary in number and intensity, and the above examples show that the number of friends a person has, i.e. whether he has many, few or no friends, is commonly thought to be an important fact about him. Specific friendships are cited and sometimes the nature of the relationship is described: 'genuine', 'close', 'extremely loyal'. Generally, the nature of friendship—loyalty, trust and so on—is taken for granted, but may be commented upon if there is something peculiar about it, '. . . her friends are wary of her . . .', or for the purposes of emphasis, '. . . generous . . . to his friends . . .', '. . . extremely loyal to her friends . . .'.

The negation of friendship and loyalty is referred to by the use of the word 'enemy' which is derived from the Old French *enemi* – Latin *inimicus* – *in*-, negative, *amicus*, a friend. An enemy is thus a person who hates or dislikes another and seeks to avoid him or to do him harm, and statements containing the word 'enemy' or 'enemies' are categorized under FRIL.

Some FRIL statements might be regarded as candidates for other content categories. For example, '. . . she cannot keep her friends . . .' has an element of ABAT or GENT in it, and '. . . she is no longer friends with the . . . host . . .', an element of SITU or LIFE. Other FRIL statements imply, indirectly, something about the stimulus person's capacity or disposition for making friends or about his life circumstances, e.g. '. . . a friend of many people . . .', '. . . never really made any close friends . . .', '. . . has made a lot of friends in a short while . . .'.

D. *Stimulus Person's Response to Others (SP–O)*

A large number of statements in ordinary personality descriptions make reference to the way the stimulus person behaves towards other people—the sorts of action he initiates and the ways in which he responds to the actions of others. This class of statements includes references to what the stimulus person thinks or feels about other people in general and in particular, i.e. his 'orientation' or attitude towards them. This facet of personality is illustrated by the following examples: 'He respects others', 'He likes people', 'He doesn't trust anyone', 'tells people', 'She succeeds in tying people in knots', 'She bullies people', 'She cannot see how difficult she makes it for her seniors', 'She is at ease with others', 'fond of people', 'tends to remain aloof (from others)'.

In the interests of developing a reasonably comprehensive and detailed system of content categories, we have distinguished between SP–O and some other, closely related, categories of information. For example, the complementary relationship, O–SP, dealt with in the next subsection, refers to Other People's Response to the Stimulus Person and includes statements about their attitudes towards and opinions about the stimulus person, as well as statements about the actions they initiate and the ways in which they respond to his actions. Similarly, the category SP + O refers to the Joint Interaction of the Stimulus Person and Others; however, statements of this type can usually be assigned to SP–O or O–SP and we shall not deal with them separately. We also note that with SP–O, as with a number of other categories, it is not always possible to be reasonably confident, much less absolutely sure, that a statement is not intended to convey overtones, i.e. subsidiary meanings, such as the dispositional (GENT) overtone in '. . . tends to remain aloof', or the evaluative (EVAL) overtone in 'She bullies people . . .'.

An appraisal of the Stimulus Person's Response to Others (SP–O) can be seen as complementing the appraisal of Other People's Response to the Stimulus Person (O–SP). At one time, it was maintained that personality could be defined objectively in terms of a person's 'social stimulus value', i.e. in terms of the effects that a person had on other people. While admitting that such a definition makes a contribution to understanding the concept of personality, we would not give it the importance that was claimed for it, even though it corresponds very closely with one of the meanings of the term 'personality' as it is used in the ordinary language of everyday life. For us, a person's 'social stimulus value', i.e. the effect he has on other people, is only *one* facet of our knowledge of him as a person and is described by statements in the content category O–SP. As we have seen, there are thirty such facets (or categories of information), and although some are larger and more revealing than others, there is no point in restricting the range of relevant data to just one of these categories, whether O–SP or GENT, otherwise we arrive at a grossly oversimplified concept of personality.

The importance we attach to a person's social adjustment is shown by the high frequency and wide variety of SP–O statements in ordinary personality descriptions. The following examples of SP–O statements are a few taken at random for the main investigation: '... expects to be supported by his family ...', '... lets his invalid mother bring him cups of tea ...', '... will only really accept criticism from those he knows very well ...', '... says that if people don't like her the way she is then that is their look-out ...', '... can take jokes about herself ...', '... those people ... often gained his respect ...', '... ready to help ... other people ...', '... he often feels, with no real justification, that people are taking advantage of him ...', '... after two minutes conversation, this fellow opens up ...', '... she cannot keep her friends and there are many quarrels with these ...', '... takes her children with her ...', '... starts off by liking people ...', '... accuses people of having no sense of humour ...', '... her husband was ground to dust by her ...', '... sincere in his endeavours to help other people ...', '... tries to see other people's point of view ...', '... does not like unfair criticism ...?', '... does not allow herself to be put upon ...', '... loves to see people and do things for and with them ...', '... she bridges the generation gap ...', '... sometimes she does ... try to manipulate people ...'.

Included in the general category of SP–O are statements describing the stimulus person's attitude towards various well-defined social groups: members of the opposite sex, people of a given age or generation, political groups, racial groups, religious bodies and so on. The following examples illustrate some of these: '... at ease with adults ...', '... lady-killer ...', '... enjoys friendships of boys his own age or adult men ...', '... she makes it difficult for seniors and juniors ...', '... great patience with children ...', '... ill-at-ease with men ...', '... no hesitation in making overtures to men ...', '... puts on an act with men ...'.

The problem of distinguishing between one category of statement and another, to which we have already referred, can be illustrated by reference to the following borderline instances. For example, in the phrase '... the antipathy he obviously engenders in most people who come across him ...', it is not clear whether the emphasis is on the stimulus person as agent (SP–O) or on other people's response to the stimulus person as such (O–SP). It might be that the antipathy is misconceived and misdirected; or it might be that the use of the word 'antipathy' is an indirect way of referring to the stimulus person's actual behaviour. In other instances, Motivation and Arousal (MOTA) would be an obvious alternative to SP–O, for example, '... whilst wanting everybody to be happy, she was not prepared to put herself out for any individual ...', '... she loves to give little presents to people ...', '... she loves her sister ...', '... likes social life ...'.

As we pointed out, in dealing with Family and Kin (FAMK), we have chosen to classify statements about the psychological and behavioural aspects of family relationships in SP–O or O–SP rather than in FAMK, on the grounds that such statements usually have implications beyond social relationships, i.e. have a more general significance, e.g. '. . . reviles his parents . . .', '. . . concerned for his elderly father . . .', '. . . disregard for his mother's wishes . . .', '. . . has taken her younger brother and sister to live with her . . . looks after them . . . tries to guide them . . . feeds them well . . .', '. . . honours his parents . . . shows allegiance to his family . . .'.

Another class of statements confusable with SP–O is that of General Personality Trait (GENT), e.g. '. . . insensitiveness to his opportunities to be of service to others . . .', '. . . always willing to help . . .', '. . . extremely anxious to be liked by everyone . . .'. The question to be resolved is whether the emphasis is on the social behaviour itself or on the underlying personal disposition. Similarly, Specific Habits and Reactions (SPET) are confusable with SP–O as in the following examples: '. . . impatient with his family . . .', '. . . enjoys spreading gossip . . .', '. . . enjoys it when she gets annoyed with her husband . . .'. Occasionally, other classes of statement present themselves as an alternative to SP–O, as may be seen by perusing the short lists of examples for categories like LIFE, PRIN, EVAL and FRIL.

There is therefore a sort of residual, perhaps irreducible, element of arbitrariness in the content analysis of personality descriptions. But we must emphasize that vagueness and complexity should not be dismissed as unimportant or inconvenient technical issues on the one hand, or as reasons for rejecting content analysis completely on the other; but, rather, they should be used to clarify and sharpen our concepts wherever they can be successfully disambiguated and, where they cannot, they should be used to demonstrate the nature, scope and limitations of the language of personality description.

A person's reaction to other people often entails some appreciation of their point of view and intentions. This is particularly important when the stimulus person himself is the focus of other people's attention; for then he needs to form what is called a 'meta-impression', i.e. an impression of what other people think of him. Failure to form such meta-impressions may well contribute to social blunders and other deviations in conduct. Chronic inability to form meta-impressions may underlie defective socialization.

E. Others' Response to the Stimulus Person (O–SP)
The effects a person has on other people are revealed, obviously, in their actions and reactions, and in the statements they make about him. They are particularly important in the professional (clinical and social) aspects of personality study (as contrasted with the psychometric and laboratory aspects) because the reactions of other people provide much of the evidence relevant to any theory we have or assessment we make about the stimulus person, e.g. in relation to vocational guidance, marital counselling or rehabilitation. They are also important, of course, in forming our ordinary impressions of people in daily life.

In personality descriptions, the contents of Other People's Response to the Stimulus Person (O–SP) comprise statements about what actions other people initiate, and how they react, towards the stimulus person, what they think and feel about him, their intentions towards him, and so on, for example: '. . . people respect him . . .', '. . . they think the world of her . . .', '. . . people try to avoid her . . .', '. . . he makes us feel small . . .', '. . . she makes everyone feel happy . . .'.

The category O–SP is not quite as simple as it appears at first glance because it comprises not only statements about the behaviour, beliefs, attitudes, and so on, of other individuals in relation to the stimulus person, but also statements about the way people in general, or specific groups of people, behave towards the stimulus person. Where there is considerable agreement between people, this is referred to as 'consensus' or 'reputation'; we usually assume that our judgments of a stimulus person are widely shared among the people with whom we associate. Indeed, we often derive our views from such association without direct acquaintance with the stimulus person; we feel uncomfortable if we discover that our impression of the stimulus person differs from that of our associates, and we usually take steps to remedy that discrepancy either by modifying our own views or by persuading others to change their views; this reminds us of the self/other comparisons described in Chapter 1.

The concept of reputation, defined as what is generally said or thought about a person, is not as simple as its dictionary definition suggests. But for our immediate purpose—that of assimilating reputation statements to the category O–SP—all we need say is that they include words and phrases indicating how widely known the stimulus person is, whether he is well thought of or not, and statements about the specific aspects of the stimulus person's existence that are agreed on by all or most people, as follows: '. . . people say . . .', '. . . people think . . .', '. . . they say . . .', '. . . he is reputed . . .', '. . . it is widely known that . . .', '. . . not well known . . .', '. . . popular . . .', '. . . well thought of . . .', '. . . generally regarded . . .'.

Like its counterpart category SP–O, the O–SP category is extensive and varied and thus reflects the importance we attach to a person's social adjustment. The following examples of O–SP statements are a few taken at random from the main investigation: '. . . antipathy he obviously engenders in most people who come across him . . .', '. . . those people who did not have the courage to resist his bullying ways . . .', '. . . the man who committed suicide because of her lies . . . or the many others who have suffered directly or indirectly . . .', '. . . disliked by nearly everybody . . .', '. . . snubbed or left out by older children . . .', '. . . one soon begins to see through his pretence . . .', '. . . she makes no impact . . .', '. . . she seems to have the attentions of her husband and another woman's husband . . .', '. . . a hypochondriac . . . a fact well known . . .', '. . . due to his parents . . . upbringing . . . the boy is . . . spoiled . . .', '. . . is indulged tremendously . . . many children come to play with him . . .', '. . . no pleasure to visit him . . .', '. . . children (will) get a lot out of life because of their mother's efforts . . .'.

Occasionally, statements categorizable as Joint Action with Others (SP + O) make assertions about activities or states of mind that the stimulus person shares with other people, i.e. joint actions requiring the use of statements like 'they' or 'each other'. Where such statements seem to defy classification elsewhere, they may be dealt with by assigning them to either SP–O or O–SP, or by partitioning the statements and assigning one part to SP–O and the other part to O–SP, depending upon the sense of the statement. Thus: '... her mother accompanied her on the journey to Australia ...' (O–SP); '... she and her husband are very fond of each other ...' (part O–SP, part SP–O); '... they went to the Collegiate (school) together ...' (part O–SP, part SP–O); '... goes out for a drink with the lads ...' (SP–O). This procedure avoids the need for the logically possible but empirically infrequent category of SP + O statements.

As expected, some statements are ambiguous and cannot be assigned definitely to one category rather than another. The number of such ambiguities might also be reduced—we have suggested—by paying closer attention to contextual factors and style, and by establishing convenient, if arbitrary, lines of demarcation between categories by means of extended definitions, criteria for inclusion or exclusion, and definitive lists of items.

F. Comparison with Others (SPvO)

Some statements in personality descriptions make comparisons. For example, the writer may use himself as a standard of comparison, or use another actual person, e.g. '... his father ...', '... John ...', or some conventional yardstick, e.g. '... most people ...', '... her friends ...', '... typical ...', or a fictional or legendary person, e.g. '... Goneril ...'. Thus words and phrases like '... bigger than most ...', '... brighter than John ...', '... a typical boy ...', '... smarter than her friends ...', '... cruel in the way Goneril was cruel ...', '... was like his father ...', and so on, enable the subject to make judgments of characteristics for which there may be no absolute standard like there is for age and some kinds of achievement, or for which the stimulus person's relative standing is informative in an approximate way (or even more informative than an absolute judgment), e.g. '... smarter than her friends ...' rather than '... an IQ of 100 ...'.

Statements in the SPvO category include those which describe the extent to which the stimulus person conforms to (or deviates from) some sort of average or standard. They should contain an explicit or implicit reference to the actual yardstick. The stimulus person may be compared with the norms derived from social groups which are based on 'common knowledge' and expressed in terms familiar in ordinary language. In some instances, the reference to social norms and common knowledge is so remote from the subject's mind that he is not really aware of the comparative nature of the judgment he is making, and this illustrates the extent to which the language of personality descriptions is pervaded by unspoken assumptions and habits of thinking. For example, in the use of the word 'very' in '... very aggressive ...', '... very well brought up ...', the relevant standard of comparison is usually not specified and often quite obscure. Similarly, in the use of words like 'much', 'little', 'often', 'sometimes', in '... doesn't go out much ...', '... I find him a little irritating ...', '... he often gets depressed ...', and '... sometimes people tease him ...', the relevant standard of comparison is by no means clear, although we must admit that it is sufficiently well understood for such phrases to be accepted in ordinary discourse. The question of what the phrase means, the semantic question, only arises when we want to make explicit what is normally taken for granted, i.e. the linguistic and behavioural criteria which permit the formulation of such phrases and control the pattern of implications in which they are involved. These linguistic and behavioural criteria can be discovered by systematic interrogation, of the sort that is familiar in the cross-examination of witnesses in a court of law. For example, an informant who asserts, among other things, that '... she is very aggressive ...' can be asked to say what he means by this phrase. For example, what did the stimulus person do and say which led the subject to assert that '... she is aggressive ...'? What were the circumstances? Does the word 'very' imply intensity or frequency of aggression or both? In comparison with what standard does the subject judge the stimulus person to be 'frequently' or 'intensely' aggressive? It does not follow, of course, that an interrogation would elicit rational or informative replies. But such an outcome would only confirm how deeply embedded in the language of personality description our understanding of others is.

The following examples of SPvO statements are taken at random from the main investigation: '... can take jokes about herself with as much enjoyment as those who are aiming the joke ...', '... worries ... greater than lots of people are called upon to bear ...', '... he is a little older than my eldest son ...', '... (his) salary ... is quickly being overtaken by the men he superintends ...', '... a refreshing exception to so many young men today ...', '... it takes the form of standing back in a disparaging manner when his contemporaries are obviously enjoying every minute of what is happening ...', '... as far removed as possible to what his mother is ...', '... slightly reminds me of his father who is not quite as bad ...', '... tries to guide them as her mother would have done ...', '... more so than is seen in the average Englishman ...', '... he had not acquired the insolent arrogance which so many young people have today ...', '... in sporting matters he is well above the average ...', '... he lacks the arrogance of many young athletes ...', '... a real public school product ...', '... I have never met anyone so independent ...', '... honours his parents, which is not common today ...', '... one of the finest young women I know ...', '... the type who likes to ...', '... almost masculine ...', '... ladylike ...', '... a very modern young man ...', '... one of the modern set ...', '... not very feminine in some of her views ...'.

Close inspection of SPvO statements reveals that some of them contain an element of ethical evaluation (EVAL), as in '... no worse than some, better than others ...', '... a typically spoilt child ...'. We have already seen that the occurrence of evaluative statements in personality descriptions is common, and that it is difficult, perhaps even impossible, to eliminate evaluation. Indeed, we have argued that ethical evaluation is often an important facet of our impression of another person, and carries with it a variety of practical implications. In addition, we shall see that validating evaluative statements, i.e. demonstrating their 'objectivity', presents no problem in principle, since the procedural model for such validation is already well-established in jurisprudence: see Chapter 8. Social norms and ethical standards are social conventions, whatever else might be said about them, and therefore provide some of the grounds for the statements we make comparing one person with another.

Inspection of SPvO statements also reveals that the behaviour of an individual is influenced by the existence of models or standards of behaviour in others, as well as by the more subtle effects of social pressures and vicarious learning. The literature on modelling has tended to emphasize the positive (copying) effects of modelling, but it is likely that negative (contrasting) effects could be induced by comparisons with disliked other persons. Consider, for example: '. . . tries to be different from other people . . .', '. . . does the opposite of what is asked of him . . .', '. . . has learned from (that person's) mistakes . . .', '. . . tries not to be like his father . . .'.

Many comparisons are based on highly subjective standards and social stereotypes rather than on genuinely verifiable common knowledge. These imaginary standards make reference to vague collectives such as '. . . lots of people . . .', '. . . young men today . . .', '. . . what a young girl should be like . . .', '. . . persons I have ever met . . .', '. . . most women . . .', '. . . like all young ladies . . .'. The similarity between these stereotypes and those familiar to us from the psychological study of prejudice: '. . . Jews . . .', '. . . blacks . . .', '. . . bourgeois . . .', '. . . hippies . . .', needs no comment, except to say that the ideas underlying the former are probably more accessible to systematic interrogation, being less bound up with anxiety and aggression, or with social conformity.

Part of the problem of analysing the language of personality descriptions is that a statement is not, as it were, self-explanatory or self-sufficient. It has to be understood or interpreted within the framework provided by the language, the situation and the phenomena being referred to (since not all knowledge and experience can be formulated in words). As a result, an initial personality description in ordinary language is a kind of roughly drawn map, the quality of which depends on the writer's experience and intellectual resources. It can provide a starting point for an interrogation—or a self-examination—to elicit clarifications and further details, but it tends to remain a sketchy, incomplete account: see Mair (1970).

Why is it that we seem to manage so well in daily life with such scant information as that provided in one person's account of another person? There are two main reasons. First, much of our behaviour in daily life is closely regulated by social prescriptions, and since we usually know what is expected of a person we need only that information which indicates the likelihood of his *not* doing what is expected of him. Second, by definition, we share 'common knowledge' about the way people in general (and some people in particular) behave, and we share a common linguistic system for the communication of ideas about people, so that we do not need to be told the 'full story' about (or given a 'detailed map' of) the stimulus person. Once we have been given some information we can fill in much of the remainder because it is *implied* by the rules of linguistic usage and by common knowledge about the behaviour of people.

We note that SPvO statements may describe similarities and differences between the stimulus person and other people in respect of almost any kind of characteristic, such as physical appearance, life-history or expressive behaviour. Rather than classify them as PHYS, LIFE, EXPR and so on, however, it seems more useful to recognize their particular function in showing the standards of comparison commonly used in personality appraisals in everyday life.

III. Content Analysis Categories: Relationships with the Subject

G. Stimulus Person's Response to the Subject (SP–S)

The term 'subject' or 'informant' is used to refer to the writer of the sort of personality description we are referring to. An informant has direct acquaintance with the stimulus person he describes in his report, since he is asked to write about people he knows or has known reasonably well. It is therefore not surprising that informants often make statements about their own personal reactions to the stimulus person (S–SP) and about his reactions to them (SP–S). In addition, there are often statements expressing some kind of joint action or shared attribute (SP + S). We recall that a similar set of content categories exists in connection with statements pertaining to social adjustment, namely SP–O, O–SP and SP + O, although the last of these is redundant because statements in this category occur infrequently. Statements in the category Joint Action with the Subject (SP + S), however, occur sufficiently frequently to warrant its retention as a separate content category.

Statements in the category Stimulus Person's Response to the Subject (SP–S) are fairly straightforward. They include statements about the things said or done by the stimulus person which are directed towards the 'subject', i.e. the person who is writing the report; sometimes the statements refer to attributes or dispositions of the stimulus person which relate directly to the 'subject'.

The importance of SP–S statements does not arise because SP–S statements have any special merit as evidence for assessing the stimulus person, but because subjects are often inclined to present a personal (subjective) account rather than a shared (objective) account. They have easy and familiar access to their own experiences with regard to the stimulus person, and indeed their impression may never have been subjected to or influenced by comparisons with other people's impressions of the stimulus person. Thus one facet of the stimulus person reflects the impression formed of him by each informant (observer or subject). Consider the following examples: 'He has always treated me as an equal', 'He makes me feel uncomfortable', 'She is always pleasant with me', 'He dislikes me', 'She has been kind to me'. The second of these is a little ambiguous because it could be construed as meaning either 'He behaved in such a way as to make me feel uncomfortable' or 'I feel uncomfortable when I am with him' or both. The statement would be assigned to SP–S if the stimulus person is held responsible, or to S–SP if the subject holds himself responsible, for the discomfort. As with all statements, the test of equivalence (and therefore of categorization) is whether two or more phrases can substitute for one another.

The following SP–S statements were taken at random from the main investigation: '... when she has told someone, usually me ...', '... tries to take a rise out of me in public ...', '... he is kind to me ...', '... does not mind taking an old duck like me to dinner occasionally ...', '... she will always help me with advice, or if I am in a jam ...', '... he was in a position to enlarge and improve my outlook upon life ... he introduced me to a club and (persuaded) me to do a little social work ...', '... he was responsible for teaching me a great deal ...', '... he has never taught me ...', '... he even flirts (or tries to) with me ...', '... we have never heard from her ...', '... he knows I am a retired ...', '... she had long disliked me for succeeding to her husband's post ...', '... she refers to me as ...', '... she encourages me to ...', '... she agrees with everything I say ...', '... she would understand what I was trying to say ...'.

The word 'you' is sometimes used in place of 'I' or 'we', as in the last example, and possibly in '... she is under the impression that you are definitely below her ...'.

H. Subject's Response to the Stimulus Person (S–SP)

Statements describing the Subject's Response to the Stimulus Person (S–SP) are the counterpart of those dealt with in the previous subsection, i.e. category SP–S. They refer to those things said or done by the writer of the description in relation to the stimulus person, and to any attributes or dispositions of the 'subject' which relate directly to the stimulus person.

Again, the importance of S–SP statements does not arise because they have any *special* merit as evidence for assessing the stimulus person, but simply because they are regarded by ordinary people as relevant to the task of describing a person. Consider the following examples: 'I suppose I am jealous of him', 'I get exhausted by him', 'He worries me' or 'I am worried about him', 'I found her an attractive person', 'I have not discovered her lesser qualities', 'I disliked him'.

From the above examples, it will be seen that the use of the first person singular is, in some instances at least, a stylistic feature of the subject's description—in the sense that the same information could have been transmitted without reference to its subjective origin, e.g. 'He is exhausting', 'She is attractive'. Conversely, one could argue that many of the third person singular assertions in personality descriptions actually have a personal and subjective origin, and that the first person singular statement is intended to reveal or emphasize the subjective basis of the assertion: e.g. 'It seems to me that he respects others' rather than simply 'He respects others', or 'I trust him' rather than 'He is trustworthy'. Where the first person singular is an obvious stylistic feature—not signifying a truly personal reaction but rather one which the informant supposes is objective and about which there is some consensus—the statement has been categorized according to its main content or as O–SP.

The following S–SP statements are a few taken at random from many in the main investigation: '... I confided in her often ...', '... it is no pleasure to visit him ...', '... one gets the impression that ...?', '... I have been ... attracted to (her) for several years ...', '... I felt I wanted to help (him) ...', '... she attracts me physically ...', '... I do like her ...', '... (he) is not only disliked by myself

...', '... I was fortunate to spot his conniving ...', '... I have not seen him since ...', '... I know her in a work situation ...', '... it would be wrong to say that I dislike her ...', '... I have to ask her for money from time to time and it is like getting blood out of a stone ...', '... I am very surprised that anyone can live with her from choice ...', '... I should think she waters the milk ...', '... this is possibly why I dislike him so much ...', '... in my opinion ...', '... to some extent I can say I dislike her ... yet I am more sorry for her ... than actually disliking her ... for this I forgive her a lot ...?', '... (she) was known by me many years ago ...', '... I have not met her socially and wouldn't want to ...', '... sometimes I feel sorry for her ...', '... I have known this lady for a few years ...', '... was a colleague of mine until recently ...', '... I did not approve of all she did ...', '... I always found her to be someone with whom I could talk, I confided in her often ...', '... I often felt I wanted to physically comfort her ...', '... I am not in a position to say a lot about this person, although I have known her for three years ...', '... I know this person fairly well ...', '... I dislike the way he treats his wife in public ...', '... a friendship that I do not treasure ...', '... I greatly admire her for all the help she has given them ...', '... rolls her own cigarettes, which I find, for some obscure reason delightful in a woman ...', '... only rudeness would penetrate ...', '... I first met him about twelve years ago ...', '... this might just be an impression I have formed ...', '... I usually feel at ease in his company ...', '... makes one feel better for knowing her ...', '... I know I shall follow his life with interest ...', '... I would rather like to think ...', '... I first met (him) about eighteen months ago through my husband ...', '... I admire the way ... he ...', '... I work with this man ... and always take every opportunity to avoid his company ...', '... I have a great deal of respect for him ...', '... a few minutes of his company are more than enough (for me) ...', '... I have a downright dislike of her way of life ...', '... I was the victim on a number of occasions ...', '... I found the best treatment was to ignore her ...', '... I have no ill feeling towards her ...', '... (she) gave the impression of having ... no confidence in me ...?', '... (I) always left her feeling inadequate and at odds with the world ...', '... she receives my accolade as one of the finest young women I know ...?'.

The number and variety of statements categorized as Subject's Response to the Stimulus Person (S–SP) indicate that the subject's thoughts, feelings and desires about the relationship between himself and the stimulus person form a major facet of his impression of that person. In our brief review of the developmental psychology of person perception in Chapter 1 we saw that the young child's egocentrism exerts an important directing and limiting influence on the impressions he forms. Our present examination confirms that the adult's 'personal point of view' continues to be a major influence. The difference, of course, between the adult and the child, is that the adult is not 'bound' by his own personal point of view, he can accept that it might be mistaken and that it might be different from the impressions formed by others. Nor is his personal point of view affected only by the way the stimulus person's behaviour affects him; his personal view is also shaped by all sorts of evidence about the stimulus person's behaviour towards others, his circumstances, life-history and so on. Indeed, his overall impression often incorporates other people's impressions of the stimulus person.

The 'personal' aspects of the adult subject's overall impression of a stimulus person are often separated out by the subject, and this is reflected, in natural language, by the use of phrases like: '. . . my impression is . . .', '. . . in my opinion . . .', '. . . I see him as . . .', '. . . he appears to me . . .', and so on. In using such phrases, most subjects are clearly aware that their assessment is personal, subjective and tentative rather than neutral, comparable with others, objective and final; although no doubt, for some subjects, such phraseology is simply a manner of speaking, a habit.

Some of the phrases that fall into the S–SP category constitute a point of departure for the rest of the description—for example, phrases that tell one how long the subject has known the stimulus person, how they first met, what the nature of the relationship is and how it has changed or is expected to change. Such phraseology: '. . . she is a friend of my wife . . .', '. . . we grew up together . . .', '. . . I met her recently at work . . .', is similar to that found in testimonials which begin by stating the nature and duration of the referee's relationship to the applicant. It seems reasonable to suppose that statements of this kind are relatively irreducible and provide anchorage points for more important observational and inferential statements; in this respect, some of the S–SP statements function rather like IDEN and PHYS statements in that they serve to introduce the stimulus person, to identify him, and to provide a firm basis for the introduction of evidence and arguments relevant to the assessment of the stimulus person. The quasi-judicial character of S–SP statements is obvious—in a court, a witness called upon to testify about a person's character might be questioned as to the extent and nature of his acquaintance with that person; the witness's responses to such questions provide the court with indications of the witness's credibility, and therefore help them to assess his testimony. In a similar way, in daily life, we tend to accept or discount one person's assessment of another according to our knowledge of the nature and duration of their relationship. A young man's assessment of his fiancée, for example, would be interpreted rather differently from an assessment made by the girl's teacher or employer.

The last-mentioned point reminds us that even written personality impressions are often imbued with feeling—revealed by affect-laden words and phrases expressing, directly or indirectly, suspicion, sarcasm, like, dislike, fear, hostility, anxiety, hope and disappointment, as in the following examples: 'no pleasure', 'attracted to', 'feel sorry for', 'enjoy', 'detest', 'admire'. In fact, a substantial proportion of phrases express a personal evaluation, of a strongly positive or negative sort, or express ambivalence or uncertainty in vacillating between the two: '. . . I cannot say I dislike this person . . . but I cannot like him . . .', '. . . to some extent I can say I dislike her . . .'. Perhaps because of the public nature of the investigation, subjects did not disclose intimate details of their relationship with the stimulus person, but it was obvious that for some subjects at least there would have been no difficulty in supplying a host of further details. We have argued that written personality descriptions are considered, emotionally controlled, expressions of opinion as compared with spoken descriptions, and that the 'affective' content of statements is not part of our present interest. A content analysis of affect in spoken statements has been reported by Gottschalk and Gleser (1969).

Occasionally, informants make comparisons between the stimulus person and some other real or imagined person, e.g. '... if she were my daughter ...'. Such comparisons are normally categorized separately—under Comparisons with Others (SPvO) or Comparisons with the Subject (SPvS). Occasionally, however, a comparison seems to be an element in the personal relationship and to belong to the category S–SP.

The exploratory and inferential character of some statements is revealed by phraseology like: '... I am surprised that ...', '... leads me to believe ...', '... I wonder if ...', '... I suppose ...'. Such remarks usually preface a claim and an explicit inference. This problem is dealt with briefly in Chapter 2 in the sections dealing with the organization and syntax of personality descriptions.

Conspicuous by their absence were higher-order meta-perspective (recursive) statements, e.g. those describing the subject's impression of the stimulus person's impression of the subject's impression of the stimulus person. These would have been statements of the form, 'He thinks I think he thinks so and so', or 'I hope he thinks I want so and so' or 'I expect he feels I know so and so'. We saw that simple meta-perspective statements occurred in category S–SP, e.g. 'He thinks I think', etc. One is drawn to the conclusion that higher-order meta-perspective statements are very infrequent in the ordinary language of personality description, no matter what prominence is given to them in the study of interpersonal relationships: see Laing, Phillipson and Lee (1966). Indeed, meta-perspectives are so complicated, in comparison with simple direct perspectives (impressions), that one wonders what level of intelligence, experience and psychological insight is needed to sustain them. We note in passing that they are also rare in personality descriptions written by children and adolescents. Even probing (guiding) questions frequently failed to elicit meta-perspective statements in educationally subnormal children, see Bilsbury (in preparation), so that one is reminded of the limitations placed on socialization by this apparent inability to take the other person's viewpoint into account. The relatively late development of meta-perspectives implies, as we have suggested, that they are not basic to person perception and self/other comparisons, but rather derivative.

I. Joint Action with the Subject $(SP+S)$

Some statements in personality descriptions refer to activities, relationships, circumstances and the like which are mutual for the stimulus person and the subject (the person who writes the description). Thus, statements using the first person plural, or some equivalent construction, and referring to things shared between the stimulus person and the subject (to their interaction, their joint action, or a mutual action/reaction) would be categorized as Joint Action with the Subject (SP + S). This category excludes mutual comparisons, categorized as SPvS, and 'one-way' social relationships, categorized as SP–S or S–SP. Consider the following statements: '. . . we have dropped out of contact now . . .', '. . . we dislike each other . . .', '. . . he and I . . .', '. . . her friendship with me began . . .', '. . . a neighbour of mine for years . . .', '. . . a member of the same church . . .'.

As we saw in connection with categories SP–S and S–SP the subject's personal involvement with the stimulus person is a large and prominent feature of the subject's impression, and the categories SP + S and SPvS may provide additional information about this feature. However, some SP + S statements could be split into two components and apportioned equally to the categories SP–S and S–SP. For example, '. . . we have dropped out of contact (with each other) . . .' could be rephrased as '. . . he has dropped out of contact with me . . .' and '. . . I have dropped out of contact with him . . .', and each half assigned to SP–S and S–SP respectively. In some instances, it is difficult to decide whether a statement is mainly about the subject's relation with the stimulus person, or the stimulus person's relationship with the subject, or about both equally.

The following examples of SP + S statements are taken at random from the main investigation: '. . . we got to know each other quite well . . .', '. . . no real conflict between us . . .', '. . . we do not argue . . .', '. . . we can still enjoy a night at a club . . .', '. . . (we) diverge or even disagree . . . enough to preserve interest when we meet . . .', '. . . we are able to visit each other's house . . .', '. . . each of us has always confided in the other . . . although we meet so irregularly . . .', '. . . we have been friends since junior school . . .?', '. . . still manage to pick up our friendship where we left off . . .?', '. . . we have a number of topics of conversation . . .'.

Thus, like the category SP + O, which is a logically and grammatically possible type of statement but occurs too infrequently to be worth classifying separately from SP–O or O–SP, SP + S is a legitimate category, since statements of this kind occur a little more frequently; if necessary, however, they could be assimilated without difficulty to other categories. The only question is whether there is any particular psychological significance in such conjoint statements.

J. Comparison with the Subject (SPvS)
An important aspect of self-understanding and understanding others is the process whereby we make comparisons between ourselves and other people. Self/other comparisons are important throughout life, but are supposed to be particularly prominent during adolescence and middle age. It is likely that they are prominent whenever the individual finds himself in social transition and required to adopt new roles, to modify his values and perspectives, and to take on a fresh or modified identity, e.g. following bereavement, disablement, migration or change of occupation.

Statements categorized as Comparison with the Subject (SPvS) describe how the stimulus person compares with (or contrasts with) the person writing the description. If we were dealing with *self-descriptions*, the equivalent type of statement (SvSP) would describe how the subject *himself* compares or contrasts with another person. It is not easy to decide whether an SPvS (or SvSP) statement derives from the subject's egocentric point of view or whether it is simply pragmatic. In the latter case, the subject refers to himself as a convenient yard-stick against which the stimulus person can be measured, just as he may refer to the stimulus person as a yard-stick against which he can measure himself. We do not propose to examine the problem of egocentricity in any detail, but we must remember that it may affect the processes (and therefore the products) of person perception in adults; and in our review of the developmental psychology of person perception, see Chapter 1, we saw that the young child's egocentrism is an important feature of the growth of his understanding of other people and that it gives way, eventually, to a more 'objective' or 'socialized' kind of understanding.

Statements in category SPvS obviously overlap with statements to be found in self-descriptions, in the sense that they are bound to make some reference to the self (the subject) and therefore to appear somewhat 'self-centered' (egocentric). Consider the following examples: '. . . he is taller than I am . . .', '. . . I am not as clever as he is . . .', '. . . he is more ambitious, than I am . . .', '. . . she lives close to me . . .', '. . . she is similar to me . . .', '. . . she is different from me . . .', '. . . she is less aggressive than I am . . .', '. . . he is like me in some respects, different in others . . .'. Phraseology of this sort enables self/other comparisons to be made over practically the whole range of topics—appearance, circumstances, traits, social relationships and other content categories. This is one reason why we have chosen to group statements into conceptual categories like SPvS and SPvO— they bring out important aspects of personality descriptions that might be neglected if they were simply assimilated to these other categories. The disadvantage is that it makes the method of content analysis more difficult.

The following examples of SPvS statements are taken at random from the main investigation: '. . . his occupation is the same as mine . . .', '. . . we are both teachers . . .', '. . . engaged in . . . Red Cross work as I am myself . . .', '. . . we hold equal rank . . .', '. . . he has much longer service than myself . . .', '. . . he is leader of a group as I am myself . . .', '. . . she is not an old age pensioner as I am . . .', '. . . she did . . . some things I would not have the courage to do . . .', '. . . I feel that he and I are very alike in character . . .', '. . . he knows most of the people I know . . .', '. . . he cherishes moral values more than I do . . .', '. . . many of her interests are similar to my own . . .', '. . . humour of the same brand as my own . . .', '. . . we believe in the same sort of ideas . . .', '. . . she is considerably older than me . . .'.

Almost any facet of personality can be incorporated in one person's concept of the identity of another person and it is not difficult to see in SPvS statements, like those illustrated above, an attempt on the part of the subject to delineate and stabilize the identity of the other person, and in the process to delineate and stabilize his own identity.

As we saw in our discussion of self/other comparisons in the context of language development in childhood and adolescence, in Chapter 1, the process of forming impressions of and describing oneself and the process of forming impressions of and describing others seems to have a reciprocal influence. An awareness on the part of the subject, that the stimulus person has a certain characteristic, sensitizes him to the presence (or absence) of that sort of characteristic in himself, i.e. it helps him to become aware of features of his own personality, his circumstances and life history, and so on. Similarly, an awareness that he (the subject) has a certain characteristic, sensitizes him to the presence (or absence) of that sort of characteristic in other stimulus persons. In the process, the subject tends to acquire a better understanding of himself and others. In view of all this, it seems reasonable to suppose that self/other comparisons play an important part in person perception: they affect the development of the self-concept; they affect our impressions and descriptions of ourselves and others throughout the life span; they are relevant to the study of personal adjustment and social relationships; they are relevant to the philosophy of personality study, especially in its concern with personal identity, continuity of the self, and knowledge of other persons.

IV. Content Analysis Categories: Evaluation and Residual Information

K. Evaluation (EVAL)

The category Evaluation (EVAL) includes statements in personality descriptions which make a moral judgment about, or assess the 'worth' or 'merit' of, a person or personal characteristic. It includes statements which refer to socially desirable or undesirable physical attributes, behaviour or psychological characteristics, and statements which express a sort of blanket approval or disapproval— whether from the subject's personal point of view or from a more objective standpoint. Consider the following examples: '... lacks physical beauty ...', '... plain ...', '... ugly ...', '... nice ...', '... nasty ...', '... likeable ...', '... hateful ...', '... interesting ...', '... dull ...', '... attractive ...', '... unattractive ...', '... pleasant ...', '... unpleasant ...', '... ordinary ...', '... pleasing ...', '... lovely ...', '... good ...', '... rude ...', '... polite ...'. It has been said that such terms should describe an *external* social judgment rather than an *internal* disposition or personal characteristic; this was the distinction that Allport and Odbert claimed to make in their psycholexical study of trait-names: see Chapter 3. But we have questioned the feasibility of assigning a fixed and definite meaning to words and phrases, and have shown that the same word or phrase may often be used to refer either to a personal characteristic or to a social judgment, e.g.honest, nasty. One of the features of ordinary language is that we can relate one frame of reference or perspective to another, e.g. observational evidence and ethical evaluation, or psychological disposition and overt behaviour. All that is required are the rules, criteria and procedures for establishing such relationships. That these rules are sometimes obscure and questionable and subject to continual revision is another way of saying that language is a form of life and evolves.

From a commonsense point of view, the ordinary behaviour of everyday life is explained, in part, by reference to dispositions, such as traits, motives, values, and so on, *within* the person. Through the process known as 'socialization' the individual's behaviour is shaped and regulated to fit the prescriptions of the society in which he lives. But it is not just his behaviour that is affected; it is rather his whole character—the internal system of motives, dispositions, beliefs and values underlying conduct—that is shaped and regulated by society. His conformity to or deviation from these prescriptions provides the basic data for social and ethical evaluations.

In the early decades of the twentieth century, moral qualities were regarded as important behavioural dispositions in respect of which individuals might differ. The classical investigation by Hartshorne, May and Shuttleworth (1930) used objective methods for the assessment of honesty, truthfulness, and so on, but concluded that personal morality was situation-specific, or 'field dependent', rather than a general disposition to behave ethically. This investigation has been the subject of controversy up to the present day. We mention it only to show some of the historical origins of personality study. Spranger's investigations into values, see Spranger (1928), also demonstrate the emphasis given to ethical characteristics in the early history of personality, and provided the basis for the Allport, Vernon and Lindzey (1960) psychometric method for the study of values. Other research work has been directed to the developmental aspects of morality: see Kohlberg (1973) for example.

Statements making Evaluations (EVAL) do not all fulfil the same sort of function. First, there are statements which pass a social judgment on the value or worth of the stimulus person, without being very specific as to which characteristics or actions warrant such praise or censure, e.g. '. . . nice . . .', '. . . rotten . . .', '. . . disreputable . . .', '. . . good . . .', '. . . bad . . .', '. . . incorruptible . . .'. Second, there are statements which select a specific feature or standard of performance of the stimulus person for blame or praise, e.g. '. . . loyal worker . . .', '. . . a nasty temper . . .', '. . . drinks too much . . .', '. . . a womanizer . . .', '. . . very good physical characteristics . . .', '. . . has wonderful understanding and compassion towards the really old . . .', '. . . a very good section leader . . .', '. . . cheats at cards . . .'. Third, there are statements which are non-evaluative in themselves but assign ethical principles (beliefs, values, standards, etc.) to the person, e.g. '. . . Christian . . .', '. . . honest . . .', '. . . reliable . . .'. Fourth, there are statements which express social desirability without implying praise or blame, e.g. '. . . good-looking . . .', '. . . fun to be with . . .', '. . . interesting . . .', '. . . dull . . .'.

Naturally, we expect evaluative statements to be mostly positive in descriptions of liked stimulus persons, and mostly negative in descriptions of disliked stimulus persons. We also expect outright evaluative statements to be difficult to distinguish from partially evaluative statements, especially those expressing social relationships and comparisons.

The following examples of evaluative statements are taken at random from the main investigation: '. . . sometimes unfairly outspoken . . .', '. . . entirely harmless . . .', '. . . (he) was a martinet . . .', '. . . almost likeable . . .', '. . . nice temperament . . .', '. . . very nice . . .', '. . . good appearance . . .?', '. . . good carriage . . .?', '. . . know-all . . .', '. . . clinically best described as a psychopath . . .', '. . . a nasty piece of work indeed . . .', '. . . too cocky . . .', '. . . interesting mind . . .', '. . . most interesting teacher ...', '... his behaviour is wholly intolerable ...', '... a very sound character indeed ...', '... a good husband ...', '... a Nosey Parker ...', '... a brittle person ...?', '... a false superiority ...', '... (I think) he was detestable ...?', '... quite untrustworthy ...', '... a rather nasty woman ...', '... one great virtue ... aimiability ...', '... rather a conventional person ...', '... she's a bigot ...', '... makes the most outrageous statements ...', '... pathetic ...', '... she has one of those faces that look spiteful and it seems ... a true reflection of her personality ...', '... there does not seem to be a trace of venom in his make-up ...', '... a fundamentalist ...', '... a very minor physical defect ... may have given him this twist of character ...', '... a very weakwilled man ...', '... he hasn't a nice personality ...', '... a horrible habit ...', '... no personality ...', '... makes her look hideous ... the perfume she uses is awful ...', '... lacking in manners ...', '... her moral integrity leaves much to be desired ...', '... attractive to look at ...', '... rather a cold fish ...', '... a most unpleasant man ...', '... innocent in his outlook ...', '... habit ... not in good taste ...', '... her conversations were hollow ... her opinions were superficial ...', '... growing up very naturally ...', '... well-balanced ...', '... nice temperament ...', '... is not too perfect ...', '... has human failings ...', '... great strength of will and of character ...', '... a wastrel ...', '... pleasant young lady ...', '... pleasant in her manners ...', '... he is either in one mood or the other and each one is equally loathsome ...', '... still very immature ...', '... she would make an unpleasant enemy ...', '... extremely rude ...', '... (she) was slightly warped ...'.

It might be possible to subdivide the category EVAL into four sections as described above: ethical evaluation of the person; ethical evaluation of a personal characteristic; statements about the stimulus person's character (social principles); statements about the stimulus person's social attractiveness—though statements of this last sort could be assimilated to the category O–SP.

The frequency and variety of evaluative statements are impressive, especially when we take into account the fact that many of the statements assigned to other content categories carry evaluative overtones. There is obviously no question of excluding evaluative statements from consideration on the ground that they have no part in the scientific study of personality—the ordinary language of personality description is pervaded with evaluative words and phrases. The problem is discussed further in Chapter 8.

The main danger in the use of evaluative statements in personality descriptions is that of not recognizing the difference between an evaluative perspective and an observational perspective. In essence, an observational perspective reports the things said or done by the stimulus person in given situations; though it may go further, in the sense of generalizing, summarizing and making inferences which can be checked by competent observers. An evaluative perspective, on the other hand, begins where the observational perspective ends, i.e. with the facts of observation; it examines these facts to see whether or to what extent they conform to a prescribed code of conduct and then judges them accordingly as good or bad. This account greatly oversimplifies matters, and is intended to describe what should happen in theory, rather than what actually happens in practice. In practice, as we have seen, observational and evaluative perspectives are often hopelessly confused; the existence of several different sorts of evaluation contributes to this confusion.

We must not omit to mention the tendency for evaluative statements to be heavily laden with affect. This has a number of consequences; for example, it leads to circumlocutions, euphemisms, sarcasm and metaphor, e.g. '. . . he hasn't a nice personality . . .', '. . . her moral integrity leaves much to be desired . . .', '. . . not the most engaging of people . . .', '. . . brittle . . .', '. . . wooden . . .'.

L. Collateral or Irrelevant Information (COLL)
When an issue comes before a court of law, rules of evidence are employed so as to exclude, as far as possible, all matters which are not relevant to the issue: see Chapter 8. Some of these rules have been introduced in the interests of fairness and justice, others in order to simplify matters and save the time of the court. Basically, the question of whether an item of information is or is not relevant to an issue is settled by asking whether the information makes any difference—does it add to the weight of evidence for or against the issue? If it does make a difference it is relevant; if not, not. As far as personality descriptions are concerned, therefore, the question is whether a statement contributes any information that makes a difference to understanding, or knowing about, the stimulus person. If it adds little or nothing then it is categorized as Collateral or Irrelevant Information (COLL). Collateral information is information which is connected with the main issue but is so remote from it as to have no immediate relevance.

Consider the following examples: '. . . I knew her husband for many years . . .', '. . . I blame her parents . . .', '. . . most boys go through a phase which aggravates me . . .', '. . . if I don't like a person I don't go out of my way to get to know them . . .', '. . . no one knows why his friend puts up with him . . .'. It could be argued that if these sorts of statements were deleted from a personality description it would make no difference to the impression; that is, it would not affect the meaning of the description. There are of course, some borderline statements, e.g. '. . . her parents are very nice . . .'. And in most instances it is necessary to examine the context before deciding that a statement is or is not irrelevant or merely collateral.

As a consequence of the method of collecting the data in the main investigation, some subjects wrote statements in their personality descriptions which were actually comments or 'asides' on the exercise itself, e.g. '. . . I find this most difficult . . .', '. . . there are several women in this category . . .'. They occasionally included explanatory comments—such as occur in casual conversations—intended to help the reader (or listener) to assimilate the information, e.g. '. . . the occasions were in connection with some social events being organized for a local charity . . .', '. . . her parents are friends of mine . . .', '. . . whether they have any effect is a different matter . . .'. Statements like these add little or nothing to the personality description and so can be ignored as far as our inquiries are concerned. But this is not to say that collateral and irrelevant statements have no psychological significance whatsoever—they reveal further aspects of the respondent's beliefs, attitudes and values. Systematic study would probably show individual differences in their frequency of occurrence, and very likely an increase with age in adult life—in keeping with the older adults' reduced capacity for ignoring and excluding irrelevant information.

Chapter 8

The Psychological Case-study

I. Introduction to the Quasi-judicial Method

A psychological 'case-study' is a scientific account, in ordinary language, of an individual person in normal or problematical circumstances. These circumstances form a substantial episode (or group of related episodes) in that person's life. A psychological 'life-history', by contrast, is a comprehensive account of the person's tendencies and characteristics revealed through an analysis of the principal episodes making up that person's life, i.e. the formative, critical or culminant episodes, together with the causal analyses (explanations, interpretations) which make that pattern of episodes significant. A case-study usually deals with a problem of adjustment during a relatively short and self-contained segment of an individual's life, although the case-report may contain some life-history information as context. A case-study may also deal with a relatively stable and enduring 'life style' if the person has adapted to his environment: see Chapter 9.

A person's life consists of a series of psychobehavioural episodes set in a matrix of surrounding circumstances. The circumstances can be analysed at various levels of abstraction: at the most concrete level are 'behaviour settings'—see Barker (1963); but a particular setting is only one of a number in the overall behavioural context—the 'total situation'. The psychobehavioural episodes themselves can be analysed, or sorted and grouped, in various ways and at different levels of abstraction; they can be represented in ordinary language by a behaviour narrative, which gives an orderly account of a sequence of behaviour. The simplest narrative is a running commentary on the individual's behaviour as it occurs: see Livesley and Bromley (1973, pp. 241–63); it gives a relatively unselected and objective record of observations. Such 'behaviour specimen' records, see Barker (1963), are usually obtained for special purposes, such as psychological research, criminal investigations, time and motion studies, and so on; they are mentioned here only in order to show the lower limits of empirical evidence in case-studies and life-histories.

Close inspection at the 'molecular level' of psychobehavioural events reveals a fine structure which can be further resolved only by resort to the techniques and language of physiology. At a more macroscopic level, however, larger segments and structures exist, as actions, traits, relationships, and so on. A case-study deals with psychobehavioural processes and environmental circumstances on a relatively large scale, so that it is obliged to take many of the small-scale functions for granted. The level of analysis is relative, however, because from, say, a life-history point of view or a sociological point of view, case-study details appear to be small, and vice versa.

Another sort of basic empirical evidence in case-studies is provided by the products, traces and consequences of the individual's behaviour: material artifacts, financial accounts, personal documents, domestic arrangements, the reactions of other people, and so on. These may have particular value as unobtrusive measures of personality and adjustment: see Webb et al. (1966).

A case-study is essentially a *reconstruction* and *interpretation*, based on the best evidence available, of part of the story of a person's life. It is a reconstruction because the events it deals with are in the past and are known only partially and for the most part indirectly; it is a reconstruction in the same sense that the story of a crime is a reconstruction from the evidence adduced and the arguments presented at a trial. It is an interpretation because the particular causal connections said to hold between one event and another are conjectural and could be otherwise.

A psychological case-study therefore presupposes that the psychobehavioural episodes associated with the person under investigation can be reconstructed from the available evidence in sufficient detail for a reasonable explanation about them to be formulated. A case-study gives an account of how and why a person behaved as he did at that time in those circumstances. Since we do not have 'privileged access' to the thoughts, feelings and desires of the person concerned, we must ascertain them as best we can from the person's disclosures, from direct observation of his demeanour and actions, and from other relevant evidence. The empirical content of a case-study, the evidence, includes observational reports by witnesses of things said and done by the person, of things left unsaid and undone, and of his circumstances and his interactions with other people. The person himself, through his own testimony, is a particularly important witness, for he can provide evidence and leads that other observers cannot provide, e.g. reports about subjective states, and actions not observed by others.

Empirical evidence, in the form of facts and observations, must be distinguished from the interpretations that can be placed upon that evidence: the facts of observation do not speak for themselves, but have to be spoken for. Moreover, they can be used to tell different stories, depending upon how they are selected, arranged and interpreted. A structure or pattern of meaning can be imposed on evidence by putting it in the form of an argument. This argument need not be of the formal, syllogistic variety, and is usually informal and to a large extent implicit and incomplete. The overall argument which organizes the case-study should consist of a network of arguments each of which cites evidence, proposes an inference, reaches a conclusion and makes reservations: see later. In a well-constructed case-study, therefore, good empirical evidence is organized and presented by means of a cogent, rational argument so as to provide a scientific (if partial) account of the person and his circumstances. The use of rational and empirical methods makes it possible to test explanatory hypotheses against the facts of observation.

It is important to assess the relevance of evidence: evidence is relevant only if it makes a difference to the argument and has a bearing on the main issues. The degree of credibility of a source of evidence must be taken into account in assessing its worth, as in a court of law. The rules of evidence in the preparation of a psychological case-study are analogous to those in jurisprudence, which provide a model for comparison.

A case-study is not exhaustive in its description and interpretation of the evidence. It is, rather, selective, in the sense that some issues and facts are regarded as more important, more interesting or more relevant than others. This selectivity is determined more or less at the outset, when the problem is formulated, by the aims of the exercise; these provide the case-study with an initial focus and direction of inquiry. Like a trial in a court of law, a case-study is centred on the 'facts at issue'; its purpose is to conduct an inquiry, following acceptable procedures, so as to settle the matters in dispute. Issues are assertions or hypotheses about the person under investigation which are required to be settled one way or the other by reference to empirical evidence and rational argument. The findings may provide a basis for guidance, treatment or other action.

The issues in psychological case-studies range widely over many different topics. For example, they may be connected with scholastic or occupational failures, with marital problems and other problems of interpersonal adjustment, with physical and psychological maladjustment, or, by contrast, with personal success and achievement. More concretely: one might prepare a case-study in order to help a Juvenile Court reach a decision about a delinquent boy; one might study a politician in relation to some political matter, or a scientist in relation to a scientific discovery, or a soldier in relation to a battle. The focus of the inquiry is on the person and his circumstances. The main point is that the inquiry is organized around one or a small number of issues, which restricts its scope and determines the relevance of the evidence and arguments.

There is no standard format appropriate for *all* case-studies, and lack of space forbids the presentation of specimen cases. We shall examine the quasi-judicial case-study method closely in order to see what is required in the way of *ideal standards* of rational and empirical inquiry in the study of individual cases; this may help to rehabilitate a sadly neglected scientific method.

The 'uniqueness' of the individual can be handled by showing that the diverse particular facts about him can be grouped, classified, measured or otherwise investigated in a scientifically methodical way. Different individuals can be described, and compared and contrasted without loss of identity, in terms of a common conceptual and empirical framework, i.e. in terms of the psychological case-study and its associated 'case-law' (which may exist, however, only in rudimentary form).

It is impossible for a case-study, or even a life-history, to tell the 'whole story', for the simple reason that the whole story is infinitely detailed. But it is possible to tell the story in such a way that the addition of further information makes little or no difference to understanding the main structure of the events under consideration and their causal relationships. A case-study, therefore, is really a theory about how and why a person behaved as he did in a given situation; this theory has to be tested by collecting evidence and formulating arguments relevant to the claims put forward in the theory. Such an inquiry will be inadequate and biased unless a scientifically acceptable procedure is used. This procedure will be referred to as the 'quasi-judicial' method. It is based on methods evolved in law for ascertaining the truth and conducting fair trials; it has been adapted as a scientific method with particular reference to the preparation of case-studies in clinical psychology, social case-work, and other sorts of professional reporting on people. The quasi-judicial method requires, among other things: that the main issues be stated clearly at the outset, that sufficient empirical data be available to support or refute claims, that evidence be admissible and relevant to those claims, that arguments be relevant and rational, and that conclusions which have important practical implications be supported by a greater weight of evidence than conclusions of lesser importance.

A life-history is a systematic and integrated account of the major episodes or adjustments in a person's life. Each major episode could become the focus for a separate case-study—as a major incident in an historical biography can become the focus of a more detailed investigation. It is obvious, however, that if the major episodes in the person's life are not adequately investigated or reported, then the life-story as a whole will give a poor scientific account of the person (no matter how good it is as a fictional representation!). Conversely, if for any reason the main outline of the life-history is wrong, it may be difficult to construct a valid case-study with regard to one of its major episodes.

A life-history is, however, more than the sum of its parts, since examination of the relationships between different episodes may reveal aspects of character and environment not discernible in episodes looked at in isolation. Thus one may see consistency or design running through a series of episodes, rather like one sees a trait expressed in a person's consistent reactions to different situations. Many events in the life of a person have systematic historical and functional connections, in the sense that what a person becomes in the future depends upon what he is now, which in turn depends upon what he was in the past. Thus it may be possible to explain the natural history of a psychological disorder or a delinquent career, or to explain why a marriage failed, or why a scientist or writer was able to make a success of his work: the literature of psychoanalysis, as well as biography and autobiography, provides ample illustrations. We have already made the point that consistency and regularity in human behaviour is not so much an empirical fact as a conceptual presupposition: we *assume* that human behaviour is orderly and meaningful, we can accept *apparent* inconsistencies but not *real* ones. Unfortunately, it is easier to make retrospective inferences about why life-history events took the course they did than to make useful predictions about future behaviour. Psychobiographical analysis is an important but relatively neglected area of personality study: see Munter (1975) and Bannister (1975).

A life-history has a further advantage: it enables us to collect a host of small pieces of information about the person. Any one of these taken by itself may signify very little, but many of them taken together may signify much, e.g. social contacts, expenditure patterns, leisure activities. The piecing together of many small fragments of evidence may be necessary and informative in case-studies which are not amenable to normal methods of investigation. Detective work, espionage, some kinds of journalism, and some kinds of biographical work, call for the patient sifting of evidence and the ability to see connections and implications.

Although a case-study usually needs to be put into the sort of historical perspective or context provided by life-history data, the amount of background information needed depends upon the facts at issue and the nature of the investigation. Evidence which is 'merely collateral' is omitted in order to save time and effort, and to avoid clouding the main issues. On the other hand, if evidence directly relevant to the main issues is insufficient, it may be necessary to use circumstantial and indirect evidence. A particular danger is the tendency to give undue weight to facts which are similar to the facts at issue but only remotely connected with them, e.g. in case-studies dealing with neuroses, crimes and occupational failures. The prior existence of facts about the person similar to the facts at issue may lead one to suppose that similar causes are at work, but proof requires evidence that is more directly connected with the facts at issue. For example, the fact that P_1 has made P_2, P_3 and P_4 unhappy does not *prove* that he has made P_5 unhappy, although it may create that suspicion; the assertion should be validated *independently* of previous 'similar facts'. In some cases, however, the similarities go beyond mere coincidence to indicate design, disposition or consistency, i.e. they indicate that responsibility should be attributed to the person and not to chance or to circumstances.

A common reason for preparing a case-study is to provide information on which practical advice and decisions can be based, as in vocational guidance and selection, marriage guidance, and other sorts of psychological counselling. Such advice and decision-making is, however, sometimes based on insufficient grounds: partly through lack of resources, partly through lack of suitable concepts and methods. The most obvious way to investigate the validity of important decisions about the management of individual cases is to examine the evidence and arguments on which they are based, i.e. to ask searching questions about the reasons for the decisions.

We are not concerned in this discussion with the kinds of decision that can be arrived at by actuarial methods: see Sines (1966). It is well known that, where basic information from case-records is available on, say, life-history or test performance for a sizable sample of people, it can be unitized or quantified, and a relatively simple actuarial formula may be used to arrive at a decision or prediction about a particular person, as in the prediction of academic success, performance on a clinical training course, delinquency, longevity, psychiatric breakdown, or the formation of friendships. The 'quasi-judicial' method has an affinity with the 'natural history' approach in science. The use of the term 'clinical' has been deliberately curtailed in this discussion because of its 'bedside' connotations; the 'quasi-judicial' method studies the person in a much wider 'ecological' sense. This method has little in common with the so-called actuarial (or statistical) approach. The major difference between them is that the actuarial method is quantitative and 'atheoretical' and concerned only with finding the formula which best predicts a particular outcome for subjects on average, whereas the quasi-judicial method is largely non-quantitative and concerned with reaching conclusions about individual cases (often in the absence of any quantifiable data or adequate standards of comparison) in relation to a theory about particular facts.

Decisions reached by means of the quasi-judicial method are not mechanical, i.e. they are not the outcome of a clerical and computational routine. However, they can be adapted to the practical consequences associated with alternative decisions: the problem is to use the risks of error to determine what strength of evidence is required to sustain a verdict. In a murder case, for example, the consequences of finding an innocent person guilty are regarded as worse than those of finding a guilty person innocent; therefore, the balance of evidence has to be adjusted so as to reduce the former risk. Reducing the former risk, however, increases the latter risk (a similar problem exists in statistical decision-making). The reasons for a decision about a case may very well include statements referring to social values, i.e. to the costs and benefits of alternative outcomes. Similarly, a medical diagnosis is supposed to be based on good evidence and an awareness of the risks of error; the treatment prescribed should take the associated costs and benefits into account. The importance of cost-benefit analysis in decision-making in psychological case-work is obvious when one considers the wide range of social and personal factors associated with, say, marriage guidance, planning for retirement, vocational guidance and selection, psychological counselling and behaviour modification, family therapy, middle-life readjustments, geriatric rehabilitation, delinquency management, vocational adjustment, and the use of leisure time.

Assessment and treatment, in social, medical or psychological settings, cannot always be carried on under ideal conditions; often there is a shortage of time and resources. Hence the attraction of short, objective methods of assessment which promise to provide adequate information quickly and cheaply in unfavourable circumstances. Unfortunately, it is often difficult to validate brief methods of assessment. An argument that is sometimes used against the detailed study of individual cases is that the practical decisions that have to be made are few and simple and are not improved by the preparation of elaborate case materials. The social and economic restraints on the preparation of detailed psychological case-studies must be recognized and dealt with in whatever way a community decides is appropriate. But, in addition to practical applications, there are theoretical and conceptual grounds for the intensive study of individual cases; indeed, it is scientific investigation, in the broad sense, that must provide the rationale for professional and commonsense ways of handling individual people in the sorts of setting mentioned above. The danger is that case-studies carried out in a sloppy and perfunctory manner serve no useful practical or theoretical purpose and bring the method itself into disrepute. Even a brief case-study should offer more than a string of facts. It should present an *organized* account of the person and his situation in as much detail as is required for the specified purpose, and meet professional and scientific standards.

It is a serious criticism of personality study in psychology that it has not yet built up a satisfactory body of psychological 'case-law'. Some case-studies have been published in the literature of psychoanalysis, but these are surprisingly fewer and briefer and less adequate than one would have supposed: see Sherwood (1969). Case-studies have also been published in the literature of social work and sociology, but again they are not numerous; they are brief, and they are not carried out in terms of an agreed method. Social case-studies are often used either singly or multiply in order to illustrate aspects of sociology (see Blankenship, 1974, for example) including the sociology of language, deviance, family life and social agency work, or to provide model cases which illustrate the workings of, say, social provision for the elderly or for unmarried mothers. The case-study method in clinical psychology (see Bolgar, 1965), as in psycho-analysis, has been based largely on the concepts and procedures of clinical medicine (see Slater and Roth, 1969), that is, with an emphasis on the signs, symptoms and history of a psychological disorder, which, when properly diagnosed may, like a physical illness, respond to a specific treatment. Recently, however, there has been an emphasis on behaviour modification in the natural environment, whereby the behaviour of the patient or client is studied in relation to the available patterns of reinforcement. The terms of reference of this sort of 'functional analysis' are obviously different from those of a psychodynamic approach, but the quasi-judicial method of studying individual cases is equally applicable to both: see Kanfer and Saslow (1965) and LeVine (1971, 1973). Thus, our purpose is not to denigrate previous work in personality study but to build on it, and show how the study of individual cases (and individual differences) might be pursued more effectively and with reference to an agreed method. There is as yet little agreement on how personality study should be pursued: see Rychlak (1968), Mischel (1969), Carlson (1971), Goldfried and Kent (1971), Meehl (1972) and Cohen (1973).

Two noteworthy attempts to demonstrate the value of case-studies in psychology are Jean Evans's study of three men, see Evans (1954), and White's analysis of lives in progress, see White (1975). They are landmarks in the history of the study of individual cases, using a remarkable blend of clinical psychology, social skills, detective work and literary craft. Other published accounts of individual cases include the following: Murray *et al.* (1938), Weinberg and Hire (1962), Zax and Stricker (1963), Allport (1965), Cleckley (1964), Shaw (1966), Burton and Harris (1966), Holt (1969). The wide differences in method are obvious: see also Eysenck (1965, pp. 95–131) in connection with Freud (1953). Most case-studies in the literature of clinical psychology and social work are brief; they are short on 'content' as regards personality description, and are concerned mainly with focal or critical causal connections and social relationships.

Again, many case-studies—more so in the literature of social work than in that of clinical psychology—describe what is essentially a 'human predicament', i.e. a problem of adjustment which would have arisen anyway, almost regardless of the personal qualities of the individual concerned. In some instances, the relevant aspects of personality and adjustment are common to most people, or to large numbers of people, and the case-study becomes simply an account of how the situation arose and how it might be dealt with. In other instances, the relevant aspects of personality and adjustment are less common, and the case-study is more concerned with the problem created by the personal qualities of the individual concerned, and with how these personal qualities are to be modified or managed. In yet other instances, it is difficult to assess the relative importance of personal qualities and situational factors in creating the problem, and it may be that an investigator attributes a personal quality, e.g. childishness, to the individual because it helps him, i.e. the investigator, to explain how the social predicament arose; alternatively he may prefer to explain it by attributing a special circumstance, e.g. temptation or stress, to the situation.

In this way, by contrasting 'personal' and 'situational' factors in the explanation of human adjustment, we see that clinical and social case-work occupy rather different, although overlapping, parts of the same conceptual and methodological continuum. In works of fiction, we find corresponding differences between stories about 'characters' and stories about 'situations', although we take it for granted that character and situation are mutually dependent: see Chapter 10. This close relationship between character and situation comes out very clearly in marital problems, for example, where one partner's character forms a major part of the other partner's situation (in general, one man's personality is another man's environment!).

Strong emotional or deviant reactions on the part of the stimulus person may lead even a professional investigator to form an impression which gives these reactions undue importance in comparison with many other features of personality which are not salient but are nevertheless important in the person's overall adjustment. Emphasis on the more dramatic aspects of personal adjustment may thus lead to a relative neglect of contextual factors, as shown in the history of personality study. However, one must recognize the clinical view that prominent or deviant characteristics which have a long history in the life of the person concerned are important in the sense that they *seem* to have a commanding influence on the person's adjustment. The question is whether their influence is as great as the observer supposes.

One of the difficulties in studying the process whereby we attribute qualities to other people is that the attribution may not be either specific or explicit. It is not always simply a matter of knowing that one thinks that another person is, say, 'sociable', 'well-thought-of' or 'rich'; in addition to explicit and specific attributions of this sort, we sometimes react to people 'as if' we had attributed certain qualities to them without actually realizing it. We sometimes unwittingly expect other people to have exceptional, even magical, qualities: e.g. when we suppose that a social worker or psychiatrist can solve our problem for us, or that someone in authority can pull strings. This tendency arises in part from our need to deal with our social predicament; but, perhaps because of infantile attitudes (feelings of powerlessness, for example), psychological defence mechanisms and transference effects, we are led unwittingly to distort and misinterpret the situation in the direction of simple wish-fulfilment. We thus behave 'as if' the other person had the attributes that would satisfy our unconscious wishes; and the failure to modify our behaviour in accordance with the *real* qualities of the other person is likely to make for maladjustment. In this connection, we can think of 'unconscious' thoughts, feelings and desires as latent forms of experience which *tend* to become realized and verbalized (i.e. conscious, manifest and explicit); but the process of realization occurs in a context of countervailing tendencies such as feelings of guilt and anxiety, and may become distorted or blocked by self-protective reactions.

The 'quasi-judicial' nature of the case-study in social work was recognized sixty years ago (see Richmond 1917), but the *scientific* merits of this method seem not to have been fully explored. It was seen as a procedure for defining, and finding solutions for, problems created when people are not able to deal effectively with their particular social situation. Alternatively, it was seen in 'quasi-medical' terms as a procedure for diagnosing and prescribing treatments for localized social ailments. The concepts and methods of social case-work have been described by Timms (1968) and Hollis (1972). The concept of personality has long been of interest to sociologists: see Burgess (1929) and Spitzer (1969), for example.

II. Basic Rules

There are six basic rules for the preparation of a psychological case-study. The first and most important rule is that the investigator must report truthfully on the person, his life and circumstances, and must be accurate in matters of detail. The relevance and importance of any particular fact must be established by rational argument and not by resort to rhetoric or special pleading. The second rule is that the aims and objectives of the case-study should be stated explicitly and unambiguously. We have already seen that case-studies vary in content and organization depending upon the purposes they are designed to fulfil; a case-study is usually carried out in order to understand and influence a person's reactions to a predicament. The third rule is that the case-study should contain an assessment of the extent to which the stated aims and objectives have been achieved. The point of this rule is that, for practical or other reasons, it may not be possible to investigate all the psychological and environmental factors that seem relevant, or it may not be possible to conceptualize the person satisfactorily, i.e. to make sense of his behaviour. For example, information about some of the precipitating and predisposing factors in a case of suicide may be unobtainable, so that it is impossible to choose between several different explanations of the act. The factors which prevent the attainment of the objectives must be described.

The fourth rule is that if, as is often the case, the inquiry deals with episodes of deep emotional significance to the person, then it can be carried out properly only by someone trained and equipped to establish and manage a close, fairly long, and possibly difficult, personal relationship. The reason for this is that the disclosure of very private thoughts, feelings and desires requires trust which can usually be built up only over a long period of time. Furthermore, psychologically significant episodes usually have considerable ramifications—in the sense that they are associated with events earlier in the person's life and influence many aspects of his current behaviour and circumstance. Considerable time is required to explore these ramifications and influences, to collect the evidence needed to corroborate the person's testimony, and to cross-check its internal consistency; systematic, friendly interrogation decreases the likelihood of accidental errors and omissions and of deliberate misrepresentation.

The fifth rule is that the person must be seen in an 'ecological context'; that is to say, a full account must be given of the objects, persons and events in his physical, social and symbolic environment. The proper focus of a case-study is not so much a 'person' as a 'person in a situation'. This rule reminds us that in case-studies of normal people in the ordinary circumstances of everyday life, the focus of the inquiry often shifts from short-term 'adjustment' to long-term 'adaptation' or life-style. A case-study is, however, usually undertaken either because the personal qualities of the individual are unusual or because the surrounding circumstances are unusual, or both. Among the psychological and situational factors commonly found in human maladjustment are those associated with interpersonal relationships. The individual person belongs to a number of small, primary, social groups whose memberships overlap and whose functions interlock. It is within these informal, human groups that the person's main satisfactions and dissatisfactions are to be found. His problems of adjustment are generally associated with his basic emotional relationships with one person or, at most, a few other people. The family is perhaps the most influential of these groups because it provides the formative experiences, and acts as the main agent for the transmission of culture from one generation to the next. The 'ecological context' referred to in this fifth rule, therefore, is a context not only in a primary or biological sense, but also in a secondary or cultural sense. The cultural context includes all the man-made systems in which we live: the built environment, the social organization, the communication system, the economic and political system, the value-attitude system, and so on.

The sixth basic rule is that the report of a case-study should be written in good plain English in a direct, objective way without, however, losing its human interest as a story. The writer should present the individual's point of view, rather as a barrister presents his client's case in a court of law. This can be done with sympathy and imagination and with due regard for high standards of evidence and argument.

The length of the report depends upon the purpose of the investigation, the complexity of the problem, and the resources available to the investigator, as well as on the investigator's abilities and other personal qualities.

Case-studies may be done well or badly, but the standards against which they are judged are the scientific ones incorporated in what we are calling a 'quasi-judicial' method.

III. Procedural Steps

There are ten procedural steps. They show the complexity and rigour of a method concerned with both 'individual cases' and 'general laws'. As a first step, the problems and issues should be stated as clearly as possible. The second step is to collect background information to provide a context in terms of which the problems and issues are to be understood. Third, on the basis of information available at the time when the problems and issues are raised, *prima facie* explanations and solutions (about the individual's personality and predicament) can usually be put forward immediately, and it is these obvious and simple *prima facie* answers that should be examined first of all, otherwise one may needlessly complicate the investigation (sometimes, of course, the obvious and simple answers are incorrect). Fourth, examination of these more obvious explanations guides the investigator's search for additional evidence; but they may not, in the end, fit the available evidence, so that further explanations (conjectures) have to be thought of. The various possible answers, both initial and subsequent, have implications as regards what should or should not be the case, i.e. they may be compatible with some of the evidence but not with it all. Fifth, the next step is to search for and admit for consideration sufficient evidence to eliminate as many of the suggested explanations as possible, in the hope that one of them will be so close to the truth as to account for all the evidence and be contradicted by none of it. The evidence may be direct or indirect; but it must be admissible, relevant and obtained from competent and credible sources. Sixth, the sources of evidence, as well as the evidence itself, must be clearly examined; in the case of personal testimony, this is analogous to cross-examination in a court of law; otherwise it amounts to checking the consistency and accuracy of all items of evidence. Seventh, there must be a critical inquiry into the internal coherence, logic, and external validity of the whole network of argument claiming to settle the issues and solve the problems. Eighth, it is likely that some lines of argument will be obviously inadequate, whereas others will be possible or even convincing; as mentioned in step five, the 'most likely' interpretation is selected, provided it is compatible with the evidence. Ninth, the formulation of an acceptable explanation for the person's behaviour usually carries implications for treatment or other action, and these have to be worked out. The tenth step is to prepare the case-report as a 'scientific account' of the person; it should contribute to psychological 'case-law' in virtue of the abstract and general *principles* employed in explaining the tactical adjustments or strategic adaptation of the person dealt with. Psychological case-law evolves out of systematic comparisons and contrasts between individual cases.

IV. The Contents and Organization of a Case-Report: Discussion of Related Issues

We deal with the question of what information might be included in a fairly detailed case-report, and with the question of how that information might be organized and presented, by dividing the report into ten sections. Each section deals with a number of general issues that might be raised in any case-study, and then discusses their psychological significance. The organization of a report on an actual case is governed partly by a fairly natural order of presentation of the information, and partly by the main and subsidiary arguments which impose a rational structure of meaning and inference on the empirical evidence.

The ten sections deal with the following topics (the capitalized abbreviations refer to the content categories dealt with in Chapters 5, 6 and 7):

- (i) The problem under investigation and the authorship of the report, including a statement of its purpose and terms of reference.
- (ii) The identity of the individual, his physical appearance, location and other routine information: IDEN, PHYS.
- (iii) The life-history and present circumstances of the individual and related issues: LIFE, SITU, PROS, ROUT, MATP, INCS, HLTH.
- (iv) The psychological attributes of the individual: GENT, SPET, EXPR, MOTA, ABAT, ORFE, PRIN, SELF, OBJE.
- (v) The social positions and social relationships of the individual: SOPO, FAMK, FRIL, SP–O, O–SP, SP+O, SPvO.
- (vi) The relationship of the individual to the investigator (or informants): SP–S, S–SP, SP+S, SPvS.
- (vii) An evaluation of the individual in terms of accepted and explicit ethical standards: EVAL.
- (viii) A review of the evidence and arguments in relation to the purposes and terms of reference of the investigation.
- (ix) A summary of the methods used in, and the conditions governing, the investigation, together with any associated reservations or implications.
- (x) Conclusions: findings, recommendations and forecasts.

As a general rule, in the organization of a case-report, issues and evidence *need not* be dealt with under all the separate headings and sub-headings we have listed, especially if some of them form a very small part of the case-study (or if the case-study itself is brief). Instead, they should be assimilated to the most relevant main category, so that, finally, the case-report is much simpler and more sharply focused than it would otherwise be, the issues and evidence being concentrated under a few main headings.

(i) Problem and Purpose

This section of the report answers the following questions: Why is the report being prepared? What are its terms of reference? As we have seen, there are many different practical reasons for preparing a case-study: reports on individual people may be needed by a court of law, by a medical or welfare agency, by a selection committee, employer, vocational advisor or marriage counsellor, by a newspaper or magazine, radio or television broadcasting company, by a school or university, and so on. Naturally, the type of information wanted and the nature of the report vary from one agency to another—a political profile in a newspaper looks rather different from an obituary or psychiatrist's case-report, in spite of the fact that they belong to the same general class of 'personality descriptions'. The terms of reference common to these descriptions is, 'To report on P_i (a particular person) in relation to S_j (a given situation)'. A political profile in a newspaper, for example, describes the individual's personality in relation to political circumstances; an obituary attempts to sum up the main landmarks and achievements as represented in the individual's reputation; a psychiatrist's report describes the individual's psychopathology, its symptoms, aetiology and prognosis.

In practice, the terms of reference of an inquiry are often not stated very clearly. More usually, the nature of the problem and the relevance of information made available become clearer as the investigation gets under way. Indeed, the nature of the problem and the scope of the inquiry may not become settled until the report of the case-study is complete. In this respect, the quasi-judicial method, as employed in the preparation of a psychological case-study, differs from the judicial method proper, as employed in criminal or civil cases, where the 'issues' are clearly stated at the outset and govern the admissibility of evidence and thus the subsequent scope of the inquiry. This comes about partly because, in law, much of the preliminary work is done before a case comes to trial, and the trial itself is a kind of formal test of the relative merits of two well-rehearsed, fully documented, arguments presented according to the rules of a clear and accepted procedure.

One of the limitations of the case-study method as traditionally practised in psychology and social work is that it tends to present a one-sided account of the person in a situation, i.e. it fails to consider and compare alternative accounts (perhaps because the relevant case-law is lacking or not appreciated), and so fails to show that one account is more acceptable than another when judged in terms of a common standard of evidence and argument. This limitation is more likely in case-studies carried out by one investigator than in case-studies carried out by a team, where discussions at case conferences bring out different points of view.

In the sections that follow, we again discuss the content categories in personality description, either individually or in groups, with reference to their place and function in the quasi-judicial method of studying personality; but we do not repeat the lexical and semantic analyses of personality descriptions presented in Chapters 5, 6 and 7 except where it is desirable to do so in the interests of continuity and cohesion. In addition, we make use of opportunities to discuss a variety of topics associated with our concepts, methods and empirical findings.

(ii) Identity (IDEN) and Appearance (PHYS)

This section of the case-report offers an answer to questions like, 'Who is the subject of this report?', 'How can he be recognized, identified and located?'. In other words, it gives information which enables the reader to identify the particular individual to whom the report refers, and to distinguish him from other people. This information normally includes some or all of the following 'formal' defining characteristics: full name, present address, date and place of birth, age, sex, religion if any, nationality and racial or ethnic group, distinguishing physical characteristics, e.g. birthmark, photograph, fingerprints, identity or other reference number. In addition to this sort of 'formal' or routine information about personal identity (IDEN), one may include any other information the primary function of which is to *identify* or to *introduce* the particular person. Some information about physical appearance (PHYS) can thus be conveniently included in this section, although it is possible that other aspects of physical appearance might be more relevantly placed elsewhere in the report.

The report itself should be a properly identifiable, documentary record showing a title, reference number, date and the author's identity. For research and teaching purposes, the real identity of the subject of the case-report should be kept confidential; if necessary, information may be altered, omitted or added in order to safeguard the confidentiality of the report, provided a note to the effect that some non-significant changes have been made is attached.

A large number of diverse facts contribute to the person's identity; any fact which validly distinguishes him from other people (especially those with whom he might reasonably be confused), and any fact which makes him recognizably the same person from one occasion to another, contribute to the notion of identity. The person's sense of his own identity is different from the objective identity he has for other people; subjective identity has much in common with the self-concept and is concerned not so much with recognizing and distinguishing the self (except perhaps in childhood) as with establishing stable, consistent and satisfying self-references, e.g. social role and status, reputation, achievement and response from others.

(iii) Life-history and Present Circumstances

This section of the case-report deals with the following categories of information: Life-history (LIFE); Contemporary Situation (SITU); Future Prospects (PROS); Routine Habits and Activities (ROUT); Material Circumstances and Possessions (MATP); Actual Incidents (INCS); Physical and Mental Health (HLTH). Corresponding to these sorts of information are the questions they are intended to answer. These questions and related issues are discussed in the following subsections.

Life-history (*LIFE*). This subsection answers questions like: 'What is the story of the person's life so far?', 'How did he become the person he is now?' This part of the case-report includes most of the historical information relevant to understanding the current problem. The reason for including life-history information is that it provides a wider context within which the particular problem can be viewed in a better perspective. The use of life-history data in a case-study, however, raises an important methodological issue. From a strict behavioural-science point of view, an explanation of the person's adjustment to his environment should be given in terms of 'proximal' causes, i.e. of factors operating at the time, and not in terms of 'distal' causes, i.e. of factors operating some time previously. In practice, however, the investigator may be unable to validate (or even to conceive) an exclusively 'proximal' explanation; he is obliged, or may prefer, to invoke 'distal' causes, e.g. maternal deprivation, absence from school, or sibling rivalry. If pressed, he might try to translate these 'distal' factors into their 'proximal' equivalents, and refer, for example, to lack of trust in others, low scholastic attainments, or fear of failure. But the point is that there may be no direct evidence for these proximal factors, even though they may be very relevant to the problem; this is why they have to be inferred, indirectly, from life-history evidence.

The methodological issue becomes clearer when we consider how a problem of personal adjustment might be dealt with in terms of behaviour modification. This approach calls for a detailed investigation of the relevant reinforcement contingencies (proximal factors) operating in the person's environment. It is not necessary to inquire into the person's reinforcement history (distal factors)—even though it is this reinforcement history that has led to his present problem—except in so far as such inquiries may alert one to current contingencies. When the baseline conditions have been worked out, the reinforcement contingencies are gradually changed, in the expectation that the person's behaviour will be shaped to the required pattern.

Thus, for both psychodynamic and behaviouristic approaches to personality study, formative (distal) factors have an historical but not a functional connection with present behaviour. The topic was discussed many years ago by Allport (1937, 1961). We emphasize the distinction between distal and proximal factors in the explanation of individual behaviour because we are recommending a quasi-judicial approach to personality, and it is well-known that the judicial method proper demands that explanations be in terms of proximal causes, e.g. in an explanation of how a person came to be raped or killed.

In spite of the precautions taken in judicial procedure to avoid relying on evidence about 'similar facts', it is quite common in psychological case-studies for an investigator to search the person's past life for indirect evidence about that person's present qualities (values, traits, abilities, motives, attitudes, and so on). In so doing, he often uncovers 'similar facts', i.e. facts which cannot be reasonably regarded as unrelated or coincidental but seem to have something in common. Thus, a series of occupational failures, or psychiatric breakdowns, or peculiar patterns of interpersonal relationships, might each seem like a set of 'similar facts' related to a common factor, e.g. low intelligence, neuroticism, or psychopathy, respectively. The danger of reasoning in terms of 'similar facts' is similar to the danger of reasoning indirectly from distal to proximal causes: see above. The assertion that certain empirical facts are 'similar' is not an observational statement but a conjecture; that is to say, we *construe* the facts as similar. In this way, when compiling life-history information, we seem to see regularities, consistencies and trends, i.e. stable personality characteristics, such as traits, motives, beliefs, abilities and values. For example, in making a case-study of a person with marital problems, a counsellor might work carefully through that person's life-history and find evidence of 'similar facts' suggesting aggressiveness, social anxiety, dependency and gullibility. He might then suppose that these personal characteristics contributed to the client's present difficulties.

Clinical case-histories are replete with examples of how events at one stage of life can have long-term consequences. It is sometimes argued that the main pattern of adult adjustment is determined by formative experiences in infancy and childhood. It seems reasonable to suppose that early experiences are very influential, but that the longer the person lives the more likely he is to integrate his experience and his behaviour into a consistent pattern, and the less likely he is to be changed by later experiences—although profound changes in personal adjustment may occur following stress or conversion to new values or change of circumstance. In one sense, the story of a person's life is the story of the evolution of his behaviour and states of mind as he tries to adjust to normal or abnormal changes in his psychobiological make-up and to the constraints and opportunities of his changing environment: see Chapter 9.

In a case-study of a young child presenting a problem of intellectual retardation or serious maladjustment, one would, as a matter of routine, inquire into pre-and post-natal circumstances and family resemblances. This might be followed by an inquiry into several aspects of the child's developmental history: his intelligence, attainments, physique, social behaviour, and so on. The evidence might be obtained from documentary records and the first-hand testimony of family members, teachers or other reliable witnesses, and from conversations with the child.

In case-studies of adults, where there is considerably more evidence available and where the relevant issues are usually more numerous, it may be desirable to deal with the life-history in terms of a number of well-defined phases; and within each phase it may be desirable to identify a limited number of important themes. For example, one might deal with the person's educational history and report on his progress and adjustment through school. Alternatively, one might deal with the person's occupational history, and report on the factors leading to occupational choice, on his progress and adjustment at work. Another possible theme might deal with the person's social and leisure-time activities: describing his relationships with other people, particularly those outside the family circle, and the deployment of his spare time, money and energy. There are obviously many basic themes in the person's life-history which *might* be investigated. In fact, most facets of personality can be dealt with in this way, e.g. the self-concept (SELF) or values (PRIN), since they can be expected to change over time.

As we saw in Chapter 6, one can conveniently, though somewhat arbitrarily, describe the person in terms of past history (LIFE), present circumstances (SITU), and future prospects (PROS). What we have called the 'distal' factors in personal adjustment are dealt with as life-history data (LIFE), whereas the 'proximal' factors are dealt with in terms of the contemporary situation (SITU). It is a matter of judgment whether aspects of the person's *recent* history are regarded as part of his life-history or as part of his current problems of adjustment.

Contemporary situation (SITU). This subsection answers questions like, 'What are the major features of the person's circumstances at present?', 'How has the situation arisen?', 'What are the actual constraints and opportunities in his environment, i.e. what behavioural options does he have?'.

As we have seen, this subsection of the case-study examines the 'proximal' factors in the individual's adjustment to his environment, and those parts of the life-history which are sufficiently recent to be regarded as part of the present situation. Some of the individual's circumstances may endure for a considerable time, months or longer, and there is no hard and fast line to be drawn between facts which belong to the individual's life-history and those which belong to his present situation.

The importance of this subsection is based on two considerations. First, the basic purpose of the case-study is to investigate, and to make recommendations for the solution of, the predicament in which the person is presently placed. Second, the present situation shows 'where the action is', i.e. where the life-history is being made; it shows how the individual's behaviour, personal qualities and circumstances are evolving; it shows how historical trends help to determine future prospects (PROS). A person's adjustment is often 'future-oriented' (see Allport, 1955), and we want to know what will become of him.

As in the life-history (LIFE) subsection, an investigator may be able to identify different aspects of the contemporary situation, e.g. circumstances at school or work, social isolation, delinquency factors, family discord or other stress. The identification of such features of the situation is a matter of experience and judgment; the particular issues to be investigated vary from case to case.

Not the least important of the issues relevant to an analysis of the person's situation is that concerned with the individual's subjective experience, particularly his orientation to himself (his self-concept and personal future) and to those parts of his environment relevant to his predicament (or achievement): see the content category ORFE. The counterpart to this subjective analysis is an objective analysis of the 'total situation', i.e. the web of circumstances in which the person is *actually* enveloped. The person and the situation are bound together by actions and their consequences, and by stimuli and the responses they elicit, as expressed in the formula: $P_i \times S_j \rightarrow B_{ij}$. The case-study attempts to describe and explain these relationships between the person and his environment.

Future Prospects (PROS). This subsection answers questions like, 'What is the person's future likely to be?', 'What will be the longer-term consequences of his present actions and circumstances?', 'What possibilities are open to him?'. Or, colloquially, 'What is to become of him?'. The time perspective adopted in this section is partly a matter of what is appropriate to the problem under consideration and partly a matter of what is possible in the way of forecasting. In some cases, it will be a matter of making fairly straightforward short-term predictions based on ample evidence and well-tried principles; in other cases, it will be a matter of making good guesses about what might or might not happen in the long run. One of the basic problems of prediction in clinical psychology and social case-work is to formulate the prediction in a sufficiently general way—so as to encompass a class of possible actions in a given set of circumstances, but also in a sufficiently particular way—so as to specify what would count as an action in that class (and what would count as a set of circumstances equivalent to the one foreseen). For example, what actual behaviour is to count as a 'delinquent act' an 'occupational failure', or an 'improvement in academic achievement'? What is to count as a 'normal home', 'occupational stress' or 'adequate opportunity to study'?

Predictions about people are often phrased in a vague or general way, such that a variety of behavioural outcomes can be seen as compatible with the prediction (hence the fortune teller's apparent success), e.g. 'will manage reasonably well'. Similarly, we often feel that the behaviour that actually occurred *could have* been predicted, e.g. suicide, divorce, or professional success, because it is nearly always possible to find a *post hoc* explanation for such events.

The forecasting of individual behaviour on a clinical basis (as opposed to an actuarial basis) is a surprisingly neglected topic. In this section, we shall briefly discuss some of the more familiar methods of forecasting, in keeping with our interest in ordinary language and commonsense.

One such method, as we have seen, is to rely upon one's knowledge of role-prescriptions, and to predict that the individual will do what is *expected* of him (by the appropriate reference group) in a given situation. So much of our behaviour is regulated by role-prescriptions that often we do not need to make personality appraisals at all (in the sense of forming an impression of a person as a unique individual). Instead, we deal with him in terms of his social role, and *expect* that he will act accordingly. People vary, of course, in the 'accuracy' of their 'stereotypes' about human behaviour. They also have differing 'response sets': for example, emphasizing a person's good (or bad) qualities, and seeing people as more (or less) similar.

Perhaps the simplest method of judging a person's prospective behaviour is to say that he will continue to behave as he has been behaving. If people are indeed regular and consistent, then this is an effective method—it is rather like predicting that tomorrow's weather will be like today's.

However, just as we have ways of forecasting *changes* in the weather, so we have ways of forecasting *changes* in the behaviour of individuals (though we lack the sort of notational system and theory that the meteorologist possesses). Hence it is sometimes possible to discern trends in a person's behaviour and to extrapolate accordingly (making such adjustments as we feel are necessary with regard to the circumstances which we expect will then exist), e.g. educational development, improvement in mental health or marital harmony.

Formal logical reasoning also enables us to make predictions, in the sense of drawing a conclusion which tells us what to 'expect'. Thus:

P_1 is an hysteric.
Hysterics condition poorly.
Therefore P_1 will condition poorly.

Another example would be as follows:

P_1 is more intelligent than P_2.
More intelligent persons do better at this job than less intelligent persons.
Therefore P_1 will do better at this job than P_2.

Again, in everyday life, if we know that Betty is pretty, and that boys are attracted to pretty girls, then we can predict that Betty will find herself attracting boys.

The existence of logical classes and relationships provides the basis for actuarial prediction and for the kind of 'clinical inference' described by Sarbin, Taft and Bailey (1960).

A similar sort of formal logical reasoning is found in the formation of personality impressions when one attribute is assumed to imply another. We have argued that commonsense and ordinary language operate a system of connectives and qualifiers which enable us to express quite complicated quasi-logical statements. Thus, for example, we might say, 'P_i tends to get depressed if he has not eaten for several hours' or 'If the situation is one in which people are behaving rather formally, then P_i will behave in a casual and off-hand way if he thinks that they expect him to conform to standards that he does not uphold'.

If we have a 'theory' about the organization of behaviour which is applicable to the person concerned, we can use it to explain the connections between what we claim or predict about the person and the evidence we have available. The problem of explanation is dealt with in Chapter 9. All we need to note for the time being is that the number of psychological concepts fulfilling an explanatory (and predictive) function in the ordinary language of commonsense seems to be quite small, namely: role, motive, trait, habit, attitude, constraint. In addition, however, there are technical concepts in academic and professional psychology and social work, e.g. conflict, reinforcement, repression, alienation. Our 'theories' about human behaviour determine our expectations about classes of people and about individual persons. But we often fail to examine the internal coherence of our 'theories' and their correspondence with the facts, and fail even to make our 'theories' (assumptions) explicit.

Reasoning by analogy is a common basis for predicting a person's future prospects and behaviour, e.g. 'P_1 is like P_2, therefore he will behave in a similar way', where P_2 may be drawn from literature or real life: see the content categories SPvO and SPvS.

Finally, we must be aware that our expectations about what a person will or will not do are not always rational predictions based on empirical evidence, but sometimes irrational expressions of desires and feelings outside our personal awareness. Our hopes and fears lead us to confuse the wish for a particular outcome with the likelihood of that outcome. The essential uncertainty about a person's prospects fosters this sort of 'projective thinking'; it is particularly likely to occur when one person is emotionally involved with another person's future.

Routine Habits and Activities (*ROUT*). This subsection answers questions like, 'How does the person live his life?'. The answer to it not only provides a broad perspective within which particular problems can be studied, but also raises new issues and new information.

A schedule of typical activities of daily living covering a small but representative period of time may reveal interesting facts about a person and his environment, dealing as it must with sequences of work, recreation, sleep, nutrition, personal hygiene, social interaction, travelling, and so on. A detailed daily schedule is difficult to compile, it requires the stimulus person or observers to keep a log of his activities. Failure to disclose significant facts, whether about actions, circumstances, or states of mind, of course, reduces the value of such a schedule. Even so, it should reveal evidence about the person's sources of satisfaction and stress, his abilities and inclinations, values and aspirations, and so on.

An examination of the way a person lives his life should enable an investigator to infer his main strategies of adjustment. It is sometimes the case, however, that the person's 'problems' exist largely in his own mind, rather than in his external circumstances; so his strategies of adjustment may be inappropriate and unrewarding, as in shyness, over-cautiousness, or jealousy.

The foregoing account of the contribution that an analysis of the contemporary situation (SITU) makes to the case-study reminds us that the quasi-judicial method of investigation is closer to natural history than to laboratory experimentation; it also shows that we have adopted what is, basically, an ecological and evolutionary approach to the study of individual cases. In other words, we are interested in how the individual person and his habitat come to terms with one another, and in the evolution of these relationships.

Material circumstances and possessions (*MATP*). This subsection answers questions like, 'What physical or material conditions characterize the person's environment?', 'What financial and material resources does he have at his disposal?'.

It is obvious that the possession of financial resources, tools, books, transport, recreational facilities, and so on, greatly increases the range of a person's behavioural options; conversely, lack of money, poor housing, or poor equipment, greatly reduces the use that person can make of his natural abilities and inclinations. It follows, therefore, that personality development, throughout childhood and adult life, cannot be dissociated in practice from material circumstances. Similarly, since psychological assessment by means of quasi-judicial methods depends upon behavioural evidence, any environmental constraint on the range of an individual's behaviour must limit the inferences that can be made about him.

It might be regarded as a point in favour of psychometric tests of personality that they attempt to provide an assessment of personality without reference to the environment, rather as intelligence tests attempt to provide an assessment of intellectual ability without reference to school attainment and cultural advantage (or deprivation), but see Mischel (1968). To the extent that personal characteristics can be assessed without reference to the circumstances in which they normally function, we may be justified in referring to them as personal dispositions which are 'field independent'. The question is whether characteristics such as neuroticism, extraversion, intelligence, and other dimensions of individual differences, can be sensibly attributed to people without reference to the contexts in which they normally function, i.e. to P_i rather than $P_i \times S_j$. Although it may be convenient to attribute operationally defined characteristics to individuals, especially when we want to study differences between them, such characteristics are nevertheless 'field dependent' in the context of an individual's personal adjustment.

It is clear from some parts of the history of psychology, e.g. phrenology and faculty psychology, that we can deceive ourselves into thinking that our concepts and statements correspond to something 'real'. The validity and utility of the concepts and methods used in the psychometric approach to personality study have been critically examined and questioned; it remains to be seen whether, or to what extent, the claims of the psychometric approach will be vindicated. There has been an extensive debate on the relative merits of 'situationism', 'dispositionism' and 'interactionism' in an attempt to account for complex patterns of personal adjustment: see Mischel (1968), Argyle and Little (1972), Bowers (1973), Bem and Allen (1974), Jaccard (1974), Bromley (in press).

The approach to personality we are advocating is systematic and naturalistic. It does not depend on psychometric concepts or psychometric data; but it can make use of them as one kind of evidence among many. It can even incorporate psychometric concepts and methods of questionable validity and utility, because reservations about them can also be incorporated. If psychometric evidence is the 'best evidence' available on a particular issue, then the quasi-judicial method requires that it be introduced; but psychometric evidence may also be introduced if only to explain why it carries little or no weight in a particular case.

Although evidence about material circumstances and possessions (MATP) is not commonly used in personality appraisal, it may have its uses, as we have seen, and it does at least remind us of the fact that the psychological significance of an action depends on the context of circumstances in which it occurs.

Actual Incidents (*INCS*). This subsection answers questions like, 'What has the person actually said and done (or failed to say and do) that is relevant to assessing his personality or understanding his behaviour in this particular situation?', 'What were the relevant circumstances surrounding the action?'.

The main aim of personality appraisal is to provide some general conclusions about the person, rather than to present a catalogue of particular facts. For this reason, information about actual incidents may not be common in personality descriptions. Although the quasi-judicial method makes it absolutely necessary to introduce actual incidents, i.e. behavioural episodes, as evidence, the incidents themselves are not likely to figure in the general conclusion or assessment. They form part of the 'infrastructure' of the appraisal (rather as the particular responses to a questionnaire, intelligence test or projective test provide the basis for a psychometric assessment). It is one of the merits of the quasi-judicial method that it obliges the investigator to take an interrogative attitude towards his informants (including the person who is the focus of the case-study), and towards the evidence they provide. He cannot accept general statements at their face value, but must inquire into the observational evidence for them. Thus, for example, before the general statement, 'He is cruel' can even be considered meaningful, there must be reliable testimony, or other good evidence, from a credible source, describing actual incidents involving the person. The investigator is simply seeking to translate terms which refer to a covert (psychological) process or to a social (evaluative) judgment into terms which refer to an overt (behavioural) process. Whether the person's actions are then still regarded as 'cruel' is another matter. In a similar way, general statements about environmental conditions, e.g. 'He is under stress' or 'Her friends give her lots of help' must be translated into empirical statements about actual events and circumstances.

Physical and mental health (HLTH). This subsection answers questions like: 'Are there any important facts about the person's physical or mental condition that need to be taken into account?'.

It is well known that there are many anatomical and physiological factors in personality and adjustment: e.g. endocrine functions, brain damage, disease and disability. Such knowledge is derived, in the main, from cases in which these factors have been abnormal to a marked degree. Within the normal range of health, the precise effects of variations within and differences between individuals in these factors are difficult or impossible to ascertain.

In many cases, evidence about a person's general physical and mental health may not be particularly relevant—simply because that person is normal and there is nothing about his health that makes any difference to the pattern of meaning we impose on the behavioural evidence. Moreover, the person is presumed to be physically and mentally normal unless evidence to the contrary is produced. But this presumption should not prevent the investigator from enquiring briefly and routinely into the individual's health.

An investigator would need to show the relevance of any *systematic* inquiry into the person's physical and mental health. But, of course, such inquiry is highly relevant in a variety of cases, e.g. suicide or attempted suicide, psychiatric disorder, sexual problems. In such cases, the ideal procedure would be for the person to have a medical and psychiatric examination and for a record of his medical history (or such parts of it as seem relevant) to be made available as evidence. Even in cases where there is fairly obvious physical or mental abnormality, it is not always possible to demonstrate a causal connection between that abnormality and the actions of the individual. The investigator may just 'presume' that the health factor was a contributory cause of the individual's behaviour, e.g. physical illness in suicide, psychiatric illness in crime, physical disability in occupational maladjustment. Where the facts of physical and mental health are known at a commonsense level of understanding, they enter into an observer's implicit theory of human behaviour to help generate expectations about people.

The selection and interpretation of facts about a person's physical and mental condition is thus not as simple or as straightforward as one might suppose. For example, wrinkles and loss of teeth may have little direct medical significance, and may be quite normal, nevertheless they may have a considerable psychological importance for particular people; similarly, poor colour vision may be unimportant for some aspects of adjustment but be critically important for others; again some symptoms of ill-health, such as skin disorders or insomnia, may have no demonstrable organic cause and yet be relevant to the individual's maladjustment.

The medical relevance of conditions like drug addiction, including alcoholism, is obvious. In cases of this sort, it might seem that the quasi-judicial method is overelaborate, and that all that is required is a valid diagnosis and suitable medical treatment. There are two points to be made here: first, a medical diagnosis is itself a type of 'quasi-judicial' inquiry (the clinical method generates a kind of medical 'case law'), and it might be that the case could be dealt with adequately within this medical framework; second, a medical condition exists in a psychological and social context, and may be understood properly only when these contextual factors—attitudes, beliefs, and family relationships, for example—are taken into account. The applicability and importance of a rigorous quasi-judicial method in social medicine should be obvious.

The routine appraisal of a person's physical and mental health naturally includes consideration of any special physical assets and disabilities such as might be relevant to a particular occupation: e.g. those relating to vision, hearing and balance, and to conditions like asthma or epilepsy.

The individual's attitude towards his own physical and mental condition must not be neglected in a case-study, and sometimes it might be preferable to deal with it under the present heading (HLTH) rather than under the self-concept (SELF) heading. The person's 'body-image' is a substantial and important component in his self-concept and may be associated with feelings of inferiority, low levels of achievement and aspiration (both physically and socially), and with psychosomatic or compensatory reactions. The person's attitude towards his physical health and appearance, his bodily functions, his medical condition, his medical history and prospects, may be very relevant to understanding his behaviour—particularly in relation to puberty, sex, middle age and old age—see Bromley (1974).

This brings us to the end of our discussion of that section of the case-study dealing with life-history, present circumstances and related issues. The next section deals with the psychological attributes of persons.

(iv) Psychological Attributes
This section of the case-report deals with the following categories of information: general personality traits (GENT); specific personality traits (SPET); expressive behaviour (EXPR); motivation and arousal (MOTA); abilities and attainments (ABAT); orientation and feelings (ORFE); moral principles (PRIN); self-concept (SELF); matters towards which motivation and orientation are directed (OBJE). Corresponding to these sorts of information are the questions they are intended to answer. These questions and related issues are discussed in the following subsections.

General personality traits (GENT). This subsection answers questions like: 'How is the individual disposed, in general, to behave?' or 'What regularities and consistencies characterize his behaviour in different situations?'.

As we have seen, one of the commonest ways of summing people up is to specify their salient personality traits, e.g. steady, reliable, humorous. We have argued that representing the person in this way is oversimplified and misleading. It is oversimplified because there is much more to being a person than having a few characteristic ways of behaving. It is misleading because it neglects the situational determinants of conduct. A case-study is concerned with the person in a situation, and it must state whatever is important and relevant to understanding the person in that situation. Nevertheless, a person's actions often *seem* more comprehensible if we can attribute them to an underlying trait.

We accept that it is a matter of linguistic convenience to define a personality trait in general terms, so as to indicate broadly the range of meanings available for it. We do not regard a trait name as having a fixed meaning; on the contrary, a trait name, like most other words, can create a variety of meanings depending upon the situational and linguistic context in which it occurs. A number of personality factors have been described by Cattell (1943, 1947, 1965, 1973), who has argued that a person can be characterized by his unique profile on a set of operationally defined standard measures. We recall that the *meaning* of a trait is not restricted to its operational definition, its 'meaning in use' is field dependent. Cattell recognizes that there are 'characteristics' other than traits, e.g. values, abilities, beliefs.

Allport (1937, 1961) rejected the idea of standardized psychometric measures of personality but accepted the idea of a consensus of informed opinion about a person which might provide a relatively small number of 'personal dispositions' tailored to fit that individual, and so not necessarily the same as the 'personal dispositions' of any other individual. The problem of trait-specificity as formulated by Allport (1937, 1961), however, is a semantic or conceptual problem, not an empirical one.

Our description and analysis of the language of personality descriptions has shown that trait names form natural clusters or sets. Cattell has used elaborate statistical procedures to demonstrate that correlations between traits can be accounted for objectively in terms of basic factors. Eysenck (1970) has used similar procedures to show systematic relationships between traits and the two basic factors of neuroticism and extraversion. There are, of course, many ways of classifying personality traits; the problems are psychometric as well as taxonomic: see for example, Campbell and Fiske (1959), Guilford (1959), Norman (1963), Peterson (1965), Passini and Norman (1966), Fiske (1971), Shweder (1975), Howarth (1976) and, with reference to abnormal traits, Lorr, Klett and McNair (1963).

Trait names or dispositional terms can be used to refer to many kinds of behavioural consistencies, temperamental qualities, abilities, beliefs and moral qualities. Knowing that a person has such and such an attribute leads us to have expectations about his behaviour; these expectations are of a general sort, but if we also know the kind of situation that person will be in (and what kind of behaviour that situation usually elicits from people of that sort), then the person's actual behaviour becomes more predictable.

Specific personality traits (SPET). This subsection answers questions like, 'How does he usually behave in this sort of situation, and how does he behave in that sort?'.

We have seen that statements in a personality description can be constructed to fit an endless variety of individual characteristics ranging from the most abstract and general sort of attribute to the most concrete and particular fact. Specific personality traits are words and statements at an intermediate level of abstraction and generality; they describe more than, say, a mannerism or a routine performance, but less than a broad disposition. In other words, they convey information about how the person is likely to behave in response to a *type* of situation (not only in a particular or actual situation). The examples we gave in an earlier section included: 'Careless of his appearance', 'Careful with money'. In other words, statements about *specific* personality traits are not unlike statements about *general* personality traits which have been qualified and organized to make their meaning narrower and more precise, i.e. less general, less abstract.

Many of the items in questionnaire measures of personality, such as Cattell's 16 PF test, refer to specific personality traits; and in so far as a respondent answers sets of questions consistently and correctly he reveals his underlying *general* traits. In a quasi-judicial investigation, similarly, statements about specific personality traits and actual incidents are closely tied to the empirical evidence; they convey information in their own right apart from providing a basis for the attribution of *general* personality traits. It is of interest to note that all the items in Cattell's 16 PF test can be classified in terms of our system of content categories.

Expressive behaviour (EXPR). This subsection answers questions like, 'What relevant information, if any, can be obtained by studying the individual's manner and demeanour?', 'What is known about his expressive behaviour? What does this tell us about his mood and temperament?'.

The importance of evidence about expressive behaviour is that involuntary non-verbal behaviour seems to reveal some important central aspects of personality and adjustment, as well as providing clues to the person's momentary states of mind, his social relationships and circumstances—provided we take into account group and individual differences. Unfortunately, expressive behaviour and affective states are particularly difficult areas of psychological research and we shall not attempt to analyse them further: see Chapter 5. Adults, especially those with a professional scientific training in psychological assessment, should have sufficient understanding of the normal range of emotional expression to enable them to assess its value in a quasi-judicial inquiry and to assess the demeanour of a client or informant.

Motivation and arousal (*MOTA*). This subsection answers questions like, 'What was the person trying to do?', 'What did he want?', 'What were his hopes and fears?', 'What is known about his likes and dislikes?'.

Such questions can be answered only by conjectures attempting to make sense of observational data, since motivation and arousal are covert psychological processes. Relevant information may be available about the person's expressive behaviour, life-history, routine habits and activities, actual incidents, and other sorts of behavioural and circumstantial evidence.

The importance of motivation and arousal as factors in understanding personal adjustment is obvious, since they are supposed to explain the direction and intensity of the major behavioural paths taken by the person. The long-range goals and basic motives can be equated with the person's strategic aims and objectives; the short-range goals and momentary inclinations can be equated with his tactical intentions. If we fail to recognize the motivational basis of a pattern of behaviour we cannot understand what the individual has to gain from it (or what he has to lose by acting otherwise); as we saw in Chapter 4, self-organized voluntary action can be explained in terms of motives and reasons.

We have argued that motivation is *intrinsic* to behaviour, and that the main problem is not how motivation is initiated and sustained but how it is inhibited and regulated. The regulation of motivation requires internal 'administrative machinery' to determine the allocation of resources and the programming of activities; this machinery takes account of the individual's beliefs and values, and estimates the likelihood that a particular outcome can be attained. At least, this is the case for the rational and non-routine aspects of personal adjustment; much of the time, however, human conduct follows speedy well-established practices, and motivation scarcely comes into awareness. Such routinized control is an important end in itself (a manifestation of the individual's adaptation to a 'behavioural niche'); the risk is that of imposing outmoded values and decision processes, thus reducing the person's behavioural options and preventing the realization of personal potentialities. Neurotic defensiveness provides an example of serious faults developing in the regulation of motivation by the central 'administrative' (or regulative) functions of the self. By contrast, apathy appears to be a state in which motivation and arousal have become abnormally low. Some forms of criminal behaviour illustrate the effects of insufficient self-regulation.

Reference to a person's motivation enables us to explain the organization of his behaviour in terms of dispositional and mentalistic processes which instigate, sustain and direct his actions towards more preferred end states and away from aversive situations. Motivation, however, is only one of many factors in personal adjustment; so the achievement of *maximum* satisfaction, measured by some sort of cost/benefit analysis, is an ideal state of affairs that occurs rarely if at all. In a quasi-judicial case-study, evidence and arguments about motivation may be relevant and important, but they must be considered in relation to other aspects of personality.

Abilities and attainments (*ABAT*). This subsection answers questions like, 'What was the person able to do?', 'How competent was he to cope with the demands of the situation?', 'What was he *unable* to do?'.

We have already explained that in ordinary language and commonsense we do not always make fine distinctions between different kinds of personality characteristics; so that statements about abilities and attainments on the one hand, and about general or specific traits on the other, may be condensed into statements which express both ability and disposition. For the purpose of scientific analysis, however, it is worth separating out evidence of what the person *can* (or cannot) do from evidence about what he *wants* (or does not want) to do, and from what he is *disposed* to do (or is in the *habit* of doing).

A scientific explanation aims to give as full an account as possible of the causes and conditions of the behaviour in question. It is not enough to specify the motivation, we must also specify the circumstances, the dispositions or habits, the abilities and attitudes, and any other factors that seem, in the context of a case-study, to determine behaviour. Some of these factors limit the scope and nature of the opportunities open to the individual; some of them predispose him towards one line of action rather than another; some raise or lower the likelihood of his taking effective action and achieving a satisfactory outcome. The psychological case-study, in theory at least, attempts to give a full account of the determinants of behaviour. In practice, of course, the requirements are much less exacting, and an investigator may be satisfied with an approximate answer that deals with some of the factors at work.

Orientation and feelings (*ORFE*). This subsection answers questions like, 'How did he see the situation?', 'What did he anticipate?', 'What did he think and feel about the way things were going?', 'What options did he think were open or closed to him?'. Note that we have used the past tense simply because the case-study is partly a reconstruction of the past.

Since there is usually a motivational component in orientation and feeling, another question would be, 'What was his attitude?'. It would take us too far afield to analyse the concept of attitude, except to say that it is a general readiness to act in a certain way based on what the person believes he wants in relation to what he thinks his environment can offer; it gives rise to specific intentions and eventually to actions of one sort or another. The connections between beliefs, motives, attitudes, abilities, intentions and actions, however, are by no means simple and direct; and in a quasi-judicial inquiry it is necessary to establish precisely what point is at issue, and what evidence is relevant to it.

As we have pointed out, people tend to react to a situation as they see it; so that failures of adjustment, in either the strategic or the tactical sense, can arise from misunderstanding the situation and not just from facing a difficult problem. We must remember too, that the person's orientation and feelings are important in understanding his adjustment, since he may misunderstand himself and not just have personal qualities that are difficult to regulate; these issues are normally dealt with separately in the subsection dealing with the self-concept (SELF).

Principles, character and moral values (*PRIN*). This subsection deals mainly with the first of two complementary questions: 'What are the person's basic beliefs, values, and rules of conduct?' and 'What basic beliefs, values and rules of conduct are relevant to the evaluation and appraisal of this person's character?'. The second question is dealt with later in connection with the subsection on ethical evaluations; we refer to it at this stage in our account of the case-study method because the investigation is bound to take place in some kind of ethical framework, and the investigator must be clear in his own mind as to what that framework is and how it might affect the quasi-judicial inquiry. Thus questions arise as to how far, or in what ways, the person's behaviour matches up to or fails to match up to the ethical principles he acknowledges, and those that the investigator acknowledges.

The individual's morality both drives and regulates behaviour, but it is not always possible to identify moral characteristics separately from other aspects of personality. The individual's moral character, as it were, *pervades* his personality. The importance of moral principles in the organization of human behaviour can hardly be exaggerated. The psychological analysis of moral development and individual differences in morality have received considerable attention. We cannot, however, embark on a survey of this work, since it would take us too far afield, but see Chapters 5, 7 and 10.

Self-concept (*SELF*). This subsection answers questions like, 'What is the person's attitude towards himself, i.e. what does he think and feel about himself, what does he want of himself?', 'How does the person's view of the way he is (real self) compare with his view of the way he feels he ought to be (ideal self)?', 'What does the person incorporate in his sense of self?', 'How would the person describe himself in respect of each of the many facets of personality?'.

The person's assessment of himself is sometimes a closely guarded secret, although most people, in the kinds of situation for which the quasi-judicial method is appropriate, are willing to disclose at least some of this private information to the investigator. A variety of counselling and examining techniques are available for the study of the self-concept. Certain kinds of counselling problems have as their main focus the exploration, analysis and modification of the client's self-concept.

The self is a particularly difficult concept to analyse, but it is well enough understood at a professional level, and at a commonsense level, for it to be dealt with effectively in a quasi-judicial inquiry. Although the contents of self-descriptions range over more or less the same categories of information as do descriptions of others, there are some differences in emphasis, and some content categories are obviously not applicable to self-descriptions. The contents and organization of self-descriptions will be the subject of a future publication, but see Livesley and Bromley (1973, pp. 236–40).

It could be argued that the self-concept is an essential element in the study of personal adjustment because it represents a subjective appraisal of the way the person has adapted to his environment. The individual's access to his own private thoughts, feelings and desires puts him in a privileged position when it comes to assessing his own behaviour. Unfortunately, the self-concept is liable to defensive distortions; hence, the way to make a comprehensive personality appraisal is to combine the best features of the objective biographical and subjective autobiographical methods, a combination which is provided for in the quasi-judicial method and widely used in clinial psychology.

Matters towards which motivation and orientation are directed (*OBJE*). The person's environment contains many objects, circumstances, ideas and events related to his motivation (MOTA) and orientation (ORFE), and the information appropriate to this aspect of personality description is dealt with implicitly in the subsections dealing with motivation and orientation. It answers questions like, 'What things are important to this person?', 'How does he regard them?', 'How does he relate to them, i.e. how does he organize his behaviour with regard to them?', 'What reinforcement contingencies are influencing his behaviour?', 'How are the person's life and circumstances interlocked?', 'What are the main situational determinants of his behaviour?'. Professional clinical psychologists or social workers should have no difficulty in adapting questions like these (and those in other sections) to the kinds of cases they deal with.

When the main 'objects' of the person's feelings and desires are other people, as they frequently are, the evidence elicited by these questions may be assimilated to some other category under the general heading of social relationships: see below.

The main purpose of emphasizing the fact that motivation and attention are directed towards 'something' is to reaffirm the *ecological* nature of human adaptation, and the need to study human behaviour in relation to the surrounding environment. The person's actual adjustment to his environment is simply one pattern in a wide range of possible patterns; this issue is dealt with in detail in our general theory of personal adjustment: see Chapter 9.

(v) Social Positions and Relationships

In the notation we have employed, the abbreviation SP, in SP–O, for example, refers to the stimulus person (the person under investigation). The letter O stands for other people with whom the SP is associated or compared. The letter S, in SP–S for example, stands for the writer of the case-report (or his primary informant) whose personality impression it describes. In earlier chapters cataloguing statements under the various content categories of personality description, the letter S referred to any 'subject' in the author's sample who had written the personality impression from which a statement was taken. In a case-study, the writer of the personality description is usually the principal investigator; he may be in a position to report on his direct observations of and relationships with the stimulus person, e.g. transference relationships. In other investigations there may be no relationships to report between the stimulus person and the writer of the report.

This section of the report deals with the following seven categories of information: social position, roles and statuses (SOPO); family and kin (FAMK); friendships and loyalties (FRIL); stimulus person's response to others (SP–O); others' response to the stimulus person (O–SP); mutual interaction of the stimulus person and others (SP+O); similarities and differences between stimulus person and others (SPvO). Corresponding to these sorts of information are questions designed to elicit them. These questions and related issues are discussed in the following subsections.

Social position (*SOPO*). This subsection answers questions like, 'What is the individual's position in society?', 'What do other people expect of him at work, at home, or in other key social settings?', 'In what esteem is he held?', 'How does he see his role relationships in comparison with the way they are seen by his role partners?'.

Information about a person's social roles and status is important because it describes the broad patterns of social behaviour expected of him and implies a great deal about his values, attitudes, abilities and daily routines. In other words, such information describes part of the social context of personal adjustment, and so helps to explain why, for example, a person who has moved educationally and occupationally into a higher social class may have problems of adjustment in relation to family and friends in a lower social class. Social roles and status are associated with income, life-style, values, leisure activities, and a wide range of other characteristics. Their influence is so extensive that it is possible to interact effectively with a person in terms of his social role and status without knowing him on a personal or individual basis. Most people behave as they are expected to behave in role relationships and in situations governed by social prescriptions; and to this extent personality characteristics, in the sense of individual qualities, are irrelevant. It is only in situations and relationships for which behaviour is *not* socially prescribed that understanding the person as an individual becomes important, or in situations where the person's behaviour transgresses social prescriptions or has become problematical. The quasi-judicial method can be used in the study of discrepancies between individual conduct and social expectation. This may lead to attempts to modify or constrain the behaviour of the individual, or to change his social arrangements, or both.

Family and kin (*FAMK*). This subsection answers questions like, 'What is his family like?', 'Who are his closest relatives?'.

Questions about the psychological aspects of family relationships are included here if the person's main problem of adjustment lies in his relationships with his family, e.g. 'What exactly is the nature of the person's family relationships?', 'How do they affect his personal adjustment?'. But if this is not the case, and his behaviour in relation to kin is simply part of a more general problem of adjustment, then questions about the psychological aspects of family relationships are dealt with under another heading.

Friendships and loyalties (*FRIL*). This subsection answers questions like: 'Who are the person's friends (or enemies)?', 'To whom is he friendly and loyal (or unfriendly and disloyal)?', 'What form do these friendships (or enmities) take?'.

The importance of evidence about friendships and loyalties, including enmities, is that this area of personal adjustment is often at the centre of a more general problem. The numerous subcategories of information included under the general heading of social relationships make it clear that individuals usually encounter their frustrations in relation to other people, especially their close associates. Failure to explore this aspect of personal adjustment would usually constitute a serious omission in a case-study.

Stimulus person's response to others (*SP–O*). This subsection answers questions like, 'What is the person's attitude to people in general, i.e. what does he think about other people, what does he want or expect of them?', 'How does he treat other people?', 'How does he react to them?'. The answers to these questions are usually given in general terms; and even where particular people and circumstances are referred to, the intention is usually to illustrate a person's general attitudes towards them.

Naturally, questions may be asked about the stimulus person's response to particular people, and the formulation of such questions presents no difficulty. Indeed, such questioning would be an inquiry into the stimulus person's impression of another person and could in theory range over all facets of personality. In practice, however, one is likely to be interested only in the stimulus person's attitude towards those aspects of the other person's behaviour which have a bearing on the problem under investigation, i.e. the personal adjustment of the stimulus person. Evidence about 'meta-perspectives' in interpersonal perception may be important, e.g. in family therapy: see Laing, Phillipson and Lee (1966).

We recall that statements about the stimulus person's response to others occur with considerable frequency in personality descriptions—testimony, perhaps, to the recognition, in commonsense, of the importance of social adjustment. Included among them are statements about social attitudes, e.g. attitudes towards fairly well-defined social groups, such as members of the opposite sex, older or younger generations, political, racial and religious groups, and so on. Attitudes towards people in general, groups of people, and individual persons, are so numerous and so important in personal adjustment that it is desirable to deal with them separately from attitudes towards the non-human aspects of the person's environment.

Others' response to the stimulus person (*O–SP*). This subsection answers questions like, 'How do people in general react to the stimulus person?', 'What is the general attitude of people to him, i.e. what do people think and feel about him, what do they want or expect of him?'. Again, the answers to these questions are given in general terms; and even when particular people and circumstances are referred to, the intention is to illustrate a common attitude towards the person, i.e. his reputation.

Naturally, questions may be asked about the responses of particular people, or groups of people to the stimulus person; and the formulation of such questions presents no difficulty, since one would simply be inquiring into the impression that other people had formed of the stimulus person, which could in theory range over all facets of personality.

The assessment of 'reputation', however, presents something of a problem. While it is relatively easy to determine what is commonly believed and felt about a person, it is difficult to validate the grounds of such beliefs and feelings. In a court of law, evidence about a person's reputation may be introduced in the form of testimony by one or more witnesses, but no cross-examination is allowed because it would raise too many collateral issues. The quasi-judicial procedure is not so closely bound by the rules of evidence in law; so it is up to the investigator to decide, in a particular case, how far he needs to go in exploring a person's reputation. The study of reputation belongs properly to social psychology, and although it would have been interesting to analyse the concept of reputation alongside the concept of personality this would have made our analysis of the language of personality descriptions even more complicated than it is now, and we prefer to deal with the social psychology of reputation in a separate and subsequent research report.

The great frequency of O–SP statements in personality descriptions further confirms the importance of social relationships in personal adjustment.

Mutual interaction of the stimulus person and others $(SP + O)$. This subsection answers questions like, 'What main activities does the stimulus person share with other people?', 'Is the problem an individual one or is anyone else closely involved and facing the *same* problem?', 'Can the problem be dealt with more effectively in terms of social (rather than individual) psychology?'.

It sometimes happens, as in marriage or family relationships, that several people are involved in a problem; so that the quasi-judicial inquiry is called upon to study the personal adjustment of several individuals in relation to each other. It must somehow deal with the factors common to all and those peculiar to each. Such investigations are obviously more complicated than individual case-studies, but the quasi-judicial concepts and procedures can be adapted to cope with them. If the inquiry is dealing with one person, however, evidence about mutual interaction between the stimulus person and others $(SP + O)$ should be assimilated to the information categories SP–O and O–SP, since it is likely to form a very small part of the total evidence.

We repeat that as a general rule in the organization of a case-report, issues and evidence *need not* be dealt with under *all* the separate headings and subheadings we have listed, especially if some of them form a very small part of the case-study (or if the case-study itself is brief). Instead, they should be assimilated to the most relevant main category, so that, finally, the case report is much simpler and more sharply focused than it would otherwise be, the issues and evidence being concentrated under a few main headings.

Similarities and differences between the stimulus person and others $(SPvO)$. This subsection answers questions like, 'How does the person compare with other people?', 'What social frames of reference are being used to assess the person?',

'Is the person being assessed against appropriate standards of behaviour and ability?'.

The relevance and importance of evidence relating to questions of this kind is easy to see. We have few absolute objective measures of psychological characteristics, and the need for at least relative and standardized measures is amply demonstrated in the immense amount of effort that has been devoted to the development of psychometric tests of personality, intelligence, motivation, attitudes, and other psychological and performance characteristics.

The issue of whether the available psychometric measures can provide the evidence needed in psychological case-studies is not one that we need to pursue further. The issue continues to be debated in the technical literature of personality and psychometrics; and it is the responsibility of a particular investigator to decide what use to make of psychometric evidence in his study of a particular case. We have argued that evidence derived from standardized assessment procedures may, or may not, be helpful, and that, in any event, such evidence is only one sort of evidence among the many diverse kinds normally available to the diligent investigator. Among the more obvious cases in which standardized psychometric evidence would usually be appropriate are, for example, those associated with scholastic and vocational adjustment and those with definite psychiatric symptomatology.

In many psychological case-studies, however, formal psychometric assessment is not possible—for want of sufficient resources or a suitable assessment method—or not necessary because sufficient relevant evidence of another, more pertinent, kind is available. We have argued that the psychological case-study focuses on 'the person in a situation', i.e. it uses what we have termed a 'behavioural ecology' framework for the study of personal adjustment. This framework requires an investigator to cast the net for evidence very widely, far beyond the scope of psychometric and laboratory measurement, and to study the situational context of personal adjustment as closely as the personality itself; it is described more fully as a 'general theory' of personal adjustment in Chapter 9.

Statements about similarities and differences between the stimulus person and other people, when valid, show how the person is placed relative to other people with whom he can reasonably be compared: in respect of, say, academic performance, co-operativeness, social isolation, and so on. Such standards of comparison, or 'yard-sticks' as they have been called, are commonly used in personality descriptions, and are often explicitly called for in requests for testimonials (referees' reports). As we have seen, standards of comparison with others are implicit in the very words and phrases we use to make statements about people. Indeed, it is obvious that a common language of personality description implies a socially shared frame of reference which must take account of the similarities and differences between individuals (as well as the similarities and differences in behaviour between different occasions for one and the same person). The logic of comparative judgments is that, if we know something about the average and range of behaviour of people of a certain kind, the reference group, and if variations in their behaviour are associated with certain other facts or outcomes, e.g. marriage, occupational failure, or whatever, then knowing how a person's actions or personal characteristics compare with those of the reference group enables us to make a more confident prediction about these associated facts.

As we have already explained, social comparisons may be more, or less, objective, and more, or less, evaluative. We do not wish to imply that the ease and confidence with which we make statements comparing one person with another reflects the validity and reliability of such statements. Much of the time, social standards of comparison are vague rather than precise, and normative rather than empirical.

(vi) Relationships with the Investigator
This section of the case-report deals with the following four categories of information: stimulus person's response to the investigator (SP–S); investigator's response to the stimulus person (S–SP); mutual interaction of the stimulus person and investigator (SP + S); similarities and differences between the stimulus person and the investigator (SPvS). Corresponding to the four sorts of information listed above are the questions designed to elicit them; these questions are discussed in the following subsections. These four categories of information are similar to four of the categories in the previous subsection, namely SP–O, O–SP, SP + O and SPvO. The reason for making a distinction between them and using the notation, it will be recalled, is that the investigator or primary informant himself is sometimes closely involved with the person under investigation. This may be so, for example, when the case-study is carried out as a class exercise by a student. When the case-study uses facts and inferences supplied by a primary informant who is closely associated with the stimulus person, it can be helpful to separate out that particular line of evidence and argument from others. Sometimes, in virtue of his comparability with the stimulus person, an investigator can use his own personal qualities and behaviour as a yard-stick against which to assess the stimulus person.

Stimulus person's response to the investigator (SP–S). This subsection answers questions like, 'What is the stimulus person's attitude to the investigator, i.e. what does he think and feel about him, what does he want or expect of him?', 'How does he treat the investigator or primary informant?', 'How does he react to him?'.

The answers to these questions naturally refer to fairly specific ways of behaving, and they have a bearing on the validity and usefulness of the evidence that the primary informant provides. For example, a statement to the effect that the stimulus person is suspicious of the investigator implies that the stimulus person has grounds for not co-operating, or will try to mislead the investigator; a statement to the effect that the stimulus person feels himself to be dependent in some way upon the primary informant implies that the stimulus person will try hard to create a favourable impression. In both instances, the stimulus person's words and actions are affected by the relationship he has with the observer and must be interpreted accordingly.

Questions about the stimulus person's reactions to the investigator or primary informant could, in theory, range over all facets of personality, since this subsection is concerned with the subjective personal elements in the stimulus person's impression (personality description) of another person. In practice, however, one is interested only in the stimulus person's attitude to those aspects of the investigator's behaviour that have a bearing on the problem under investigation.

Investigator's response to the stimulus person $(S–SP)$. This subsection asks questions like, 'How does the investigator (or primary informant) react to the stimulus person?', 'What does he think and feel about him?', 'What does he want and expect of him?'. Again, the answers to these questions naturally refer to fairly specific ways of behaving, and they have a bearing on the validity and usefulness of the evidence that the investigator provides. For example, a statement to the effect that the investigator likes or dislikes the stimulus person implies that the evidence he provides, and any personality description he gives, is likely to be selected and distorted in one way or the other; or, a statement to the effect that the investigator associates frequently with the stimulus person implies that his assessments are based on reasonably large and representative samples of the stimulus person's behaviour.

The formulation of questions to inquire into the investigator's subjective reactions to the stimulus person presents no difficulty because what is being inquired into is part of his personal impression (personality description) of the stimulus person; and such questions could, in theory, range over all aspects of personality. In practice, however, one is interested only in those aspects of the investigator's impression which have a bearing on the issues in the case-study.

Statements in the category S–SP may constitute a major facet of the investigator's impression (personality description) of the stimulus person, partly because a personality impression is usually a personal and subjective reaction, and is often conveniently expressed in first person singular statements. But if an investigator is successful in obtaining evidence about the stimulus person from a number of independent and competent observers (secondary informants) he is in a strong position to establish areas of inter-subjective agreement and to correct any distorting tendencies and omissions arising from his own personal and sub-jective reactions, e.g. from race prejudice or transference.

Mutual interaction of the stimulus person and the investigator $(SP + S)$. This subsection asks questions like, 'What main activities, if any, of the stimulus person are shared with the investigator (or primary informant)?', 'Is the problem a personal one or is the investigator (or primary informant) himself involved in it?'.

Any evidence supplied by an informant about affairs with which he is closely involved is bound to be viewed rather sceptically, even though the informant is well-placed to provide relevant evidence. The problem is that if the informant has an 'interest' in the outcome of the investigation, he cannot be regarded as a credible witness since, apart from deliberate lying and withholding of infor-mation, his view of the stimulus person may be unwittingly selected and distorted. On the other hand, the informant's personal involvement puts him in a good position to provide important evidence about the stimulus person, evidence which may not be available from any other source. In judicial inquiries, considerable care is needed in handling evidence of this kind, since a witness may not wish to incriminate himself or to be seen to break confidences that he may have entered into with the stimulus person. In quasi-judicial inquiries, on the other hand, the situation is less fraught with difficulties, and it is up to the investigator to assess the relevance and admissibility of evidence of this kind.

Statements about the mutual interaction of the stimulus person and the investigator (SP + S) are relatively infrequent and can usually be assimilated without difficulty into the categories SP–S or S–SP. As with SP + O statements, SP + S become problematical only when the case-study is plural, i.e. concerned with two or more closely involved people, and when one of these is the primary informant, as in marital counselling.

Similarities and differences between the stimulus person and the investigator (SPvS). This subsection asks questions like, 'How does the stimulus person compare with the investigator (or primary informant)?', 'Are such comparisons appropriate?'.

The information needed to answer questions of this sort is clearly different from that provided by reference to commonsense social norms or psychometric standards—these are agreed between competent observers; but there are no such standards of reference in the personal and subjective comparisons categorized as SPvS. However, provided the personality of the primary informant (S) is reasonably well understood, then comparative statements of the SPvS variety can be informative, and can range over most facets of personality. Quite often, SPvS statements reveal something of the identification characteristics used by the informant himself in establishing and confirming his own personal identity (self-description).

(vii) Ethical Evaluation (EVAL)

This section of the report deals with questions like, 'What moral considerations, if any, are relevant to the assessment of this person?', 'What ethical rules and standards are appropriate?', 'What ethical considerations, if any, has the person himself been influenced by?', 'What can be said about the social desirability or undesirability of this person's tendencies and characteristics?'.

We have argued against the policy of pretending that personality assessment can be made objective in the sense of excluding value judgments. We have preferred instead to follow the logic of the quasi-judicial procedure, which enables us to use an objective, rational, empirical, socially agreed method for making value judgments. The quasi-judicial method is concerned with empirical evidence and psychological inference, but it is also concerned with social norms and values, if only because much of the behaviour that it has to investigate depends upon internal and external ethical factors: see Chapters 5, 7 and 10.

(*viii*) *Review of the Evidence and Arguments*

The purpose and the terms of reference of a case-study may undergo some revision as the investigation proceeds, but by the time the report is being written up, these can be clearly stated. The subsequent sections: identity, life-history and present circumstances, psychological attributes, social relationships and evaluation, present whatever information and arguments are available for dealing with the issues in the case-study. This next section of the report, therefore, is analogous to the judge's 'summing up' in a judicial inquiry: it restates the basic questions; it summarizes and simplifies the empirical evidence and logical inferences presented in the previous sections; it considers the possible findings and recommendations.

The language of quasi-judicial investigations—of the kind typically encountered in clinical psychology, social case-work, biography and high-grade journalism—is closer to ordinary language than is the precise and formal language of court proceedings.

We repeat that issues and evidence need not be dealt with under *all* the separate headings and subheadings we have listed, especially if some of them form a very small part of the case-study (or if the case-study itself is brief). They can be sharply focused and concentrated under a few main headings.

We also repeat that there is no standard format appropriate for *all* case-studies, and lack of space forbids the presentation of specimen cases. Our account of the quasi-judicial method has shown what is required in the way of *ideal standards of scientific inquiry* in the psychological study of individual cases.

Even casual personality descriptions in everyday life frequently include an explanatory framework, i.e. simple inferences and arguments. Unfortunately it is not always easy to see the structure of 'commonsense' arguments, since they are sometimes incomplete and confused, apart from being invalid or untrue. A scientific, quasi-judicial, account of a person's adjustment must not only report systematically what has been observed, it must impose a convincing 'pattern of meaning' on that evidence.

The kinds of case-study we are concerned with usually preclude the exclusive use of actuarial argument; and, in spite of the attempt by Sarbin, Taft and Bailey (1960) to demonstrate the applicability of formal logic in clinical assessment, psychological case-material does not lend itself to this kind of analysis. The most effective way of demonstrating the internal logic of empirical arguments expressed in ordinary language is that developed by Toulmin (1958). The applicability of this method to the analysis of arguments in clinical case-studies was demonstrated by Bromley (1968); in a further study, Bromley (1970) showed in detail how Toulmin's logic worked in practice in the analysis of empirical arguments in social and behavioural science. We described the method briefly in Chapter 2 (using the notation: D, so Q, C, since W, on account of B, unless R, for a simple argument in standard form).

In the kinds of informal argument we are referring to, it is understood that one need not state *all* the conditions that must be met if the argument is not to be rebutted, but one should state those which might reasonably be called in question. Regrettably, even in professional and scientific writings, arguments are often incoherent and incomplete; and many facts, assumptions and relationships are not stated explicitly.

The following informal argument in standard form illustrates one of several possible 'constructions' imposed on an actual case-study:

D: There was no evidence in the life-history data on the patient to indicate any predisposition to neurosis, and the presenting symptoms did not clearly fit any of the standard patterns. The patient's condition did not improve over a period of time.

Q, C: So, presumably, the patient was not suffering from a neurosis precipitated by the stress of the accident (a head injury) and the subsequent circumstances (absence from work, boredom).

W: Since stress reactions tend to decrease with time after the stresses are removed, and neurosis is usually associated with a predisposition to maladjustment.

B: On account of the accepted concepts and findings described in the literature of psychopathology.

R: Unless the term neurosis is taken to include the condition referred to as 'compensation case'; or unless the cumulative effects of ageing, alcohol and occupational stresses, have lately increased the patient's predisposition to neurosis; or unless the patient's life-history and present circumstances have not been adequately investigated.

Arguments in ordinary language can be transformed into their explicit 'standard form' and connected with one another to form a 'network' by virtue of the fact that some of them have statements in common: for example, the C of one argument is the D of another. Each of the six component parts of an argument may consist of several sentences. Taken together, the component statements form a complex quasi-logical network or structure. Some of them may be accepted without question as assumptions, others may be disputed. Disputes give rise to further arguments until the parties to the dispute can find common ground for agreement. Such 'disputes', of course, may take place within the mind of one investigator as he works out the implications of his own theories and observations. Eventually, some of the statements come to be regarded as established or not in dispute, or used simply as assumptions or definitions, and these provide anchorage points for the system as a whole. The problem is to develop the network of argument so that it is capable of dealing with the 'facts in issue'—capable, that is, of leading to a reasonable conclusion, either by finding evidence and arguments which deal with the problem directly or by finding circumstantial evidence and indirect arguments.

In theory, this approach to the analysis of case-material is an informal, open, logical system capable of assimilating all kinds of data, definitions and concepts. In practice, the problem is to derive, from the ordinary language of the case-study, those propositions which form the component statements in C, D, W, Q,

R and B. Actually, the explicit or manifest argument is usually derived from a much larger system of implicit or latent arguments, and the validity of the main explicit argument can be established only by working through the ramifications of these subsidiary arguments.

We have seen that statements about personality and adjustment may have quite complicated syntactical structures, expressing complex logical relationships. The connection between the logical expressions referred to then and the logical arguments referred to now is fairly straightforward. A statement of the form: 'P_i is A only when S_j is X', e.g. 'He is depressed only when there is pressure at work', might operate as a component in an argument about a person's occupational adjustment. As we have seen, a simple 'argument' in 'standard form' consists of a sequence of statements, as follows: D, so Q, C, since W, on account of B, unless R. A 'network' of arguments is an interrelated system of arguments in standard form, usually arranged so that the key issues can be settled by reference to them: see Bromley (1970).

This method of analysing the logical structure of a complex argument goes well beyond ordinary language and commonsense in the degree of explicitness, precision and comprehensiveness that it calls for. Nevertheless, it does not have the exactness of completeness characteristic of formal logic; and for want of a better name we have referred to it as 'informal logic' or, to use Toulmin's original term, 'substantial logic': see Toulmin (1958).

The basic aim of a quasi-judicial case-study is to formulate a cogent argument, i.e. a rational and empirical argument, which will explain the problematical behaviour of the person under investigation. Such an argument is, in effect, a *theory* or *explanation* about that person's adjustment, and is therefore open to question and subject to continual revision in the light of fresh evidence and new ideas. Ideally, the case-study eventually reaches a stage at which it makes good sense: it is internally coherent; it corresponds with the empirical evidence; it successfully predicts how the individual will behave; and it is accepted by competent investigators working independently of one another. We can then say that we 'understand' the stimulus person (or at least that aspect of his personality which is under scrutiny). In general, to understand the *logic* of human conduct (as expressed in correct explanations) is to understand the *psychology* of human conduct.

We have already described some familiar concepts in ordinary language and commonsense which we use to impose orderliness and predictability on human behaviour: concepts like role, motive, trait, habit, attitude (or state of mind) and constraint. Such concepts fulfil an explanatory function. We have also referred, very briefly, to the technical and professional concepts used, for example, in clinical psychology and social case-work. Thus behaviour can be 'explained' in terms of psychodynamic mechanisms, stress reactions, genetic flaws, psychophysiological functions, social factors, developmental sequences, schedules of reinforcement, cognitive processes, political bargaining, family dynamics, and so on. Such explanatory notions may find a place in case-studies. Indeed, they can be regarded as conceptual routines for making psychological sense of certain *classes* of problematical behaviour, e.g. neurosis, accidents, interpersonal conflict; and in this respect they have a bearing on the development of psychological 'case law'.

An adequate explanation for a person's behaviour in a given situation is one which contains enough empirical evidence, marshalled by a sufficiently cogent and comprehensive argument, to convince a competent investigator that he understands something that previously puzzled him. When the issues are dealt with in the 'informal' but systematic way that we have proposed, it is easy to see how a psychological case-study can be dealt with effectively by means of a quasi-judicial procedure. A psychological case-study presents a problem—one that calls for understanding and practical action. On the basis of preliminary inquiries, the issues are stated and the inquiry gets under way by verifying the basic facts and collecting evidence relevant to the main issues. Gradually, various lines of evidence and argument are followed up, leading eventually, by recognized procedures, and with varying degrees of confidence, to reasonable conclusions and recommendations. Clinical and social case-work, using a quasi-judicial procedure, assess the extent to which a psychological theory can be tested against the available evidence. A theory, as we have seen, is simply a way of organizing a network of substantial (informal) arguments so that sensible conjectures imposed on good evidence lead convincingly to conclusions which can be held with some confidence.

In one sense, an explanation supplies the information which dispels the puzzlement felt by the person seeking an explanation. A simple fact or relationship may be all that is needed to dispel the puzzlement. In general, when we seek an explanation for a person's behaviour we are looking for the evidence we lack, or we are looking for some sort of interpretation or relationship which has so far eluded us. To find an explanation is to be able to impose a pattern of meaning on the information we have available. Metaphorically speaking, it means getting those additional pieces of the jig-saw puzzle which enable us to put the whole picture together. Sometimes, however, we do not have all the pieces of the puzzle, and the pieces we do have can be put together in different ways, so that we cannot be sure which is the correct way.

Strictly speaking, the quasi-judicial procedure is designed not to establish what is true but to refute what is false. The conjectures we make, as investigators, about why the person behaves as he does can be regarded as 'proto-theories': simple arguments about facts and relationships. The problem then is to propose explanations for the problematical behaviour and to attempt to refute them by reference to the evidence. Thus, in the end, when the ramifications of the network of argument have been worked out, we have a complex web of evidence and inference which is compatible with some conclusions but incompatible with others.

The quasi-judicial case-study provides a paradigm for the study of personality and adjustment in clinical psychology, social case-work, and other areas of work with individuals. It is not difficult to state the rules that govern the relevance and admissibility of evidence, the credibility of witnesses, the significance of personal disclosures, the significance of personal involvement in the case on the part of informants or the investigator himself, the significance of documentary and psychometric evidence, experimental evidence, and so on. Such rules are modelled on those of judicial procedure, and include those relating to corroboration, circumstantial evidence, confessions, and the like: see, for example, Trankell (1972).

Ideally, clinical psychology and social case-work should have principles based on a body of 'case law' accumulated through the rigorous use of the quasi-judicial method applied selectively but systematically and making psychologically significant comparisons and contrasts between individual cases.

In reality, all we have is a few detailed case-studies, together with an assortment of brief descriptions or illustrative fragments of cases. We are aware, of course, that the proposal to rely on 'case law' as the foundation for a 'science' of personality is so radical that its philosophical and methodological implications are difficult to appreciate.

(ix) Methods and Constraints

This section of a case-report answers questions about the methods used and the conditions under which the case-study was carried out. For example, it shows who took part in the investigation and what contributions they made. Where appropriate, it refers to non-directive interviewing, psychological testing, experimental results, systematic interrogation and cross-examination, unobtrusive measures, reports of observers, letters, testimonials, diaries and other personal documents, and any other sort of method. This section describes any restrictions imposed by time, resources and other circumstances; and it attempts to show what effects, if any, these restrictions have had on the case-study. This section of the report should conclude with a statement of what evidence is still outstanding and what further lines of inquiry are worth pursuing.

(x) Conclusions: Findings, Recommendations and Forecasts

This section of the report simply restates as concisely as possible the findings reached in the 'Summing Up'—omitting the supporting evidence and arguments; it also recommends whatever practical action is appropriate, with regard to therapy or training, for example. It attempts to forecast the way the individual will react to these measures or to future circumstances, such as occupational stress, divorce or adoption, in the light of the assessment arrived at in the case-study.

V. Final Checks

Before we conclude this chapter, we need to list the final checks that an investigator should make in order to be confident that he has made a satisfactory case-study. These checks are as follows: that the report fulfils its aims and purposes; that it satisfies its terms of reference, contains no serious omissions, and makes good psychological sense; that subjective factors have been reduced to a minimum, preferably by the incorporation of several independent opinions; that matters of detail are correct and each part is given its due weight; that the sources of evidence and methods of investigation are clearly stated and properly evaluated; that evidence and inference are not confused; that arguments are made explicit and as cogent as possible; that reasons are given for whatever conclusions are reached and for whatever action is recommended; that the evidence and its sources are properly catalogued, so that, in the event of another investigator taking over the case, the original data can be re-examined.

If the investigation is limited to fact-finding, as it might be if called for in connection with a judicial inquiry proper, care should be taken that no inadvertant selection and interpretation has been imposed on the empirical evidence, i.e. that the issues have not been 'pre-judged'.

VI. Postscript on Training

Our account of the quasi-judicial case-study method has been entirely theoretical, and concerned with ideal standards, but the practical applications are fairly obvious. It would have helped greatly to have presented a few detailed cases and a variety of summary reports (analogous to case law reports) by way of example. Unfortunately, the inclusion of such materials and the associated analysis would have added greatly to our already lengthy account. Psychological case-materials in Evans (1954), White (1975) and elsewhere show how the individual person can be described in ordinary language: these and other sources, e.g. political profiles, biographies, can be used to illustrate some of the concepts and procedures in the study of individual cases if looked at in terms of the quasi-judicial method.

The author has used the method for several years in undergraduate psychology training, and many satisfactory case-studies have been written by students. Case-studies prepared as training exercises have a few special features: the person to be investigated should be reasonably well-adjusted, unrelated to the investigator, and able to understand the nature of the exercise in which he is taking part; the nature of and the reasons for the exercise should be explained to the stimulus person, who must freely agree to take part (though some friendly persuasion and reassurance may be necessary); the investigation should be entirely confidential, to the point of altering or eliminating data on personal identity when writing up the report; the investigator should not become emotionally involved with the stimulus person but should maintain a neutral scientific (rational, objective) attitude; there need be no 'invasion of privacy' since the stimulus person will be prepared to disclose enough personal information to satisfy a practice exercise. Since everyone has problems of adjustment of one sort or another, there should be no difficulty in finding a suitable focus (or main issue) for the investigation— the investigation can, of course, deal with the stimulus person's life-style, i.e. his strategic adaptation to a fairly stable and congenial environment; there may be some small benefit to the stimulus person from the opportunity to talk about himself with someone who is prepared to listen, to ask relevant questions, and to discuss problems with him in an informed, dispassionate way.

A possible method for improving self-understanding and understanding others has been suggested by Mair (1970). It calls for a gradual but systematic mutual analysis of interpersonal disclosures through personality descriptions written by two cooperating subjects.

The quasi-judicial method is dealt with again briefly, in a somewhat different way, in Chapter 9, which describes a 'general theory' of personal adjustment, and includes a note on the advantages and applications of a 'quasi-judicial' approach to the study of persons.

CHAPTER 9

A General Theory of Personal Adjustment

I. Introduction

In this chapter, we put forward a theory of personality and adjustment which incorporates the advantage of ordinary language and the quasi-judicial method. It is difficult to find a suitable name for this theory. It attempts to develop a *comprehensive* account of the adaptation of an individual to his circumstances; so it could fairly be called a 'general theory' of personal adjustment.

How is the theory best presented? This question is easy to answer, thanks to the publication of *Personality Theories: A Comparative Analysis* by Maddi (1972 rev. ed.). In order to compare and contrast a wide range of personality theories, Maddi identifies a number of formal and substantive features. First, there are certain core tendencies and characteristics common to all normal people. Second, there are certain peripheral tendencies and characteristics peculiar to the individual or to particular types of individual; naturally, peripheral characteristics must be observable (preferably measurable) and capable of revealing a range of differences between individuals for a given characteristic. Third, there are developmental processes associated with the interaction of core factors on the one hand and environmental factors on the other, which lead to the manifestation of peripheral tendencies and characteristics. Fourth, there are procedures for the collection and analysis of empirical data, so that the reasoning that takes place within the framework of the theory can be related to the facts of observation.

We shall not review Maddi's method of comparative analysis, which is remarkable for the insights and perspectives that it achieves, but we shall adopt his terms of reference, as outlined in the previous paragraph. It is of particular interest to note that our attempt to develop a general theory of personal adjustment has revealed a few omissions in Maddi's meta-theoretical framework, and we shall refer to these in the appropriate place.

II. Basic Assumptions

A. Core Tendencies and Characteristics

According to Maddi, all theories of personality make assumptions about what he calls the 'core of personality'. This consists of what is essential and universal in normal human nature; the core is inherent and unlearned. Theories usually make reference to one of three central features, namely, the resolution of conflict, the fulfillment of potentialities, the integration of behaviour and experience. The term 'core tendency' refers to a basic function or purpose in human life, e.g. tension reduction, achievement, consistency; the term 'core characteristic' refers to a basic psychological structure or process, e.g. ego, defence, balance.

What does our 'general theory' of personal adjustment say about the central features of personality? With regard to 'core tendencies' it says that human beings evolve long-range strategies of adaptation (life-styles) through the selective reinforcement (or extinction) of varying patterns of behaviour. In response to demands and changes within himself, in relation to the constraints and opportunities in his environment (as he perceives them), the individual exhibits various forms of short-term tactical adjustment. Through contingencies of reinforcement, coupled with the complex effects of internal psychophysiological processes, he acquires, in time, relatively stable behavioural adaptations to his environment. Non-contingent changes in the person and in his environment create a continual demand for readjustment between the two.

Our general theory of personal adjustment identifies *one* core tendency, namely, 'adaptation'. But, in the light of Maddi's comparative analysis of personality theories, we can say that adaptation has at least three aspects: the tendency to reduce tension and to resolve conflicts—both within the person and between the person and his environment; the tendency to fulfil potentialities—in the sense that people tend to explore their environment and exercise their capabilities; the tendency to reduce or eliminate inconsistencies—in the sense that people seek to organize their behaviour and experience coherently.

Note that whereas the long-term strategic process of adaptation tends towards conflict resolution, the fulfillment of potentialities, and the elimination of inconsistencies in behaviour, the short-term tactical processes of adjustment may be accompanied by tension, failure and dissonance.

What does our general theory say about the 'core characteristics' of personality? Since it is mainly concerned with the psychological aspects of adaptation, it must take much of the biological basis of behaviour for granted. The theory naturally assumes that there is a physical basis for human behaviour and experience, and sees it as consisting of peripheral receptor/effector structures with sensori-motor functions and of central organizational structures with dispositional and mentalistic functions.

The dispositional and mentalistic functions in the organization of human behaviour and experience are not understood to anything like the same extent as those of sensori-motor functions, so it is worth examining these 'core characteristics' at least briefly. It is possible to distinguish at least eight varieties of central organizing function, all of which may (or may not) come into conscious awareness. The first such function is *directive*, i.e. behaviour tends to be linear, moving towards one state and away from another; this function may be experienced as desire, interest and intention. The second is *selective*, i.e. behaviour tends to be focused and restricted, oriented towards one aspect of the environment rather than another; this function may be experienced as attention, expectancy and set. The third is *associative* and *inferential*, i.e. behaviour tends to be internally connected, so that one sort of action is related to another (partly via rules and generalizations); this function may be experienced as learning and remembering. The fourth is *evaluative*, i.e. behaviour tends to be costed, the costs and benefits of one course of action are compared with those of another; this function may be experienced in feelings and attitudes. The fifth is *implicative*, i.e. behaviour tends to be deductive, inferences are derived from rules, generalizations and assumptions; this function may be experienced as reasoning and problem-solving (which is not necessarily formal or valid). The sixth is *executive*, i.e. behaviour tends to be put into effect, action is taken with regard to a situation; this function may be experienced as decision, choice and volition. The seventh function is *reflexive* and *defensive*, i.e. behaviour can be directed towards the self as well as towards the external environment; actions and mental states can refer to the subject (agent) as if he were an object, i.e. capable of being considered and acted upon by himself; this function may be experienced as self-awareness and self-control, but it is not necessarily complete or rational, and, like other functions, may take place without awareness. The eighth function is *speculative* and *creative*, i.e. behaviour is not confined to responses to actual, here-and-now situations, but can be detached, hypothetical and prospective (future oriented); this function may be experienced as imagining, exploring, planning, experimenting and daydreaming.

This brief excursion into the dispositional and mentalistic aspects of human behaviour is sufficient to show that our 'general theory' of personality and adjustment can incorporate what are elsewhere called 'ego functions', and can describe the self as an 'agent', i.e. a person capable of acting with some degree of independence from his external environment. It is not restricted to the mere description of overt behaviour, but attempts to analyse the *organization* of that behaviour by reference to a variety of hypothetical central organizing processes. In so doing, it shows the connections between the study of personality and adjustment on the one hand and much of the rest of scientific psychology on the other—connections which do not figure prominently, if at all, in other theories of personality.

The foregoing description does not pretend to have solved the many philosophical and psychological problems associated with concepts such as 'self' and 'consciousness'. But at least it attempts to show the connections between psychological processes and overt behaviour. The basic problem is probably semantic—that of developing a language which will co-ordinate the meaning of, and allow easy transitions between, terms referring to overt actions and terms referring to the covert organization of behaviour and associated experiences (including states of self-awareness).

Before we leave the topic of core tendencies and characteristics we must refer to the 'developmental process' whereby the individual's life-style or pattern of personal adjustment evolves out of the interactions between his core tendencies and characteristics on the one hand and his social and physical environment on the other. This developmental process accounts for what Maddi calls the 'concrete peripheral characteristics' of the individual, namely, his motives, traits and beliefs: characteristics that he acquires through learning and experience. Our general theory of personal adjustment adopts an ecological and evolutionary approach to this developmental process. It assumes that the behaviour and experience of the individual may vary or may stabilize, depending upon whether he is willing or able to produce variant forms of behaviour and experience in response to the opportunities and constraints of his environment. It also assumes that the environment itself may vary or remain stable, being partly within and partly outside the control of the individual.

The environment brings selective pressures to bear on the varying forms of behaviour produced by the individual. There is an obvious analogy, therefore, between the ontogenesis of individual behaviour and the phylogenesis (evolution) of species. The term ontogenesis refers to the historical development of a person's adaptation to his environment; the term phylogenesis refers to the genealogical history or biological evolution of a species. In this analogy, the person responds to his environment, but, in turn, the environment responds to the person. In virtue of the consequences of an action (or response), the person is more (or less) likely to reproduce the same or a similar action (or response) in the same or similar circumstances on another occasion. But the inborn psychobiological capacities of human beings include a tendency for their behaviour to vary *independently* of the environment, and the consequences of that behaviour on the environment then help to determine whether that sort of behaviour is more (or less) likely to be 'reproduced', i.e. repeated, on another occasion. The tendency for behaviour to vary independently of the environment plays a part in the development of personal adjustment analogous to the part played by genetic variations in the evolution of species. This may prove to be an important insight into the psychology of personal adjustment, because the idea that human behaviour can vary independently of the environment has been greatly overshadowed by the contrasting behaviourist idea that variations in human behaviour depend upon the shaping effect of environmental contingencies. Nevertheless, both commonsense and scientific observation confirm an essential and intrinsic variability in individual behaviour, see Fiske (1961), associated with the interplay of many different determining factors and inbuilt random processes as well as with intrinsic creative and exploratory functions.

Briefly then, the 'developmental process' in personal adjustment consists of the selective reinforcement of some forms of behaviour from among the variant forms produced by the individual, and of the rejection (extinction) of other forms. This does not mean that the individual is constantly moving towards a greater fulfillment of his potentialities or towards a more effective adaptation to his environment. We know only too well that some individuals evolve unsatisfactory, inefficient and maladaptive forms of behaviour. The drift of behaviour is towards the establishment, preservation and exploitation of a 'behavioural niche'.

B. Lifespan Changes and the Developmental Process

In this section and the two that follow we deal with an aspect of personality theory neglected by Maddi. Almost without exception, traditional theories of personality and adjustment have been concerned with juvenile development and young adult status. The more influential theories, indeed, have claimed that the main personality characteristics and strategies of adjustment are fashioned in the experiences of infancy and early childhood, and that subsequent patterns of behaviour are repetitions and variations of these basic themes.

Our 'general theory' cannot accept such restrictions on the nature and scope of personality study. It must take account not only of the differences *between* individuals but also of the variations *within* individuals at different times of life. It therefore regards personal adjustment as consisting of a finite series of ontogenetic and evolutionary adaptations between the person and his environment, beginning with conception and ending with death. We use the phrase 'adaptations between the person and his environment' to remind ourselves that adaptation is a two-way process: the person changes, and is changed by, his environment. The proper study of personality and adjustment is, therefore, the study of persons in situations.

The 'developmental process' referred to at the end of the previous section may have been taken to refer only to the juvenile period—the formative years. Indeed the very use of the word 'development' seems to imply a systematic and progressive expansion of behavioural capacities. But a moment's reflection on the post-developmental aspects of the human life-span shows that adult life and old age normally occupy about five-sevenths of the total life span: a period during which a variety of changes in personality and adjustment occur. A general theory must take these changes into account.

The life-span as a whole comprises a juvenile and an adult phase: see Bromley (1974) for a detailed account of concepts, methods and findings in the study of human ageing. The juvenile phase is normally characterized by the programmed maturation of psychobiological capacities (core tendencies and characteristics) and by the acquisition, through learning, of a wide range of associated behaviour patterns, dispositions and forms of experience (peripheral tendencies and characteristics). The nature of these peripheral qualities changes as development progresses, e.g. through middle childhood and adolescence, but the genetically based programme of juvenile development moves steadily towards its completion in early adult life. At this stage, and for a number of years thereafter, the normal adult is capable of surviving, thriving and reproducing his kind; at least he can in a congenial environment. He has developed a broad repertoire of responses, and can choose among a wide range of environmental circumstances.

Traditionally, theories of personality have been concerned with the structure and dynamics of the normal adult personality and its formation during the juvenile period; in addition they have been concerned with deviations from the normal and with psychopathological development. A general theory of personality and adjustment must take account of personality changes (and personality perception) in adult life and old age, see Bromley (in press). Many of these changes are not developmental in the strict sense, although others are; and the general pattern of change in the adult period is one of gradual but cumulative deterioration in psychobiological capacities accompanied by a systematic reduction in the individual's repertoire of responses and a shrinkage in the range of environmental opportunities for him to select from.

In adult life and old age, biological deterioration undoes the work of maturation carried out in the juvenile period. It follows, therefore, that the core tendencies and characteristics of personality change as the individual grows older. In addition, the environmental conditions surrounding the individual are different in adult life and old age from what they were in childhood and adolescence. So it follows, further, that the interaction between core tendencies and characteristics on the one hand and environmental conditions on the other gives rise to peripheral tendencies and characteristics which are different in the adult period from what they were in the juvenile period. Sometimes, especially in middle life, the changes are so gradual that they are hardly noticed; at other times, the changes are rapid and obvious, e.g. at critical ages like adolescence, the menopause, retirement, or at times of stress.

The term 'development' seems to be apt enough when applied to the growth of juvenile patterns of personality and adjustment and to their culmination in early adult life; but the term is not altogether apt when applied to later adult life and old age, since the process is mainly one of 'deterioration'. In spite of diminishing capacities for psychological development, there are often residual capacities for the expansion and improvement of personal adjustment even late in life.

The early stage of adult life is normally a period of gradual change in which the individual seeks to optimize his adjustment to his environment by exploring its opportunities and testing its constraints, at the same time discovering his own capacities and limitations. This generally takes place within a well-ordered social framework which prescribes the general nature and direction of the individual's behaviour; the effect of this is to reduce the range of individual differences and to encourage relatively standardized, normative, forms of behaviour. The pressures towards the stabilization of individual behaviour are therefore quite strong, particularly when the individual has to adapt to the existence of other individuals, e.g. at work, and through marriage and child-rearing.

In normal conditions, the environment in which the individual finds himself is relatively congenial, in the sense that it tends to be the best among the available alternatives, and makes demands well within the range of the individual's competence. In other conditions, however, where stress or deprivation occur, the demands of the environment may push close to or even beyond the limits of the individual's ability to cope, with the result that he becomes physically injured or ill, mentally ill, maladjusted or inefficient. The individual seeks an environment with which he can cope, and with which he can come to terms at a tolerable cost-benefit level.

The concept of adaptation (and of adjustment) implies a two-way relationship; the person adapts to his environment and the environment adapts to the person. Since the 'environment' includes other people and many man-made features, e.g., rules, regulations, symbols, machines, buildings, and so on, it is not wholly passive, but has the properties of an active agent. It is certainly no effort for the individual to regard his environment *as if* it were *active* in relation to him. He may change in response to the demands of the environment, and he may change the environment in response to his own demands.

This two-way relationship varies over time depending upon changes in the person and in his environment and upon the conditions governing the way they come to terms with each other. In the early, juvenile, dependent phase of life, for example, the social environment tends to be supportive, as it also tends to be late in life, taking account of the elderly person's infirmities. At least, this is the ideal state of affairs; although we know that in some cases life can be severely stressful at these ages. So stressful in fact that the person becomes physically and psychologically damaged; and, in extreme cases, unable or unwilling to go on living. At other times of life, by contrast, say in early or middle adulthood, the individual's psychobiological resources—and especially his accumulated experience, material resources and social relationships—may be greatly in excess of the routine demands of daily living, so that he has resources to spare, as it were, for the intensification and diversification of his own behavioural activities, and is thus able to engage in exploratory activities, cultural and scientific pursuits, technological innovations, and so on. It is sometimes under these relatively well-adapted conditions that the individual produces 'variant forms' of behaviour (although we normally think of necessity as the mother of invention), thus increasing the likelihood of improving his 'ecological niche'. In the process, he helps to create more of the man-made environment, although the consequences of his activities are not always clear to him. In particular, his behaviour in relation to religious, economic and political features of the social environment is likely to be affected by the normative nature of his ideas, in comparison with the positive nature of his knowledge of the material world.

Thus, the study of personality and adjustment cannot be pursued without reference to the man-made, cultural, aspects of the environment. Indeed, for modern man, these aspects of the environment are the most important, since the activities of daily living have been brought under close control by many generations of social and technical organization.

C. *Short-term Learning and Tactical Adjustment*

The mnemonic expression: $P_i \times S_j \to B_{ij}$ reminds us that behaviour (and experience) is a function of the interaction between a particular person and the particular situation he is in. Ordinary language enables us to state this relationship in a straightforward way, and to give a narrative, episode by episode, account of a series of personal adjustments: see Livesley and Bromley (1973, pp. 241–64) and Barker (1963). Episodic (momentary or tactical) adjustments can be thought of as segments in the serial organization of behaviour.

The changing person and the changing environment are partly dependent on, and partly independent of, each other: they have partial autonomy in the production of actions and circumstances respectively. The episodic nature of human adjustment can be illustrated by reference to Figure 3, representing one behavioural episode. The figure illustrates the simple idea that an individual person in a given situation acts in a particular way which has consequences for that person and for the situations in which he will find himself; moreover, both the person and the situation he is in are affected by factors acting independently. The complexity of events and their relationships sometimes makes it difficult for the person to act in accordance with the realities of the situation and of his own nature.

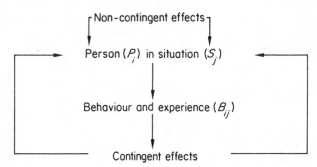

Figure 3. The cycle of events in psychobehavioural episodes.

A person's actions have short-, medium-, and long-term consequences for the person himself and for his environment. These consequences may be called 'contingent' in the sense that they depend on the person behaving in a particular way, although the actual effects also depend on factors other than the person's behaviour. In other words, just as the person's response occurs in a situational context, so the *effects* of that response occur in a context. As far as effects on the person are concerned, these range all the way from simple physiological effects, such as those following physical effort, to effects on motivation, such as diminished interest; the person's mood and dispositions may also be affected, e.g., elation and optimism, as may his capacities, e.g. increased knowledge and skill. As far as effects on the environment are concerned, these include simple physical effects like those of opening a door or steering a vehicle, as well as complex social, technological and ecological effects. A rational analysis of the sequence of antecedent and consequent events should enable one to decide the extent to which a particular effect can be attributed to a person's actions, as in a court of law.

The non-contingent effects on the person and his situation include all those factors that are relevant to understanding the person and his situation but are not attributable in any way to the person's previous behaviour. Such non-contingent effects would include, say, tension attributable to unavoidable social stress, and lack of information or incentive. Some effects may be contingent on the person's behaviour without his being aware of the fact, e.g. migraine following the ingestion of certain foods, or relief from anxiety when working hard. There are so many diverse and interacting factors at work in the creation of the situations that a person has to deal with that there is no point in attempting to explain their particular causal connections, unless, as in a judicial or quasi-judicial investigation, there is some reason for inquiring into them. For example, one might want to know the sequence of events leading to a scientific discovery, a suicide, a broken marriage or a failed examination; and some of the connections between one event and another in a sequence might be quite fortuitous, e.g. an overheard conversation, access to a drug, economic recession or a cold.

The individual is rarely, if ever, in full command of his environment; and his environment is in a constant state of flux. The individual is not even in full command of his own person and his own behaviour, since many of his psychobiological functions are outside his control and his awareness. Thus, when we speak of the person being partly autonomous we are saying no more than that he seems to have *some* capacity for reflection and for the self-regulation of his behaviour.

In the organization of behaviour, 'mentalistic' and 'dispositional' functions subserve the adaptive aspects of personal adjustment (comprising the motivational, attentional, associative, evaluative, rational, executive, reflective and speculative processes to which we have already referred). Briefly: in a simple situation, the individual is directed towards (or away from) some state of affairs, so that he is particularly attentive to certain features of his own environment and his own being; he attempts to relate his previous experience to his current situation and examines the pros and cons of various possibilities before taking action. This, at least, is the pattern for a fairly rational sort of behaviour. Often, however, the individual's behaviour is badly organized, in the sense that the dispositional and mentalistic functions are not operating effectively; he may have conflicting or detrimental desires, be unable to concentrate sufficiently, have mistaken ideas, confused values, insufficient intelligence, poor self-understanding, or lack grounds for decision. As a result, he fails to adjust well in the short-run and jeopardizes his chances of making a good medium-or long-term adaptation to his environment. There are some aspects of his behaviour, called 'expressive', e.g. unlearned emotional reactions, that may have contingent effects, especially on other people; but we would not regard such behaviour as organized in the same sense that 'coping' behaviour is organized.

In the ideal, rational, well-adjusted case, the dispositional and mentalistic functions govern particular phases of the activity cycle: rather like the 'drive, cue, response, reward' sequence familiar in the description of animal behaviour. Thus the individual is continuously motivated in one way or another; this leads him to take up some sort of selective orientation to his actual environment, and to the further possibilities of that environment; he then uses his experience and ability to 'realize' one or other of these possibilities; his actions may be more (or less) successful, and he sets in motion a causal sequence of events which includes physiological and psychological changes in himself, as well as physical and social changes in his environment.

A 'situation' is usually embedded in a set of wider circumstances with varying durations and complex interconnections. Thus, a wedding ceremony is embedded in the more inclusive arrangements of the wedding day, which in turn is embedded in a pattern of social relationships and economic circumstances. Again, a school lesson is embedded in a school day, a syllabus, a pattern of pupil-teacher relationships, classroom conditions, school organization, and so on. The 'meaning' of a situation depends on its context. In addition, because of the complexities of human existence and the operation of chance factors, situations arising from quite independent causes can become interconnected and give rise to new situations, as when two people meet by chance, or when a person is injured in an accident. For these reasons, adjustment has to be flexible, and effective long-term adaptation demands continuous variation and evolution in the organization of behaviour, not merely the repetition of standard forms of behaviour.

The term 'activity cycle' is appropriate to describe those routine forms of behaviour which comprise regular patterns of response to normal environmental conditions. The most obvious of these are the basic biological cycles associated with nutrition, excretion, sleep and sex. But culturally acquired habits of adjustment to a congenial and orderly environment also have the form of 'activity cycles', e.g. work, leisure and domestic activities. These routine activities of daily living in a man-made environment are analogous to the behavioural ecology of animals in their natural habitat.

D. Long-term Learning and Strategic Adaptation (Life-style)

We have used the phrase 'tactical adjustment' to refer to a relatively short-term pattern of behaviour exhibited by the person in coping with a fairly well-defined situation of rather limited duration. We obviously need another phrase to refer to a relatively coherent long-term pattern or system of tactical adjustments by means of which the individual comes to terms with the more enduring features of his environment. The most obvious phrase to use is 'strategic adaptation'. The terms 'tactics' and 'strategy' are familiar in relation to military and political matters, and in relation to games. The idea is that a general method or policy can be adopted in order to achieve a basic or distant aim; but the particular actions or moves by means of which the method is implemented depend upon the actual circumstances operating at the time.

The concept of personality itself refers to a stable set of characteristics and tendencies attributable to individual persons; these characteristics and tendencies are thought of as enduring over relatively long periods and as accounting for psychological similarities and differences among people. Personality has its basis in the individual's biological endowment and social upbringing, but is usually thought of as referring to the main psychological and behavioural themes of personal adjustment. Thus, although personality is 'realized' in the context of the immediate, existing situation, i.e. at the level of tactical adjustment, the concept itself refers to the somewhat idealized psychological structures or themes, i.e. dispositions, in the organization of behaviour, which have evolved as strategic adaptations to the general terms and conditions of the person's environment.

The distinction between strategy and tactics in the analysis of personal adjustment is important because case-studies and personality assessments are based on the assumption that it is possible to ascertain some of the more enduring (strategic) features in the organization of the person's behaviour. Thus, the formula $P_i \times S_j \rightarrow B_{ij}$ can express two rather different ideas: first, the determinants of a *particular* action; second, the determinants of a *characteristic* action. *Characteristic* behaviour (and experience) is a function of stable personal qualities interacting with recurrent and familiar circumstances. In our normal existence, we engage in certain recurrent cycles of activity, namely, those connected with biological functions and the habitual activities of daily living. These become fairly standardized or routinized patterns of adjustment associated with stable and congenial (or at least tolerable) environmental conditions; they constitute behavioural adaptations in the ontogenetic, evolutionary sense. They demonstrate the establishment of what is, in effect, an 'ecological niche' for the person concerned.

In addition to the strategies developed by the individual for coping with the ordinary activities of daily life, there are strategies for coping with life's uncertainties; and we often think that personality characteristics are more clearly revealed in rare unfamiliar situations than in frequent familiar ones. Most people have personal qualities and resources well in excess of those required by the ordinary demands of everyday life. Sometimes, however, the problem is to assess how a person will cope with new, perhaps stressful, situations that arise from time to time. Does he have the abilities, the inclinations, the values and attitudes, the experience and other personal qualities, to adjust to the circumstances envisaged? Does he seem to have them to a greater or lesser extent than other people with whom he can reasonably be compared? The answers to these questions tell us something about *strategic* considerations in the organization of individual behaviour (not forgetting his material assets and social contacts).

The last three sections have dealt with important aspects of personality and adjustment which are neglected in Maddi's comparative analysis. In the next section, however, we return to Maddi's framework.

E. The Description of the Person(ality)

Maddi (1972, pp. 404–521) discusses the ways in which empirical data are related to a variety of theories of (approaches to) personality and adjustment. The problem is to construct valid methods for the observation and measurement of each of the empirical manifestations of personality referred to by the descriptive terms of a theory. Those aspects of personality which can be empirically validated correspond to what Maddi calls the 'periphery of personality'; they are aspects of the organization of behaviour specific to that individual—being the products of the interaction between that particular person and the environmental circumstances to which he has been exposed. For the purposes of comparison, however, (and because people from a given stock brought up under similar cultural conditions develop broadly comparable patterns of personality and adjustment) it is necessary to construct methods for the observation and measurement of these peripheral characteristics, which are applicable to people in general (or at least to certain classes of people). This is merely saying that in the scientific study of personal adjustment we must relate our observations and measurements on particular people to a common frame of reference. The same principle applies in the formulation of *explanations* about the behaviour of individuals: see Chapter 8.

Particular manifestations of personality, i.e. peripheral characteristics, are found across the whole range of human behaviour, since each person is biologically unique and each person is influenced by a unique pattern of external circumstances, and has an individual history. Thus, differences between individuals are observable at all levels in the hierarchical and sequential organization of behaviour, from simple characteristics like the amount of pressure used to press a button and the frequency and duration of rest pauses in a standard test of continuous performance, to more complex characteristics like social attitudes and general traits.

Some of the more important personal characteristics are associated with social adjustment; and, as we have seen, most personal characteristics are associated with a greater or lesser degree of social desirability. Accordingly, we regard some people as more friendly, tolerant and trustworthy than others, on the basis of what we know of the way of their behaviour is organized, e.g. being pleasant and interested in other people, being able to accept differences and faults, and keeping their word. These social aspects of personality are, presumably, the products of a complex process of development relating the genetically-based morphological characteristics of the individual to the conditions of his environment and upbringing.

Descriptions of the observable manifestations of personality, i.e. peripheral characteristics, take the form of statements about a person's motives, traits, abilities and beliefs, e.g. 'He has a strong need for the company of other people', 'He is a competent car mechanic', 'He thinks his wife loves him'. If the person is systematically investigated, as in a case-study, it is usually possible to integrate observations and assessments like these, so that a coherent account can be given of the 'type' of personality to which the person belongs, and of the 'life-style' (type of strategic adaptation) that the person has evolved in coming to terms with his environment. The identification of distinctive 'personality types' or 'life-styles' through systematic comparisons and contrasts between individual cases shows how psychological 'case law' can lead to *scientific* generalizations.

The main question for this section, therefore, is, 'What sorts of empirical data and descriptive categories are relevant to a general theory of personal adjustment? But we have already answered this question in some detail through our analysis of the contents of personality descriptions in Chapters 5, 6 and 7, and through our analysis of the procedures and evidence in quasi-judicial case-studies in Chapter 8.

We must appreciate that the terms 'empirical data' and 'descriptive categories' do not have the same meaning. Strictly speaking, the term 'empirical data' refers to whatever can be objectively observed or measured with little or no inferential reasoning. The term 'descriptive categories', on the other hand, refers to whatever can be reasonably and conveniently referred to as evidence relevant to issues raised about a person's adjustment. Thus statements about physical appearance (PHYS) and actual incidents (INCS) refer fairly directly to empirical data (which may be used as evidence), whereas statements about traits (GENT), abilities (ABAT) and motivation (MOTA), if used as evidence must be backed up by empirical data. For example, descriptive evidence about an elderly person's mental status may be based on empirical observations of his responses to a standard mental status questionnaire. The use of descriptive categories thus greatly simplifies the problem of organizing information about personal adjustment; they provide a kind of bridge between theory and data. However, it is not the data that impose the descriptive categories on the theory, but the theory that must come to terms with the data by imposing meaningful descriptive categories on it.

One of the most difficult problems in the study of personality and adjustment has been that of linking personality theories with empirical data through meaningful descriptive categories, since the descriptive categories must be an integral part of the theory, but must also fit the empirical data. Our 'general theory' of personality and adjustment solves this problem in a straightforward way: first, by surveying the ordinary language of personality description and cataloguing the main descriptive categories and explanatory concepts; and second, by developing a quasi-judicial procedure for the study of individual cases, by means of which many sorts of empirical data can be considered to see whether or not they constitute evidence relevant to a particular case.

In a general theory of personal adjustment, it is unwise to limit the descriptive categories unnecessarily. Maddi, for example, seems to argue that there are only three: motives, traits and schemata (belief systems). It is obvious, however, that abilities and social relationships, for example, feature in the description of personality, and the important thing is to take account of all relevant data. Until a simpler system for describing peripheral personality characteristics can be shown to be preferable on both rational and empirical grounds, we prefer a relatively open, extended system, one that can assimilate any and all of the varieties of evidence relevant to understanding the individual person (including the comparisons and contrasts between that person and other people).

In our general theory of personality the 'peripheral personality characteristics', as Maddi would call them, have been grouped as follows:

External characteristics (nine content categories: IDEN, PHYS, HLTH, LIFE, SITU, PROS, ROUT, MATP, INCS);

Internal characteristics (nine content categories: GENT, SPET, MOTA, ORFE, ABAT, OBJE, EXPR, PRIN, SELF);

Interpersonal characteristics (eleven content categories: SOPO, FAMK, FRIL, SP–O and SP–S, O–SP and S–SP, SP+O and SP+S, SPvO and SPvS);

Ethical evaluation (one content category: EVAL).

The justification for regarding EVAL as a 'peripheral personality characteristic' is that it is possible to make an ethical evaluation of a person on the basis of empirical data about those aspects of his behaviour covered by a moral code. There are two further 'peripheral personality characteristics' in our general theory: short-term adjustments to situations (tactics); and long-term adaptations to the environment (strategy or life-style). The idea of 'adaptive strategy' or 'life-style' corresponds roughly to the notion of 'personality type'. Adaptive strategies (personality types) can be identified by reference to the quasi-judicial method in clinical psychology and social work where case-studies representative of a *class of similar cases* are available and can be used to illustrate the broad features common to such cases, e.g. delinquent careers, marital relationships, adaptations to old age, attempted suicides and neuroses. Similarly, in psychometric assessments of personality, it is possible to classify subjects according to the similarity of their score patterns and to refer to the average pattern as a 'personality type'.

At this point, it is convenient to make a distinction between 'personality measurement' and 'personality appraisal'. The term 'personality appraisal' refers to the assessment of persons by means of the broad range of concepts and methods used in the quasi-judicial approach to individual cases, which can (but need not) incorporate evidence derived from standardized, quantitative measures of personality. The term 'personality measurement' refers to the assessment of persons by means of a relatively narrow range of concepts and quantitative methods used in the psychometric approach to personality. The various types of psychometric method, see Cronbach (1964), and Goodstein and Lanyon (1971), measure the peripheral personality characteristics referred to in our general theory of personal adjustment, e.g. traits, abilities, interests, the self-concept.

Personality appraisal and personality measurement both contribute to the *basic* science of personality by developing standard concepts and methods (procedures) for the objective assessment of persons. It thus becomes possible to compare and contrast individuals, and to find relationships, including causal relationships, between one variable and another. Personality appraisal and measurement also contribute to the *applied* science of personality by providing evidence (based on empirical data) relevant to the treatment and practical management of individual cases, e.g. in educational and vocational guidance, marital counselling, behaviour modification (including attitude change) and psychotherapy. The practical advantages of personality measurement are obvious, provided the necessary requirements regarding reliability, validity, standardization and utility can be met. These requirements, however, are often not met; furthermore, psychometric methods of personality assessment are based on doubtful concepts and assumptions. Measurement is a desirable aim in, but it is not an essential feature of, personality study.

The quasi-judicial procedure for the study of individual cases, set in the context of a general theory of personal adjustment, provides a basic scientific method for personality appraisal and co-ordinates the empirical and applied aspects of case-work with the conceptual and theoretical aspects of case-law. We recall that the psychometric approach to personality assessment is embedded in a larger non-quantitative conceptual framework formulated partly in technical and partly in ordinary language. Although the psychometric approach, in the narrow sense referred to above, is compatible with our general theory of personal adjustment (since it can be used to generate data and test hypotheses), yet some of the assumptions underlying the use of psychometric methods seem to be less, if at all, compatible: see Mischel (1968).

What is so far lacking in the quasi-judicial approach to personality assessment is an extensive, systematically classified, collection of case-studies on the basis of which a body of psychological 'case law' could be established, as in jurisprudence. At present, the psychological and social work literature consists of an unsystematic collection of cases, and fragments of cases, investigated by means of an assortment of methods, and described and analysed in terms of different sorts of concepts. Thus, the literature on individual cases in clinical psychology and social case work does not yet provide the necessary basis for a body of 'case law', although it illustrates a variety of psychological theories and principles, and describes a number of unusual and interesting people: see Evans (1954) and White (1975). The attempt to formulate general laws to acount for similarities and differences between individual cases is a perfectly sound scientific endeavour. Lack of space prevents us from considering the psychoanalytic endeavour in this connection, but see Sherwood (1969) for an account of the logic of explanation in psychoanalysis. Case-law is to the quasi-judicial method what norms and standards are to psychometrics.

III. The Explanation of Behaviour

The general problem of how we explain a person's behaviour is an interesting issue in philosophical psychology: see Chapters 2 and 4. The general problem must be distinguished from the particular problems encountered in explaining why this or that person behaves as he does. These individual patterns of behaviour may be explained by reference to ordinary concepts, such as habit, motive or expectation, or by reference to technical concepts, such as institutionalization, displaced aggression, anxiety.

In a particular case, the problem is to specify the components in the expression $P_i \times S_j \rightarrow B_{ij}$ in sufficient detail to satisfy the curiosity of the investigator. But explanations are always relative to the understanding of the person seeking an explanation; one person may lack knowledge of a simple item of empirical evidence, another may not understand the causal connections because he does not know the appropriate psychological theory. A full understanding of the expression $P_i \times S_j \rightarrow B_{ij}$ requires information about facts and relationships for each component in the expression. To begin with, however, one has only partial knowledge and partial understanding, and one's puzzlement motivates the search for relevant information. For example, one may understand the individual's personal characteristics and have knowledge of his behaviour, but not appreciate the circumstances he is in; or, one may appreciate his circumstances and have knowledge of his behaviour but lack information about his personal characteristics. Again, one may know the individual's personal qualities, his circumstances, and his behaviour, and still not understand why that sort of behaviour should result from the interaction of those personal qualities and situational factors; in this instance, what is lacking is a 'theory' about that sort of behaviour—a theory which would enable us to explain the ' $\times$ ', i.e. 'interaction', and the ' $\rightarrow$ ', i.e. 'resultant', in the expression $P_i \times S_j \rightarrow B_{ij}$.

From what we have said already about the difference between tactical adjustments and strategic adaptations, it should be obvious that at least two different levels of explanation are called for. At the level of tactical adjustments, we need explanations about short-term processes in the organization of behaviour—explanations that involve the use of *mentalistic* terms like 'wants', 'intends', 'expects', 'remembers', 'feels', 'supposes', 'thinks', 'chooses', and so on; these terms refer to experiential states accompanying overt behaviour (they may also be described in 'as if' terms). At the level of strategic adaptations, we need explanations about long-term processes in the organization of behaviour— explanations that involve the use of *dispositional* terms like 'motive', 'habit', 'trait', 'attitude', 'ability', 'belief', 'value', and so on; these terms refer to regular and consistent patterns of overt behaviour, or rather to the covert central processes that organize them.

These two levels of explanation are also required to say something about the short-term 'situation' and the long-term 'environment' respectively, because the person's behaviour is partly a function of the immediate situation and partly a function of the wider environment. At the level of tactical adjustments, we need explanations which refer to the actual objects, persons, events, and other real features of the individual's *immediate* situation, which may be influenced directly or indirectly by the person's actions and may affect the person contingently or non-contingently. At the level of strategic adjustments, we need explanations which refer to *all the relevant realizable conditions of the wider world in which the person lives*, e.g. those governing personal security, companionship, financial resources, material assets and social status. The general terms and conditions governing their realization constitute the realities of life for a person although he may be unaware of them. The distinction between the subjective and objective environment is familiar to psychologists.

Something of a paradox arises when we consider the person's adjustments (and adaptations) to himself. We saw, in connection with our brief analysis of central organizing functions, that human behaviour can be reflexive—in the sense of the person becoming the object of his own actions and tendencies. For this reason, it may be necessary to refer to the 'self' in order to explain why the person behaves as he does. For example, the explanation of suicidal behaviour or of depression may well include statements about the person's self-concept; and many problems of adjustment involving social relations may require explanations making use of the notion of self/other comparisons: see Chapter 1. Indeed, the classical problems of neurosis are said to be explicable in terms of inadequate strategies for dealing with the realities of one's personal tendencies and characteristics (some people have difficulty in 'labelling' their personal qualities and states of mind). It is not uncommon in the ordinary affairs of everyday life for us to have to make *tactical* adjustments in relation to our self-concept, as when we 'force' ourselves to work, or hold our temper in check. Socialization during the juvenile period is regarded by some as being mainly concerned with the acquisition of self-control and self-understanding and of community-oriented ways of behaving, i.e. with *strategic* adaptations of the self-concept. The classical failures of socialization are explained in terms of inadequate strategies for dealing with self–other relationships. Tactical adjustments to other people in everyday life commonly require a fairly clear conception of at least some aspects of the self, e.g. one's identity, social role, values and attitudes, otherwise one is likely to be confused about what to do in a particular social situation. Hence, explanations about our tactical adjustments to particular people, and about our strategic adaptations to the social environment in general, often include references to the way we organize our behaviour *reflexively*, in relation to our own tendencies and characteristics.

As we have already stated, *any* fact or relationship may fulfil an explanatory function if it provides information relevant to the question being asked. The adequacy of an explanation is relative to the understanding of the person seeking an explanation. It is desirable, but by no means necessary, for us to understand a causal chain completely and in detail; it is sometimes sufficient to be able to validate the main causal relationships.

We have argued that there are several kinds of explanatory concept: one kind refers to mentalistic processes, another to dispositional characteristics, a third to environmental conditions (including social conditions), and a fourth to the self-concept. In addition, it may be necessary to introduce technical concepts, such as the biomedical factors in brain damage or other physical disability, fatigue or intoxication, or the psychodynamic factors in neurosis, delinquency, and so on.

The problem of 'explaining' the behaviour of an individual arises in two rather distinct forms. The first is when the behaviour in question falls within the normal range—in the sense that it is familiar or comprehensible in terms of the ordinary language of everyday life. The second is when the behaviour falls outside the normal range—in the sense that it is unusual, deviant, inexplicable in ordinary language, or incomprehensible to common sense.

It is unfortunate, in some respects, that the early study of personality was more strongly influenced by consideration of abnormal behaviour than by consideration of normal mechanisms of adjustment. The result has been an attempt to assimilate 'normal' behaviour to the theories and concepts of psychopathology, e.g. those of psychoanalysis, rather than to extend the theories and concepts of normal psychology to take account of 'abnormal' behaviour.

We shall not review the numerous technical concepts and methods that have been developed in psychopathology. We shall simply point out some of the basic concepts in ordinary language and commonsense that are used to 'explain' ordinary behaviour. It will be seen that all of them may be utilized in accounting for some aspects of abnormal behaviour, although they usually do not provide a sufficient account.

There are six main sorts of psychological explanation familiar to commonsense and embedded in ordinary language. The most frequent of these involves the concept of 'motivation' in one form or another; ordinary language words like 'want', 'desire', 'wish', 'try', 'intend', express the idea of goal-directed processes within the person which instigate, direct and sustain his behaviour until the need is satisfied or displaced. A second type of explanation involves the concept of 'habit'; this notion is based on the commonsense belief that a person's behaviour is shaped by experience so that he acquires relatively automatic, reliable dispositions to react in particular ways in particular circumstances, e.g. consumer habits and other daily routines. The third type of explanation requires the notion of a 'generalized personality trait', a notion with which we are now very familiar; traits are thought of as relatively enduring dispositions (ability plus inclination) to behave in characteristic ways in a wide variety of circumstances and over long periods of time; ordinary language terms like 'aggressive', 'sociable', 'intelligent', 'shy', express this idea. The fourth type of explanation is similar to what we have referred to as 'orientation and feeling' in that it refers to the way a person's attitudes, expectations and feelings, or other temporary states of mind, such as being suspicious or angry, exert a controlling influence on his actions. The fifth type of explanation shows how easily commonsense and ordinary language connect the person's behaviour to the situation he is in, for it introduces the familiar concept of 'surrounding circumstances' which provoke or encourage some sorts of action and inhibit or discourage others; the phrase in ordinary language, 'In the circumstances . . .' conveys the general idea. The sixth type of explanation refers to the way a person's behaviour is conditioned by his social position; certain forms of behaviour are expected of persons occupying certain social roles; these are backed by powerful sanctions and feelings of obligation; the ordinary notions of 'duty', 'professional standards', even 'normal behaviour' express this general idea. These six varieties of explanation of normal behaviour are easily detected in the ordinary language of personality descriptions in everyday life, and to some extent can be translated into the professional language of clinical psychology and social work.

Although it would be interesting to survey the explanatory concepts in psychopathology, especially those relevant to the study of personality and adjustment in its normal forms, we cannot embark on such a major investigation, and in any event we should find that explanatory concepts cannot be detached from the theoretical context to which they belong, e.g. defence and fixation in psychodynamics, reinforcement and generalization in behaviourism. In fact, a survey of explanatory concepts, and their theoretical contexts, in personality and adjustment has been carried out by Maddi (1972) in his comparative analysis of personality theories. A theory is, after all, simply an explanation or argument in which facts and principles are interrelated in a coherent way to make them meaningful and useful.

In Chapter 8, we describe a method for analysing 'informal arguments' and showed what was required for the construction of scientific, i.e. rational and empirical, explanations. Explanations about a person's conduct can be analysed as informal arguments, in which the sorts of terms we have referred to above—mentalistic functions, dispositions, circumstances, the self, and so on—enter into a network of statements giving rise to a 'pattern of meaning', subject to revision, of course, in the light of additional evidence and fresh inferences (constructions).

IV. Methodology

We draw attention to the fact that most theories of personality and adjustment do not raise epistemological questions, i.e. questions about the grounds or theory of knowledge. Yet some of the more serious criticisms of personality theories arise in connection with the credibility of their basic assumptions, and the meaning of their basic terms, e.g. mental structure and psychosexual development in psychoanalytic theory. Claims to explain human behaviour by means of theories purporting to use formal logic must be treated with some scepticism, since analytical reasoning requires a closed system of clearly defined classes and relationships, whereas arguments about human behaviour form an open system, i.e. a system open to new facts and relationships, and result, at best, in *approximations to knowledge.*

Maddi (1972) indicates, but does not emphasize, the extent to which concepts, methods and findings of a particular approach to personality are all interdependent. Methodological assumptions and procedures, however, are a fundamental part of any theory. Moreover, a theory is selective with regard to the data (evidence) it admits as relevant, for the simple reason that its concepts and claims do not exhaust all the issues that fall within the scope of personality study; witness the differences, for example, between psychanalysis, personal construct theory and personality factor theory. Even when different theories deal with the same sorts of data collected by means of similar methods, they may still conceptualize these data differently, e.g. the contending schools of psychoanalysis or of factor analysis. A 'general theory' of personal adjustment should be capable of assimilating the concepts, methods and findings of particular theories, or of showing that they are invalid, irrelevant, or meaningless. In any event, each particular theory provides little more than a loosely integrated framework of ideas within which certain problems, concepts, methods and findings can be discussed. They do not usually generate testable alternative explanations for the *same* phenomena, and so have relatively little value at the tactical level of research in personality; their main function is strategic.

Our general theory incorporates a quasi-judicial method for the study of individual cases; it has six basic features. First, it uses ordinary language and assimilates new technical and professional terms to its 'commonsense' framework (or it brings ordinary language and commonsense into line with these new scientific developments). In other words, it attempts to reconcile a scientific (rational, empirical and approximate) account of personal adjustment with a pre-existing 'social construction' of human reality. Second, it provides a systematic investigative procedure comprising a series of steps analogous to those required to settle issues in a court of law. Third, it provides an 'informal logic' for the analysis and synthesis of explanations (arguments) about human conduct. Fourth, it is capable of incorporating the specialized, technical or quantitative, methods associated with particular theories of personality. Fifth, it recognizes the practical limits of personality study: it does not attempt to deal with the 'whole person' (except in terms of a lengthy biography) but to study this or that particular issue. Sixth, it proposes the establishment of a body of 'case-law' to express the abstract and general principles of personal adjustment.

V. Advantages and Applications

Some of the conceptual advantages and practical applications of our general theory of personal adjustment have been mentioned in passing, but it is worth bringing them together at this point to remind ourselves of the scientific merits of the approach we have outlined and to consider whether there might be other advantages and applications.

The main advantage of a 'general theory' is that it integrates personality study with the rest of psychology through its use of psychobiological and social psychological concepts. The theory also promises to integrate personality study with other biological and social sciences because of its emphasis on broad ecological concepts.

The next most important advantage is that a 'general theory' provides a satisfactory conceptual framework for the co-ordination and integration of narrower and more specialized theories of personality, for example those described by Maddi (1972), together with their associated methodologies.

A further advantage is that it provides a 'life-span' conceptualization of personality, i.e. one adequate for dealing with both juveniles and adults, and one capable of conceptualizing the biosocial transitions from one stage of life to another.

It might be argued that our 'general theory' does not solve any of the problems of adjustment described in the literature of psychopathology, e.g. the neuroses and psychoses. But we have argued that the study of abnormal cases and exceptions is secondary to the study of normal cases and general rules. It is possible that a systematic reconsideration of the 'normal range' of personal adjustment will force us to revise our ideas about psychopathology. Indeed, recent criticism of the 'medical model' in the study of psychopathology gives weight to this suggestion.

However, a systematic reconsideration of the 'normal' range of human behaviour, within the framework of a general theory of personality and adjustment, would be a major undertaking. It would seem to require the building up of an immense number of rigorously conducted studies, which would give substance to the general theory and from which would be derived the much-needed 'case-law'. This 'case-law' in turn, would provide the rules, relationships and classifications needed to impose systematic patterns of meaning on to the infinitely varied forms of personal adjustment that come under scrutiny in case-studies; and it might well have important implications for psychopathology, where rudimentary forms of case-law already exist. On the other hand, if 'informed' commonsense and ordinary language can be relied upon to give a reasonably valid account of normal behaviour, then psychological 'case-law' would be required only in specialized areas, e.g. delinquency, marital counselling, and in areas of abnormal behaviour, e.g. neurosis, psychosis, psychopathy.

Among the more obvious practical applications of our 'general theory' is the prediction of individual behaviour. We have considered, although somewhat briefly, the concepts and modes of argument used in explaining and predicting individual behaviour: see also Chapters 2, 4 and 8. We saw that there were both similarities and differences between the ordinary language of commonsense and the professional language of clinical psychology and social case-work. Hitherto, 'clinical' prediction has fared badly in comparison with 'actuarial' prediction. It may be that part of the reason for this is that clinical psychology, unlike clinical medicine, has not had a rigorous conceptual and methodological framework within which to operate (except that derived from clinical psychiatry: see Slater and Roth, 1969, pp. 33–55). Such a framework would be provided by our general theory and its associated quasi-judicial methodology. A particular advantage is that this conceptualization refers mainly to normal behaviour in normal circumstances and so complements that of clinical psychiatry and social case work. It provides a systematic way of appraising, i.e. describing, analysing and explaining, personality. Hence, it is useful as a guide in structured interviewing for a wide variety of assessment purposes, and in writing systematic self descriptions and descriptions of others. It can be used as a guide in practical training exercises for students in psychology, social work and elsewhere, who are learning to investigate individual cases and interpersonal relationships: see Mair (1970), for example. It shows how evidence about individuals can be dealt with rigorously and objectively, not only by means of psychometric testing and formal interviewing, but also through direct observation in the natural environment, the use of documents, the evidence of informants, and so on.

The approach we have advocated can be put to practical use in education and industry, where its main advantage is that it deals with concepts that are familiar to commonsense and couched in the ordinary language of everyday life. It provides a framework for the development of educational curricula, for use in schools and universities, dealing with human beings in their natural habitat. It provides a framework for the various levels of personality appraisal required in industrial organizations. It contrasts sharply with the pseudo-scientific techniques with which personality appraisal is plagued. It encourages a sensitivity to language and an awareness of the complexities of personal adjustment.

Finally, some individuals who experience difficulties in personal relationships might be helped by a system of rational psychotherapy in which they learn to observe, describe and analyse their own behaviour and the behaviour of other people using the concepts and methods we have outlined. A weakness in our approach so far, however, is that we have not yet examined the *affective* characteristics of language in relation to personality description, but see Chapter 10 and Bilsbury (in preparation). It is usually the affective factors that give rise to difficulties in personal relationships. Nevertheless, our approach recognizes the importance of feelings and emotions and there is no reason why they should be excluded from consideration in this sort of rational psychotherapy.

VI. Conclusions

We have sketched a general theory of personality and adjustment partly in terms of Maddi's comparative approach to personality theories. It incorporates many features from existing theories and introduces considerations not previously dealt with adequately, e.g. life-span changes, and the distinction between tactical adjustments and strategic adaptation (but see McCall and Simmons, 1966). It provides an epistemological basis for its explanatory and methodological framework. Its essential aim is to promote a 'biosocial' approach to the study of human nature by studying individual cases and developing general laws of personal adjustment in terms of the evolution and ecology of individual behaviour.

Personality appraisals based on quasi-judicial case-studies are conceptual systems built up by investigators in order to make sense of their data; they are not in themselves data, but constructions imposed on data. But these conceptual constructions are intended to apply to whole classes of psychological cases, not just to the particular case for which they were first formulated. Psychological 'case-law' thereby provides the abstractions and generalizations needed for a *science* of personality and adjustment.

CHAPTER 10

Characterization in Fiction

I. Introduction

This chapter is an elementary analysis of the language of personality description in fiction, based on the novel as a distinct literary form, from its eighteenth century beginnings: see Leavis (1948), Allott (1959), Kettle (1962), Watt (1963) and Harvey (1965). It is, of necessity, a simple and selective account and does not attempt to give any sort of historical perspective. A novel can be conveniently defined as a fictitious prose narrative dealing with psychological and moral issues in the way people attempt to come to terms with life and with themselves.

The novel became a distinctive literary form not only because it attempted to render a *realistic* account of the daily lives of ordinary people, and of the key features of human nature, but also and perhaps mainly because it described *diverse* forms of personal adjustment. This required an objective (public or external) account describing the person's actions and circumstances and a subjective (private or internal) account describing the person's motives, attitudes and states of mind.

At first glance then, the novelist's aim seems to have much in common with that of a clinical psychologist or social worker concerned with the study of individual cases and with its attendant 'case-law'. The novelist would also seem to have much in common with the social psychologist interested in social adjustment and interaction. Further inquiry, however, soon reveals major differences in aim and method, for the novelist's product is a fictional account and does not even pretend to tell the truth about particular empirical facts (no matter what status it acquires as literature), whereas the psychologist's product is factual (in the sense of empirical) and attempts to render as truthful an account as possible of particular facts. 'Fidelity to the real world' is one of the criteria for

228

assessing the scientific merit of a psychological case-study, but it seems curiously inappropriate when applied to a novel, depending upon what 'truth' the 'fiction' is supposed to show. On this test, biographical and serious journalistic accounts of persons are closer to the psychological case-study than to the novel. One problem is that the boundaries between different literary genres are often vague, and the diverse aspects of human nature can be represented in words in all manner of ways.

We have seen fit to question the principle that fidelity to actual human experience and behaviour is an important criterion in the evaluation of a novel. In view of what we have just said, this presents a paradox which we shall examine in due course. What then does a novel do if not report actual facts about real people? It attempts to demonstrate, by means of artificial data, a moral evaluation and an implicit theory (see Chapter 9) about some aspect of human nature and personal adjustment; it tries to persuade the reader that character, environment and fate are interrelated. The nature of these literary accounts of human behaviour can be made explicit by answering questions about the structure of the novel and separating the moral issues and psychological analysis from other literary considerations. A novel is not a scientific product, and is not required to meet the normal requirements of scientific method; its value must be assessed by literary standards. Of what advantage is it then to compare personality in fiction with personality in behavioural science? We shall pursue this question throughout the present chapter, but for the time being we shall assume that there are three advantages. First, there is still a surprising lack of detailed and comprehensive case-material in psychology, and until such case-material has been produced we might do worse than consider possible insights into human nature demonstrated by novelists' methods. Second, the novelist's handling of certain forms of inner experience—the states of mind his characters have—is a method of representing subjective states in human nature that complements that of the psychologist (consider the reproduction in dramatic form of case-studies in clinical psychology or social case-work). The third, and main, advantage is that the language of human behaviour and experience in the novel is relevant to our investigation of the language of personality description.

The very use of the term 'novel' implies that something new and strange is represented, by means of a prose narrative portraying interesting but largely fictitious aspects of the lives of individual characters. The implication is that human lives are not simple and all alike, but constitute an almost infinite variety of forms to be portrayed, analysed and evaluated. The problem is to demonstrate basic forms of human adjustment and interesting variations, by a sort of natural history method, without undue repetition or excessive detail. We need not concern ourselves with the novel as a product of the writer's personal adjustment.

Watt (1963, p. 15) tells us that Defoe, and subsequently Richardson and Fielding, in breaking with literary tradition, 'allowed his narrative order to flow spontaneously from his own sense of what his protagonists might plausibly do next'. Eventually, this emerging literary method called for the interlocking of character, circumstance, action and consequence to demonstrate important moral and psychological insights. Thus the novel pursues in fiction what the psychological case-study pursues in fact, namely the representation of an individual person (or persons) in a particular situation using not merely descriptive data, but also a 'logical structure' to impose a particular pattern of meaning.

The difficulty that the novel, as a literary method, faced was the same difficulty faced in the scientific study of personality—that of reconciling a 'nomothetic' approach (dealing in general laws and universals) with an 'idiographic' approach (dealing in particular facts and individual cases): see Allport (1937). As regards the novel, Watt refers to this as 'the controversy between neo-classical generality and realistic particularity', (p. 17); but it could be argued that Chaucer and Shakespeare faced the same difficulty. Both the novel and the case-study go beyond the available data by proposing a logical structure and a psychological or moral significance, i.e. an interpretation and evaluation of the data, which goes beyond the *individual* case to the *class* of similar cases.

The approach to personality that we are advocating shares with the novel the assumption that both the person and the environment (situation) he is in require analysis; if not in detail, at least in respect of their key features. The novelist's attempt to 'particularize' a character, by giving him a name, a location, a certain physical appearance and so on, is also an attempt to give that character an 'identity'. Characters in fiction often portray basic human values (or their opposites) and may be appropriately named. Writers often go to some lengths to find a name that 'fits' their characters, even when those characters represent individuals rather than types. We discussed the problem of identity in Chapter 6. But we should remind ourselves that personal identity is both a psychological issue and a philosophical one. Psychologically, personal identity is associated with the self-concept and with interpersonal comparisons; philosophically, personal identity is associated with the epistemological status of proper names and, presumably, of other words and phrases which are used to distinguish one person from another: see Strawson (1964, 1974). The notion of personal identity is closely tied up with that of self-awareness. Self-awareness ranges over past and present experiences; it can project one into future or imaginary situations; it enables one to make comparisons between oneself and others. Normal people are usually aware of a sort of continuity in, and a centralized organization of, their identity and personal experience. The novelist's attempt to portray his fictional characters as individuals, expressed in part by his careful choice of a proper name for them, contrasts with the more traditional literary method of identifying the character with an historical or legendary figure or with some abstraction or type, nobleman or warrior, that is, not a person but a personification. According to Watt (p. 284) the classical tradition in literature avoided '... the intimate and confessional approach to personality; and in any case the philosophical problems of self-consciousness had only begun to receive attention some six centuries after Aristotle in the works of Plotinus'.

In real life, ignorance of what is going on 'within' a person is a serious handicap to understanding, predicting and influencing his behaviour. Similarly, the reader of a novel must be able to share the fictional character's thoughts, feelings and desires, otherwise he cannot understand the meaning, or appreciate the significance, of the story he is reading. Of course, in writing about these matters the author may be referring to wider issues such as the purpose of human existence or morality. Even so, the issues must be dealt with in terms of *human* nature, otherwise the writing becomes transcendental and scientifically meaningless, as in the fiction preceeding the emergence of the novel: see Watt (p. 83).

Access to the individual's personal experience, his subjective point of view, is an important ingredient in a novel as in a case-study. Some novels in fact are composed either largely or entirely of the subjective experience of a character, the so-called 'stream of consciousness' novels. Whether it is possible to have a strictly 'behaviourist' novel, i.e. without any reference to inner-personal experience, is debatable: the French 'anti-novels' are said to have attempted this.

Moreover, it is not sufficient simply to describe the particular characteristics and inner experiences of a *person*; one must also describe the particular characteristics and significance of the objects, other persons, events and circumstances that make up the *environment* of that person. Human actions are the joint product of personal and situational factors, and the writer must somehow fuse his analysis of subjective character with his account of objective reality.

A writer might introduce characters into a novel for reasons other than 'characterization'—e.g. to further the plot, to give local colour and authenticity, or to entertain. Such characters are not developed, i.e. the narrative does not go on to disclose an inner life or to show different facets of the individual's psychological make-up by describing his behaviour in different situations. But the prime function of a *psychological* novel is to provide the 'inside-story', of thoughts, feelings and desires, and of dispositions, to accompany the 'outside story' of actions, circumstances and events.

In F. Scott Fitzgerald's book *The Great Gatsby* the author describes the physical characteristics and expressive behaviour of his characters, and the events in which they are involved, but does not directly reveal their states of mind (excluding Nick the narrator and Gatsby himself). This is not unlike the situation we face with regard to person perception in daily life. But even with this technique, the novelist can provide us with several different views of the same character, which is often not possible in daily life. The use of a relatively neutral or a central character as a narrator is a common technique in writing fiction; another possibility is for the author to assume a sort of omniscience and to describe both the external facts and internal experiences of his characters, e.g. Henry James in *The Portrait of a Lady*.

The events that make up the major episodes in a person's life occupy time, and their description, in a psychological case-study for example, requires a kind of causal analysis (or story) showing how one event leads to another. Similarly, in a novel, there is an underlying serial order of events, supposedly occupying real time, although the novelist in the exercise of his literary craft may deliberately change the order of presentation of the events in his novel so that it no longer coincides with the way events would have happened had those events been real rather than fictional. He may also manipulate the time factor in order to achieve special effects such as surprise, tension or clues to character. Some novels (and some psychological case-studies) make compelling reading because, like a detective story, they 'unfold' the evidence and the arguments, beginning with the problem and gradually disclosing its circumstances and origins. A strictly causal analysis, however, may call for a more straightforward account in which events move forward in time.

As E. M. Forster pointed out in *Aspects of the Novel* (1962), the basis of a novel is a story about events in real time, although the narrative may not describe them in their sequential order. 'A plot is also a narrative of events, the emphasis falling on causality. "The king died and then the queen died", is a story. "The king died and then the queen died of grief", is a plot.' (p. 93.) The plot explains the connections between events in the story (narrative).

Both the novel and the psychological case-study (or life-history) rest on the assumption that there is a logical and causal structure in human behaviour and experience, with the implication that an analysis in terms of chance, coincidence, supernatural intervention, and the like, will not do. Moreover, facts and events need not be reported in their entirety; only those facts and events which are relevant to the underlying argument, the causal analysis and moral evaluation, need be reported. This is why neither the novel nor the psychological case-study provides an exhaustive narrative of events; and this is why the time scale in a novel is reduced and distorted. On the other hand, it may be necessary, in order to provide a meaningful context for the description and analysis of a person's behaviour, to provide an extensive and detailed background and history, as in historical novels, or in the psychological analysis of personality in politics and history.

Another aspect of the time factor in the analysis of personal adjustment is the duration of the episodes under investigation and the degree of detail required for their description: see Livesley and Bromley (1973). Watt (p. 25–6) compares the novelist's use of finely detailed descriptions with the film producer's use of close-ups (to which we might add slow motion, replays and stills). We note in passing that the motion picture, play and television documentary or dramatization have given us other ways of 'representing' the sorts of issues dealt with in novels, case-studies, biographies and autobiographies. A pictorial dramatization accompanied by an interpretative commentary can provide a particularly compelling demonstration: see Chapter 1, in connection with self/other comparisons. It is obvious that, regardless of how we present a causal analysis or moral evaluation of personal adjustment, we should focus on the critical issues, select only the relevant evidence, and describe in fine detail only those aspects of behaviour that require close examination.

A novel, a psychological case-study and a biography, are in some respects similar. Each represents human beings in terms of their 'individual ecology'— the way they adapt (or fail to adapt) to changes in their local environment (habitat) or to changes in their own psychobiological development. Each provides a narrative of events describing the serial organization of actions and experiences of individual people in their particular and changing circumstances. Each has some internal coherence (or logic) and moral significance. Finally, each is capable of demonstrating continuity of character and personal identity running through the variations in behaviour. We have argued, however, that consistency and continuity in personality are not facts that we confirm by observation, but rather *presuppositions* without which our experience of the behaviour of others would be meaningless. In this sense, consistency and continuity are *a priori* notions.

A novel is a story about people—or, rather, imaginary people. A novel is not a biography, an autobiography, or a piece of social history, or a psychological case-study, although it may masquerade as one of these, and they in turn may masquerade as a novel. The differences between works of fact and works of fiction concern both aim and method: factual studies employ rational argument and empirical evidence to create a scientific argument about the real world; fictional studies employ a variety of persuasive devices and imaginary data to create a work of art, evoke a vicarious experience and pass a moral judgment. The existence of hybrid forms softens the contrasts we have made, and perhaps justifies the comparisons.

Human actions occur in their particular settings, and it can be shown that some kinds of setting are particularly effective in eliciting behaviour which is appropriate. Games are a case in point, since the physical arrangements, equipment, rules and so on, tend to prescribe and enforce some sorts of behaviour and to proscribe and prevent others. But all settings and situations generate expectations and inclinations, because the individual carries within him, as it were, the effects of his reinforcement history, in the form of habits, expectations, plans and reasons, which make him partly but not wholly subject to 'stimulus control'. We cannot even discount the effect of what are called 'subliminal stimuli', which affect the person's behaviour without his being aware of them; these are analogous, in a sense, to the subliminal proprioceptive and other sensory stimuli which are relegated to control centres outside awareness, e.g. those controlling some aspects of posture, movement and vision. Thus, it may be vitally necessary to analyse a situation in very fine detail in order to locate subtle features having a profound influence on the person's behaviour. Furthermore, we are to some extent the architects of the settings in which we find ourselves; a detailed analysis of the ecological conditions in which our behaviour occurs can provide clues to the analysis of character: clues like the objects that surround us, the people with whom we are involved, the circumstances and events that happen to us. It is also part of the writer's craft to describe behaviour settings so as to achieve special effects, e.g. to demonstrate social class differences, to create 'atmosphere' or tension.

Exact and detailed descriptions of the character's daily surroundings can be used to give an impression of verisimilitude which adds to the reader's acceptance of the fictional character, e.g. details pertaining to university life, to the Army, or to a prison camp. In the early history of the novel as we know it, such descriptive detail was an important source of satisfaction to readers because it confirmed and amplified their own experience or gave them insight into the lives and circumstances of people they could never encounter socially.

The presentation of a detailed description of an individual's actions and states of mind, and of the particular circumstances in which they occur, gives the reader of a novel the impression that he is 'getting' an authentic account of a real person. We need the inelegant verb 'to get' to express the idea that what a reader 'gets' from a novel may not be what he 'gets' from a more straightforward personality description or psychological case-study: in the former he in enjoying a vicarious experience, in the latter he is studying a document. There is a kind of personal involvement and immediacy in a novel, partly attributable to literary art, which tends to be absent from a case-study. The difference, however, is one of degree rather than kind, and depends on how the material is presented. How we get this kind of experience, this quasi-reality, from the pages of print in a novel is a mystery and a major concern of literary criticism.

A writer can represent a character both externally (by describing his overt behaviour) and internally (by disclosing his covert states of mind), and he has at his disposal a range of literary techniques for combining these approaches to achieve a realistic presentation which readers find absorbing and convincing. Whether what he has to say is worth saying may be judged by the relevant scientific, literary or moral standards. Forster asserts that the novel can do what no empirical study can do, that is, reveal the hidden, inner, psychological life of a (fictional) person *directly*, at its source, as it were. An empirical study may speculate about a person's inner states and may provide good, first-hand evidence, e.g. the person's own admissions and demeanour, in support of such speculation. But it can never present them *as part of the evidence* as the novel does. The novel, in other words, gives us 'privileged access' to the psychological states of (fictional) persons. An autobiography or personal diary may seem to give the same sort of direct privileged access to the writer's state of mind; but a moment's reflection shows that all it gives us is a verbal account, and for all we know the writer may be lying and denying his own personal qualities and states of mind (a common enough occurrence in real life).

Thus, one of the main functions of the sort of novel that we are interested in is to represent, and reveal directly, mentalistic states (thoughts, feelings and desires) that are not revealed directly in behaviour. Such states of mind are important in the organization and direction of human behaviour though they are not necessarily rational, coherent, fully open to reflective awareness, or capable of being expressed exactly in words. A novel may thus help a reader to understand his own behaviour—clarifying his states of mind by formulating them in language: see Chapter 1. As for the characters in the novel, the reader may feel he knows them better, through privileged access to their inner life, than he knows the real people around him.

In a novel, as in real life, we do not need a comprehensive catalogue of facts about a person in order to perceive his actions and respond adequately to him. We do, however, need some sorts of information, about identity, expressive behaviour, social role, and so on. Such information is made available quickly and easily in a novel and is not essentially different from the categories of information we have listed and discussed at length elsewhere: see Chapters 5, 6 and 7. These categories of information include mentalistic and dispositional characteristics, i.e. psychological attributes which, as we have seen, may be given directly in a novel, but have to be inferred in real life.

The need for immediacy and personal involvement on the part of the reader of a novel is met by combining the descriptive (referential) function of language with its relational (inferential) and its evocative (affective) functions; for example, by the choice of words and the use of imagery. In a scientific description, by contrast, the relational function is more explicit and the affective function is reduced to a minimum. We need not concern ourselves with the way the language of the novel differs from other literary forms.

Watt (pp. 31–2) seems to argue that the realism of the novel was an aspect of the growth of reason and empiricism during the Enlightenment, and that the art of the novel may be defined as a literary craft and philosophical procedure which produces a realistic imitation or representation of human life. We are offering no historical perspective on the novel, but we understand that 'missionary zeal' on the part of authors has given way to 'personal expression and communication'. It is interesting, from our quasi-judicial point of view (see Chapter 8) to note that Watt makes a direct comparison between the craft of the novel and judicial procedures, arguing that both the reader and the jury member want to be presented with all the particular details of evidence relevant to the issue. The obvious objection to this line of argument is that the novel is, by definition, fiction and not fact. It cannot, by definition, be a *true* representation of human life unless one adopts a metaphysical view, e.g. of 'moral truth'. Therefore, it must have some other function.

The disciplines which had their beginnings in the growth of reason and empiricism during the Englightment, and attempted to tell the truth, i.e. the empirical facts, about human life, were, of course, the biological, medical and social sciences. Psychology, particularly clinical psychology, developed relatively late; but it is the psychological case-study, not the novel, that attempts to represent the true, i.e. the particular and general, facts of personal adjustment. In that earlier age, of course, there would not be the same kind of narrow specialization in the arts and sciences that we find today, and it may be that some novels are not as fictitious as they claim to be (and others not as factual as they claim to be). Or, as we have suggested above, novels attempt to demonstrate general principles by presenting and interpreting fictitious and idealized data not available to observation (or not available for public verification). The aim is to clarify complex psychological issues and provide a more persuasive com-munication than could be achieved with empirical data and rational argument.

A serious examination of the novelist's method shows that, apart from being instructive, novels are often entertaining or refining. The novelist is not necessarily being false to his craft if his concern with entertainment and aesthetics leads him to neglect scientific realism. But even a novelist who wishes above all to instruct does so by demonstrating principles in idealized conditions, not by reporting empirical facts.

The formal realism of the novel, according to Watt, is analogous to evidence in judicial procedure. Novels can be badly written just as judicial inquiries can be badly conducted. But even at its best the formal realism of the novel represents an *imitation* of human life, whereas the psychological case-study represents a *true* account of a *real* person. Traditionally, the clinical case-study has tried to account for behaviour which is inexplicable and barely describable within a framework of ordinary language and commonsense; the novel, on the other hand, has usually given us accounts of human behaviour within the normal range of experience and comprehension.

One of the most disappointing features of the scientific study of personality has been its failure to give continuous *scientific* attention to the natural history of personal adjustment; it has left human biography to novelists, historians and others. Even the psychoanalysts, and others concerned with abnormal psychological conditions, have not provided us with a *science* of human biography; Sherwood (1969, p. 69) claims that there is scarcely a worthwhile case-study in the whole of the literature of scientific psychology; see also Bannister (1975).

Personality descriptions, whether presented directly as assessments or case-studies or indirectly as fiction or drama, tend to be phrased to suit the intended audience. So we must not be surprised to find a very wide range of usage even within the particular areas we are comparing, the novel, the psychological case-study, the biography, the autobiography and the journalistic article, since authors may be writing with rather different audiences in mind. Associated with these audiences are economic or ecological factors which also affect the way the personality descriptions are phrased: e.g. editorial policy, fashion, innovations in vocabulary, new knowledge, market forces, and so on.

II. Individualism and Social Values

Watt (pp. 62–3) argues that the novel was associated with the rise of 'individualism' in society and sought to describe the daily lives of ordinary people. Economic individualism provided the leisure, opportunity and motivation for more people to read novels; it also provided the novelist with the opportunity to describe for his readers the diverse sorts of people and activities which capitalist specialization had created and separated. The novel (and other forms of fiction) enable the reader, vicariously, to cross social and geographical boundaries and to experience ways of living from which he is segregated in normal life—as the poor are segregated from the rich, the law-abiding from the criminal, commoner from royalty. The tensions and the traffic between these partially segregated social groups also provide material for the novel's plot: the 'rags to riches' story, the story of conflict between desire and duty. Moreover, the boundary between fact and fiction is permeable.

People, however, are segregated not only by contemporary cultural boundaries but also by historical differences. Watt (pp. 191–2) seems to argue that the shift from rural to urban living associated with eighteenth century economic change began to break down the centuries old community-based adaptation to nature, i.e. to seasons, crops and cattle, and to substitute for it a new individualism based on adaptation to circumstances created by men, i.e. to cities, technologies and social systems. With this new individualism came a greater rivalry (for material goods and social status) and a sense of personal independence (or separateness, isolation and self-consciousness) combined with a correspondingly greater emphasis on deep personal relationships with a few other individuals. This provided a cultural basis for the novel and brought about the shift of interest from 'community character' to 'individual personality' which was to affect the way the social and behavioural sciences studied human nature. Psychology and sociology studied individuals in urban societies, although anthropology studied the 'community character' of simple societies. It has been argued that suburban life, the theme of not a few novels, represents a sort of compromise between the extremes of rural communality and urban isolation, achieving privacy without sacrificing companionship.

In this connection we should mention an obvious aspect of the novel which Watt fails to mention, namely, the vicarious enjoyment of activities forbidden by law or convention: sexual activities including perversions, aggression and crimes of all kinds, political and religious deviation, and so on. It is well known that human beings entertain, in imagination, thoughts, feelings and wishes which they cannot translate into action because of personal and social constraints. To some extent censorship sets limits to what the novelist can publish; this is relevant to the social history of the novel, but we are interested only in examining the claim that the novel is 'true to human life'. To the extent that novels have explored these extensions to and deviations from what is typical or prescribed, they have obviously gone beyond observation and description to speculation and fiction. This argument, of course, adds to rather than detracts from the value of a novel as an art form since it opens up possibilities for new (variant) forms of behaviour and experience. Nevertheless, what is advantageous in a novel may be disadvantageous in a case-study or biography where fidelity to the facts, being 'true to life', is essential.

It is often the case that what is revealed when a person's character is subjected to deep and detailed analysis is not very edifying, for the simple reason that those aspects of his personal morality that he tends not to disclose are usually the ones that are regarded as reprehensible. Censorship has had profound effects on literature and science throughout their long history; and even today it is not unusual to find resistance to the investigation of the inner workings of human behaviour and experience on the grounds, for example, that it offends people's moral sensibilities, or the individual's right to privacy.

The relevance of all this to the language of personality description is that in our descriptions and appraisals of other people we recognize, and are able to state explicitly, the distinction between what the person actually does and what he would like to do or what he might be capable of doing, between what he says and what he thinks or feels; in other words, we can reveal aspects of the other person's character that are not directly manifested in his behaviour. The novelist's portrayal of the inner-personal, or subjective, states of mind of his characters is an important mark of his ability as a novelist (and quasi-psychologist); it enables the reader to make sense of and to appreciate the actions and circumstances of these fictional characters, just as the same sort of information would help him to make sense of his own behaviour and the behaviour of other people in real life. The 'stream of consciousness' technique shows how important this aspect of the novel is. The importance of and emphasis on subjective personal states in 'psychological' novels probably has a bearing on our search for meaning in nature and for personal identity in society, through observation, reflection and self-examination, and has a parallel in personal revelations in autobiography (a novel may, indeed, be autobiographical).

Individuality and diversity have a psychological as well as a biological dimension. The study of personality, via nomothetic and idiographic methods, is based on the assumption that the study of systematic differences and individual cases is scientifically meaningful. We are aware of the possibility, however, that such an assumption may be ideological; in which case, we might expect the psychological novel to give way in due course to the sociological novel as the communal trends in human society gradually curtail the range of individual differences and interpersonal relationships. Again, this is a problem which requires more historical perspective than we can provide. It is likely, however, that individuality and communality are essential but counterbalancing (and often conflicting) forces in the evolution of human nature; indeed the history of the novel reflects different facets of, and shifts in the balance of, these essential forces, as expressed, for example, in the works of Jane Austen or Conrad. As far as human values are concerned, 'individualism' represents one side of a single coin which bears 'socialism' (for want of a better word) on the other. It could be argued that socialism has produced its own forms of the novel, not concerned with the individual as such, but with society as lived by individuals. No doubt one could identify extreme examples of individualistic or socialistic novels, but it is likely that the ideal novel reveals both sides of the coin. The side that we are concerned with is the individual, but the individual has no meaningful existence without social relationships. And, as we have already seen in the chapters on content analysis, the stimulus person's social relationships form a major component of the impressions that people form of him.

Watt (p. 69) claims that *Robinson Crusoe* expresses the economic individualism of Defoe's society — an ideology which organizes human life around, and subordinates it to, the production and utilization of material wealth. This particular brand of individualism may seem psychologically immature in that it is egocentric and motivationally simple. But it represents a common enough notion of what is meant by 'personality' or the 'individual', as shown by the use of statements about material possessions, routine activities and occupational role, in personality descriptions, or by the economist's notion of man as a producer/consumer. Watt (p. 76) says, '*Robinson Crusoe* is certainly the first novel in the sense that it is the first fictional narrative in which an ordinary person's daily activities are the centre of continuous literary attention'.

Authors are often direct and fairly explicit in expressing the values of their time, e.g. as regards patriotism or religious beliefs; but they may inadvertently and indirectly express implicit values, i.e. values that they are scarcely aware of, such as the inferiority of women, or social class values. The importance of 'values' in the description of personality has been recognized for a long time, certainly since Spranger (1928) attempted a systematic description of them: see Allport *et al.* (1960) and Kohlberg (1973). In the novel, as in real life, values are one aspect of character that contribute to the organization of behaviour, and they are commonly mentioned in personality descriptions, as we have seen.

So far, then, we have argued that the novel and the psychological case-study have points of similarity and difference. Both are concerned with individual persons, with social relationships, with patterns of personal adjustment; the individuals they are concerned with live their lives in a secular world free from supernatural influence or unlikely coincidences, and they have both an outward (public or behavioural) aspect and an inward (private or psychological) aspect. The difference, however, is that the novel presents a story for what is basically its moral worth, its aesthetic merits, its psychological insights and its entertainment value, whereas the psychological case-study presents a story for its *scientific* worth.

Whether the economic and moral individualism which provided the historical context for the rise of the novel also prepared the way for the scientific study of individual cases is a matter for historical research; it seems more likely that the latter was a natural method in nineteenth century psychiatry which was in turn derived from European, especially French, clinical medicine.

It is of particular interest to us that, according to Watt (p. 202) Richardson's *Clarissa*, written in the 1740s, contains the first recorded use of the word 'personalities' to refer to 'individual traits'—long before the singular term 'personality' acquired its modern meaning as the set of traits distinguishing one person from another (but see Allport, 1937).

III. Methods, Aims and Comparisons

In its simplest form a novel describes a patterned sequence of actions and events in which the main character pursues some compelling objective or gets caught up in circumstances not of his own making, and exhibits, in his characteristic actions and states of mind, a salient attribute, be it courage, moral turpitude or other trait. In some respects, the main character behaves like an ordinary human being and faces a normal range of social circumstances; but in other respects his life is peculiar, he has an odd quirk of character, he faces an unusual situation, or there is an unusual combination of circumstances which create new possibilities for human behaviour and experience. *Robinson Crusoe*, for example, demonstrates the accomplishments and joys of unfettered individualism, not only in the overall structure of the plot and through the words, deeds and thoughts of the main character, but through a host of minor literary touches. But, as explained above, the novel demonstrates with fictional, i.e. artificially contrived, data; and in the case of *Robinson Crusoe* the author forgets, or chooses to neglect, facts which, in real life, would press insistently on the theory propounded in the book, such as social necessities, long-term effects and so on. In some instances, the fictional narrative is an allegory representing people and events indirectly and metaphorically, as in *Animal Farm* or *Lord of the Flies*. In other instances, the fictional narrative is a patchwork of observational and autobiographical material suitably distorted and camouflaged, and leavened with psychological and moral insights.

Social relationships and role systems offer unlimited scope for the novelist to think up all kinds of combinations and permutations, and to portray those that he thinks have some psychological, social and moral significance, as in *A Passage to India*, *The Grapes of Wrath*, *The Way of All Flesh*. Social relationships and role systems vary from one culture to another and from one historical period to another, and it is an exceptional novelist who can construct a story which is universal and timeless in its appeal. The novelist often relies upon the reader's familiarity with ordinary social arrangements to demonstrate some of its less familar but interesting possibilities, e.g. treachery, sacrifice, adventure and intrigue.

Within the general framework of plot, character and morality, the novelist has a choice of methods for representing and demonstrating his views about human behaviour and experience. He often makes use of what a behavioural ecologist would call a 'behaviour narrative', i.e. a detailed description in episodic form of things said and done by a person, together with an account of the circumstances and events associated with the actions. However, the 'behaviour narrative' is often presented in the novel by one of the characters, perhaps the main character, or by someone, e.g. the narrator or author, who has insight into the psychological states to which the behaviour in question is related. In such cases, the narrative goes beyond the description of overt behaviour and real circumstances by introducing psychological information. In a similar way, the author can present either an external account of the surrounding circumstances as seen by his characters, or he can 'let the reader in' on information about those circumstances that his characters do not have. Hence, the reader can see a number of possibilities for action and a number of different chains of consequence; and his attention is held, in part, by the uncertainty of what will happen.

The analysis of human character by means of a narrative that describes a sequence of behavioural episodes, in which people behave in a certain way in response to the situation as they see it, is a basic method in fiction. This basic method, however, can take many forms—it can emphasize either the subjective experience or the objective action, it can be prosaic or poetical, it can be adapted to suit a particular sort of audience, it can be used as the vehicle for the propagation of the author's views on a whole variety of issues from gardening to politics, it can proclaim morals, attitudes, values, fashions and a host of other matters of social and psychological interest.

We must not expect an author to be perfectly consistent in his use of literary techniques, indeed he may not be fully aware of how he composes his material; so that, in a sense, it is not entirely within his conscious control. The psychological case-study, by contrast, ideally adopts a quasi-legalistic procedure in that it follows explicit and agreed rules for the introduction and analysis of evidence relevant to specific issues. There are literary standards for judging the worth of a novel, and there are scientific standards for judging the worth of a psychological case-study: see Chapter 8. But these standards are different, as we have seen, and the language is different also, being more detached (a kind of 'meta-language') in the psychological case-study. We are concerned mainly with rational and empirical descriptions of personality, and we venture into fiction only to explore the limits of *scientific* language.

Internal consistency is an important criterion of literary merit in a novel, just as it is an important criterion of scientific merit in a case-study. The notion of internal consistency, however, is not quite as simple as it appears to be at first glance. To begin with, it is a presupposition; that is to say, it is an *assumption* that we have to make in order to adjudicate between acceptable and unacceptable arguments or descriptions. Thus, although a person might be said to 'behave inconsistently', yet our account of how and why he behaves in this way cannot itself be inconsistent, e.g. it cannot say that a person is both stupid and intelligent or that he is both happily and unhappily married, at least not without considerable qualification. In saying that we cannot allow our account of a person's behaviour to be inconsistent, we are assuming that there is some logic in it; though we may have difficulty in demonstrating that logic because we lack empirical evidence or an understanding of the processes at work in that person's adjustment. The criterion of internal consistency clearly excludes a wide range of poorly constructed stories: those that omit significant information or contain contradictions, those that rely too much on chance, supernatural intervention, and the like. But neither the novelist nor the psychologist has to *prove* that the character he is studying is consistent, since we already *know* (or rather assume) that he must be consistent, in the final analysis at least. What the novelist and the psychologist have to demonstrate is that their account of the person is consistent as far as it goes; if that account is incomplete or leaves issues unresolved, the writer's purpose may be fulfilled even if he has presented only a partial solution and the reader is left with some questions unanswered.

A narrative does not normally have a uniform scale; it does not describe each and every episode in the same detail. A narrative is like a series of maps, or like a series of images seen at different levels of magnification through a microscope. Thus some of the maps (or images) are on a large scale; they show the wider context within which smaller parts are set. Ordinary language enables us to describe human behaviour and psychological processes at various levels of abstraction—from minute movements and momentary feelings to complete achievements and stable traits. Similarly, ordinary language enables us to describe the physical and social environment in fine detail or in general terms, or at whatever level of analysis is appropriate. The question is, 'What information is relevant to the issue being considered?' A novel is not subject to all the restrictions imposed upon a scientific case-study; the novelist can afford to use the narrative method, and to vary the level of detail in it, according to his diverse literary purposes. But selectivity and 'scale' are features of both scientific and literary descriptions, and one of the problems, perhaps more pronounced in works of fiction, is to integrate the large-scale and small-scale sections into a coherent narrative. This task is comparable to that of drawing a map which combines the benefits of large-scale and small-scale surveys, e.g. a large-scale map with a number of small-scale inset maps occupying space which is relatively unimportant and tagged so that their true position is known. A similar technique is used in biological and technological illustrations. We note, in passing, that scale, order and organization (structure) are general properties of cognitive representation and in no way restricted to the language of personality description.

Variations in descriptive detail, in the manner and order of presentation, and in the overall organization of the material, are matters which affect the coherence of a narrative and the readability or comprehensibility of a personality description. Since the novel usually deals with issues which go beyond the analysis of character, the problem of coherence is very much greater than it is in the psychological case-study; but we need not concern ourselves with coherence and style in literature, e.g. with regard to collateral detail, temporal reversals, separation of related issues, sentence length, vocabulary and grammar.

We cannot leave this issue, however, without pointing out that when we talk about ordinary language being used in the scientific description of personality and adjustment we are talking about the 'plain' language of observational report and rational argument—the language intended to deal with matters of fact; we are not talking about the 'coloured' language of emotional reactions and evaluative judgments. In other words, the scientific report is intended to convince by appealing to empirical evidence and logical inference, whereas the fictional report supplements the plain language of psychology with the affective language of literature. When reading a novel, one becomes personally involved with the people and events portrayed; it evokes a quasi-real experience and congruent feelings which amplify the reader's rational convictions. We must remember, however, that although a psychological case-study may include reports of affective language used literally, such reports are part of the evidence; affective language is eschewed in the accompanying commentary. In the novel, however, there is no such distinction, and the uncritical reader is led by his feelings, as it were, to the conclusions which the author has prepared for him. Serious journalism and biography occupy a sort of intermediate ground, closer to the case-study.

The coherence and internal consistency of a novel and a psychological case-study are enhanced by the imposition of a structure of relationships between and within its main components, e.g. morality, characterization, circumstance and causality. The existence of such a structure can be illustrated by reference to the way novels and case-studies can be analysed and summarized. Thus, for example, one may be able to identify several interlocking themes and sets of related behavioural episodes; within each theme and set, one may be able to identify subthemes and subsets of episodes. It is partly through these structural relationships that the particular events and circumstances of the novel or case-study achieve their psychological and moral significance.

Since coherence and consistency refer to the pattern of events in a story, the story must be terminated at some point, and it must be relatively self-contained. The manner in which the various components of a novel are brought into relationship with one another is a literary rather than a psychological concern, since the writer may deliberately withhold information in order to heighten tension in the reader, as with a detective story, or juxtapose items for the purposes of humour or contrast. Writers, of course, vary in their attachment to the realities of human behaviour on the one hand and to the craft of fiction on the other. Psychological case-studies are sometimes disappointing because they are incomplete; much of the enjoyment of the novel, however, lies in its presentation of a finished story; novels which contain omissions, loose-ends and uncertain outcomes are also disappointing, unless the writer manages somehow to leave the reader free to complete the story as he wishes. The novel, as it were, imposes more logic, coherence and drama on human events than is normally apparent.

It is not enough simply to list the person's attributes, describe his circumstances, give a commentary on his actions and their outcomes, and then make a psychological assessment or a moral judgment; these might be adequate for a psychological case-study or even a biography, but certainly not for a novel. On the other hand, the realistic psychological novel, as it is ordinarily understood, cannot become detached from the basic conditions of human behaviour and experience, otherwise it ceases to be that sort of novel and becomes some other kind of literature, romance, fairy-tale or science fiction, for example, and free from at least some of the bonds of realism.

Straightforward narrative accounts of ordinary human behaviour are obviously unsuited both to the novel and to the case-study, for the simple reason that a great deal of human behaviour is uninteresting or mere routine. Hence, the only episodes which are worth reporting in detail or at all are those that evoke feelings, raise moral issues, or are psychologically significant, i.e. relate to some theory or interpretation (causal analysis) of the events described. Such causal analysis is usually concerned with both characterization and circumstantiation; but, where characterization is emphasized, we have what is called the 'psychological novel', i.e. a story about a particular, usually complex, kind of fictional person, e.g. Dorothea or Lydgate in George Eliot's *Middlemarch*, rather than a story about an ordinary person in a particular, rather complex, situation.

Characterization in fiction can be conveyed both directly, by statements about the fictional person, e.g. that he is stubborn, hardworking and unkind to his wife, and indirectly, by statements describing incidents incorporating his actions and states of mind, e.g. the failure of his friends to persuade him to abandon a line of action, his tendency to go to work early and finish late, his reluctance to do what his wife desires, and so on. This sort of behavioural analysis can be paralleled by a psychological analysis in which the novelist gives us a sort of 'privileged access' to the fictional person's thoughts, feelings and desires, e.g. 'He saw the logic of their arguments but could not bring himself to admit it', 'He felt ill at ease while waiting and longed to get back to his work', 'He felt a grim satisfaction as he saw the disappointment in her face'. There are many literary devices for making such disclosures.

The process of characterization, of course, is co-ordinated with the other fictional processes: circumstantiation, narration and moralization, so as to achieve the coherence and completeness referred to above. Again, the question of whether the characterization is successful is a literary one, it does not depend on the validity of a technical, psychological theory outside the range of ordinary experience, but rather on the evidence and arguments marshalled by the writer and on the literary procedures he uses to present his fictional case. The literary standards we apply to characterization in fiction are analogous to (but of course not the same as) the quasi-judicial standards we apply to characterization in real life, and in professional psychology or social work.

For a novel as for real life, we need to know something about the situation a person is in. A novel normally analyses the situational constraints in considerable detail since such knowledge is part and parcel of the reader's understanding of the character's actions and psychological characteristics. We have argued elsewhere that it is a mistake to suppose that a person can be studied in isolation from the environment in which he exists, as seems to be implied in the psychometric approach to personality.

The extent to which a novel dwells on the inner psychological states of its characters, or on the fine details of the situations they are in, depends upon the novelist's aims and methods: these are literary issues which are not our concern. But we must not exaggerate the writer's control over his writings or the coherence of the 'argument' or 'demonstration' that he is trying to present. If we examine even the best works of fiction, we find omissions, contradictions, loose ends and other flaws; which is not to say that comparable flaws do not occur in scientific case-studies. If a character's inner psychological life is revealed directly and in detail and if the contextual information is adequate, than the reader will form an impression of a person which at times seems clearer and more realistic than a real-life impression; added to which, the reader fully understands *why* the character behaves in the way he does, and this again is usually an improvement on the sense he can make of the behaviour of the people around him (and perhaps of his own behaviour!).

We have written so far as if characters in a novel were all main characters. This is not so, obviously; and yet if we are to understand the language of personality in fiction we must surely concern ourselves with the main characters, and assume that subsidiary characters do not entail any additional analysis. Forster divides fictional characters into 'flat' and 'round'. Flat characters are simple and static, often to the point of caricature. Round characters are complex, they develop with the story, they have a number of facets which are revealed in different circumstances; their behaviour varies, and they usually have an inner life which enables the reader to see consistency in their actions and states of mind and to have expectations about them (which are not always confirmed). The contrast is too sharp, of course, since intermediate characters can be portrayed.

It is in the portrayal of 'round' characters that we see how the novelist's art may part company with the psychologist's science. The novelist can select a limited number of attributes and a limited range of circumstances. He does not have to deal with evidence that will not fit, or with actions which seem inconsistent—he can make up whatever evidence he needs and eliminate inconsistencies by careful editing and rewriting.

A particular form of distortion to which the novel and the autobiography are particularly liable, in contrast with the biography or case-study, is the tendency for the author's own views and personal characteristics to find vicarious expression in the actions and fate of his fictional (or autobiographical) character. Professional psychologists make practical use of this supposedly universal human tendency when they employ projective tests to elicit phantasies whose content and organization are more a function of the subject's personal qualities than of the stimulus situation. Unlike the novelist, the psychologist who is studying a real person is fairly firmly bound by the relevant evidence; he tries not to use the case he is reporting as a vehicle for the expression of his own views and personal qualities. The novelist's portrayal of a character in fiction is on a par with the artist's portrayal of a visual scene—it can range all the way from a literal representation to a highly selective, distorted and personal view. In the extreme case, therefore, the novelist's subjective representation of character is the very opposite of the psychologist's objective endeavour.

A distinction has also been drawn between 'characters of manners' and 'characters of nature': see Watt (p. 272). Characterization in the former mode deals with the relatively superficial structure of human behaviour and experience—with the more obvious variations between people, their typical problems, reactions and relationships. Characterization in the latter mode deals with the relatively deep structure of human behaviour and experience, with the preconditions or grounds of its organization in motives, beliefs and values, and attempts to demonstrate some aspect of this deep structure by revealing its surface manifestations (and particularly by revealing the possibilities for and limits of human conduct). The analogy, therefore, is with language, in that the novelist attempts to demonstrate the 'grammar' of human nature by showing what human beings can and cannot do because of the preconditions of character. In order to demonstrate this 'grammar', however, the writer must somehow reveal the inner psychological processes. He may do this either directly by having his characters make personal disclosures, in letters or reminiscences, for example, or by his 'privileged access' to their states of mind; or he can do it indirectly by whatever literary techniques he can muster, such as imagery, symbolism, and so on.

We seem to have assumed that adequate characterization in fiction cannot be achieved in anything less than a full-length novel. But of course, we know, from our ordinary experience of personality descriptions in journalism and professional psychology or social work, that effective characterization can be achieved in relatively short descriptions. The existence of short and medium length stories in magazines and elsewhere also suggests that adequate characterization in fiction can be achieved outside the novel, since such stories commonly contain one or more characters. It would be interesting, but outside the scope of our present inquiry, to examine the differences between the novel, the short story and other literary forms with regard to characterization.

Consider, for example, Theophrastus (trans. 1973), Strachey (1933), and Dreiser (1929) in connection with Rosenberg and Jones (1972). In a short story, the main emphasis is concentrated on the fine details of one particular situation and describes the build-up and the resolution, usually in a surprising way, of the predicament in which the main character is placed. Some sort of moral or psychological issue acts as the focal point of the story, and some sort of 'demonstration' is given, as in a full-length novel, of a 'theory' about the workings of human nature. We need not discuss the literary styles and techniques that might be used in short stories, e.g. those associated with structure and tension; but it could be argued that the short story probably has little to offer in the way of new psychological insights or new ways of describing personality. Its emphasis is on circumstance, action and outcome. A short story typically describes an incident which illustrates an interesting or unusual sequence of events and contains an element of drama or humour. Its main hold on our attention is not through the psychological make-up of the main character, but through the contingencies of human life. As one might expect, there are exceptions, e.g. in the works of Gogol and Chekov, in which it might be said that the story is about the 'tactical adjustment' of a character to his immediate situation. The notion of 'tactical adjustment' is important in the scientific study of personality: see Chapter 9.

In the novel, as in law and real life, it is sometimes important to report what is not said and not done (in comparison with what could have been expected in the circumstances). We have already mentioned that novels, biographies and psychological case-studies tend to be selective, focused and coherent; a great deal of detail must be omitted so that the overall structure or pattern of meaning can be comprehended. In a novel, the author has complete control over the fictional evidence; so it could be argued that the omission of relevant evidence signifies a literary lapse. In a biography or psychological case-study, on the other hand, the author is limited by whatever evidence he happens to have at his disposal and such evidence is often partial; nevertheless, he is bound by his procedure to report when no evidence is available to test important conjectures.

The psychological study of the process of attribution (identifying the causes of behaviour) is of relatively recent origin (see Jones *et al.*, 1972) and we shall not review the technical literature. Ordinary experience tells us that a person's actions are a function of his dispositions and abilities in relation to the opportunities and constraints in the situation facing him. Thus, an 'honest' person may be forced into 'dishonest' actions, perhaps by blackmail. The sorts of evidence we use as the basis for attribution are various; they include: the personal testimony of the character under investigation, the consequences or 'traces' of his actions, the observations and assertions of privileged observers, the public actions and words of people, including the main character, and the opinions of other people, or their fictional equivalents. In real life, characterization and attribution may be marred by an unavoidable lack of information and psychological insight; but in the novel such inadequacies are the responsibility of the author and lead to faults such as implausible characters, unlikely circumstances, contradictions within the narrative, and so on. In other words, while it is reasonable and often desirable in the interests of literary style to refute the expectations which the reader has developed, it is not reasonable to leave them unexamined. It is part of the novelist's art to take the reader's reactions into account by introducing or excluding material, by adopting one order of presentation rather than another, or by using other literary devices. In the novel, real life may be subordinated to literary merit; although mechanical craftmanship is no substitute for psychological and moral insight.

One of the main purposes of a novel is to demonstrate, by means of fictitious (but not fantastic) data, some kind or moral or psychological theory, dealing, for example, with interpersonal conflict or contradictions within character; or, to put it another way, the novel works out, makes explicit, the writer's understanding of human behaviour and morality. So, although it accepts a 'real-life' framework, the novel is often a speculative account of what *might* happen, given certain facts, *if* the author's 'theory' about human behaviour and morality were correct. To the extent that the writer's views are incomplete, inconsistent or poorly expressed his story will be unconvincing and lacking in literary merit.

We should mention that the difference between a moral theory and a psychological theory is that the former is normative whereas the latter is positive. The test of a moral theory is its ability to formulate and resolve moral dilemmas; the test of a psychological theory is its ability to identify and solve puzzles about the behaviour of individuals.

The writer's tendency to express (project) his own ideas and personal qualities (or those of the society to which he belongs) has its counterpart in the reader's tendency to interpret the story according to his (the reader's) own ideas and personal qualities. It is not surprising therefore to find that readers see meanings (ironical, political, psychological, moral) that the author had not intended or would not agree with, especially if author and reader are separated by cultural or historical circumstances. Similarly, readers sometimes fail to see meanings the author had intended.

Omissions, contradictions and inconsistencies are not acceptable in a novel, autobiography, biography or case-study; their existence permits too much freedom of interpretation, and indicates a failure to measure up to accepted literary or scientific standards of appraisal.

We cannot hope to deal with all the different psychological themes that run through works of fiction, such as jealousy, greed, physical and moral courage, heterosexual and homosexual love, family relationships, aggression, and so on; the list is too long and too varied, covering as it does the whole range of human behaviour and experience. It would be interesting to examine the psychology of the novel with special reference to the comparative approach to personality described by Maddi (1972). For example, psychological themes in novels might be classified in the way Maddi has classified personality theories, i.e. by identifying their 'core' features, namely, fulfilment, conflict, consistency, and their 'peripheral' manifestations: see Chapter 9.

Any of the themes we have mentioned could be used in a fictional demonstration of a psychological theory; and each theory could give rise to numerous idealized fictional demonstrations, through the domestic love stories in women's magazines to the more complex issues which provide the focus for serious full-length novels. We note that the language used to describe human behaviour, human experience and human personal qualities is basically the same in all these sorts of literature. There are, of course, differences associated with the educational, moral or literary functions of the subject-matter. The lexical, syntactical and semantic aspects vary in the sense that some literary forms draw on a wider range and more complex levels of language. Nevertheless, it is basically the language we use to describe human affairs in ordinary life. It is a language which can handle all the objects, events and relationships that make up the circumstances in which human actions and experiences normally occur. The language of fiction can incorporate inference and explanation although it is usually descriptive and evocative. Given the immense range and flexibility of language, it is not difficult to see how fictional and quasi-fictional persons can be described and analysed, and how their lives can be used to argue a variety of issues from the sublime to the ridiculous—from self-sacrifice to the proper way to open a boiled egg.

Novels and their pictorial equivalents do not merely rehearse the ordinary familiar facts of everyday life—that would be too tedious. Instead, they introduce elements of surprise, novelty, drama; and so, in a sense, they are constantly exploring the limits of individual variation and interpersonal relationships. Although the novelist is able to speculate more richly than the ordinary person, he is still to a large extent a prisoner of his time and circumstances; it is not surprising, therefore, that he should concern himself with issues that are important for the society to which he belongs. Courtship, marriage and family life are themes which continue to attract the attention of many novelists; sex, conflict, deviant behaviour and moral problems are also popular themes, as are social life, work and personal achievement. The novel, after all, needs a readership: it must appeal to and satisfy an audience with broadly similar needs, outlooks and personality qualities.

It follows that the language of personality description must have some sort of evolutionary history; for example, in the kinds of moral and psychological issues dealt with and in their surface manifestations, since the needs, values, attitudes and abilities exhibited by, or of interest to, human beings today are different in many respects from those in former times. One of the features of an outstanding novel may be that it reflects, and even contributes to, the evolution of language and human nature. There is, after all, some correspondence between words, ideas and actions. Among other things, however, a good novel identifies the 'preconditions' of human nature, and at the same time works out possibilities for new forms of behaviour and experience, e.g. changes in social class relationships, changes in the relationships between men and women, changes in family life. The range of human behavioural variation seems to be limitless, and novels (not merely science fiction) can provide us with fictional variants not encountered in real life. Although the novel appears to deal with a particular person in particular circumstances, the theme running through it is usually supra-individual; in other words, it deals with universal and perennial human problems, such as adjustment to external demands and internal conflicts, achievement and failure, and so on.

One of the main differences between fictional and scientific studies of personality is that the former tend to be unorganized and speculative, whereas the latter tend to be systematic and empirical. The latter, in other words, being scientific, are concerned with the evolution, integration and stabilization of knowledge; they are (or, rather, should be) grounded in the epistemology and philosophy of behavioural science; the former, by contrast, are concerned primarily with exploring the infinite possibilities of human situations and, in particular, with the crystallization and expression of new values, ideas and feelings associated with social evolution.

Without wishing to make prescriptive statements, one could say that 'good' novels deal with basic human issues, and are sensitive to newly evolving forms of behaviour and experience; yet a great deal of their effort is spent in exploring language as a medium of communication and evocation. Scientific studies, by contrast, are simple and straightforward; their capacity to convince is a function of empirical evidence and rational argument, not of literary magic, i.e. imagery, suggestion, the selective use of information, timing, and so on. As we have said, the existence of hybrid forms blurs the distinction we are trying to make. Literary magic apart, a novel may convincingly demonstrate a psychological or moral theory through the presentation of realistic (though fictional) data; and much of the interest, excitement and entertainment of a novel lies in following the details of the 'argument' until its final implications are worked out. The 'argument' in a novel is analogous to, but not the same as, the 'argument' in a psychological case-study or some other scientific study of personality.

Another major difference between a novel and a psychological case-study is that the psychological case-study presents the person as a sort of specimen for clinical dissection (we are reminded of medicine both historically and scientifically); so the reader, often a professional psychologist or social worker, can achieve the sort of 'psychological distance' necessary for impartial examination. The novel, on the other hand, presents a 'realistic' (but not a 'real') person with whose actions and experiences the reader becomes personally involved. Much of this vicarious involvement is the effect of literary techniques: convincing first-hand description, authentic detail, evocative imagery, absorbing narrative, privileged access to the states of mind of the fictional characters, and so on. Where the events presented in the novel are sufficiently close to the reader's experience and imagination, he becomes almost a 'participant observer' as his thoughts, desires and feelings are evoked by what he reads. The psychological phenomenon of vicarious experience is familiar in daily life and is probably more effectively induced by films and plays than by the printed word, but as yet we have no satisfactory explanation of how these symbolic representations evoke such partial, vicarious experience. It is not part of our present endeavour to embark on an exploration of the difficult problem of imagery and its relationships with cognition, language and sense perception; and we are not equipped to explore the literary aspects of imagery, metaphor, symbolism and related issues.

We tend to forget that, although in theory a novelist has complete control of his material, in practice he is constrained and directed by his own psychological make-up and by language, as well as by the validity of the 'theory' he tries to demonstrate in his novel. A novel can therefore be viewed from several different standpoints: literary technique, authorship and psychological validity. As regards authorship, one might be interested in the novel as an expression of its author's character and cultural background. It has been said that in literature there are always three matters; the man, the moment and the work; the interplay between the first and second gives rise to the third.

IV. Communication and Meaning

The relationships between language and experience are complex and not sufficiently well understood for us to use them in our account of character in fiction. It is obvious, however, that experience can be communicated by and evoked by words, and that other symbolic means, e.g. moving pictures or music, can achieve comparable effects, in so far as they can engross the attention of an audience and shape their thoughts, feelings and desires. Oral language, with its emotionally expressive features, and mime similarly, are particularly effective ways of communicating and evoking affect—film is even more effective. The written (printed) word, by contrast, is probably less effective in this respect. Written language, on the other hand, is usually more articulate and durable and more capable of being reflected on; the novel, therefore, is better suited to the expression of complex thoughts and feelings than crude passions. One interesting possibility, referred to indirectly by Watt, is that printed words (unlike spoken words) tend to have an independence, a permanence, and a reality of their own, rather like the facts they portray would have if they were not fictional, and this helps them to carry conviction. We accommodate ourselves to the printed page by allowing our experience to be shaped into the pattern of meanings represented there, usually in a solitary and receptive state.

It is through such engrossment in the circumstances, states of mind, actions and personal relationships of the characters in a novel that identification with and appreciation of them is achieved on the reader's part—provided the 'psychological distance' is not too great and the literary standard not too low (or too high!). We must remember, however, that a character in a novel is identified with (consists of) bundles of words, though we read the meaning of the words 'as if' they referred to external facts. There seems to have been surprisingly little research into the effects of reading novels.

The novel's concentration on subjective experience is not simply a means to an end, not simply a device to make the character's circumstances and actions more realistic by revealing the 'inside story'. Rather, the subjective experience is itself a reality, a sort of inner psychological world of human nature that men must explore, map, change and come to terms with. It is not surprising, therefore, that novelists have been concerned, in their own way, with some of the issues that interest clinical and social psychologists: interpersonal relations, love, hate, success, failure, and so on. The sorts of issues which Maddi (1972) regards as lying at the heart of personality study, namely fulfilment, conflict and consistency, may also lie at the heart of great novels and express the supposed 'preconditions' of human conduct.

Although we have had occasion to refer to it several times, there is one aspect of characterization in fiction that does not directly concern us as psychologists, namely, literary technique. We have mentioned the main compositional features of the novel: dramatic narrative, subjective experience, objective action, plot, character, situation, interpersonal relationships and morality. In developing these features, novels use various modes of presentation, e.g. an exchange of letters, a running commentary on events by an omniscient observer, personal narration by one of the characters, and so on. Humour, tempo and imagery contribute a great deal to the novel as an art form without necessarily adding anything to the psychological insights of its characterization. The actual information supplied, either directly or indirectly, by an author about a character is in no way remarkable. In fact, in comparison with the numerous and diverse aspects of personality that an author might refer to (see Chapters 5, 6 and 7) the usual selection is quite small and restricted in its variety. Statements about physical appearance, as we have seen, are often used to introduce a character and to convey psychological significance; these may be supplemented by statements about expressive behaviour. Statements about life-history, the reactions of other people towards the character, his social roles, his abilities and attainments, and other familiar kinds of information, are used by novelists to portray their characters in ways which are not very different from the manner in which ordinary people are represented in the ordinary language of personality descriptions. This raises the question of what it is in his readers' psychological make-up that the novelist addresses himself to. The novelist, presumably, has a view of what his readers want and how they will react to what he writes. We have discussed elsewhere the general problem of 'meta-perspectives' in understanding others.

The *contents* of personality descriptions, whether in a novel or in the social exchanges of everyday life, have to be *selected* and *organized* in the interests of comprehension and usefulness. This aspect of the ordinary language of personality description is complicated, to say the least: see Chapter 2. For example, there is the overall structure or 'informal logic' of the representation, and there are the problems associated with attribution (including causality), and other psychological relationships and distinctions. These matters affect the credibility of the characterization. Much characterization is indirect; that is to say, the reader is left to construe many of the character's personal qualities from the behaviour narrative and circumstantial evidence presented by the author. We need not concern ourselves with the subtleties of literary techniques except in so far as they enable us, as psychologists, to represent real persons *scientifically*. For this reason we would regard the order of presentation of information about a person as a matter of logic rather than as a way of achieving literary effects such as tension, surprise or humour. On the other hand, we would regard the novelist's use of behavioural indices of character as potentially useful in so far as it draws our attention to aspects of human action that we had not hitherto noticed; these might include, for example, the inconsistencies caused by confused love relationships or by lack of personal insight, the unusual forms of relationship resulting from the interaction of two or more characters with particular qualities, the 'logic' underlying apparent contradictions in behaviour.

Naturally, the method of characterization evolves with the novel as an art form just as the social, psychological and moral issues with which novels are concerned also evolve. The economic, sociological and religious conditions which contribute to the rise of the novel, e.g. economic individualism, have given way to new conditions; moreover modern novels are being written in the context of a century of psychological research. From this, one might conclude that only the best and most recent novels have any psychological interest; and this is probably true in so far as such novels can be expected to say something *original* about human behaviour. On the other hand, it can be argued that the important insights are those which reveal the basic features (preconditions) of human nature underlying the infinite variety of its particular manifestations in individual behaviour and experience. These basic features recur throughout the long history of literature in general, and can be demonstrated independently of time and circumstance. It is not only in the novel that their universality and the diversity of their particular manifestations in individual experience has been demonstrated, but also, and perhaps especially, in Renaissance drama.

We are not in a position to say how much more we have to learn about the psychological and social features of human nature (excluding its biological foundations); some would argue that we already have a fairly complete account, the accumulation of several thousands of years of human experience; others, however, would point to the relatively recent discoveries associated with psychodynamic psychology, socialization and stress, as evidence that modern psychology is changing our conception of human nature. Moreover, writers (some of them psychologists) were not slow in incorporating Freudian ideas into their novels, although psychodynamic processes (the 'unconscious'), e.g. dreams, psychological defences and disturbances, featured in literature before Freud.

One way of contrasting the psychological case-study with the novel is to say that the latter is governed by its own 'fictional imperatives' (Watt, p. 228), the former by its quasi-judicial 'scientific imperatives'. Because a case-study is conjectural and empirical we take for granted the possibility that some of the ideas and evidence in it may be wrong; but in a novel, too, part of our absorption and enjoyment comes from the realization that we cannot necessarily accept the character's actions and states of mind at their face value, because the character may misrepresent his own feelings, deny his own motives and fail to understand the situation he is in. The failure of a character to 'know himself' is a common theme in fiction, as is the conflict between reason and passion, and the realization that another person is not all that he appears to be.

Much of Freud's writing was devoted to case-material. Not that he followed a a strict quasi-judicial procedure; on the contrary, the logic and method of psychoanalysis left much to be desired—see Sherwood (1969) and Eysenck (1965). Psychoanalytic case-studies had much in common with fiction: a narrative history, personal disclosures of the most revealing sort, situational analysis, characterization, psychological complications, moral conflict, suspense, symbolism and structural cohesion. Freudian theory not only provided a stimulus for deeper characterization in fiction but also contributed to the literary evaluation of pre-Freudian fiction and its writers. Until the advent of psychodynamic theory, psychological interpretation was limited largely, although not entirely, to commonsense notions (we can ignore the often prevalent misconceptions, fallacies and supernatural interpretations). Afterwards, however, when the fundamental drives and relationships associated with nutrition, sex, aggression, security, and so on, were acknowledged, together with the psychological defences that repressed and distorted them, many aspects of behaviour which had hitherto been puzzling or disturbing became comprehensible (within a psychodynamic framework, at least). Advances in understanding the psychopathology of human behaviour extended the boundaries of commonsense; so that some of the minor deviations, delinquencies, perversions and peculiarities of human nature could be considered rationally and empirically rather than dismissed as incomprehensible. Although psychoanalytic theories may not be correct in some respects or not applicable in some instances, it is right that they should be tested to their limits. A framework of beliefs can create the *illusion* of understanding and provide grounds for action without being true. Ordinary language and scientific language can exert that kind of regulation of human experience and conduct. Scientific method is a way of bringing beliefs into closer correspondence with facts.

A novel or a case-study can legitimately be concerned with an individual whose predictament is peculiar to him; but each is expected to deal, in a way, with issues of a more general sort, i.e. with perennial and universal human problems of the sort to which we have already referred. Each is expected to have a sort of metaphysical dimension, like a parable, in the sense of stating a general principle about human life. In novels, such principles are usually normative and implicit; in case-studies, they are (or should be) positive and explicit. Case-studies are not simply exercises in applied psychology; they contribute to our theories about human nature, through the development of psychological 'case law'.

So far we have concentrated on the idea of the novel as the literary analogue of a psychological case-study, in the sense that it has as its main focus, and deals in detail with, the actions and experiences of one person in relation to a particular set of circumstances. There are, of course, novels of other kinds; for example those that deal with adventure, comedy, crime, life on other planets, sex, and so on, and contain little in the way of characterization. Even when such books appear to present the thoughts, feelings and actions of individuals, the intention is not usually to 'characterize' them but to contribute to the book's main purpose: adventure, humour, or whatever. There are also novels which deal on a large scale with whole groups of characters in complex social relationships; such novels might be of great interest to social psychologists, but in so far as the characters are composed in the interests of elucidating sociological relationships (rather than psychological processes) they are not directly relevant. In other words, we are interested only in the *psychological* novel, i.e. the novel that deals with the intricate patterns of thought, feeling and desire woven into the deep and complex relationships that one person has with other people. The possibility that such *personal* relationships occur in a sociological framework need not displace the psychological analysis and may in fact give it greater significance.

In a novel as in a psychological case-study or in daily life, character cannot be studied in isolation from its history and environmental context. Hence, characterization in a novel is difficult, if not impossible, without plot and situation (or, in a case-study, without some life-history data and environmental analysis). In a psychological novel, the emphasis is on the deep structure of character, whereas in novels of suspense or humour the emphasis is on the unfolding of events and the interplay of circumstances. The difference in characterization is one of degree rather than of kind, since character and plot are inseparable in fiction as in fact. Watt (p. 291) says, '. . . the importance of the plot is in inverse proportion to that of character'. There are, of course, other points of view.

Some people adapt successfully to their environment, some do not. But in either case the explanation is to be found in the psychobiological make-up of the individual and in the life circumstances with which he is faced. From a biosocial point of view, human beings can be thought of as complex organisms exhibiting wide ecological variations in adaptation; usually, they settle into some kind of 'ecological niche', i.e. they 'come to terms' with their environment. At times, however, they are obliged to explore new ground, react to threat from predation or stress, cope with changes in themselves and their environment, and otherwise respond to life's challenges. Often, the individual is incapable of coping with the demands of life and fails, in one way or another, to make a satisfactory adjustment.

Characterization in fiction deals in part with the possible ways in which psychological dispositions determine a person's fate, by showing how they affect his actions in relation to the constraints and opportunities of his environment. In the process, we have suggested, writers reveal a view of the 'grammar' and 'moral logic' of human action by showing its causes and consequences. The central issues of human action include: adaptation to demand, the resolution of contradictions and conflict, and the evolution of new forms of being. Psychological novels deal with inner-personal morality and choice, whereas 'environmental' or 'social' novels, if we may so call them, portray a kind of external logic or morality to which human beings are subject. In simpler novels of adventure, crime and humour, this external logic or morality may be of a very simple sort: courage and true love win, crime does not pay, and so on; the characters are simple and static, i.e. they have no moral options, the implications of which evolve out of the situations in which they find themselves. In more complex novels, approaching epic proportions, the external logic or morality is correspondingly more complex and more closely interwoven with the diversity of people in the story, as in Tolstoy's *War and Peace*.

By means of detailed descriptions of actions and circumstances in the appropriate literary terms an author may give us better 'access' to a character than the character himself seems to have. Our attention is drawn, as it were, to those aspects of the character's actions (especially his expressive behaviour and his choice of words) and dispositions which the character himself seems not to be fully aware of—actions which 'betray' or 'reveal' his basic traits, beliefs, values and motives. Naturally, we do not mean that the access we are given is 'real', since the character does not 'really' exist; and we cannot 'know more' about him because there is no more to know (unless there is a sequel to be read!). The character in a work of fiction is completely defined by what the writer says or implies about him. Discussion of the fictional character is limited by that fact.

Novels dealing with complex psychological processes depend upon the assumption that the individual has some control over his own actions. To assume otherwise implies that human nature is stable, and that character, i.e. personal responsibility, is fixed and unable to evolve new forms. According to the classical view, stories about human behaviour are simply variations on fixed themes. According to the modern view, however, individuals differ widely, and new forms of human behaviour evolve in response to new environmental conditions. The evolution of an individual's character, i.e. the 'realization' of what is possible through the interaction of his psychological make-up and his circumstances, provides the theme for modern psychological novels. The basis of this evolution is the individual's capacity, as an active agent, continually to reinterpret his past and to influence his future; in other words, to help make his own personal history. Individuals seem to differ in the extent to which they feel constrained by 'internal' and 'external' factors.

In a novel, the plot incorporates the ordinary activities of daily life but the action depends on the personal qualities of the individual in the story and on the evolution of his character. The classical view, in contrast, sees the individual as a passive pawn whose fate reflects only the rules of the game (the universal, unchanging, human condition). As Watt says (p. 291) 'the organization of the narrative into an extended and complex formal structure will tend to turn the protagonists into its passive agents ...'. It would be a mistake, however, to suppose that this contrast (agent vs pawn) means that the portrayal of individual character cannot be reconciled with the portrayal of complex social and environmental circumstances, as evidenced in the works of Tolstoy, for example.

It is of some interest to note, in passing, that the novel is one of the few areas of cultural and psychological achievement in which women have equalled or surpassed men. Watt says (p. 310) of Jane Austen, 'Her example suggests that the feminine sensibility was in some ways better equipped to reveal the intricacies of personal relationships and was therefore at a real advantage in the realm of the novel'. The reasons for this possible advantage, for which Livesley and Bromley (1973) have provided some slight, empirical support, could include the following: the exclusion of women from many areas of education and work, their interest in and involvement with informal interpersonal relationships within the family and neighbourhood, their accelerated rate of psychological growth in comparison with males and, until recently, their relatively subordinate social status, which would require them to be socially sensitive and to use subtle, devious and tactful ways of influencing people as a substitute for more direct action. In an unexpected psychological footnote (p. 311) Watt reminds us that, 'One comparative study of conversations showed that 37 per cent of women's conversations were about persons as against 16 per cent of men's, citing M. H. Landis and H. E. Burtt, 'A Study of Conversations'. *Journal of Comparative Psychology*, **IV**, 1924, pp. 81–9. However, the problem of sex differences in literary talent and social intelligence is not one that we can discuss further in the present context.

V. Conclusion

Our main concern has been to compare characterization in fiction with characterization in psychological case-studies. The case-study is a relatively simple affair (see Chapter 8) in that it attempts to present an account of a real person in a real situation, and does so by means of empirical evidence and rational argument. Characterization in the novel is different in several respects and its aims and methods are more diverse. Fiction has a long history, dating back before Homer, so it is not surprising that the representation of individual cases should appear in story form long before clinical methods made it possible to construct case-studies. As a literary form, the novel has a short history, but, as we have mentioned, its evolution can be traced back a long way; it is not completely distinct from other literary genres. We have argued in some detail in Chapter 8 that jurisprudence provides the procedural model for a very effective *scientific* procedure for the study of individual cases; and Watt (p. 32) makes a similar comparison for the novel, without going into detail.

The literary and scientific approaches to personality both attempt to demonstrate important aspects of human nature by imposing some kind of construction or interpretation (explicitly in the case-study, implicitly in the novel) on the assembled data. It is the nature of these demonstrations that reveals the contrasts between the two approaches. One is positivistic and objective, the other evaluative and subjective. One proceeds by rational argument about empirical evidence, the other proceeds by idealizing and dramatizing fictional 'evidence'. One appeals to scientific interest, the other to sensibility (sensitive emotional responsiveness); sensibility may go beyond observation and reason, but lacks validity without them.

The study of personality in behavioural science has historical origins different from those of personality in literature. Our problem has been to reconcile these two contrasting approaches by showing how they complement each other in the study of human nature. Their common features are illustrated by the ease with which scientific case-studies can be dramatized like fiction, and by the fact that we can discuss the plausibility or implausibility of a fictional character in terms of what is known scientifically about human behaviour.

It is unfortunate in some respects that the psychometric approach to personality had such a dominant influence in psychology. It led to a neglect of the quasi-judicial case-study method and of psychological case law. It led to a preference for the study of individual differences over individual cases. We could argue that that the psychometric approach to personality (like the novel) had its ideological basis in economic individualism, and that it attempted to assess the person cheaply and simply in terms of his suitability for education and specialized employment in industrial society and in military organizations. Although there is some merit in this argument, it is also true that the psychometric approach to personality can be traced to academic sources, in psychology, education and social work. Furthermore, the approach was a legitimate extension of the work which had been so successful in the study of intelligence, and was in any event used to supplement the clinical (case-study) method as it developed in psychopathology.

The aims and methods of literature are not the same as those of behavioural science. A psychological case-study provides us with an objective account of a real person as seen from the outside. A literary character-study not only gives us the experience of having witnessed some revealing episodes in the life of a 'quasi-real' person, it also takes us on an imaginative exploration of human nature as experienced on the inside, as it were.

We have seen that accounts of real lives and fictional lives have features in common; for example, they illustrate moral principles and psychological theories of a very general sort. Some of the central issues in the scientific study of personality are related to presuppositions and beliefs about human nature similar to those dealt with in moral philosophy and literature—for example, in connection with conflicts of interest, aspirations to ultimate ends, relationships between people, and self-justification. Our presuppositions and basic beliefs about personality and adjustment underlie our understanding of ourselves and other people in daily life, they underlie the writer's portrayal of character in fiction, they underlie the study of personality in professional and scientific work.

Bibliography

Adinolfi, A. A. (1971), 'Relevance of person perception research to clinical psychology', *Journal of Consulting and Clinical Psychology*, **37**, 167–76.
Allott, M. (1959), *Novelists on the Novel*, London: Routledge and Kegan Paul.
Allport, G. W. (1937), *Personality*, London: Constable.
Allport, G. W. (1955), *Becoming: Basic Considerations for a Science of Personality*, New Haven Conn: Yale Univ. Press.
Allport, G. W. (1961), *Pattern and Growth in Personality*, London: Holt, Rinehart and Winston.
Allport, G. W. (Ed.), (1965), *Letters from Jenny*, New York: Harcourt, Brace and World.
Allport, G. W. and Odbert, H. S. (1936), 'Trait names: a psycholexical study', *Psychological Monographs*, **41**, 1–211.
Allport, G. W. and Vernon, P. E. (1933), *Studies in Expressive Movement*, New York: Macmillan.
Allport, G. W., Vernon, P. E. and Lindzey, G. (1960), *A Study of Values* (3rd edit.), Boston: Houghton, Mifflin.
Anderson, N. H. and Lopes, L. L. (1974), 'Some psycholinguistic aspects of person perception', *Memory and Cognition*, **2**, 67–74.
Anscombe, G. E. M. (1963), *Intention* (2nd edit.), Blackwell: Oxford.
Argyle, M. (1975), *Bodily Communication*, Harmondsworth, Penguin Books.
Argyle, M. and Little, B. R. (1972), 'Do personality traits apply to social behaviour?', *Journal for the Theory of Social Behavior*, **2**, 1–35.
Austin, J. L. (1970), *Philosophical Papers* (2nd edit.), Oxford: Oxford University Press.
Bannister, D. (Ed.) (1970), *Perspectives in Personal Construct Theory*, London: Academic Press.
Bannister, D. (1975), *Biographies as a Source in Psychology*, Psychology and Psychotherapy Association (mimeo).
Bannister, D. and Mair, J. M. M. (1968), *The Evaluation of Personal Constructs*, London: Academic Press.
Barker, R. G. (Ed.), (1963), *The Stream of Behaviour*, New York: Appleton-Century-Crofts, Meredith Pub. Co.
Beach, L. and Wertheimer, H. (1961), 'A free response approach to the study of person cognition', *Journal of Abnormal and Social Psychology*, **62**, 367–74.
Bem, D. J. and Allen, A. (1974), 'On predicting some of the people some of the time: the search for cross-situational consistencies in behaviour', *Psychological Review*, **81**, 506–520.
Bernstein, B. (1972), 'Social class, language and socialisation', in *Language and Social Context*, (Ed. Giglioli P. P.), Harmondsworth: Penguin Books, pp. 157–78.
Bieri, J., Atkins, A. L., Briar, S., Leaman, L., Miller, H. and Tripodi, T. (1966), *Clinical and Social Judgment*, New York: John Wiley.
Bilsbury, C. (in preparation), *Person Perception in Educationally Subnormal Children*, Liverpool: University of Liverpool, (mimeo).
Black, M. (1972), *The Labyrinth of Language*, Harmondsworth: Penguin Books.
Blankenship, R. L. (1974), 'Case records language: Towards a sociolinguistic perspective on deviance labelling', *Sociology and Social Research*, **58**, 253–61.

258

Block, J. (1965), *The Challenge of Response Sets*, New York: Appleton-Century-Crofts.
Bolgar, H. (1965), 'The case-study method', in *Handbook of Clinical Psychology*, (Ed. Wolman B.). New York: McGraw-Hill, pp. 28–39.
Bowers, K. S. (1973), 'Situationism in psychology: an analysis and a critique', *Psychological Review*, **80**, 307–36.
Bromley, D. B. (1966), 'The social psychology of reputation', *Bulletin of the British Psychological Society*, **19**, No. 65, p. 73.
Bromley, D. B. (1968), 'Conceptual analysis in the study of personality and adjustment', *Bulletin of the British Psychological Society*, **21**, 155–60.
Bromley, D. B. (1970), 'An approach to theory construction in the psychology of development and aging', in *Life-Span Developmental Psychology*, (Eds. Goulet, L. R. and Baltes, P. B.), New York: Academic Press, pp. 71–114.
Bromley, D. B. (1974), *The Psychology of Human Ageing* (rev. edit.), Harmondsworth: Penguin Books Ltd.
Bromley, D. B. (in press), 'Approaches to the study of personality changes in adult life and old age', in *Studies in Geriatric Psychiatry* (Eds. Isaacs, A. D. and Post, F.), London: John Wiley.
Bruner, J. S., Shapiro, D., and Tagiuri, R. (1958). 'The meaning of traits in isolation and in combination', in *Person Perception and Interpersonal Behaviour*, (Eds. Tagiuri, R. and Petrullo, L.), Stanford: Stanford University Press, pp. 277–89.
Burgess, E. W. (Ed.), (1929), *Personality and the Social Group*, Chicago: University of Chicago Press.
Burton, A. and Harris, R. E. (Eds.), (1966), *Clinical Studies of Personality* (2 Vols.), New York: Harper and Row.
Campbell, D. and Fiske, D. (1959), 'Convergent and discriminant validation by the multitrait-multimethod matrix', *Psychological Bulletin*, **56**, 81–105.
Carlson, R. (1971), 'Where is the person in personality research?', *Psychological Bulletin*, **75**, 203–19.
Cattell, R. B. (1943), 'The description of personality: basic traits resolved into clusters', *Journal of Abnormal and Social Psychology*, **38**, 476–506.
Cattell, R. B. (1946), *Description and Measurement of Personality*, New York: World Book Co.
Cattell, R. B. (1947), 'Confirmation and clarification of primary personality factors', *Psychometrika*, **12**, 197–220.
Cattell, R. B. (1965), *Scientific Analysis of Personality*, Harmondsworth: Penguin Books.
Cattell, R. B. (1973), *Personality and Mood by Questionnaire*, San Francisco: Jossey Bass.
Cattell, R. B., Eber, H. W. and Tatsuoka, M. M. (1970), *Handbook for the Sixteen Personality Factor Questionnaire* (16 PF), Champaign, Ill.: Institute for Personality and Ability Testing.
Cleckley, H. (1964), *The Mask of Sanity* (4th edit.), St. Louis, Missouri: Mosby.
Cline, V. B. (1964), 'Interpersonal perception', in *Progress in Experimental Personality Research*, Vol. 1., (Ed. Maher, B. A.), New York: Academic Press, pp. 221–84.
Cohen, J. (1973), 'The concept of personality: a symposium', *Journal of Psychological Researches*, **17**, 85–98.
Crockett, W. H. (1965), 'Cognitive complexity and impression formation', in *Progress in Experimental Personality Research*, Vol. 2., (Ed. Maher, B. A.), New York: Academic Press, pp. 47–90.
Crockett, W. H. and Meisel, P. (1974), 'Construct connectedness, strength of disconfirmation and impression change', *Journal of Personality*, **42**, 290–9.
Cronbach, L. J. (1955), 'Processes affecting scores on "understanding others" and "assumed similarity"', *Psychological Bulletin*, **52**, 177–93.
Cronbach, L. J. (1964), *Essentials of Psychological Testing*, New York: Harper & Row.
Dana, R. H. (1970), 'A hierarchical model for analyzing personality data', *Journal of General Psychology*, **82**, 199–206.

De Charms, R. (1968), *Personal Causation*, New York: Academic Press.
Dreiser, T. (1929), *A Gallery of Women*, New York: Liveright.
Edwards, A. L. (1957), *The Social Desirability Variable in Personality Assessment and Research*, New York: Dryden.
Ekman, P. and Friesen, W. V. (1975), *Unmasking the Face*, Englewood Cliffs, New Jersey: Prentice-Hall.
Estvan, F. J. and Estvan, E. W. (1959), *The Child's World: His Social Perception*, New York: Putnam.
Evans, J. (1954), *Three Men*, London: Gollancz.
Eysenck, H. J. (1965), *Fact and Fiction in Psychology*, Harmondsworth: Penguin Books Ltd.
Eysenck, H. J. (1970), *The Structure of Human Personality* (3rd edit.). London: Methuen and Co.
Feffer, M. H. (1970), 'Developmental analysis of interpersonal behaviour', *Psychological Review*, 77, 193–214.
Fiske, D. W. (1961), 'The inherent variability of behaviour', in *Functions of Varied Experience*, (Eds. Fiske, D. W. and Maddi, S. R.), Homewood, Illinois: Dorsey Press, pp. 326–54.
Fiske, D. W. (1971), *Measuring the Concepts of Personality*, Chicago: Aldine.
Flapan, D. (1968), *Children's Understanding of Social Interaction*, New York: Teachers College Press, Columbia University.
Flavell, J. H. (1968), *The Development of Role-Taking and Communication Skills in Children*, New York: John Wiley.
Forster, E. M. (1962), *Aspects of the Novel*, Harmondsworth: Penguin Books.
Freud, S. (1953), 'Analysis of a phobia in a five-year-old boy', in *Collected Papers*, Vol. III, London: Hogarth Press.
Gage, N. L. and Cronbach, L. J. (1955), 'Conceptual and methodological problems in interpersonal perception', *Psychological Review*, 62, 411–22.
Gergen, K. J. (1971), *The Concept of Self*, New York: Holt, Rinehart and Winston.
Glueck, B. C., Meehl, P. E., Schofield, W. and Clyde, D. J. (1964), 'The quantitative assessment of personality', *Comprehensive Psychiatry*, 5, 15–23.
Goffman, E. (1963), *Behavior in Public Places*, Glencoe, Ill.: Free Press.
Gollin, E. S. (1958), 'Organisational characteristics of social judgments: a developmental investigation', *Journal of Personality*, XXVI, 139–54.
Goodstein, L. D. and Lanyon, R. I. (1971), *Readings in Personality Assessment*, New York: John Wiley.
Gottschalk, L. A. and Gleser, G. C. (1969), *The Measurement of Psychological States Through the Content Analysis of Verbal Behavior*, Berkeley and Los Angeles: University of California Press.
Gough, H. G. (1960), 'The Adjective Check List as a personality assessment research technique', *Psychological Reports*, 6, 107–22.
Gough, H. G. (1965), *Adjective Check List Manual*, Palo Alto, California: Consulting Psychologists Press.
Guilford, J. P. (1959), *Personality*, New York: McGraw-Hill.
Hampshire, S. (1960), *Thought and Action*, London: Chatto and Windus.
Harré, R. and Secord, P. F. (1972), *The Explanation of Social Behaviour*, Oxford: Basil Blackwell.
Hartshorne, H., May, M. A. and Shuttleworth, F. K. (1930), *Studies in the Organization of Character*, New York: Macmillan.
Harvey, W. J. (1965), *Character and the Novel*, London: Chatto and Windus.
Hastorf, A. H., Schneider, D. J. and Polefka, J. (1970), *Person Perception*, Reading, Massachusetts: Addison-Wesley Publishing Co.
Heider, F. (1958), *The Psychology of Interpersonal Relations*, New York: John Wiley.

260

Hollis, F. (1972), *Casework: A Psychosocial Therapy* (2nd edit.), New York: Random House.

Holsti, O. R. (1969), *Content Analysis for the Social Sciences and Humanities*, London: Addison-Wesley.

Holt, R. R. (1969), *Assessing Personality*, New York: Harcourt Brace Jovanovich.

Howarth, E. (1976), 'Were Cattell's "personality sphere" factors correctly identified in the first instance?', *British Journal of Psychology*, **67**, 213–30.

Jaccard, J. J. (1974), 'Predicting social behavior from personality traits', *Journal of Research in Personality*, **7**, 358–67.

Jersild, A. T. (1951), 'Self-understanding in childhood and adolescence', *American Psychologist*, **VI**, 112–26.

Jones, H. G. (1971), 'In search of an idiographic psychology', *Bulletin of the British Psychological Society*, **24**, 279–90.

Jones, E. E., Kanouse, D. E., Kelley, H. H., Nisbett, R. E., Valins, S. and Weiner, B. (1972), *Attribution: Perceiving the Causes of Behaviour*, Morristown: General Learning Press.

Jones, R. A. and Rosenberg, S. (1974), 'Structural representations of naturalistic descriptions of personality', *Multivariate Behavioral Research*, **9**, 217–30.

Kanfer, F. H. and Saslow, G. (1965), 'Behavioral analysis: an alternative to diagnostic classification', *Archives of General Psychiatry*, **12**, 529–38.

Kelly, G. A. (1955), *The Psychology of Personal Constructs*, New York: Norton.

Kettle, A. (1962), *An Introduction to the English Novel* (2 vols.), London: Arrow Books.

Klages, L. (1929, trs. 1932), *The Science of Character*, London, Allen and Unwin.

Kohlberg, L. (1973), 'Continuities in childhood and adulthood moral development', in *Life-Span Developmental Psychology, Personality and Socialization*, (Eds. Baltes, P. B. and Schaie, K. W.), New York: Academic Press, pp. 161–207.

Laing, R. D., Phillipson, H. and Lee, A. R. (1966), *Interpersonal Perception*, London: Tavistock.

Lawton, D. (1968), *Social Class, Language and Education*, London: Routledge and Kegan Paul.

Leavis, F. R. (1948), *The Great Tradition*, London: Chatto and Windus.

Leach, G. (1974), *Semantics*, Harmondsworth: Penguin Books.

LeVine, R. A. (1971), 'The psychoanalytic study of lives in natural social settings', *Human Development*, **14**, 100–109.

LeVine, R.A. (1973), *Culture, Behavior, and Personality*, Chicago: Aldine.

Lewis, M. and Brooks, J. (in press), 'Infant's social perception: a constructivist view', in *Infant Perception*, (Eds. Cohen, L. and Salapatek, P.), New York: Academic Press.

Livesley, W. J. and Bromley, D. B. (1973), *Person Perception in Childhood and Adolescence*, London: John Wiley.

Lorr, M., Klett, C. J. and McNair, D. M. (1963), *Syndromes of Psychosis*, New York: Macmillan.

McCall, G. J. and Simmons, J. L. (1966), *Identities and Interactions*, New York: Free Press.

Maddi, S. R. (1972), *Personality Theories: A Comparative Analysis* (rev. ed.), Homewood, Illinois: Dorsey Press.

Mair, J. M. M. (1970), 'Experimenting with individuals', *British Journal of Medical Psychology*, **43**, 245–56.

Mead, G. H. (1934), *Mind, Self and Society*, Chicago: University of Chicago Press.

Meehl, P. E. (1972), 'Reactions, Reflections, Projections', in *Objective Personality Assessment: Changing Perspectives*, (Ed. Butcher, J. N.), New York: Academic Press, pp. 131–89.

Miller, G. A., Galanter, E. and Pribram, K. H. (1960), *Plans and the Structure of Behaviour*, New York: Holt.

Minnis, N. ed. (1973), *Linguistics at Large*, St Albans, Herts: Paladin.

Mischel, T. (1964), 'Personal constructs, rules, and the logic of clinical activity', *Psychological Review*, **71**, 180–92.

Mischel, T. (Ed.), (1969), *Human Action—Conceptual and Empirical Issues*, New York: Academic Press.

Mischel, T. (Ed.), (1974), *Understanding Other Persons*, Totowa, N.J.: Rowman and Littlefield.

Mischel, W. (1968), *Personality and Assessment*, New York: John Wiley.

Munter, P. O. (1975), 'Psychobiographical assessment', *Journal of Personality Assessment*, **39**, 424–8.

Murray, H. A. *et al.* (1938), *Explorations in Personality*, New York: Oxford University Press.

Newtson, D. (1973), 'Attribution and the unit of perception of ongoing behavior', *Journal of Personality and Social Psychology*, **28**, 28–38.

Newtson, D. (1974), 'Dispositional inference from effects of actions: effects chosen and effects forgone', *Journal of Experimental Social Psychology*, **10**, 489–96.

Norman, W. T. (1963), 'Toward an adequate taxonomy of personality attributes: Replicated factor structure in peer nomination personality ratings', *Journal of Abnormal and Social Psychology*, **66**, 574–83.

Ogden, C. K. (1932), *Bentham's Theory of Fictions*, London: International Library of Psychology, Philosophy and Scientific Method.

Palmer, F. (1971), *Grammar*, Harmondsworth: Penguin Books.

Passini, F. T. and Norman, W. T. (1966), 'A universal conception of personality structure', *Journal of Personality and Social Psychology*, **4**, 44–9.

Peevers, B. H. and Secord, P. F. (1973), 'Developmental changes in attribution of descriptive concepts to persons', *Journal of Personality and Social Psychology*, **27**, 120–128.

Peters, R. S. (1960), *The Concept of Motivation* (2nd edit.), London: Routledge and Kegan Paul.

Peterson, D. R. (1965), 'Scope and generality of verbally defined personality factors', *Psychological Review*, **72**, 48–59.

Piaget, J. (1926), *The Language and Thought of the Child*, New York: Harcourt Brace.

Piaget, J. (1929), *The Child's Conception of the World*, London: Routledge and Kegan Paul.

Popper, K. (1972), *Objective Knowledge*, Oxford, Clarendon Press.

Richardson, S. A., Dornbusch, S. M. and Hastorf, A. H. (1961), 'Children's categories of interpersonal perception', Final report June 1961, National Institute of Mental Health Research, Grant 7-2480.

Richmond, M. E. (1917), *Social Diagnosis*, New York: Russell Sage Foundation.

Rosenberg, S. and Jones, R. (1972), 'A method for investigating and representing a person's implicit theory of personality: Theodore Dreiser's view of people', *Journal of Personality and Social Psychology*, **22**, 372–86.

Rosenberg, S. and Sedlak, A. (1972), 'Structural representations of implicit personality theory', in *Advances in Experimental Social Psychology*, Vol. 6, (Ed. Berkowitz, L.), New York: Academic Press, pp. 235–97.

Rychlak, J. F. (1968), *A Philosophy of Science for Personality Theory*, Boston: Houghton Mifflin.

Ryle, G. (1949), *The Concept of Mind*, London: Hutchinson's University Library.

Sarbin, T. R., Taft, R. and Bailey, D. E. (1960), *Clinical Inference and Cognitive Theory*, New York: Holt, Rinehart and Winston.

Scarlett, H. H., Press, A. N. and Crockett, W. H. (1971), 'Children's descriptions of peers: A Wernerian developmental analysis', *Child Development*, **42**, 439–53.

Selman, R. L. (1971), 'Taking another's perspective: Role-taking development in early childhood', *Child Development*, **42**, 1721–34.

Shantz, C. U. (1975), 'The development of social cognition', in *Review of Child Development Research*, (Ed. Hetherington, E. M.), Vol. 5, Chicago: University Chicago Press.

Shaw, C. R. (1966), *The Jack-Roller: A Delinquent Boy's Own Story*, Chicago: University of Chicago Press.

Sherwood, M. (1969), *The Logic of Explanation in Psychoanalysis*, New York: Academic Press.

Shweder, R. A. (1975), 'How relevant is an individual difference theory of personality?', *Journal of Personality*, **43**, 455–84.

Sines, J. O. (1966), 'Actuarial methods in personality assessment', in *Progress in Experimental Personality Research*, Vol. 3, (Ed. Maher, B. A.), New York: Academic Press, pp. 133–93.

Slater, E. and Roth, M. (1969), *Clinical Psychiatry* (3rd edit.), London: Ballière, Tindall & Cassell.

Smith, H. C. (1966), *Sensitivity to People*, New York: McGraw-Hill.

Smith, M. B., Bruner, J. S. and White, R. W. (1956), *Opinions and Personality*, New York: John Wiley.

Spitzer, S. P. (ed.), (1969), *The Sociology of Personality*, New York: Van Nostrand Reinhold.

Spranger, E. (1928), *Types of Men* (transl. by P. Pigors), Halle: M. Niemeyer.

Stone, P. J., Dunphy, D. C., Smith, M. S. and Ogilvie, D. M. (1966), *The General Inquirer: A Computer Approach to Content Analysis in the Behavioural Sciences*, Cambridge: M.I.T. Press.

Strachey, L. (1933), *Eminent Victorians*, New York: Modern Library.

Strawson, P. F. (1964), 'Persons', in *Essays in Philosophical Psychology*, (Ed. Gustafson, D. F.), New York: Doubleday, pp. 377–403.

Strawson, P. F. (1974), *Subject and Predicate in Logic and Grammar*, London: Methuen.

Tagiuri, R. and Petrullo, L. (Eds.), (1958), *Person Perception and Interpersonal Behavior*, Stanford: Stanford University Press.

Theophrastus (1973), *The Characters* (trans. by P. Vellacott, 2nd ed.), Harmondsworth: Penguin Books.

Thurstone, L. L. (1934), 'Vectors of the mind', *Psychological Review*, **41**, 1–32.

Timms, S. N. (1968), *The Language of Social Case Work*, London: Routledge and Kegan Paul.

Tolstoy, Leo (1932), *War and Peace*, London: J. M. Dent.

Tomkins, S. S. and Izard, C. E. (Eds.), (1966), *Affect, Cognition and Personality*, London: Tavistock Publications.

Toulmin, S. E. (1958), *The Uses of Argument*, London: Cambridge University Press.

Trankell, A. (1972), *Reliability of Evidence: Methods for Analyzing and Assessing Witness Statements*, Vallingby, Sweden: Beckmans.

Vernon, P. E. (1964), *Personality Assessment: A Critical Survey*, London: Methuen.

Vygotsky, L. S. (1962), *Thought and Language*, Cambridge, Mass.: M.I.T. Press.

Waldron, R. A. (1967), *Sense and Sense Development*, London: Deutsch.

Wallace, J. (1966), 'An abilities conception of personality: Some implications for personality measurement', *American Psychologist*, **21**, 132–8.

Warr, P. B. and Knapper, C. (1968), *The Perception of People and Events*, London: John Wiley.

Watt, I. (1963), *The Rise of the Novel*, Harmondsworth: Penguin Books.

Watts, A. F. (1944), *The Language and Mental Development of Children*, London: Harrop.

Webb, E. J., Campbell, D. T., Schwartz, R. D. and Sechrest, L. (1966), *Unobtrusive Measures: Non-Reactive Research in the Social Sciences*, Chicago: Rand McNally.

Weinberg, H. and Hire, A. W. (1962), *Case Book in Abnormal Psychology*, New York: Alfred Knopf.

Wessman, A. E. and Ricks, D. F. (1966), *Mood and Personality*, New York: Holt, Rinehart and Winston.

White, R. W. (1975), *Lives in Progress* (3rd edit.), New York: Holt, Rinehart and Winston.

Whorf, B. L. (1956), *Language, Thought and Reality*, (Ed. Carroll, J. B.), New York: John Wiley.

Wishner, J. (1960), 'Reanalysis of "impressions of personality"', *Psychological Review*, **67**, 96–112.

Wittgenstein, L. (1953), *Philosophical Investigations*, Oxford: Basil Blackwell.

Worrall, N. and Worrall, C. (1974), *First and Second Impressions of Personality*, Final Report to the Social Science Research Council, London: University of London, Institute of Education.

Yarrow, M. R. and Campbell, J. D. (1963), 'Person perception in children', *Merrill-Palmer Quarterly*, **IX**, 57–72.

Zax, M. and Stricker, G. (1963), *Patterns of Psychopathology: Case Studies of Behavioral Dysfunction*, London: Collier-Macmillan.

Author Index

Subject Index

272

274

Objective knowledge, 55, 57–58, 59, 223
Objectivity, in content analysis, 110: *see also* Objective knowledge
Object of an attitude (OBJE): examples, 112; in case-report, 190; mentioned, 38, 110–112 *passim*, 185, 190
Observation, contrasted with evaluation, 159–160
Operational definition, 43, 45, 55, 97, 182
Opinions, personality descriptions as, 46
Ordinary language: comparison with others implicit in, 23–24, 26, 194–195; contrasted with scientific and technical language, 28, 59, 60; complex, 29–30; and operational definition, 43; holophrastic, 47; terms for personal dispositions, 62–63; and abnormal behaviour, 80; explanation in, 81–82; statements not taken literally, 100; average adult's use of, 101–102; convenient conceptual shifts in, 109; interrelated frames of reference in, 157; in fiction, 227–256 *passim*; analysis of behaviour and psychological processes, 240; mentioned *passim*: *see also* Commonsense; Language
Orientation and feeling (or attitude) (ORFE): to self, 106; in explanation of behaviour, 106; as attitude, 107, 111, 188, 192; in fiction, 107–108; in relation to time and possibility, 108; latent or manifest, 108; uncertainty, 108; examples, 108, 109; and overt behaviour, 109; in case-report, 188–189; mentioned, 99, 105, 106–110 *passim*, 112, 126, 131, 140, 178
Others' response to the stimulus person (O–SP): scope of category, 145; examples, 146, 147; in case-report, 192–193; mentioned, 39, 139, 141, 142, 143, 144, 145–147, 150, 151, 155
Overt behaviour: relation to covert psychological processes, 6, 100, 109, 183; children's understanding of, 11; abstract terms for, 15; construed in different ways, 71; and dispositions, 71, 76, 77, 185; plans and rules in the organization of, 107; realization of a programme, 110; directed to objects, 110–111; coping and expressive aspects, 113; non-verbal, 113; perception of, 136; narrative of, 162–163; traces of, 163; situation as determinant of, 185; regulated by social

prescriptions, 134, 191: *see also* Behaviour; Cycle of behaviour

Passage to India, A, 239
Pattern of meaning, imposed by informal argument, 223
Pawn: *see* Agent
Perception: *see* Overt behaviour; Person perception
Peripheral tendencies and characteristics, 205, 215–216
Person: as active agent, 110, 129
Personal adjustment, requirements for a general theory of, 223
Personal construct theory, 4
Personal disclosures, 189
Personal dispositions: individualized traits, 61–62, 185; terms in ordinary language, 62–63; and ethical evaluations, 63–64; *see also* General trait (GENT); Traits
Personal identity, 156, 229: *see also* Identity (IDEN)
Personality: approaches to, 45, 61, 77, 111; problem of, misunderstood, 61; and character, 64, 117, 189; implicit theories of, 69; intelligence excluded from, 77; ways of representing, 79, 231; motives, key to, 86; in behavioural ecology, 98; table of external aspects, 120; Allport's definition, 121; continuity of, in time, 126, 129; social aspects of, 143, 216; concept of, 214–215; realized in tactical adjustments, 215; idealized psychological structures, 215; individual differences, 216; and ideology, 237; mentioned *passim*: *see also* Character; Personality appraisal; Personality description; Personality impressions
Personality appraisal: profound influence of language, 6; contrasted with measurement, 218; constructs in, 226: *see also* Character; Personality description; Personality impression
Personality description: defined, 1; in juvenile development, 1–27 *passim*; depends on shared experience, 3; diverse kinds of, 3; consistency and meaningfulness, 5–6; disjunctive and conjunctive elements in, 8; no definitive system of analysis, 9; serial changes in, 10; fluency in, 11, 12, 15, 16; spoken or